Sexual Culture in Ancient Greece

OKLAHOMA SERIES IN CLASSICAL CULTURE

Sexual Culture
in Ancient Greece

DANIEL H. GARRISON

UNIVERSITY OF OKLAHOMA PRESS : NORMAN

ALSO BY DANIEL H. GARRISON

Mild Frenzy: A Reading of the Hellenistic Love Epigram (Wiesbaden, 1978)

The Language of Virgil (New York, 1984)

The Student's Catullus (Norman, 1989)

Horace: Epodes and Odes,
A New Annotated Latin Edition (Norman, 1991)

Library of Congress Cataloging-in-Publication Data

Garrison, Daniel H.
Sexual culture in ancient Greece / by Daniel H. Garrison
p.   cm. — (Oklahoma series in classical culture ; v. 24)
Includes bibliographical references and index.
ISBN 0-8061-3237-x (alk. paper)
1. Sex—Greece—History.   2. Sex customs—Greece—History.   3. Sex—Mythology—
Greece.   4. Sex in art.   5. Sex in literature.   6. Civilization, Classical.   I. Title.   II. Series.
HQ18.G8 G37 2000
306.7'0945—dc21   99-049026

Sexual Culture in Ancient Greece is Volume 24 of the Oklahoma Series in Classical Culture.

1   2   3   4   5   6   7   8   9   10

Contents

Apollo displays himself to a muse. Athenian covered cup, ca. 450 B.C. (Henry
Lillie Pierce Fund. Courtesy, Museum of Fine Arts, Boston)

Preface

The tug-of-war that went on in ancient Greece between partisans of a high sexual culture and those who felt that virtue should be made of sterner stuff has never, to my knowledge, received its due share of attention. Michel Foucault recognized the significance of repression, social power, and domination in Greek sexual culture, but in appealing to a principle of "isomorphism between sexual relations and social relations" (1985, 215), he prepared the way for scholarship in which Greek love of power was seen to determine a monolithic sexual culture bent on control of the self and domination of others. My own interest is less tightly focused, and it has produced a more complex view.

When I began studying Greek sexual culture more than twenty years ago, there was little of a general nature either in anthropology or in cultural history on which to model my work on the Greeks. Since then, a flood of work has appeared on modern European societies, as has a substantial bibliography (of which the one in this book is only a sample) on sexual issues in Greece and Rome. For reasons that are not far to seek, most of what now exists has to do with two contemporary concerns: sexual inequality and homosexuality. It can now be learned in detail how male attitudes curtailed female participation in public life, literature, and the arts and what women achieved in spite of barriers erected against them. Extreme views, on the one hand that matriarchs once ruled Greece and on the other that women in classical times were kept in "oriental seclusion" at the mercy of an insecure male "phallocracy," have been effectively countered, for example, in books by Mary Lefkowitz (1986) and David Cohen (1991). The traditional Greek indifference to gender in the object of sexual desire has been amply demonstrated by K. J. Dover, Foucault, Jack Winkler, and David M. Halperin, among others. In brief, sex roles and sexual images in classical antiquity are better understood than ever before. My own thinking has been much aided by the work of the past two decades, whether or not it fell within the realm of sexuality and sex roles and whether or not I found myself in agreement. But as I studied the written and pictorial testimony of the Greeks themselves, I found my interest caught by matters only tangential to the concerns of my colleagues. My primary informants seemed to be saying in a number of ways that our questions about sexual orientation and gender equality were not as interesting to them, especially before the fourth century B.C., as they are to us. While this confirms the consensus of recent study, it begs the question of what sexual questions did engage the minds of the Greeks themselves. Without answering this question in detail, I concentrate in this book on one persistent ancient controversy: the play and place of erotic sex in human life as it should be lived.

My working assumption is that societies that accord erotic life greater importance tend to develop a higher sexual culture, in which a greater personal and social investment is made and where there is a wider variety of choices. A low sexual culture, like a low verbal culture, has a limited variety of expression and discourages behavior that exceeds prescribed limits. A high sexual culture invests erotic meaning in a large range of behavior that includes costume, grooming, art, song, theater, and literature. In modern urban culture, "sexy" is a term of approval for anything stylish and interesting—whether or not it is in fashion. Low sexual culture is fundamentalist in its ideology: sex is appropriate only for relief of an urge (Cynics) or for procreation (Stoics, early Christians). High sexual culture seeks in eros an enrichment of personal life. Far from seeking oblivion in debauchery, orgies, or other activities subversive of consciousness, such a culture finds in eros an end in itself rather than a distraction from (or a means to) more important goals. The distinction of high and low must be used with considerable caution, as they can coexist in the same culture and even in the same social class. For example, the same social class of "beautiful and good" *kalokagathoi* that admired Spartan repression of the appetites also enjoyed the "good times" of *euphrosynē* provided by hetaeras in Athens and Ionia; likewise, the most strident denunciations of eros took place in late Hellenistic and Roman cultures where both erotic bonding and sexual recreation enjoyed widespread popularity. Corinth was the sex capital of the ancient world (as early as Aristophanes, *korinthiazomai* meant "to practice fornication") and at the same time a center of Christian worship that harshly condemned fornication in the first century A.D.

It is probably impossible to talk about the subject of erotics without bringing in personal bias. I must therefore admit here at the beginning that my preference is as much for high sexual culture as it is for high literary culture and high culinary culture. If this makes me in the reader's view a porker from the herd of Epicurus, I can retort only that Epicurus was no hedonist and that the dietetic and erotic regimens of Epicurean philosophy are no more to my liking than the wholesale hedonism of the Cyrenaics. The reader should also be warned of my view that any ideology that makes its appeal to a reified "nature" has taken a path from which there is no return. Plato, the Cynics, the Stoics, and many early Christians made this error most egregiously when they ventured into the deep waters of sexual ethics. Anyone who condemns homosexuality because it is "unnatural" will get little comfort from reading this book, notwithstanding my personal heterosexual bent.

I hope the reader will agree that it is impossible to separate the achievements of classical civilization from its erotic sensibilities. The affinity of achievement and sensibility is easiest to see in Greek representations of the human body, male and female, clad as well as nude. It can be readily sensed also in its literature of all periods and dispositions, for a wary appreciation of the sexual lies at the heart of the Greek sense of life. The purpose of this book is to show that as Greek civilization was far from monolithic, little was left unchallenged about its erotic sensibility. Rather than the flabby platitudes of a Zorba, the artists and poets of ancient Greece handed down a disciplined variety of erotic encounters that put them in a class by themselves. Like all great art, theirs grew out of mixed feelings.

Though the book is titled *Sexual Culture in Ancient Greece*, I have taken the liberty to stray outside the Greek-speaking world when it seemed reasonable to do so. The Gilgamesh Epic and the Hebrew Scriptures throw light on the early Near Eastern substratum and cognate sexual myths by which Aegean Greece was influenced. For late antiquity, the Latin West is as important as the Greek East to which it was united in a more or less homogeneous urban inhabited world, or *oikoumenē*. If at the end the Latin West upstages the Greek East, my purpose from the beginning has been to explain early features of the dominant European culture that shaped the West.

This book is not so much a systematic exposition of Greek sexual culture ab initio as a series of chapters commenting on what seem to me the most significant stages of a long development. The first two chapters are preparatory to the main stages: chapter 3 looks at ways in which an emergent Hellenism distinguished its sexual culture from those of its eastern neighbors; chapter 4 explains the ascetic spirit and sexual dimorphism that is prominent in archaic literature; chapter 5 describes the development of a higher sexual culture in Athens, chapter 6 the philosophic uses of eros. Chapter 7 accounts for the aesthetic sea change in which the female nude, previously rejected, became the supreme artistic form. Chapter 8 follows the development of a romantic idealism that promoted conjugal love of men and women living as equals, and chapter 9 traces the themes that led to the final rejection of ancient sexual culture at the same time as a virulently anerotic religion—Christianity—was transforming the ancient world. In making sense of each of these stages, I have found that some of my material overlaps, and much that I could have said about my larger subject must be omitted.

The illustrations that accompany the text document my argument in ways that no words could do. It has in some cases been difficult to locate the owners of the images I have used. I apologize for any errors or omissions in the credits and, if contacted, will be pleased to rectify them at the earliest opportunity.

During the years over which this book developed, I have been influenced by personal conversations with Sir Hugh Lloyd-Jones, Paul Friedrich, Reginald Allen, Charles Fantazzi, and many others. The largest portion of my intellectual debt is reflected in my bibliography and notes. Portions of this book have been read by Christopher Faraone, Ann Ellis Hanson, Diane Legomski, Wendy Doniger O'Flaherty, Sara Monoson, Phyllis Bird, Kathleen McCarthy, Benjamin Sommer, Bob Wallace, and (again) Paul Friedrich. Each has contributed valuable suggestions. Hugh Lloyd-Jones and Marilyn B. Skinner read the entire manuscript, providing guidance in the removal of the manuscript's worst blemishes. Though they will disagree with some of the things I say, the book has benefited greatly from their criticisms. Special thanks are due to Bob Wallace for numerous historical consultations during the latest months of writing, to Anne Garrison for editorial corrections, to Sheila Berg, who edited the manuscript for the Press, to Penny Livermore for assistance with permissions to use the illustrations, and to my wife, Tina, who has enough editing of her own to do but provided necessary moral support. To her this book is dedicated in the spirit of erotic friendship.

Sexual Culture in Ancient Greece

CHAPTER ONE

Sexual Religion

THE ROOTS OF SEXUAL CULTURE

The erotic contains the least that repels the mind,
and the most that inevitably attracts.

ABHINAVAGUPTA

The prehistoric Mediterranean is a picture book without words.
The earliest pictures are colorless pieces of bone and clay, charred
remains, stone, and imprints in the earth. Real pictures, such as
Minoan carved gemstones and the paintings at Knossos and Akrotiri,
are late and exceptional, particularly for the religious prehistory of the
Greek world. Neolithic and early Bronze Age Greece, before a palace
civilization had added the color of palaces, gold, bronze, and pictorial
art, have been declared terra incognita: "We know nothing," Martin
Persson Nilsson declared in 1950 of Helladic religion. Walter Burkert,
writing in 1977, found little to add.[1] The mental leap from that world's
physical remains to its sense of life would therefore be long and
perilous, were it not that Neolithic and early Bronze Age cultures left
a distinctive imprint over a large area from Old Europe to Anatolia,
the Levant, and Egypt.[2] When the view is broad enough, the archaeological remains of early religion point to a Neolithic and Bronze Age
oikoumenē, held together in part by a common network of trade but
chiefly by a common condition of agricultural life.

A further aid to the reconstruction of early Mediterranean life is
that one of its cultures, Greece, left the most articulate record of any
known civilization in the ancient world, fully attuned to its religious
past and conservative of its traditions. Iconographic features of
Neolithic religious objects found in Greece, the Balkans, and Anatolia
can easily be related to similar objects from the Greek Bronze Age and

Figure 1.1. Fragment of an early Neolithic terracotta figurine from Sesklo, Thessaly, ca. 6000 B.C., arms placed on the breasts in a gesture suggesting nutrient powers of a life-giving goddess. The gesture remained part of the standard iconography of such goddesses for millennia: cf. fig. 1.30. The proportion of shoulders and chest to midriff here and in fig. 1.13 suggests the Homeric epithet of Trojan women, βαθυκόλποι "deep-chested," referring to the fold beneath the breasts. Cf. βαθύζωνος, "deep-girdled," in *Il.* 9.594, *Od.* 3.154. (National Archaeological Museum, Athens, no. 5942)

subsequent historical periods, even into Roman times. The continuity of Greek religion, with due allowances for changes that came with the arrival of Indo-European deities after the second millennium, is indicated by the persistence of its iconographic symbols. It may also be embedded in verbal testimony, for example, in Aeschylus' *Eumenides* (458 B.C.), where the contest over Orestes is waged by ancient chthonic female spirits against the new gods represented by Apollo. The religious message of the play is that the city must provide its oldest spirits with a place of honor even though their traditional powers are abridged: only by doing so can the city survive. Aeschylus' telescoping of time brings an awareness of already ancient history into

Sexual Culture in Ancient Greece

dramatic focus as if the contest between Indo-European, patriarchal cult and an aboriginal religion, in which female powers were more prominent, had taken place only yesterday. Aeschylus' Athenian audience was particularly well attuned to his religious viewpoint because it was autochthonous, never having been displaced by invaders foreign or domestic. The Athenian religious calendar is marked with rituals that can be traced to ancient agricultural usages. The sexually explicit content of these rituals confirms that the sexual character of Neolithic religion was not easily set aside by the high civilization that grew up in its place millennia later (see fig. 1.2).[3]

Greek poets and historians, while often scornful of non-Greeks, were quick to perceive cultural similarities, particularly in religious matters. The ecumenical spirit is close to the surface, for example, in Homer's representation of Troy and its Anatolian allies in the Trojan War. To the women of Troy, Athena is as much their goddess as she is the Greeks', and they pray to her in her temple on Troy's citadel to save their city (*Il.* 6.286–311). The assimilation of the multibreasted Anatolian goddess of Ephesus to the Greek Artemis, "Diana of the Ephesians," is symptomatic of the continuing sense of religious community. This is particularly understandable, as much of Greek language, culture, and religion came from the East during the Bronze Age. At the same time, a native Balkan Neolithic tradition persisted in the religious and imaginative life of the historical Greeks. Though later literary documents such as the *Oresteia* cannot be used to explain the practices of Neolithic religion, it would be difficult to understand much of classical art, literature, or thought without reference to that tradition.

Even before the seventh-millennium evolution of human settlements dependent on planted crops and domesticated animals, the projective and symbolic activities of people close to the Mediterranean reveal a primary concern about the sources of food. Survival and prosperity depended on the reproduction of human families, animals, and the vegetation that nourished them. Fecundity, if not sexuality, is the apparent theme of one of the earliest "Venus" figures of Paleolithic Europe (fig. 1.3); her resemblance to many steatopygous, or fat-buttocked, figurines of Neolithic cultures from Malta to the Near East is evidence of the religious continuity over millennia that makes it possible to link remote prehistory with cultures that speak for themselves by leaving a written record.

Figure 1.2. A woman sprinkles planted *phalloi*, probably for the Haloa festival. The prominence of girls and women in Attic ritual, particularly in events such as the Haloa and the Thesmophoria from which men were excluded, may be traceable to agricultural eras when power over fertility was imputed to women. Athenian red-figure *pelike* by the Hasselmann Painter, ca. 430–420 B.C. (The British Museum, no. 819)

Figure 1.3. The "Venus of Laussel," carved from a block of stone about eighteen inches high in a rock shelter in the Dordogne. She holds a horn in her right hand, possibly a symbol of fertility. Like the "Venus of Willendorf," found in Austria, and similar figurines of later date, this icon has no face. Her meaning, expressed in a series of fatty bulges, is emphasized by the gesture of an arm just long enough to reach her tumid stomach. The association of a birth-giving goddess with bull's horns is found again in a seventh-millenium shrine at Çatal Hüyük. (Erich Lessing/Art Resource, New York)

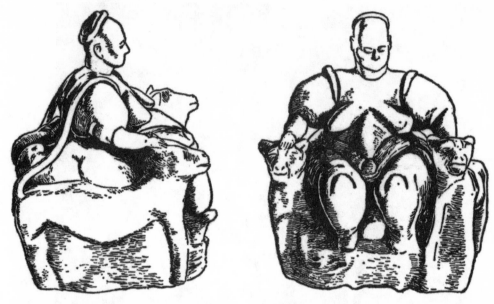

Figure 1.4. Seated on a throne flanked by two felines, this "Great Goddess" was found in a grain bin at Çatal Hüyük in central Anatolia. Though dated from the middle of the seventh millennium B.C., her iconography resembles that of Greek art from the historical period: the headpiece, or *polos* (later identified with the κρήδεμνον or battlements of a city and her role as protector of cities), and paired animals marking her as πότνια θηρῶν, mistress of animals—roles the historical Greeks would assign to Athena and Artemis respectively. (James Mellaart)

Figure 1.5. The heavy-thighed seated goddess was a standard fixture of Neolithic and early Bronze Age religion over a wide area. This terracotta seated nude (6000 B.C.) comes from Sesklo, Thessaly. (Permission of the Estate of Marija Gimbutas)

Figure 1.6. From Kato Ierapetra, Crete, this Neolithic seated goddess is ornamented with the polos and incised lines to suggest her costume. (Permission of the Estate of Marija Gimbutas)

Figure 1.7. One of the massive goddesses from Malta (ca. 3000 B.C.), whose legs taper off to points like the legs of her Cretan counterpart above (fig. 1.6). (Yale University Press)

    The "Neolithic revolution" that took place as hunting and gathering gave way to herding and planting did not require a change of imagery, but the new technology required its practitioners to become more manipulative of their environment, both physical and metaphysical. Instead of responding to their environment, Neolithic communities took nature in hand, breeding animals, sowing seeds, and cultivating the goodwill of nature and its gods in more complex ways. Reproduction (claims to the contrary notwithstanding) was understood to be sexual. Even those aspects that are not strictly sexual, such as rainfall and the germination of seeds, were likely to have been understood through sexual metaphor: rain is the semen of a paternal sky fecundating a maternal earth; crops are encouraged by a sexual act performed in a furrow above the newly planted seed. Such ideas could scarcely have been novelties for the Greek poets of later millennia. Aphrodite speaks these lines about the rain in a fragment of Aeschylus' *Danaids.*

Sexual Culture in Ancient Greece

The holy sky longs to pierce the earth, and desire seizes earth to attain her marriage; rain, falling from the bridegroom sky, impregnates earth. She bears for mortals flocks of sheep and life that comes from grain; the fruit of trees from this moist wedding comes to fulfillment. Of these things I am the cause.[4]

The basic and insistent needs of small agricultural communities focused their attention on the production of plants and the reproduction of animals, including their own species. That this focus was

Figure 1.8a–b. Kourotrophos: two versions of the divine mother and child from Hacılar VI and Horoztepe in Anatolia. (James Mellaart)

Figure 1.9. A Cypriote nursing goddess, probably related to Astarte, the Near Eastern goddess of sex and fertility. Like many Neolithic and Bronze Age goddess icons, she (and her child) has a birdlike face; note also the figure of a swan incised above the vulva. Greek myth associated Aphrodite with swans, Athena with the owl. 1400–1200 B.C. (Cyprus Museum, Republic of Cyprus)

feminine and sexual is shown by an impressive accumulation of circumstantial evidence.

First, Neolithic sites routinely yield a variety of female figurines too numerous and widespread to be dismissed as children's dolls. Occurring more frequently than male or animal figurines, they are distinguishable by the artisan's emphasis on feminine shapes—wide hips, enlarged buttocks, breasts—and sometimes on maternal function.[5] The *kourotrophos*, a mother holding or suckling a child, is a distant ancestor of the Christian Madonna.[6] Like the mother of Christ, at the same time both mortal and divine, this figure is an icon of what parents pray for: the birth of a child who will be their advocate when they are in need and the ability to nurture such a child. As goddess, she represents nature at its most benign; she later becomes the benefactor of rulers, as remembered (with a patriarchal twist) in the Homeric formula διοτρεφέες βασιλῆες, "Zeus-nurtured kings."

Second, a strong sexual theme runs through the Neolithic figurines that is not necessarily erotic but demonstrates an early awareness of the sexual role in reproduction and calls attention to its power. The most overt expression of the sexual theme is genital representation. Figurines are often carved to represent and even exaggerate the vulva, even in otherwise schematic representations such as the headless fiddle-shaped and "frying pan" artifacts from the Cyclades (figs. 1.10, 1.11). The sexual emphasis sometimes even transcends the ordinary limit of gender, as in hermaphroditic figurines (e.g., figs. 1.11, 1.12) that combine a phallic neck and head with breasts and vulva. Perhaps the most difficult problem facing the interpreter is how to distinguish between *sexual* religion, rituals, and artifacts and *fertility* symbols. Like distinguishing between sacred and secular in the medieval world, any such attempt is anachronistic and futile, because the two are so closely linked in the archaic mind. A symbol need not be sexually arousing to be sexual; it need only represent sexual success, like the nursing or pregnant woman, or sexual readiness, like the phallic satyr. Sex and fertility are an unbroken iconographic continuum.

Male sexuality plays a part in all phases of Neolithic art in the Mediterranean *oikoumenē*; as we have already seen, the phallus is a detachable and portable symbol (see Gimbutas 1982, figs. 219–226)

Figure 1.10. Cycladic "frying pan" terracotta from Syros. Of unknown function, this is one of the most abstract of art objects from a period with a marked penchant for abstraction. The running spirals of sea and sky surround a boat with oars; below, set off by an incised triangle, is a vulva. The stubby handles are legs. The association of feminine imagery with ships and the sea is ancient and persists in poetry (e.g., through a variety of sea nymphs such as Achilles' mother, Thetis, and her attendant nereids) throughout antiquity. Aphrodite's birth from sea foam is part of this tradition. (National Archaeological Museum, Athens, no. 4974)

Figure 1.11. Fiddle-shaped Cycladic figurine with phallic, headless neck and vulva set off by an incised triangle as in the preceding figure. Though the basic representation is schematic, the artist has incised double lines for a necklace and four lines to suggest an ornamented girdle. (N. P. Goulandris Collection, Museum of Cycladic Art, Athens, no. 338)

Figure 1.12. Sexual forms merge in this late Neolithic marble nude from Glypha in Paros (ca. 3200 B.C.), with phallic head and neck, breasts, and vulva. The slender shape and rectilinear forms of Cycladic figurines were influenced by the hardness of the medium and the limitations of the saws used to fashion them. (National Archaeological Museum, Athens, no. 4762)

Figure 1.13. This marble figurine from Sparta, ca. 6000 B.C., is iconographically similar to a seventh-millennium figurine found in Nea Nikimedia, Macedonia, with the addition of a headpiece like that of the "Great Goddess" of Çatal Hüyük, fig. 1.4. As in the previous figures, her face is without detail. (Permission of the Estate of Marija Gimbutas)

and continued to be so into historical times. The horned, masked phallic dancer, a very early example of which was found in the Trois Frères cave by the Abbé Breuil, has a Neolithic counterpart in a masked, originally horned figure (fig. 1.14) of a man holding his penis (which is painted red, like the phallic costume in Aristophanic comedy). The horn was from the start an emblem of virility, endowed with ritual potency; combined with female figures in the Venus of Laussel and the "Birth-giving goddess" of Çatal Hüyük, or mounted on the heads of males, it is a part of sexual iconography into Roman times.[7] In classical Greek myth, phallicism plays out into representations of Hermes, the phallic guardian of boundaries,[8] Pan, the amorous, goatish Arcadian god regularly represented as Hermes' son,[9] and (especially) the satyrs, whose hornlike ears and grotesque phalli marked them as insatiably libidinous.

Figure 1.14. Masked, ithyphallic figures distantly related to the performers in Greek Old Comedy can be traced as far back as the fourth millennium B.C. This terracotta figurine, originally horned, holds his red-painted penis. Late Vinča (central Balkans). (Permission of the Estate of Marija Gimbutas)

The sexual character of Neolithic religion and its tradition is not exhausted by the display of anatomy. By themselves, male and female represent potential, but its fulfillment comes in the fruitful union of the two. This is graphically represented in a very early set of images found in a shrine at Çatal Hüyük (fig. 1.19), perhaps intended as a narrative representation: an embracing couple on the left, mother and child on the right. That these are a divine family can be inferred from later Greek analogies; this would be the *hieros gamos*, or holy marriage, the union of goddess and god that provides the paradigm for all human unions,[10] and the *kourotrophos* who holds the divine child. Figurines of embracing couples are found in widely distributed parts of the Neolithic Mediterranean *oikoumenē*; everything that is known or surmised about the earliest art points to a religious interpretation.

The male was not necessarily the dominant partner in such hierogamies, though he probably was in actual social institutions. Early traditions from the ancient Near East point to an immortal goddess

Sexual Culture in Ancient Greece

Figure 1.15. Throned male figures were part of the Neolithic Greek pantheon, as attested by this figure from the sixth-millennium B.C. Sesklo culture found at Pyrasos, Thessaly. The great plains of north central Greece were the first center of Neolithic Greek culture. The stylized combination of legs and throne may be related to the myth of the Centaurs, wild and oversexed horse-men of Thessaly whose defeat by the Lapiths symbolized the triumph of civilization over barbarism. A comparable earlier figure from Porodin, southern Yugoslavia (Gimbutas fig. 231) shows that this type of figure was not unique in the area. (Permission of the Estate of Marija Gimbutas)

of nature in the female role, with the male played by a year god who (like the vegetation) must die and be reborn annually.[11] The pattern is variously reenacted in myths of eastern origin—the union of Egyptian Isis and Osiris, Sumero-Accadian Astarte/Ishtar and Tammuz, Sumerian Inanna and Dumuzi, Phrygian Cybele and Attis, western Semitic Anat and Baal—and is related to the pattern of the Sorrowing Mother that survives in the Christian figure of the *Mater Dolorosa.* The youthful sensuality of the Virgin Mother's face in Michelangelo's *Pietà* (fig. 1.21) coincides with the original character of the primeval myth, in which the bereaved goddess is the ever-youthful lover of the deceased nature god.[12]

Sexual Religion

Figure 1.16. As Paleolithic "Venus" figures were bodies without faces, Greek Herms were faces without bodies, featured only with the erect phallus that warded off trouble. Rural Herms were often aniconic: rocks placed at boundaries of a farm. The sanctity of Athenian Herms placed at house doors was so great in fifth-century Athens that when a large number were mutilated in 415 B.C. on the eve of the Sicilian expedition, "the whole affair was taken very seriously, as it was regarded as an omen for the expedition, and at the same time as evidence of a revolutionary conspiracy to overthrow the democracy." (Thuc. 6.27, tr. Rex Warner). This Herm, from Siphnos, is dated ca. 520 B.C. (National Archaeological Museum, Athens, no. 3728)

Figure 1.17. An ithyphallic Pan pursues a startled goatherd, while an even more ithyphallic Herm looks on. Ca. 470 B.C. Throughout antiquity, the Greek and Roman art market exhibited a tireless interest in sexual motifs from early cult. (James Fund and by Special Contribution. Courtesy, Museum of Fine Arts, Boston)

In various forms of the myth, the goddess is semiautonomous as sister and/or sexual partner of an annually dying god. The male partner is not always a year god, but he is always, in such unions, passive, ephemeral, and powerless. The dawn goddess Eos' male consorts include Orion and Tithonus; Aphrodite has an eastern lover in the Trojan Anchises, father of Aeneas. Like Aeneas, the hero Gilgamesh is born of the union between a divine mother (Ninsun) and a mortal or semidivine father (Lugalbanda). Though the surviving forms of the myths are late, the erotic relation and the dominance of the female are patterns of extreme antiquity, reflecting the views of early agriculturalists and cases in nature in which females outlive males.

Figure 1.18. A satyr with hornlike ears and phallus is fended off by a maenad in a scene that appears with endless variations in Classical vase painting. Symbolic of insatiable animal libido, the satyr never attains his sexual goal. A comic figure in historical times, his origins lie in prehistoric Dionysiac ritual. (Staatliche Antikensammlungen und Glyptothek, Munich, no. 2624)

The feminine theme in early religion has given rise to two forms of wishful thinking that have been exploited by popular writers. One is to translate a purely religious view of nature into sexual politics, imagining an early matriarchy that held gentle sway in the Aegean until the invasion of brutal and swinish Indo-Europeans who drove the old religion underground. While it is true, as we shall see, that patriarchal gods often drove older cults out of the center of power, the two religious layers were to a great degree absorbed into each other in the usual syncretistic fashion. And while there have been (and still are) matrilinear societies and matrilocal marriages in which the bride owns

Sexual Culture in Ancient Greece

Figure 1.19. The embracing couple on the left and mother with child on the right were found a schist plaque in shrine VI A 30 at Çatal Hüyük. Divine prototypes of procreation are common denominator of early Mediterranean, Anatolian, and Balkan religion. Given its context, this could represent a divine archetype of procreation, the *hieros gamos*, and its ult. (James Mellaart)

the house to which her husband moves, evidence has not yet been found of a society run by women.[13] A second distortion has been to project onto the Mediterranean East a single areal religion built around a (capitalized) Mother Goddess. In tacitly appealing to the patterns of organized, monotheistic "religions of the book" such as

Figure 1.20. The "Gumelniţa lovers," a late fifth-millennium hierogamy from the lower Danube. In this rough terracotta pair, the female, on the left, is marked with the pubic triangle and is more prominently represented than her male partner, reflecting the greater importance of the female in nature religion. (Permission of the Estate of Marija Gimbutas)

Figure 1.21. A remarkably youthful Virgin mourns her divine son in Michelangelo's *Pietà* (A.D. 1498–1499, completed when the artist was in his midtwenties). In addition to her nubile face, her chest band is a possible vestige of pagan iconography (cf. figs. 3.3–3.5). The archetype of death, mourning, and resurrection, purged in Christianity of its erotic content, took various forms in the pre-Christian world, all related to the annual cycle of vegetation. (Alinari/Art Resource, New York)

Figure 1.22. Suckling child or lover? This late sixth-millennium pair found at Hacılar in Anatolia has been variously identified as an erotic symplegma (Amiet 1980) or a *kourotrophos* with infant (Mellaart 1975). Either the lover is very small or the infant very large, but in the mythic framework (even if it is potentially Oedipal) one alternative does not necessarily exclude the other. (James Mellaart)

Judaism, Christianity, or Islam, such a projection assumes a uniformity as unsupported by evidence as the fantasy of ancient matriarchy. Cognate elements over a wide area illustrate common religious instincts, not a uniformity of cult. Not all figurines are female, and not all female figurines are goddesses (or The Goddess). One of the frequent difficulties of interpretation has been to distinguish worshiper from worshiped. The same figurine may be described as an orant with hands raised in prayer, or a divinity with hands raised in epiphany. The phallus may be a metonymic symbol of generative power, or a display of apotropaic magic to ward off evil spirits. The evidence of prehistoric religion in Greece, as elsewhere in the region, points to a considerable variety in local cult that forbids the supposition of a single religion. The religious rhetoric of historical Greece shows that ancient piety throve on local variety. The divinity worshiped in Argos was not The Goddess, nor was she simply Hera; she was *Argive* Hera. At the same time, the more names and attributes that could be recited in prayer, the more powerful the deity and the more effective the prayer. Here, for example, is Lucius' prayer to Isis in Apuleius' *Metamorphoses*:

> Queen of Heaven, whether you are fostering Ceres the motherly nurse of all growth, . . . or whether you are celestial Venus who in the first moment of Creation mingled the opposing sexes in the generation of mutual desires . . . or whether you are [Diana] the sister of Phoebus . . . or whether you are Proserpine . . . O by whatever name, and by whatever rites, and in whatever form it is permitted to invoke you, come now and succor me in the hour of my calamity.[14]

The ecumenical spirit of early Mediterranean religion did not flatten out distinctions, it cherished them. It did not rule out contradictions, it drew strength from them. As complex and irregular as the Greek verb, Greek piety maintained whole constellations of local cults, myths, and rituals;[15] its centrifugal character is masked by a number of historical levelers, as early as Homeric Panhellenism and as late as the Romans, the great regularizers. The resulting oversimplification is compounded today by romantic antiquarians who impose Judeo-Christian standards of orthodoxy. Greek paganism was from the beginning responsive to common themes and divine archetypes, but it was not a monolithic religion, even in historical times. So much the less when ethnic, linguistic, and political ties were undeveloped.

That the goddesses of nature were more than static sexual icons is suggested by evidence of relatively late date connecting cults of Demeter, Athena, Aphrodite, Hera, and Artemis with sexual symbolism, licentious talk, and indecent dances. The most sexually explicit of the women's festivals in Athens was the winter observation of the Haloa, held at Eleusis in honor of Demeter and Dionysus. Women carried sexual emblems and made licentious sexual jokes, just as men did in the rural Dionysia.[16] At their banquet, they had baked goods shaped to represent sexual organs, and their ritual appears to have included planting clay phalli in the ground and sprinkling them with something to make them "grow" (fig. 1.2).[17] Similar sexual symbolism was probably part of the nocturnal festival of Arrhephoria in Athens.[18]

Sexual Religion

The objects carried by the girls, considered unmentionable in the time of Pausanias, were probably comparable to the sexual cakes used in the Haloa. Nothing illustrates the inappropriateness of our conception of religious propriety better than ceremonials of the type that employ genital symbolism. On these sacred occasions associated with growth and fertility, what is normally improper becomes a ritual necessity.

The aura of decency that surrounds Demeter, the matronly respectability of Hera, and even the asexuality associated with Athena and Artemis are a poor guide to the roles they played in specific local cases.[19] Though the evidence is often late, it shows that the Greek goddesses were what Lewis Richard Farnell called "cognate forms"[20] whose worship often included sexual themes. The most persistently sanitized goddess is Artemis. She had been so thoroughly neutered by Classical times that Euripides' Hippolytus (428 B.C.) was able to fixate on her as his personal savior from the impurity of sex. But divinities often embody opposites, as Apollo is the god of plague and of healing. On the one hand, Artemis inherits the roles of the prehistoric Mistress of Animals, πότνια θηρῶν; she is goddess of the young, patroness of girls, and herself a "virgin," παρθένος (the fates of Tiresias and Acteon, who see her nude, attest her inviolability). On the other hand, she is worshiped with lewd dances such as the *kordax* and phallic paraphernalia. As Artemis *Locheia* and *Soödina*, she presides over childbirth; her association with nubile girls in dances honoring her and in her mythic retinue is colored by the fact that the dances were preludes to courtship, and more than one of her retinue were victims of rape; her cult title λυσίζωνος identifies her as the "looser of belts," goddess of sexual initiation. Finally, her title *parthenos* may be understood not as indicative of virginity but of freedom from male sexual control, that is, unmarried but not necessarily celibate.[21] She is a nature goddess, belonging to the wilderness and wildness; her animals are wild, not domesticated. She is notorious for her cruelty, especially to women, though she is a woman's goddess. She demands human sacrifice, notably that of Iphigeneia;[22] in the *Iliad*, Hera taunts her: "Zeus has made you a lion among women, and given you leave to kill any at your pleasure" (21.483 f., tr. Lattimore). Sexually, she is the countertype of Hera: "We can find scarcely any [titles or allusions] that recognize her as a goddess of marriage."[23] Her rites are often orgiastic, and she has close ties with the oriental goddesses of sexual generation. Homer

Sexual Culture in Ancient Greece

alludes to the sexual power of Artemis when he compares Helen to her (*Od.* 5.122); so also the nubile Nausicaa (*Od.* 6.102 ff., 151). Even Penelope, more notable for prudence than erotic élan, looks "like Artemis or like golden Aphrodite" (*Od.* 17.37, 19.54).

Hera's sexuality stresses control and domestication. As Artemis is worshiped in the wild, Hera is worshiped in temples, hers being the oldest known in the historical Greek world. Whereas Artemis is worshiped with the sacrifice of wild animals, Hera is worshiped with the sacrifice of cattle. The punishments of Tiresias and Acteon emphasize Artemis' jealousy of her sexual privacy; the punishment of Io, transformed into a cow and set to wander the earth tormented by a gadfly because she had turned Zeus's head, emphasizes Hera's jealousy of her sexual proprietorship. Her cultic epithets, *gamostolos* the preparer of weddings, *zygia* the yoker, *teleia* the fulfilled, reflect a woman's view of marriage as female proprietorship. Though she is not given a maternal role, her power to fecundate nature through her sexual union with Zeus is dramatized in the *Iliad* when she seduces her spouse on the summit of Mount Ida:

Underneath them the divine earth broke into young, fresh
grass, and into dewy clover, crocus and hyacinth
so thick and soft it held the hard ground deep away from them.
There they lay down together and drew about them a golden
wonderful cloud, and from it the glimmering dew descended.

(14.346–351, tr. Lattimore)

Maternity is emphasized in Demeter, whose name was believed to be etymologically derived as "earth mother."[24] Specifically, she is the grain goddess and mother of Korē, "the Girl" Persephone. Literature, such as the Homeric *Hymn to Demeter*, emphasizes the bereft mother's search for her daughter who has been abducted by Hades and the barrenness of nature while Korē is underground. But even in the historical phase of the history of Demeter and Korē, sexual themes survive. First, Persephone must forever spend part of the year with Hades because in the underworld she has eaten the pomegranate, a sexual symbol. Second, an old woman named Iambe comforts Demeter in her grief, making her laugh "with many jokes" (πολλὰ παρασκώπτουσα, *H. Dem.* 203). Apollodorus connects this with the obscene raillery exchanged by women at the festivals of Thesmophoria, Stenia, Haloa, and others. Sexual talk stimulates nature; and though Demeter and Korē emerge in literature symbolizing the bond of mother and daughter, celebration of the cult was prominently sexual in a number of ways.[25]

The pairing of Demeter and Korē is another extremely ancient phenomenon in the representation of the goddesses of nature. Like verbal reduplication, the pairing and sometimes, as we shall see, the trebling of goddesses is implicit in their nature. The close partnership of Hera and Athena to aid the Greeks in the *Iliad* may be a reflection of this tendency. The earliest example of this motif is a Siamese-twin figure from Çatal Hüyük (fig. 1.23). It is also suggested in the Balkans by an early Vinča figurine (fig. 1.25), which is simply two-headed.

Figure 1.23. The consubstantial double goddess, ca. 6000 B.C., from Çatal Hüyük in central Anatolia. The earliest of a series of multiplex goddesses, perhaps related to the Greek pairing of Demeter and Korē. (James Mellaart)

Figure 1.24. A plank-shaped variant of the double goddess motif from Crete. Early Bronze Age, 2100–2000 B.C. (Cyprus Museum, Republic of Cyprus)

Such reduplication may be related to the conception of fraternal pairs like the Dioscuri Castor and Pollux or the Theban twins Zethos and Amphion. It is certainly related to many triple goddesses and similar feminine groups: the Moirai (Fates), the Graces, the Horai (Seasons), the Muses, and the Sirens.[26] Particularly as a sexual, erotic icon, the triple goddesses have a long history, beginning with a nude

Figure 1.25. This two-headed figure found in southwestern Romania dates from the end of the sixth millennium B.C.: Vinča culture. (Permission of the Estate of Marija Gimbutas)

triad from Crete (fig. 1.28) and continuing into the European Renaissance. Conventionally represented as two frontal nudes flanking a third who faces to the rear, they are from an early date made into symbolic, even allegorical representations. The Graces, or Charites, are closely associated with the Muses, the Horai, and Aphrodite. They appear in Hesiod's *Theogony* (ca. 700 B.C.), first grouped with Desire (Himeros) and the Muses (64 ff.), then with the Horai and the Moirai as daughters of Zeus. Though in Hesiod the Horai have been politicized into chamber of commerce allegories of good government—Order,

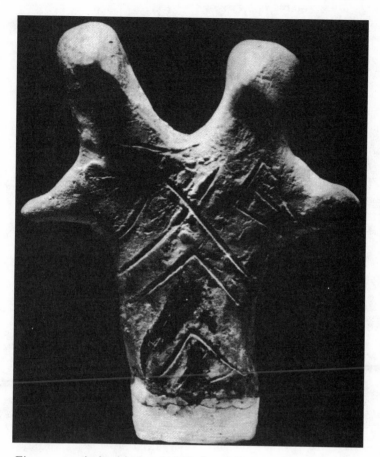

Figure 1.26. A double-headed bird goddess marked with chest bands associated in later Greek culture with Aphrodite figures. Like the preceding figurine, she bears traces of red paint. Vinča culture, early fifth millennium B.C. (Permission of the Estate of Marija Gimbutas)

Justice, and Peace (902: Ἐυνομίην τε Δίκην τε καὶ Εἰρήνην)—the Charites are fully erotic:

> Love which drops from their eyes strikes whomever they look on,
> loosening their limbs; under their brows their eyes glance with loveliness.
>
> (910 f., tr. R. M. Frazer)

Their common themes are the power to create (Horai, Moirai), attract, or even enchant, especially with song and dance (Charites, Muses,

Figure 1.27. Two women in elaborate, flounced Mycenaean costume hold a child in their lap. Found on the acropolis of Mycenae, this ivory group has been tentatively identified as Demeter and Korē with the child Ploutos. Probably fourteenth century B.C. (Archaeological National Museum, Athens, no. 7711)

Sirens). They may also be associated with death (Moirai, Sirens).[27] In Hesiod's *Works and Days*, the Graces join with Peitho (feminine Persuasion, Seduction) and the Horai to adorn Pandora. Hesiod forgets about Order, Justice, and Peace this time, making the Horai goddesses of springtime, flowers, and erotic Misrule. They are like the Graces in Botticelli's *Primavera*.[28]

Of these powerful kindred sisters, the Muses have best resisted simple trebling; like many pluralities in the Greek pantheon, they alternate between singular and plural. Hesiod trebles them twice to

Figure 1.28. A nude triad from Gortyn, Crete, seventh century B.C. The full nudity at this date marks them as oriental in inspiration; the tall *polos* is related to the headpieces in figs. 1.4, 1.6, 1.13, and 1.24. (Archaeological Museum, Heraklion, Crete)

Figure 1.29. The three Graces, detail from Botticelli's *Primavera* (1478 Florence: Ufizzi). Classical in inspiration, "with zones untied" (Hor. *Odes* 1.30.5) symbolizing their sexual freedom, they illustrate the liberation of erotic energy that comes with spring. Though more fluid than the rigid triad in fig. 1.28, they are less sexually explicit. (Alinari/Art Resource, New York)

Figure 1.30. Goddesses that give also take away. Kēres were goddesses of death and doom, like the Fates. The tetrad on this Cypriot sarcophagus (ca. 540–500 B.C.) are a multiplied variant of an eastern goddess, perhaps representing rebirth more than death. Hands held to their breasts like countless goddess figures since Neolithic times (cf. fig. 1.1), these are adorned with bead collars, necklaces, and pendant. Their hair is closely curled, with long tresses falling in front of each shoulder. (The Metropolitan Museum of Art, The Cesnola Collection; purchased by subscription, 1874–1876. [74.51.2453].)

nine (*Th.* 60), making them, as M. L. West remarks, "the largest multiple birth in Greek mythology"; this became their canonical number, though Plutarch says they were originally three.²⁹ Like other nymphs, they are associated with mountains and (especially) springs as emblems of inspiration. The fertility they represent is mental rather than physical, cultural rather than agricultural. Hesiod, for example, makes them responsible for the king's ability to make wise judgments (*Th.* 82 ff.), politicizing them as he does the Horai.

Cult also provides couture and ornament for the sexual goddesses of early religion. As in other ways they have a penchant for opposites—birth and death, propriety and lewdness—these tend to be represented either in full nudity (figs. 1.3, 1.12, 1.28, 1.30) or richly ornamented (figs. 1.24, 1.27). Typically, ornament does not mask but tends even to emphasize sexual characteristics, like the pubic triangle in the Cycladic fiddle-shaped goddess (fig. 1.11, cf. 1.20) or the exposed breasts in the elaborately costumed Minoan women (figs. 3.1, 3.3). Incised designs on the "frying pan" idol from Syros (fig. 1.10) cover the entire surface except the pubis, thus emphasizing that part. Terracotta figurines are sometimes perforated as if for the attachment of additional ornament (e.g., fig. 1.25). Headgear, necklaces, and chest bands are a standard part of the iconography of sexual goddesses from an early date; the flounced dresses of Minoan-Mycenaean goddesses and their priestesses (figs. 1.27, 3.1, 3.2) are echoed in the layered, pleated costume of Archaic Athenian korai (figs. 7.10, 7.13a-b, 7.14a-b-c)—all of which reveal and emphasize as much as they conceal. Full female nudity, after a few centuries of eclipse in Archaic and Classical Greece, returned in the Hellenistic period as a major object of veneration, to be once again submerged under Christianity until the Renaissance. Ornamentation and costuming suggest the richness implicit in the lifegiving goddesses and are emblematic of the worshipers' prosperity.³⁰ They can be understood as a tribute to the wealth that the goodwill of nature has made possible.

As sexual religion and myth take on a stronger erotic color, the love of ornament takes on added meaning. "Golden" Aphrodite, who is in most respects a Bronze Age eastern import, is significantly metallic, exotic, and costly, far from the nature goddesses with whom she shares Olympus.³¹ Though her eastern cognates were regularly nude, they are sometimes shown wearing a chest ornament with which

Aphrodite is appropriately costumed in the following scene. When Homer's Hera condescends to borrow something sexy from Aphrodite to seduce Zeus, she receives the κεστός ἱμάς, an embroidered sash that passes diagonally between the breasts and was the emblem of the love goddess:

> . . . on it are figured all beguilements, and loveliness
> is figured upon it, and passion of sex is there, and the whispered
> endearment that steals the heart away even from the thoughtful.
> (Il. 14.215 ff., tr. Lattimore)

This eastern detail, comparable to the ornament on statuettes of nude love goddesses from Mesopotamia and Syria to Iran and India, is worn singly or double in an X form, and it becomes a feature of Greco-Roman representations of Venus.[32] Hesiod's Pandora, who like Homer's Helen is a projection of Aphrodite, is carefully costumed for her mission of stealing the heart away from mankind:

> . . . the goddess gray-eyed Athena girdled and dressed her:
> the Graces divine along with our Lady Persuasion hung
> golden necklaces on her, and the lovely-haired Horai
> crowned her head by setting upon it a garland of spring flowers.
> (Op. 72–75, tr. R. M. Frazer)

Aphrodite herself is costumed in a peplos that the Graces wove for her (Il. 5.338), and though Homer does not often linger over details of clothing, he takes time to describe the regalia of Calypso and Circe, Odysseus' chief sexual distractions on his way back from Troy:

> . . . she, the nymph, mantled herself in a gleaming white robe
> fine-woven and delightful, and around her waist she fastened
> a handsome belt of gold, and on her head was a wimple.
> (Od. 5.230-232 = 10.543-.545, tr. Lattimore)

Aphrodite's love of complex ornament is further reflected in her Sapphic epithet ποικιλόθρονος, "intricately throned." Her love of complexity is summed up by Euripides: "there are many intricate things about Aphrodite" (τῇ δ' Ἀφροδίτῃ πόλλ' ἔνεστι ποικίλα, fr. 26

Nauck). Coming from Euripides, this is an ironic statement, reflecting her deceptiveness and the complicated things people do under her influence. The Greeks understood all their gods to be deceptive, none more than Aphrodite.

An earlier, less complex Aegean tradition represents its sexual goddess with an instinct for simple elegance that has struck chords in artists and connoisseurs of the twentieth century. Taking their cue from the schematic style of Neolithic art, Cycladic craftsmen adopted a simplicity of line and gesture in their religious figurines that was in part dictated by the hardness of the stone used and the limitations of the saws used to form the basic shapes. Here too an aesthetic ideal clearly enters into the expression of a sexual idea.

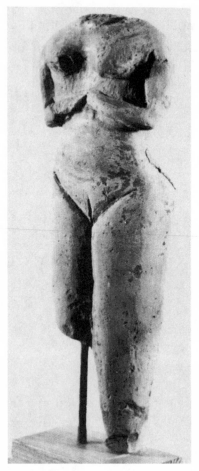

Figure 1.31. This standing nude excavated from Neolithic Lerna, like the nude from Nea Nikomedeia, anticipates the elegant simplicity of later Cycladic figurines. (Permission of the Estate of Marija Gimbutas)

Sexual Culture in Ancient Greece

Figure 1.32. A Chalcolithic icon from Cyprus, which became the most important westward conduit for the cult of Aphrodite. Her phallic head, like that in fig. 1.12, expresses her dual sexual nature, and her body is all rhythms: hips echo the arms (which are bent inward at the elbows as in fig. 1.1), pelvis echoes the breasts, and the three cleavages form a single interrupted line. Ca. 3500 B.C. (Cyprus Museum, Republic of Cyprus)

Figure 1.33. In an ingenious type of reduplication, the cruciform goddess of generation wears an amulet of herself. Steatite from Cyprus, found near Paphos, the center of Aphrodite's cult (she is often called "The Paphian") at the western end of the island. Ca. 3000–2300 B.C. (Cyprus Museum, Republic of Cyprus)

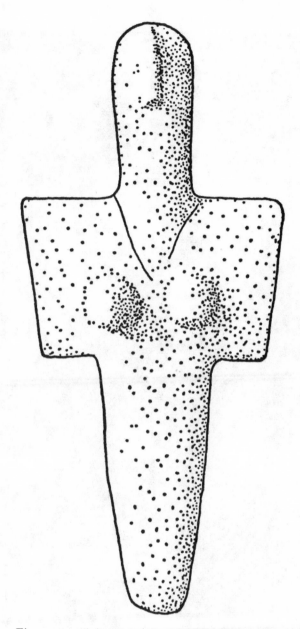

Figure 1.34. Adorned only with a necklace, the "Venus of Senorbi" is a Sardinian variant of the cruciform design. (From Trump, *The Prehistory of the Mediterranean*, 1980, fig. 33, p. 147, Yale University Press)

Figure 1.35. Cycladic figurines combine economy of manufacture with elegance of line. The saw cuts that separate the arms from the body continue the divergent lines of legs and hips, while the incision separating the legs becomes the pubic cleft. Syros, ca. 2300 B.C. (National Archaeological Museum, Athens, no. 6174)

Figure 1.36. Zeus and Hera as lovers. This late seventh-century woodcarving from Samos is a unique variation of the goddess with her hands on her breasts. The gesture, neither foreplay nor seizure, is a display of Hera's power, appropriate to the island that held the goddess's great cult center. It shares some of the ambiguity of fig. 1.22 above. Now lost from the museum at Vathy, Samos. (Copyright by DAI Athens, neg. no. Samos 2313)

Well before the beginning of recorded history, Aphrodite or her closest cognates in the Chalcolithic pantheon attracted conceptions that went beyond mere sexuality to the aesthetic and the erotic. Impulses that had little scope for development in rudimentary agricultural societies clustered around sexual figures. These icons paved the way for an easy transition from sexual religion to the erotic culture that flourishes under the conditions provided by actual civilization.

CHAPTER TWO

Coming-of-Age in the Ancient Near East

TWO SEXUAL MYTHS OF CULTURAL INITIATION

Ye shall not surely die: for God knoweth that in the day
ye eat thereof, then your eyes shall be opened, and ye
shall be as gods, knowing good and evil.

GENESIS 3:4–5

M any early communities of the Mediterranean perceived the
natural forces around them as sexual. The more religion and
custom reflected this perception of nature, the more sexual knowledge
merged with cultural knowledge. Because sexual codes may express a
people's sense of identity, the people so identified are apt to myth-
ologize the passage from nature to culture as a sexual initiation. Sexual
initiation can thus be a symbol for becoming more human, even in a
people like the Hebrews whose religion shows few of the sexual features found in neighboring cults. The centrality of sex to cultural
identity is demonstrated in this chapter by two myths, the expulsion
of Adam and Eve from the Garden into the larger world and the
initiation of Gilgamesh's companion, Enkidu, into the life of the city.
Though the story of Enkidu embodies a more positive attitude toward
the erotic, both myths express a significant ambivalence regarding the
sexual passage out of the state of nature. Neither myth is Greek, but
both shed light on the problematic character of erotic life that would
come to the surface in Greek thought.

Though it is appropriate to speak of the great transformations of
human life as revolutions—the Neolithic, the urban, the industrial

revolution—these evolved over generations, and in the case of the first two without leaving a written record. Each created larger concentrations of people, more intensive relations between cultures, and more complex social arrangements. Important as these were, the evolution of change is a less dramatic story than the sudden impact of a more developed culture on a more primitive. It is seen in Genesis when Adam and Eve encounter a serpent who knows more than they do and in the Gilgamesh Epic when the woman from the city teaches Enkidu city ways. The encounter with a higher culture happens in a way that has nothing to do with sex in the *Odyssey*. Consider, for example, what Telemachus, a western islander, says to his companion, Pisistratus, when he first glimpses the Mycenaean palace of Menelaus and Helen:

> . . . only look at
> the gleaming of the bronze all through these echoing mansions,
> and the gleaming of gold and amber, of silver and ivory.
> The court of Zeus on Olympus must be like this on the inside,
> such abundance of everything. Wonder takes me as I look on it.
>
> (4.71–75, tr. Lattimore)

The first impression, and the compelling attraction, is of a divine life, like "the court of Zeus." No one knows what the Greeks said or thought when they first encountered the great civilizations of Egypt and the Near East, but like the serpent in Genesis assuring Eve that she and Adam "shall be as gods," Homer knew that the wealth and knowledge of civilization would prompt comparisons with divinity. The effect on the newly initiated is indeed revolutionary; the effects of such encounters and the resulting transformations are a commonplace of song and story from the Gilgamesh Epic to *Sister Carrie*. With Telemachus, it is part of the story of how a youth comes of age in the age of iron, a kind of *bildungsroman*; with Adam and Eve, it is a collective experience in which the entire human race turns a historical page. The progenitors of humankind are drawn from the childlike simplicity of food gathering to the painful complexities of agricultural life:

> Cursed is the ground because of you;
> in toil you shall eat of it all the days of your life;
> thorns and thistles it shall bring forth for you;

and you shall eat the plants of the field.
By the sweat of your brow you shall eat bread . . .

(Gen. 3:17–19)

With all of its nostalgia for a primal simplicity of life, the myth employed by the Hebrews in the first chapters of Genesis is on one level Neolithic because it mythologizes the passage of mankind from a food gathering to a farming and pastoral economy. After the fall, Adam will eat manufactured food instead of tree-ripened fruit, and he will do so "in toil," by the sweat of his brow. Whatever its advantages, the Neolithic revolution is remembered in biblical myth as a calamity.

But the story in Genesis is a double myth, symbolizing two great transformations. The second cultural revolution, the conversion to the culture of cities, was another unwelcome development for the Hebrews, if we believe the priestly fulminations against the "abominations of the Canaanites" who inhabited the cities of ancient Palestine. Like the Helladic Greeks, the pastoral and agricultural Hebrews lived for a long time on the periphery of the great Bronze Age civilizations, combining in their history elements of Neolithic myth (the first chapters of Genesis) with stories of contact with Bronze Age Egypt (Abraham and the Pharaoh) and the wicked "cities of the plain."

Both phases of Hebrew protohistory are woven into scripture with a clearly discernible sexual and erotic thread. God creates Woman out of Adam's rib as an extension of him, to be his "helper."[1] In their primal state the first couple are asexual, ignorantly unashamed of their nakedness. This sexual innocence is the first thing they lose when they eat the fruit of the tree of knowledge: their eyes are instantly opened. The first thing they *know*, without a word spoken, is their sexual nakedness: "Then the eyes of both were opened, and they knew that they were naked; and they sewed fig leaves together and made themselves aprons" (Gen. 3:7). This is then the basis of God's accusation, the only evidence required that Adam has eaten the forbidden fruit: "Who told you that you were naked?" (Gen. 3:11). Adam is penalized for his disobedience by having to become a food grower. Eve's punishment, besides painful childbirth, is an erotic dependency on her husband, which forms the basis of her subservience: "your desire shall be for your husband, and he shall rule over you" (Gen. 3:16). The first knowledge of man is carnal, and his first act upon leaving Eden is sexual: "Now Adam knew Eve his wife, and she conceived" (Gen. 4:1). This fulfills the serpent's promise, which was implicitly sexual in the first place: "knowing good and evil" is a Hebrew phrase for the erotic discrimination that was thought to come with sexual maturity.[2]

The Genesis myth of mankind's Neolithic coming-of-age is nostalgic toward the original state of sexual innocence, and at best ambivalent about sexual knowledge. Sexuality is a feature that separates humankind from God, who is patriarchal but (at least in the priestly texts that were canonized as the Hebrew Bible) has no sexuality.[3] Later Bible stories evince a fixation on sexual purity that characterizes the entire Judeo-Christian ethical code and contrasts sharply with Greco-Roman culture. Some of the early biblical narratives relate encounters with neighboring cultures in which Hebrew patriarchs compromise their sexual rules to survive; the general tendency, though, shows a continual battle against assimilation of the surrounding sexual culture.

Like the Greeks, the Hebrews migrated into their homeland in the early part of the second millennium B.C., leaving behind the Mesopotamian source of their earliest myths and moving into the ambit of the Bronze Age Egyptians, Phoenicians, and Canaanites. Their natural source of food relief when there was famine in Canaan was the reserves in Egypt. When Abraham takes his wife Sarai there to wait out the famine, he pretends she is his sister so that he can lend her to the Pharaoh according to the customs of sexual hospitality familiar to the archaic nomads and pastoralists of the region (Gen. 12:11). He repeats the deception later with Abimelech, the king of Gerar—again with Sarai's connivance—but this time God intervenes to prevent the consummation of the loan (Gen. 20).[4] When Abraham's son Isaac uses the same strategy with his wife Rebekah in the household of Abimelech six chapters later, the Philistine king spots Isaac fondling Rebekah in an unbrotherly way and once again avoids offending God (Gen. 26:6-16). When powerless and needy, Hebrews are not above compromising their wives to ensure their personal safety. Each time it is God alone who intervenes to preserve the purity of his people, superimposing his will on the ancient custom of sexual hospitality.

A different kind of hospitality is displayed by Lot, the only good citizen of Sodom, who offers refuge to two angels of God disguised

Sexual Culture in Ancient Greece

as travelers. When the locals demand that he surrender his guests for sexual abuse, Lot offers his daughters instead (Gen. 19:8) rather than break the law of hospitality that demanded that he protect his guests at any cost (Gen. 19:8, cf. Judg. 19:22–26). The rescue of Lot from the subsequent annihilation of the "cities of the plain" is an object lesson in good and bad hospitality, but the secondary reading of this episode as a lesson in sexual conduct—singling out "sodomy" as a cardinal offense against God—has important later ramifications, anticipating and legitimizing the most draconian penalties for sexual offenses. To this day, even blatant anti-Semites appeal to ancient Hebrew law when attempting to legitimize the regulation of sexual behavior.

Yet some of the early stories suggest, as we have seen, that the Hebrews of antehistorical legend did not make sexual taboo and male proprietorship a categorical imperative but pragmatically let the necessities of personal safety and the laws of hospitality take priority as circumstances required. Although expurgated by later revision, such stories provide occasional glimpses into an early Hebraic culture that accepted and even assimilated sacred prostitution, fertility cults of the goddess Asherah, and sexual magic.[5] However, these same stories portray an asexual but patriarchal God to whom the protection of Hebrew sexual honor is inseparable from their religious rectitude. This theme was to be played on repeatedly by the reformist authors of Deuteronomy, Leviticus, and Kings as well as Jeremiah and such prophets as Hosea and Amos, by whom erotic rituals such as cult prostitution and sexual intercourse on threshing floors (Hos. 4:13–14, 9:1–2) are condemned as apostasy instead of tolerated as syncretism. The sexual-religious purism of the Deuteronomist tradition is not at work, for example, in Genesis 38, when Judah impregnates his daughter-in-law Tamar thinking she is a cult prostitute. But in later Hebrew writings, such abominations are mentioned, and mentioned often, as evidence of a fatal disloyalty to God and his Covenant with the Hebrews. The distrust that the Hebrew reformers of the seventh and sixth centuries B.C. felt toward the sexual and religious culture of the Near East is a frequently shrill theme of their sacred writings and an instructive contrast with the prevailing civilization of the region. It is heard in the Deuteronomic prohibition against male and female sacred prostitution (Deut. 23:17–18), in the downfall of David after his affair with Uriah's wife Bathsheba (2 Sam. 11 ff.), in speculations that the political troubles of Solomon and his son Rehoboam resulted from backsliding into sexual cult (1 Kings 11:33, 14:23–24), and in the severity with which the Holiness Code in Leviticus condemned a whole spectrum of sexual deviations. The separateness of the Hebrews from their neighbors, which they made a part of their sense of identity around the time of the Exile, was most vigorously defined with regard to cultic exclusivity and sexual behavior. Sexual profligacy was the metaphor of choice to condemn religious backsliding: "They shall no more slay their sacrifices for satyrs, after whom they play the harlot. . . . If a person turns to mediums and wizards, playing the harlot after them, I will set my face against that person" (Lev. 17:7, 20:6). Sexual crimes are almost always punishable by death in Hebrew law: adultery, some types of incest, male homosexuality, polygamy with a woman and her mother, and sex with animals are all equally mortal crimes in Leviticus 20:10–19. A man and a woman who have sex when she is menstruating are to be "cut off from among their people"; even cross-dressing is an "abomination" in Deuteronomy 22:5. By the end of the pre-Christian era, fornication was elevated to the gravest of sins: "There is no greater sin than fornication."[6]

The draconian character of Hebrew law in sexual matters is evidence that it was precisely in this area that its authors felt threatened by their neighbors. Military aggression was an overt form of hostility that could be militarily warded off. But the more active sexual culture of the Babylonians, Canaanites, and Philistines was a cultural subversion that some patriarchs and prophets feared no less and sought just as vigorously to nip in the bud. God himself demands the most drastic measures in Numbers 25, when the Israelites profane themselves by "whoring with the Moabite women" and sacrificing to their god. He commands Moses to impale the ringleaders of this sexual-religious apostasy, and when Phineas impales an Israelite and a Midianite woman with his spear while they are fornicating, God checks the plague with which he had been punishing his people. The biblical linkage between illicit sex and religious apostasy is nowhere better illustrated. The purpose of Hebraic sexual law served two purposes: to keep their sexual culture elementary and diametrically opposed to that of their neighbors and to maintain their ethnic purity.

It is not necessary to conclude that the Hebrew people were sexually repressed by nature, or even by their early culture. Granted, their culture during the Bronze Age was the simple one of poor agricultural and pastoral tribes who lived in the hills outside the "cities of the plain." The stern sexual prohibitions of the so-called Holiness Code (Lev. 17–26) may reflect ancient taboos, but their puritanical severity is the work of reformers affected by the universal myth that our ancestors were more righteous than ourselves. We can read between the lines of their insistent denunciations that the average Hebrew was all too prone to assimilate the sexual religion and culture of the region, as Abhinavagupta's dictum about the attractiveness of the erotic could have predicted. The early patriarchs, as we have already seen, were not moral zealots. David, the seducer of Bathsheba, was no Cato; his son Solomon (r. ca. 970–922 B.C.), the supposed author of the erotic Song of Solomon, married a number of foreign women, beginning with the Pharaoh's daughter (1 Kings 3:1); he eventually had a total of 700 wives and 300 concubines (if we believe 1 Kings 11:3), whose worship of the erotic goddess Astarte he not only tolerated but joined. His son and successor, Rehoboam, likewise tolerated the cult of Asherah, as the Canaanite fertility goddess was called: "For they also built for themselves high places, and pillars, and Asherim on every high hill and under every green tree; and there were also male cult prostitutes in the land" (1 Kings 14:23–24). As for the Song of Solomon itself, this collection has been variously dated;[7] it suggests the oriental splendor of Solomon's court, and its inclusion in the Hebrew Canon may be understood as a concession that physical eroticism was accepted in its proper context. The Hebrew Scriptures, in short, attest a tension between the prevailing sexual culture of the region and the determination of Hebrew reformers to carve out a separate identity and a type of archaistic "purity" that reflected the simpler erotic culture of pastoral tribes a millennium earlier.

The heated language with which Israel's religious purists denounce the neighboring religion, in particular its erotic character, throws light on the sexual culture of the ancient Near East in the same way that Christian denunciations of Classical paganism have provided significant information about Greco-Roman religion. Although the scriptural passages we have considered here took their present form just before the middle of the first millennium B.C., the culture and the cults they denounce—to which we shall return—have roots in the Bronze Age.

Some of the earliest and most impressive evidence of the erotic self-awareness of the Near Eastern Bronze Age is literary as well as physical. The text of the second-millennium Gilgamesh Epic, preserved on tablets of a later period,[8] records the exploits of a hero of the early third millennium B.C. whose name is recorded in a later Sumerian King List as the fifth ruler of Uruk. Gilgamesh, a hero whom the gods made two-thirds god and one-third man, is a wise but arrogant ruler whose warlike ways leave no son with his father and whose lust "will not leave young girls [alone], the daughters of warriors, the brides of young men." Consequently, the goddess of creation Aruru is asked to create an alter ego to contend with him and leave Uruk in peace. The creation of Enkidu from clay and his introduction to civilization by a prostitute from Uruk[9] has significant parallels to the biblical epic of man's creation and his sexual initiation. Particularly interesting in this instance is the Babylonian epic's greater emphasis on eroticism and its linkage of sex with other emblems of civilization such as bread, beer, and clothing.

When Enkidu is first created, his body is rough and covered with matted hair, the length of which makes him "like a woman." The story multiplies emblems of Enkidu's wildness, as it will later of his civilization: he roams over the steppe with wild creatures and sucks their milk, lacking all knowledge of bread and beer.[10] He helps game to escape the trapper, whose father advises him to ask Gilgamesh for a prostitute to tame this fearsome creature. Gilgamesh understands the ruse:

> . . . When he approaches the cattle at the watering place,
> She must take off her clothes and reveal her attractions.
> He will see her and go close to her.
> Then his cattle, who have grown up in open country with him, will
>   become alien to him.

When the trapper and the harlot finally spot Enkidu approaching the drinking hole with the wild herds, his instructions are even more explicit:

Sexual Culture in Ancient Greece

Here he is, Shamhat, bare your bosom,
Open your legs and let him take in your attractions!
Do not pull away, take wind of him!
He will see you and come close to you.
Spread open your garments, and let him lie upon you;
Do for him, the primitive man, as women do.

Enkidu lies with her for six days and seven nights as she teaches him the sexual art of civilization, and for this period he forgets his home in the hills." When he does try to return to his wild companions, they bolt before him, and he finds he cannot run after them: "Enkidu had been diminished, he could not run as before. Yet he had acquired judgement, had become wiser." He returns now to the harlot Shamhat, who tells him what has happened and where his future lies:

You have become [profound] Enkidu, you have become like a god.
Why should you roam open country with wild beasts?
Come, let me take you into Uruk the sheepfold,
To the pure house, the dwelling of Anu and Ishtar,
Where Gilgamesh is perfect in strength.

She praises Uruk, which is described in other ancient sources as "city of courtesans, hierodules, and prostitutes";[12] there, Shamhat continues, "young men are girded with sashes and every day is a feast day, and girls (?) [show off] (their) figures, adorned with joy and full of happiness." She divides her clothing and dresses Enkidu, thus conferring on him the first outward sign of his conversion to civilization. She takes him to the shepherds' tents, where he is given food and beer: "Eat the food, Enkidu, the symbol of life. Drink the beer, destiny of the land." Like the beer that he has shunned in his wild state, Enkidu's meal of bread and beer is literally cultured food, products of fermentation controlled by man: natural food, mediated by human culture. Now merry with drink, Enkidu rubs down the matted hair of his body and anoints himself with oil. The process is complete; Enkidu is now "like any man," no longer the frightening savage who first appeared to the trapper. Like the Genesis story, the tale of Enkidu links sex with knowledge[13] and a godlike state.

The iconography of this section of the Gilgamesh Epic is compact and unmistakable. As in the Genesis account, it is a woman who initiates the man in a multiple symbolic process that includes eating, clothing, and the erotic. There are two conspicuous differences: as we have seen, the symbolic terms of Genesis are agrarian rather than urban, and it is pessimistic, describing the protagonist's change of status as a transgression and expulsion from a happy state of innocence. The biblical comparison to a divine state—"You will be like God"— is ironic, a serpent's cynical promise. But when the prostitute tells Enkidu "you have become like a god," the hyperbole does not mask a deception so much as it highlights a transformation. What happens in Genesis is the first in a series of disobediences, apostasies, penalties, and exiles. What happens in the Gilgamesh Epic is in the end tragic for Enkidu (he loses his life and even for a moment curses the woman who introduced him to civilization), but it is tragic in the best sense also because Enkidu attains a heroic role and becomes (like Adam in Gen. 3) a full participant in the life that only civilization makes possible. The personal relation with Gilgamesh that Enkidu's transformation makes possible is one of equality, a marriage of true minds.[14] The companionate, helping relation of Eve to Adam in Genesis 2:18 is bluntly downgraded to servitude after she corrupts him with the forbidden fruit: "he shall rule over you" (Gen. 3:16).

Although it stands by itself as a positive myth of civilization, the story of Enkidu's sexual initiation and the halting of his companion's barbaric defloration of virgins are congruent with the meaning of the Gilgamesh Epic as a whole. Realizing that life is short and fame is long, Gilgamesh takes Enkidu on a series of exploits that end in the latter's death. Gilgamesh's subsequent grieving quest for everlasting life ends in disappointment when he learns from Utnapishtim in the underworld that there is no permanence and when he fails to bring back the plant that restores lost youth. The story ends on a note of triumph, though, when Gilgamesh proudly displays his city to the boatman of the underworld:

> Go up on to the wall of Uruk, Ur-shanabi, and walk around,
> Inspect the foundation platform and scrutinize the brickwork!
> Testify that its bricks are baked bricks,
> And that the Seven Councilors must have laid its foundations!

Sexual Culture in Ancient Greece

One square mile is city, one square mile is claypits, as well as the open
    ground of Ishtar's temple.
Three square miles and the open ground comprise Uruk.

The values that this epic affirms are anything but otherworldly, and
they are not even completely heroic. Though Gilgamesh is too frantic
with grief for Enkidu to heed her words at the time, the hedonistic
advice of the alewife Siduri has a positive value for the emergent
meaning of the epic:

> So, Gilgamesh, let your stomach be full,
> Day and night enjoy yourself in every way,
> Every day arrange for pleasures.
> Day and night, dance and play,
> Wear fresh clothes.
> Keep your head washed, bathe in water,
> Appreciate the child who holds your hand,
> Let your wife enjoy herself in your lap.[15]

The heroes of biblical and classical epic are made of sterner stuff, but
civilized people ignore the advice of Siduri at their peril. Such a philosophy is implicit, perhaps, in a culture of cities, though it may not
entirely define such a culture. Pleasure is one of the goals of civilization, one of the products it consciously aims to promote. The Gilgamesh Epic is the epic of Bronze Age civilization because the values it
implies are those that the cities made possible, and vice versa. Our text
begins and ends with praise for the city and its monumental walls made
of burnt brick (as opposed to mud brick, which quickly weathers
away). The copper that ornaments the wall's cornice is emblematic of
metallurgy. The hero's infatuation with warfare that leaves no son with
his father, and with sexual privilege that leaves no virgin to her lover,
suggests the abuse of extratribal political power in the culture of cities.
When Enkidu is able to halt those abuses, he advances the civilized life
of Uruk. The killing of the forest monster Humbaba in "the country
where the cedar is cut" is symptomatic of the need that cities in
southern Mesopotamia such as Uruk had for the large timbers used
in the construction of monumental buildings—another feature of
civilization. Perhaps even the love of Gilgamesh for the outsider
Enkidu is symbolic of an ethical dimension of city life, where close ties

are not only the parochial bonds within one's own clan but also alliances with unrelated newcomers. Like Plato's *Symposium*, the Gilgamesh Epic reflects the high value civilization puts on eroticism, and it sketches the passage from sexual love to the deeper personal attachments that take on a sublime character. Though Enkidu does not become personally attached to the prostitute, she is for him what Calypso, Circe, and Nausicaa are for Odysseus: a liminal character standing on the threshold of two states, a guide, and a provider of food, comfort, and clothing. Above all, she is the doorkeeper of civilization, not least because she is a professional, belonging to a class that did not exist before the division of community functions into specialties.

During the Bronze Age, the sexual female began her evolution from goddess of nature to emblem of civilization. More accurately, perhaps, a sexual female developed alongside traditional goddesses such as Ishtar and circumstantially related to her (e.g., as hierodule or temple associate) and charged with erotic—as opposed to simply sexual—power to transform. If the model supplied by the Gilgamesh Epic is symptomatic of a general Near Eastern pattern, this erotic, liminal figure, standing as she does at the threshold of a new human condition, makes Bronze Age man simultaneously more godlike and more fully human. It is no irony that Shamhat says to Enkidu "you have become like a god," while a few lines later Enkidu is "like any man." The biblical myth of mankind's transformation, while diametrically opposed to this progressive view of sexuality, necessarily adopts similar erotic symbolism to depict the passage from the original state of ignorance into one of knowledge.[16]

CHAPTER THREE

Hellenizing Greece

THE REVISION OF BRONZE AGE MYTHOLOGY

No, my child, not for you are the works of warfare.
Rather concern yourself only with the lovely secrets of
marriage, while all this shall be left to Athene and sudden
Ares.

ZEUS TO APHRODITE, *ILIAD* 5.428–430,

TR. LATTIMORE

The previous chapter showed how sexual and erotic myths figure prominently in two important Near Eastern documents whose intentions were in varying degrees both universal (telling the story of humankind) and specific to their respective culture. The myth of Adam and Eve's encounter with the serpent and the story of Enkidu and Shamat in the Gilgamesh Epic, in the context of the archaeological record of the eastern Mediterranean and the biblical fulminations against sexual cult, argue that sexual cult and erotic myth were not just prominent features but in some sense distinctive cultural markers. In seeking to define a Hebrew identity that contrasted definitively with that of their Levantine neighbors, the authors of the Torah assembled myths and taboos that distinguished their sexual culture from that of the surrounding Canaanites. This chapter considers some Homeric myths in which it is possible to detect a related Panhellenic impulse to distinguish an emergent Greek culture from that of its eastern neighbors. These myths are likewise sexual.

Greek civilization as we know it developed some centuries after the arrival in the southern Balkans of a new group of people who spoke the Indo-European parent language of Greek, Latin, and most other European languages. Important studies have endeavored to show how Indo-Europeanism shaped the politics, myth, and poetry of early Greece.[1] An equally important outside influence was Near Eastern, brought by colonists and maintained over a period of centuries by trade relations. These two formative influences overlap and intertwine, making the task of separation difficult. The Indo-European components are hard to identify with any degree of certainty; they certainly include patriarchal sky gods, chief among them *dyiaus>Zeus, *dyiaus-pitar>Jupiter, and the dawn goddess Eos (cognate to Indic Uas)—both of whom are sexually active in surviving myths.[2] The language core is Indo-European; but other structures, such as Georges Dumézil's three-part schematization of Indo-European thought and institutions into religious, military, and agricultural divisions, are more speculative.

Few questions in European history are as murky as the details of the arrival in Greece of people who spoke an early form of Greek. An invasion or migration of peoples, driven by the breakup of a Proto-Indo-European (PIE) culture somewhere, is thought to have initiated a process of cultural change that would eventually produce a distinctive, persistent, and dominant set of traits that we designate as "Greek." But the archaeological evidence is so unclear that the supposed invasion may have been only a political-military takeover and a slow evolution instead of a sharp break with the past. Even the date is disputed: instead of a time near the beginning of the second millennium—2100 or 1900 B.C.—some prehistorians are willing to accept a lower date, ca. 1600 B.C., for the appearance of an Indo-European language in the southern Balkans.[3]

The Indo-Europeans may have prevailed not by irresistible numbers of warlike invaders but by a military technology of fighting from a chariot that afforded an armored rapidity like something between a tank and a fighter plane. The masters of this technology were, in this hypothesis, the captains of a new industry—wheel making, horse breeding, and horse training—and the experts of a new craft—horsemanship and archery or spearmanship. This new elite, while not exactly a military-industrial complex, had the requisite leverage to take over the southern Balkans (as they did other parts of the ancient Near East), bringing with them Indo-European Greek as the language of the conqueror. Similarly, William the Conqueror brought French to England not by force of a migrant population but by the prestige of the court. With Indo-European language came Indo-European myth. Because chariot fighters worked in pairs of a driver and a bowman or spearman, a significant connection has been found between the "Heavenly Twins" myths found in Indic, Greek, Baltic, and Celtic mythologies.[4] Castor and Pollux are the chief Greek expression of this pairing, but anyone who has read the *Iliad* closely is aware of how often Homer pairs his heroes, even when they are not partners in the chariot: Idomeneus and Meriones, Ajax and his half brother Teucer, Achilles and Patroclus, Diomedes and Sthenelus, Sthenelus and Deïpylos, and a score of other pairs, many but not all of them brothers. Other Greek traditions paired Theseus and Pirithoos, Heracles and Iolaus, Orestes and Pylades. The tendency of later Greeks to represent Achilles and Patroclus as lovers, and the assemblage in Thebes of an entire corps of male lovers called the Sacred Band of Thebes, is one aspect of sexual identity in a culture whose earliest epic featured a warrior elite built around male partners. The extreme degree of male bonding in the Greek branch of the Indo-European family is not an inevitable result of its claimed military origins, but it may be a significant outcome because of the tendency in warlike societies such as Sparta for men and women to live separate lives. Although the pairing of men in battle stands out in the Homeric epics, there is no early evidence, nothing in Homer, that points clearly to anything homoerotic in the relations of warriors. The cult of homoeroticism in certain Greek male elites appears to have been a later development. The first statements of a Greek sexual idiom have little to do with "Greek love." Erotic male companionship may therefore be a delayed result of Indo-European warrior society, but if so it was a result that took the form it did only in Greece. Like other allegedly Indo-European features, it does not admit proof.

Lacking as we do clear signposts of a cultural spirit before writing came to Greece, we look for clues in the earliest available literary text. Because he encapsulates so much of what it meant to be Greek in the ancient world—his authority was virtually canonical throughout antiquity—Homer is a fertile source of cultural insight. The likeliest and most widely accepted dates of authorship (ca. 750-700 B.C.) place Homeric epic more than four centuries after the legendary Trojan War (ca. 1184 B.C.) and the Mycenaean world that collapsed soon after the sack of Troy. Following several generations of obscure poverty, a "dark age" in which trade with the Near East was discontinued and their culture lay in an isolated state of incubation, the Greek-speaking communities of mainland Greece and the Aegean restored their contacts with the East, and perhaps as a consequence became more aware of a separate identity. One lasting expression of this self-discovery was the establishment of quadrennial Panhellenic games at Olympia (776 B.C.) from which they dated their subsequent history. The other was the Homeric epics, which represent the distant Trojan War as a Panhellenic expedition. The *Iliad* and the *Odyssey* provide only a dim historical record of the Mycenaean age, but they give a sharply drawn picture of an emergent culture that took shape long afterward.

In contrast to Hebrew scripture, where tribal narrative gives authority to an ethnic law code (the Torah), Homeric epic dramatizes national character without laying down a code of law. Homer is normative, showing how heroes behave and quoting their discussions (more than half the *Iliad* is direct quotation). Significantly, appeals to authority or obedience tend to fail in Homer.[5] The quarrel of Achilles and Agamemnon and its consequences in the *Iliad* explore the strengths and weaknesses of Greek individualism, pitting competitive against cooperative virtues. The successful return of Odysseus dramatizes the high value the Greeks placed on self-control, intelligence, and cunning over brute force and superior numbers. In his treatment of the love goddess Aphrodite, Homer rejects the traditional Near Eastern conception of a goddess who combines the attributes of sex and warfare. Before detailing Homer's remythologizing of the sex goddess, it will be useful to review some well-known features of the religious archaeology.

The culture of Greece and the Cyclades in the Bronze Age is too diverse and obscure in its details to admit of any monolithic description. This is particularly true with respect to religion. The confidence with which Nilsson could describe "the Minoan-Mycenaean religion" in the years between 1926 and 1950[6] has given way to a caution with which authorities such as Colin Renfrew deny that there was any single Minoan-Mycenaean religion.[7] Three religious traditions or influences were at work in Bronze Age Greece: (1) the Neolithic substratum, in which goddess figures were similarly prominent but the emphasis was probably agricultural; (2) the male-dominant cult of sky gods brought in by the Indo-European speakers of proto-Greek; and (3) Near Eastern cult, as exemplified by the snake goddesses and the ecstatic dancers on Minoan-Mycenaean seals.

The early Bronze Age developments of the third millennium that so changed the cultures of western Asia and the Cyclades did not dramatically affect mainland Greece. This pre-Indo-European period, called the Early Helladic on mainland Greece, contrasts with the island culture of the Cyclades, where the nude goddess evolved into the well-known slender, elegant Cycladic figurines (fig. 1.35). On the more commercially active islands, the goddess tradition continued with both marble figurines with crossed arms and the mysterious clay "frying pan" artifacts that were sometimes decorated with genital represen-tations (fig. 1.10). Both of these types have been found in graves, suggesting that they were everyday personal talismans, perhaps also symbolic of rebirth. About the personal life of the Early Cycladic people little can be known, as many graves but few settlements have been excavated. It is not even certain what they received in exchange for their obsidian, metals, and handicrafts, but their exports are found throughout the eastern Mediterranean as far as Sicily.

Though for a time the mainlanders were minor participants in the more cosmopolitan life of the Cyclades, mainland culture remained simple, without large buildings or significant foreign contact. But the dullness of the period preceding the Minoan-Mycenaean era masks a dramatic movement of peoples that affected all of Europe, including Greece. The Middle Helladic period, beginning by most accounts soon after 2000 B.C., witnessed the arrival of the first Greek speakers—that is, of the people who spoke a proto-Greek dialect. This was an Indo-European language of the *centum* branch, not necessarily unrelated to the dialects already in use in Early Helladic Greece but distinct from them.[8]

The picture of nomadic, warlike, Indo-European "Minyans" sweeping down from somewhere on settled, agricultural, non-Indo-European "Pelasgians" and imposing a patriarchal religion of sky gods on a matriarchal religion of earth goddesses in 2000 B.C. is too tidy for the evidence to bear. In fact, the new arrivals came during the course of a cultural depression that did not end until just before the middle of the second millennium B.C., when the appearance of shaft graves at Mycenae mark the beginning of a new "international" phase.

Hellenizing Greece

The users of Minyan ware brought little to change the archaeological record of that drab period (2000-1500 B.C.). Rather than impose their culture as conquerors of the area into which they came, they mingled their religion, language, and customs with what they found, and when their culture once again reached the takeoff point, it was more through the stimulation of its Minoan neighbor on Crete than the result of indigenous development. As a myth, the invasion story is a challenging developmental model, but the evidence so far points to a culturally inconclusive migration.

An oversimplified view of early Greek cultural development collides with facts pointing to a less dramatic evolution. First, the archaeological record so far indicates that the goddess religion represented in the Neolithic by nude female idols stopped yielding artifacts of this type nearly a thousand years before the supposed arrival of the "Greeks."[9] Second, there is no linguistic or other evidence so far to show that "pre-Greek" means "non-Indo-European" (Vermeule 1964, 63). Third, whoever it was who began migrating into Greece soon after the beginning of the second millennium did not change the depressed level of the culture already in place. And fourth, well into the first millennium B.C., religious figurines on the mainland remained typically feminine, indicating that while the pantheon described by Homer sometime after 750 B.C. was male dominated, actual religious practice remained conservative of a modified form of an ancient goddess religion.

The myth continues to be useful, however, because it fits the larger pattern of middle Bronze Age developments from Egypt to Anatolia. This pattern includes the westward shift of political development from Mesopotamia to the Levant and the rise of the megalithic cultures in Western Europe. Linguistically, the spread of recognizably Indo-European languages as far east as India and as far west as the Hebrides is a complex but inescapable fact of this period, during which both Greek and Hittite took shape as "the two classic Indo-European languages of the Aegean Bronze Age."[10] The *post hoc propter hoc* assumption that underlies any account of Greece's transition from a Neolithic zone on the periphery of civilization to a major participant in the Bronze Age, tying that transition to the arrival of "the Greeks," is difficult to refute by an appeal to the actual evidence from Greece itself, given its sparseness. At the same time, we must be aware that it is a historical construct that will not tolerate rough use.

Sexual Culture in Ancient Greece

The Late Helladic Minoan-Mycenaean culture was considerably more complex, cosmopolitan, wealthy, centralized, and powerful than anything that had previously appeared on the mainland. It was a synthesis, not so much of pre-Greek and Greek, but of mainland and Minoan cultures, Minoan culture itself being a synthesis that included a strong Near Eastern component. It appears likely that the civilization of Minos at Knossos preceded and inspired the Mycenaean civilization that developed at Mycenae, Pylos, Athens, Iolkos, and other centers. The discovery of hilltop sanctuaries on Crete unlike any on the Greek mainland but comparable to those in the Levant, the tree cult illustrated in Cretan seal rings, also comparable to the cult activities under trees mentioned in Hebrew scripture, the numerous Minoan snake goddesses with their eastern analogues, the bull leaping, and the horns of consecration similar to Anatolian bull horns set in places of worship as early as the sixth millennium B.C. in Çatal Hüyük, all argue a Minoan religious culture closely tied to that of the Near East. The Linear B script common to Crete and the mainland is an early form of Greek; the undeciphered Minoan Linear A is more likely an Anatolian language such as Luwian or a northern Semitic dialect.[11]

If this reasoning is correct, we might expect the sexual culture of Minoan Crete and its Mycenaean derivative to be similar to that of the Near Eastern "cities of the plain" condemned in Hebrew scripture. The difference is that the Minoan-Mycenaean civilization lacked the urban character of the great cities of the ancient Near East. Although the population of Greece expanded in the Late Helladic phase, it remained a scattered-site population clustered around a variety of fortified palaces. The same was true on Crete, minus the fortifications. The evidence of an eastern style of luxury includes a highly developed art of painted decorations featuring lush natural motifs of birds, fish, flowers, and plants, richly dressed female votaries with well-developed exposed breasts, and an emotional, even ecstatic religious life that included a tree cult.

The last of these is important because at least two mythical figures, known to later tradition as heroines who became sexually involved with Mycenaean heroes, are linked to Minoan-Mycenaean cult: Ariadne, who fell in love with the Athenian prince Theseus, and Helen of Sparta, for Homer the sex symbol but in an earlier age a tree goddess in the southern Peloponnese.[12] Ariadne's sister was Phaedra, who

Figure 3.1. Thought to represent a religious votary, this Minoan wall painting from Thera (mod. Santorini) suggests something more than the rudimentary imagery of agricultural ritual. Though largely forgotten after the Aegean collapse near the end of the second millennium B.C., the glamour of Mycenaean life is dimly reflected in Homeric epic. Ca. sixteenth century B.C. (National Archaeological Museum, Athens)

Figure 3.2. Cult scene with women and a child. The flounced skirts and bare breasts are the common ceremonial attire of this tradition. The tree on the left is probably related to the cult in Sparta with which Menelaus' wife, Helen, is thought originally to have been connected. Gold ring from Mycenae, ca. 1500 B.C. (National Archaeological Museum, Athens, no. 992)

married Theseus and fell in love with his son, Hippolytus. The mother of these was Pasiphaë, "shining for all," the wife of King Minos whom Poseidon caused to fall in love with a white bull and who bore by it the Minotaur. The names of Ariadne (*ari-adnē* or -*agnē*, "most pure") and Phaedra (*phaidra*, "bright, beaming") point to their divine aspect. All three are celestial, possibly lunar.[13] It is significant that the tradition assigned each of these figures an erotic role, because the direct testimony we have about the erotic character of traditional religion in the Levant is missing for these western goddesses-turned-heroine.

More suggestions of the erotic content in Minoan-Mycenaean civilization lie in the early history of Aphrodite, whom tradition connected with the islands of Cyprus and Cythera, both of which were closely tied to Crete and the Mycenaean sphere of influence. Among the strands of tradition that contributed to the formation of the Greek sex goddess is the Near Eastern goddess of love. She was variously

Sumerian Inanna, Semitic Ishtar, and Phoenician Astarte/Asherah and was worshiped in Sidon and other Levantine ports in her nude epiphany.[14] This cult and the temple prostitution associated with it were present at an early stage on Cyprus. Aphrodite's most common epithet in historical times, "The Cyprian," preserves the local tradition of her origin. Hesiod represents Cyprus as her first landing place after she came into being from the foam (*aphros*) made by the falling blood of Uranos' castration (*Th.* 180–199). Her first landfall, according to this account, was Cythera, a volcanic island less than sixty miles south of ancient Sparta colonized by the Minoans. According to Herodotus I.105, the temple of Aphrodite on Cythera was built by Phoenicians from Ascalon, where the most ancient of the temples to Uranian Aphrodite/Astarte was located. The same Phoenician temple, Herodotus tells us, was the model for the Cypriot temple. Pausanias (3.23.1) adds that the temple on Cythera is "the most ancient of all the sanctuaries of Aphrodite in Greece" and that the cult statue therein is an armed *xoanon*, or wooden idol. Pieces of the ruins of this ancient temple are now built into the fourteenth-century church of Hagios Kosmas. The archaeological and later written record agrees with the Hesiodic myth, which differs only in obscuring the goddess's eastern connections.

Cyprus had an independent tradition of the nude goddess as early as the Chalcolithic, as demonstrated by figurines found at Lemba-Lakkous (figs. 1.32, 1.33). This island became a major cultural link between the Aegean and the coastal cities of Syria in the late Minoan age and continued in this role after the collapse of Knossos ca. 1380 B.C., when Mycenaean traders, drawn by Cypriote copper and the wealth of the Syro-Palestinian coast, made the port cities of Cyprus a market for large amounts of Greek pottery.[15] The early and continued existence of a Cypriote bull cult is further evidence of the common ground of Cypriot, Minoan, and mainland Greek culture. At Cition, where a late Bronze Age temple of Astarte was rebuilt in the middle of the ninth century B.C. by Phoenicians, a late Classical inscription includes male and female sacred prostitutes among the personnel of the temple.[16] At Paphos, on Cyprus's west coast, there was a great temple of Aphrodite Paphia, also referred to in inscriptions as Astarte Paphia. This mixture of cult names (and certainly also of cult practice) came as naturally to Greeks in the Near East as it did to Hebrews in

Palestine, with the exception that in Greece it was not attacked by religious reformers.

Because their literacy ran only to inventory and tribute lists, the Minoans and Mycenaeans cannot speak for themselves. The only direct literary evidence comes from Ugarit (modern Ras Shamra), a city unearthed in northern Syria in 1929, just sixty-five miles east of Cyprus. This city's heyday corresponds roughly with that of Mycenaean Greece, 1400–1200 B.C., and it traded so actively with the Mycenaeans that one part of town was inhabited by Greeks. The religious culture of Ugarit included Adonis, Asherah, and Astarte, whose cults are prominently erotic wherever they appear. Like the Canaanite neighbors of the Hebrews, they employed male sacred prostitutes, or *qedeshim*, in their temples.[17] The Ras Shamra texts, composed in the thirteenth century B.C. and found in the temple of Baal, are both religious and epic. Because of the form of the Ugaritic script in which these texts are preserved and their mutilated condition, it is not certain what their proper order, religious significance, or interpretation should be, and we are left with a series of vignettes rather than a coherent body of texts. Asherah's formulaic characterization in these fragments as "Lady Asherah of the sea" is congruent with Hesiod's story of Aphrodite's origin in the southern Aegean Sea. In the *Birth of the Gracious Gods*, El, identified with Thôr, "the bull," and head of the Ugaritic pantheon, charms two women by the size of his phallic "hand."[18] and begets Dawn and Dusk and "the Gracious Gods . . . who suck from the nipples of the [Lady Asherah's] breasts." In another text Baal, the storm god, begets offspring by a cow, perhaps his sister Anath in disguise.[19] The myth is similar to the story of the Minotaur's birth from Pasiphaë, who disguised herself as a cow to mate with Poseidon's white bull. A fragmentary text telling about Baal's mating with his sister the Virgin Anat may be cognate:

[   ]he is passionate and he takes hold of [her] vagina
[she] is passionate and takes hold of [his] testicles
[Aliyan] Baal makes love by the thousand
[The Vi]rgin Anath
[embrac]ing, conceiving and there is born
[   ] the band of Kosharot
[the Vir]gin Anath

[Ali]yan Baal

[   ] reply . . .   (Text 132, Gordon 1966, 90 f.)

The sexual activity of the Greek gods has parallels in Ugarit, whose texts further confirm the eroticism of the religion that the Hebrews of the Old Testament sought to expel from their own cult.

The western Semitic affinities of early Greek culture are further borne out in the foundation myths surviving into historical times. Europa, founder of the continent that bears her name, was a Tyrian princess, daughter of Telephassa ("Far-shining," also named Argiope, "Bright-face"). Zeus fell in love with her and approached her in the form of a bull, and when she playfully sat on his back he ran into the sea and swam to Crete, where she bore him Minos, Rhadamanthys, and Sarpedon. The story is parallel to that of "All-bright" Pasiphaë and Poseidon's bull.[20] The places in the ancient world later said to have been founded by Europa's brothers who were sent out in search of her—Carthage, Cilicia, Thynia, and Thasos—reflect the colonizing activities of the Western Semites during the Bronze Age and the consequent influence of their culture. Europa's brother Cadmus, acting on instructions from the Delphic oracle, followed a cow to Boeotia, where he founded Thebes. Danaüs, whose fifty daughters colonized Argos on the Peloponnese and whose descendants were the Danaans of Homer's *Iliad*, is linguistically connected to the Cilician Danuna or Danana on the southern Anatolian coast north of Cyprus. Homer calls the Greeks of the *Iliad* Achaeans or Dana(w)oi, "a regular Hellenization of the Semitic ethnic name *Danuna*," and the Danunians of eastern Cilicia "were Western Semites in origin, language, culture, and ethnic name" (Astour 1967, 52 f.). Egyptian inscriptions from the first half of the fifteenth century to the beginning of the twelfth referring to Danuna do not indicate their place of origin, but their characterization as hostile raiders during and after the peak of Mycenaean power supports the inference that the western Semites of Cilicia and the masters of Mycenaean Argos had strong connections.[21]

These myths and linguistic hints argue that the Minoan-Mycenaean culture of the Greeks was heavily influenced by their western Semitic connections even while their language was Indo-European Greek. This is nowhere better illustrated than in the Mycenaean Linear B syllabary, which uses Semitic pictographs to denote the syllables of

Greek words. Their system of acrophony used a pictograph of "man" (*bunushu* in Ugaritic) for the syllable *bu*, an "apple" pictograph (*tuppūhu* in Ugaritic) for the Greek *tu* sound, and so on (Gordon 1966, 37). Centuries later, when they had a need for a true alphabet, the Greeks found it on the same Phoenician coast, and they once again adapted a Semitic system to their Indo-European language. The meaning of this eastern orientation is that the infiltration of Greek speakers into the southern Balkans during the second millennium was not necessarily the most significant Bronze Age development for Greece as an evolving culture. It was not the Greek speakers but the northwestern Semites who stimulated Greek participation in the enriched life of the age of heroes. The archaeological record of the Middle Helladic shows the Greek-speaking arrivals to have been no more civilized than the tribes they invaded. The great palace civilizations of Crete and Mycenaean Greece were responses to contact with the east rather than invasion from the north. Cyprus and Crete were the stepping-stones of a sexually active Near Eastern religion and mythology that built on ancient Neolithic traditions shared by the southern Balkans with the rest of the Mediterranean littoral. The traditional European preference for an "Indo-European" Greece has tended to obscure Semitic elements. Near Eastern archaeology and the deciphering of important Near Eastern texts has made a more balanced view possible. This is particularly important when investigating the origins of Greek sexual culture.

The preference for a history that pushes Near Eastern features into the background was not invented by modern scholars, however. It can be traced to the archaic Greeks themselves, who began at about the same date as the Hebrew compilers of the Torah to sense and give mythic shape to a distinctive national identity. When a Panhellenic sensibility emerged in the eighth century B.C., its spokesmen produced a highly mediated account of the past. Some of this mediation can be attributed to the vagaries of an oral tradition, but the Homeric Catalogue of Ships in the second book of the *Iliad* shows that such a tradition was capable of impressive precision when its poets chose to keep an accurate record.[22] In part, the Homeric poems show a composite picture of Mycenaean and eighth-century customs, armor, and other features of the age of heroes. The poet of the *Iliad* appears to want to give a credible image of the past with which his audience, newly interested in their Bronze Age roots and vaguely familiar with its ruins, can identify. The language of the Linear B tablets, which distinguished the great king, or *wanax*, from the lesser lord, or *pasireu* (*basileus* in Homer), is often recognizable in Homer's epics of the Trojan War and its aftermath, but the religion is very different. The goddesses of nature, sex, and fertility who were so plentiful in the Near East, the frenzied scenes of worship recorded on Mycenaean gems and gold jewelry, the splendidly attired, bare-breasted female votaries, the bull cult, the snake cult, and the tree cult so vividly pictured in artifacts from Asia Minor, Palestine, Crete, and Mycenae—all of these profusely documented features of Mycenaean religious culture are nowhere to be seen in Homer's world. Male gods are in control, and even though the goddesses have their place as divine consorts, quarrelsome spouses, spiteful enemies, or personal patrons, they are (with the exception of Athena) characteristically subordinated in a patriarchal system.

Unlike the biblical writers, Homer was neither prophet, priest, nor propagandist, but he worked at a mythmaking craft that we must assume reflected the views of his audience. His divine mythology is strongly anthropomorphic, with similarly behaved gods and mortals. At the same time, he rationalized cult in the world he portrayed, excluding any ecstatic or mystical element. Dionysus, who appears (at least by name) on the Mycenaean tablets found at Pylos, is significantly downplayed in Homer. Homeric prayers are *do ut des* propositions, offering past or future service for a specific favor, not including fertility. Sexuality is very much a part of Homer's picture of the heroic world, but even when invested in Aphrodite, it is a rationally apprehensible power rather than an abstract, numinous presence. It is also an ambivalent power capable of great mischief, in fact a kind of loose cannon on the rolling deck of history rather than the guarantor of prosperity, symbol of vitality, and doorway to the life of the gods that Eastern religions sometimes perceive in sexuality.

Homer makes sex problematic by predicating the Trojan War on the eroticism of Helen, whose escapade from Sparta to Troy with her Trojan lover Paris is the casus belli. Legend has transformed the one-time tree goddess of Sparta[23] into a mortal woman and translated her sexual power to bless and fructify into the power to lead men astray. This is one of a series of demotions that took place in the mytholo-gizing of the Bronze Age by the storytellers of the Iron Age and later.

It was not entirely the work of Homer. Europa, the Eastern goddess of dusk and the evening star, became a king's daughter, like the Argive Io and the Cretans' Pasiphaë, Phaedra, and Ariadne. Only Pasiphaë and Ariadne are mentioned at all by Homer, briefly noted as shades in the underworld.[24] This reverse Euhemerism that demoted gods to heroes was the first step in rewriting Bronze Age myth into Greek *mythos*. Like the Hebrews of the eighth century B.C., the Greeks of Homer's time inherited a tradition of syncretism with Semitic sexual religion. Although they did not outlaw its usages as did the priestly authors of the Hebrew Holiness Code, they sought to leave Near Eastern sexual cult behind by shaping an alternate set of myths. If we read Homer in this context, a constellation of meanings and values comes into perspective.

Rather than condemn the great sexual icon of the heroic age as an agent of fatality (as the chorus of old men do in Aeschylus' *Agamemnon*), Homer separates a decent and respectful Helen from her erotic power. The condemnation is more credible coming from her own mouth. This is what she says to Priam:

> Always to me, beloved father, you are feared and respected;
> I wish bitter death had been what I wanted, when I came hither
> following your son, forsaking my chamber, my kinsmen,
> my grown child, and the loveliness of girls my own age.
> . . . slut [lit. bitch-eyed] that I am. Did this ever happen?
>
> (*Il.* 3.172–180, tr. Lattimore [cf. 6.344])

By making Helen the only character in the *Iliad* besides Achilles who is capable of self-blame, Homer places her and the power she possesses in a special category above simple moralizing but not beyond good and evil. Helen's self-consciousness renders her ambivalent about the mischief she has caused. When first seen in the *Iliad*, she is weaving a red robe embroidered with the struggles the Greeks and Trojans have endured for her sake (3.125–128), but later in the same book, when Aphrodite summons her to comfort Paris after his rescue from a duel with her husband, Menelaus, she refuses: "Not I. I am not going to him. It would be too shameful. I will not serve his bed." Aphrodite bluntly reminds her of her obligation: "You wretch, do not provoke me lest I become angry and abandon you" (410–414). Helen's exit is shrouded in irony and pathos:

So she spoke, and Helen daughter of Zeus was frightened,
and went, shrouding herself about in the luminous spun robe,
silent, unseen by the Trojan women, and led by the goddess.

                                (3.418-420, tr. Lattimore)

Helen's ambivalence extends to her lover Paris:

So you came back from the fighting. Oh, how I wish you had died there
beaten down by the stronger man, who was once my husband.

. . . .

Go forth now and challenge warlike Menelaus
once again to fight you in combat. But no: I advise you
rather to let it be . . . you might very well go down before his spear.

                                (3.428–436, tr. Lattimore)

By this means Homer preserves the epic luster of Helen while somewhat diminishing the glamor of her affair with Paris—just as he
counters the romanticism of the Trojan War itself by having the
Achaeans stampede to their ships when Agamemnon imprudently
suggests that they should give up and go home (2.142–154).

    Although Helen blames herself for the evil effects of her sexuality,
Homer is at pains to imply that the gift is not her fault. It is the nature
of any *areté* or preeminence that it is a divine gift over which the
recipient has no control. In the beginning of the *Iliad*, Agamemnon
taunts Achilles: "If you are very strong indeed, that is a god's gift"
(1.178). So when Hector rebukes Paris for having no virtue but his
good looks, the latter's defense is unrefutable:

                                     . . . yet do not
bring up against me the sweet favors of golden Aphrodite.
Never to be cast away are the gifts of the gods, magnificent,
which they give of their own will; no man could have them for
wanting them.

                                (3.63–66, tr. Lattimore)

Similarly, Priam's first words to Helen in the *Iliad* are conciliatory: "I
am not blaming you: to me the gods are blameworthy," which adds

meaning to the Trojan elders' refusal a few lines earlier to blame either Greeks or Trojans for fighting over her because "her face is dreadfully like the immortal goddesses" (3.155–164).

If humankind is merely the vessel in which eroticism is placed, it is Aphrodite herself and not her human avatars who will best reward scrutiny of Homer's intentions. Like other Homeric characters, her appearance is not described. Her only visible emblem is the embroidered sash that she wears down between her breasts (ἀπὸ στήθεσφιν, 14.214)—an ancient emblem, as the Near Eastern figurines in figures 3.3–3.5 show.[25] The embroidery on "Aphrodite's Girdle," as it has been misleadingly called, is more directly symbolic than the pictures on Helen's robe showing the trouble caused by her misbehavior. Its "pictures" are erotic abstractions: charming delights, love, longing, and tête-à-tête persuasion. The word translated by Lattimore as "beguilements" is Homer's *thelktēria*, a word whose ambiguities include bewitchment, propitiation, charm, and delight. These *thelktēria* are paratactically subdivided into (1) *philotēs* ("loveliness" above), the only word in Greek that can mean both goodwill and sexual love; (2) *himeros*, or desire; and (3) *oaristys parphasis*, the intimate persuasion to which the logomaniac Greeks would be particularly vulnerable.

That Aphrodite still could be recognized as the Queen of Peace in matrimony (as well as a home wrecker) is implicit from the episode in which her iconic sash is mentioned. In this moment of the *Iliad*, Hera wants to borrow the sash to seduce her husband, Zeus, but she must conceal this purpose from her adversary, Aphrodite. She therefore pretends that she wants to settle a conjugal dispute between Ocean and Tethys.[26] As the goddess of marriage, Hera has a presumptive function to heal the matrimonial divisions of the gods; her need of sexual *philotēs* (198, 207, 209) to accomplish the task is interesting, as conjugal eroticism was not commonly emphasized in Greek discourse about marriage until the end of the fifth century B.C. Homer does not give us this without an ironic twist, however. The actual reason Hera wants to seduce Zeus is to induce a postcoital nap so that he will not see Poseidon helping the Achaeans contrary to his express command. The proximate cause of her seduction is resentment of the threat he poses to her plan: she sees him sitting on Mount Ida overlooking the Trojan plain,

*Figure 3.3*a–b. Elaborately coiffed female idol from Susa, end of the third millennium B.C. The sash between the breasts, sometimes two crossed sashes, was later emblematic of Greek Aphrodite and is described in Homer's *Iliad*, 14.214 ff. The patterning at the groin is stylized pubic hair rather than a garment, as the rear view shows. (Musée de Louvre) (Photographs by Jean Mazenod)

Figure 3.4. An early ancestress of "golden Aphrodite," this Anatolian nude goddess in silver and gold found at Hasanoglan wears a saltire of crossed sashes. End of third millennium B.C. (Anatolia Civilization Museum, Ankara, Turkey)

Figure 3.5. This bronze nude from Cyprus wears the sash that identifies her as the goddess of love. This is the love charm that Hera borrows from Aphrodite in *Iliad* 14 to help her seduce Zeus. (The Metropolitan Museum of Art, The Cesnola Collection; purchased by subscription, 1874–1876. [74.51.5680]. All rights reserved, The Metropolitan Museum of Art)

and in her eyes he was hateful.
And now the lady ox-eyed Hera was divided in purpose
as to how she could beguile the brain in Zeus of the Aegis.

(14.158–160, tr.Lattimore)

So the ostensible appeal to Aphrodite is to the Queen of Conjugal Peace, but the real need is for Our Lady of Confusion, and the attendant emotion is hatred.

Hera's belief in the sex goddess's disorderly tendencies is justified by Aphrodite's erotic pairing with Ares in the *Odyssey*'s Song of Demodocus (8.266–366). In this comic *chronique scandaleuse*, the disreputable god of ruinous battle has little trouble seducing Aphrodite with some gifts and dishonoring the bed of her husband, Hephaistos. When Hephaistos traps his wife with Ares in flagrante delicto, he denounces his "bitch-eyed" wife (the same epithet Helen had applied to herself in the *Iliad*, and does again in the *Odyssey* (4.145): "she is beautiful," he declares, "but unrestrained."

Something more needs to be said about the pairing with Ares. The roots of this association are once again in the ancient Near East, where Ishtar and her look-alikes were goddesses of love and war. This dualism is a recurrent theme in religions of the East: Siva, himself much given to contradictions, has a voluptuous wife, Parvati, whose alternate manifestation is the hideous Kali, a Medusa-faced hag with a necklace of human heads. When Ishtar was Hellenized as Aphrodite, the Greeks stripped her of her warlike character and left her only an affection for Ares as a vestige of her former power. That her dual attributes in the Bronze Age persisted for centuries after Homer is shown by Pausanias' discovery of armed Aphrodites at Cythera, Sparta, and Corinth (3.15.10, 3.23.1, 2.4.7). There were others elsewhere in the Greek world far into Roman times.[27] It would appear that Homer himself thought it necessary to urge Aphrodite's demotion on his audience. In the fifth book of the *Iliad* the warrior goddess Athena expresses a certain gratuitous malice toward Aphrodite when she warns Diomedes to steer clear of gods in the heat of battle: "if a god making trial of you comes hither, do you not do battle head on . . . but only if Aphrodite . . . comes to the fighting, her at least you may stab with the sharp bronze" (5.129-132). When he later encounters Aphrodite trying to rescue her son Aeneas, "knowing her for a god without warcraft" he stabs her in the hand in a passage that parodies the wounding of a mortal in battle and shouts defiance in a way that is conventional for a god or a warrior warning off a lesser antagonist: "Give way, daughter of Zeus, from the fighting and the terror. Is it not then enough that you lead astray women without warcraft?" (5.330–349).[28] Aphrodite shrieks, drops her injured son Aeneas to fend for himself, and borrows Ares' chariot for a tearful retreat to Olympus. Her mother, Dione, comforts her with other tales of outrage against the gods, but Zeus drives home the point that Diomedes made: "not for you are the works of warfare!" (5.428).[29] It is often remarked that this episode makes Aphrodite look like a little girl who runs crying to her parents when her childish games go awry and she skins her hand. That is exactly the point. This scene in the *Iliad* along with the comic song about her infidelity in the *Odyssey* effectively reduce the dread goddess of procreation and battle to a mischievous second-rate player on the Hellenic stage. The arts of war are reassigned to an asexual Athena and to a callow Ares whom the gods despise.

The firm hand with which Homer strips Aphrodite of her Bronze Age rank does not of course diminish his interest in her character, or in the charisma of eroticism itself. Different aspects come forward as the occasion demands; if she is childish in the scene where Diomedes wounds her and feckless when she jumps into bed with Ares, she is stern when she exacts obedience from a mutinous Helen in book 3 of the *Iliad*, and urbanely Mephistophelian a moment later when she draws up a chair for her other protégé, Paris:

> Aphrodite the sweetly laughing drew up an armchair,
> carrying it, she, a goddess, and set it before Alexandros.
> > (3.424–425, tr. Lattimore)

Homer's epithets help to indicate his placement of Aphrodite in the scheme of things. She is second only to Athena as "Zeus's daughter," her most common epithet. This is a vestige of their common Bronze Age roots (love, war, and the protection of cities), but it is also significant in terms of their subordination to the centralized, patriarchal governance of heaven that was so important to both Homer and Hesiod. The most common of her special epithets is "golden," a quality that has strong connotations for Homer and is used to call up the

Sexual Culture in Ancient Greece

splendors of the heroic age. The root *chrys-*, "gold," is in fact Semitic, appropriately evoking the luxury and wealth of the East, which were always proverbial for the Greeks of historical times—as no doubt also in prehistory. The goldenness of Aphrodite is multivalent because it also connotes her celestial aspects as a sky goddess in the tradition of Egyptian Nut (Uranian Aphrodite), her astral associations through Sumerian Inanna and Phoenician Astarte, and her northern roots as a PIE goddess of dawn.[30] Another special epithet, *philommeidēs*, usually translated "laughter-loving" with reference to the euphoria that goes with sexual excitement or fulfilled eroticism, may mean "genital-loving" if it is derived from *mēdea*, which means specifically male parts. This was Hesiod's own view, on the grounds that she was created from the foam of Uranos' severed genitals (*Th.* 200). If we accept this interpretation, which has the authority of Hesiod's near-Homeric antiquity, it gives Aphrodite a specificity that the later phrase *ta aphrodisia*, "sexual matters," did not necessarily have because it implies a feminine attraction to male sexual anatomy. This feature recalls the Hebrew myth of woman in Genesis 3:16 ("your desire will be for your husband"), and it reflects a widespread folk belief that women are more sexually dependent on men than the opposite, and more unstable because of their sexual craving.[31]

While the *Iliad* reflects a tendency to demote the mighty Near Eastern goddess of sex, it does not include a corresponding puritanical rejection of eroticism. Homer makes sex problematic, but he freely admits the humor, energy, and color with which it enriches his epic tableau. Some of his most unforgettable vignettes are erotic, as when Hera consummates her scheme to distract Zeus in the *Dios apatē* (the Fooling of Zeus) near the center of the *Iliad*:

> . . . The son of Kronos caught his wife in his arms. There
> underneath them the divine earth broke forth into young, fresh
> grass, and into dewy clover, crocus and hyacinth
> so thick and soft it held the hard ground deep away from them.
> There they lay down together and drew about them a golden
> wonderful cloud, and from it the glimmering dew descended.
>
> (14.346–351, tr. Lattimore)

This is the earliest appearance in Greek poetry of the grassy and floral harmonics of eroticism, though the connection was perhaps already conventional as an aspect of the *hieros gamos*, the sexual union of god and goddess that was celebrated in this part of the world. This annual ritual was attended by the seasonal renewal of nature when the dry season ended and vegetation sprang up even in usually dry places. The cloud and the dewiness (348, 351) of this divine union are thus a component of the scene's iconography, which merged with the erotic language of early Greek poetry.[32] The passage is of special interest because of the merging of sacral eroticism with a secular erotic scene of great delicacy and charm.

The sexual union of Zeus leads to a peaceful nap in the course of which his brother Poseidon is able to bring much-needed relief to the embattled Achaeans. Paris' union with Helen at the end of *Iliad* 3 gives him the exuberant freshness of a stallion in a simile that is a masterpiece of latent eroticism:

> As when some stalled horse who has been corn-fed at the manger
> breaking free of his rope gallops over the plain in thunder
> to his accustomed bathing place in a sweet-running river
> and in the pride of his strength holds high its head, and the mane floats
> over his shoulders; sure of his glorious strength, the quick knees
> carry him to the beloved places and the pasture of horses;
> so from uttermost Pergamos came Paris, the son of
> Priam, shining in all his armor of war as the sun shines,
> laughing aloud, and his quick feet carried him . . .
>
> (6.505–514, tr. Lattimore)

The glamour of the heroic past includes a certain sexiness that Homer regards with an affectionate detachment, neither indifferent nor censorious. Love and war are regarded with an equal eye that takes in both the excitement and its dreadful cost. The luster that gilds the tragic events of the *Iliad* is not applied to the *Odyssey*, where Homer combines the romance of a fairy-tale world (bks. 9–12) with the realism of postheroic Greece. The backward looks at the old world are often admiring: Telemachus is dazzled by the sight of the Mycenaean palace of Menelaus and Helen (4.71–75, see above p. 48), and we are left to imagine for ourselves his powerful reaction when Helen, looking like an Artemis whose sexual power was still strongly felt,[33] sweeps into the great megaron hall and recognizes him instantly as the son of great-

Sexual Culture in Ancient Greece

hearted Odysseus (4.121–146). The comic song of Ares' mischief with Aphrodite that Demodocus sings in the great hall at Phaeacia (8.266–366) is perfect for the gracious style of Odysseus' overcivilized hosts in book 8, but neither the half-repentant glamour of Helen nor the bland affluence of the Phaeacians fits the realities of Iron Age life in the western islands. Telemachus sensibly refuses the three horses that Menelaus offers as a guest gift ("there is no one of the islands that has meadows for driving horses," 4.607) just as Odysseus politely declines the hand of the nubile Nausicaa.[34]

The practical values of the *Odyssey* call for an unadorned life in which sexual pleasures are an encumbrance rather than an ornament of life. A double standard is tolerant of the infidelities of a great lady such as Helen or a goddess such as Aphrodite. Penelope comments mildly on Helen's misbehavior (23.218–224) while holding rigidly to her own wifely honor; the gods in Demodocus' song laugh about Aphrodite's fling with Ares (8.326), but the household women at Ithaca who have slept with the suitors are strung up without mercy (22.457–472). Likewise, Odysseus dallies a long time in the beds of the nymph Calypso and the enchantress Circe without relinquishing his ultimate fidelity to Penelope, but in spite of a complicated mind that makes her a fit wife for cunning Odysseus, "careful Penelope" (her epithets *periphrōn* and *echephrōn* emphasize her thoughtfulness) never lowers her guard in preserving her husband's rights. Yet the concentration of her focus on Odysseus does not make Penelope a less sexual character: her tests of his identity when he returns do not end until she tricks him into describing their conjugal bed, one leg of which is an olive tree still rooted in the earth. Odysseus too has his sensuous side: he likes to wear next to his skin a silky fabric of a type that women admire (19.232–235; see n. 9. chap. 4); he loves hot baths (8.450–454); for all his legendary toughness and self-control, he has such a good time with Circe that after a year his men have to remind him that it is time to leave for home (10.467–474).

As in the *Iliad*, Homer does not so much condemn eroticism in the *Odyssey* as build it into a system of values in which it is not the supreme good or the highest goal. The *Odyssey* is the bible of a sturdy small-town elite: mobile, acquisitive, adaptable, versatile, sometimes combative and always hardheaded, but with a controlled hedonism that acknowledged the claims of sex. Hesiod's world in the *Theogony* and the *Works and Days* is no less tough and hardheaded, but without the spaciousness. His mythical history is ultimately dependent on Near Eastern sources, which perhaps explains why, in spite of his distaste for eroticism in marriage or anywhere else, he places Eros in the first generation of created powers (*Th.* 120; West 1966, 195–196).[35] The account of Aphrodite's birth from the foam of Uranos' severed genitals and her first landfalls on Cythera and Cyprus (*Th.* 180–206) are a complex etiological myth combining an explanation of Uranian or "heavenly" Aphrodite, the form of her name (*aphros* = foam), her epithet *philommeidēs*, and the antiquity of her two island cults.[36] While Hesiod's Eros appears at the beginning of creation and makes possible the sexual generation of the gods, his Aphrodite accounts for the erotic life of gods and mortals alike:

> flirtatious conversations of maidens, smiles and deceits,
> sweet delight and passion of love and gentle enticements.
> (*Th.* 205–206 Frazer)[37]

But like the similar Homeric description of Aphrodite's chest band in the *Iliad* (14.215 ff.), this is not by way of celebrating sex in human life. Soon after, sexual love (*philotēs*, 224) is listed with deceit, old age, and strife among the baneful children of Night. Hesiod's distrust of most things feminine is clear, as this is the gender of most of his bogeys. His Eve figure, Pandora, comes as the price of Prometheus' stolen fire: an "evil to balance a good," a "sheer inescapable snare for men" (585, 589 Frazer). Fashioned out of clay, she looks like a modest virgin, but on the crown that Athena gives her there are terrible monsters; she is a drone among men who work like bees, and the women descended from her are "an evil for men and conspirers in troublesome works" (601). Men who refuse to marry have no one to care for them in their old age and no heirs, while the best a married man can hope for is an endless alternation of good and evil. Hesiod repeats this myth at the beginning of his practical advice in the *Works and Days* to explain why hard work without hope is the lot of man. Pandora (acting, we are left to surmise, on curiosity—but Hesiod is uninterested in her motive) lifted the lid of the (forbidden?) *pithos* and put it back only after all of its contents except Hope had escaped.

The Hesiodic Pandora myth has the marks of a much more ancient myth with a radically different meaning that has been rewritten to support an ideology that is apprehensive of women, their sexual power, and their capacity for mischief.[38] The name *Pandora*, which Hesiod explains as a punitive "gift of all the gods," can also mean "all gifts," and other sources identify her variously as the wife of Prometheus, the mother of the eponymous Graikos, an earth goddess, or the mother of Deucalion. Hesiod himself is associated with these alternative traditions.[39] The weight of evidence suggests therefore that the story of Pandora in the *Theogony* and the *Works and Days* is another piece of revisionism intended to demote the old Pandora who bestows everything good to a new Pandora who is Our Lady of Irony, responsible for the bad things that men must endure. Since Hesiod was considered by the later Greeks as an authority second only to Homer, this reworking of the Bronze Age tradition did in fact lower the prestige of what Hesiod called "the female race" (γένος, *Th.* 590)[40] and consequently the bond between the sexes on which a high sexual culture depends.

The Delphic oracle is another place to find a feminine, orgiastic cult supplanted by a masculine, rational, par excellence "Apollonian" institution. Literary tradition makes Earth the predecessor of Apollo;[41] the female Python who guarded the cleft in the rocks at the Castalian spring can be identified with the various serpents of Near Eastern and Minoan-Mycenaean cult.[42] The displacement of the early female proprietors by a new male arrival is celebrated in the Homeric Hymn to Apollo as the slaying of a dragon, but the feeling that this displacement was an act of excessive violence is reflected in the tradition that Zeus made Apollo atone for his act with nine years' exile in Thessaly.[43] There is also a pattern of concessions to female participation in Delphic ritual during the historical period: the Pythia who delivered the god's oracles from the center of his shrine in an unknown language was always a woman; Dionysus became closely associated with Delphi no later than the sixth century B.C., and women's rituals in his honor continued there into the time of Plutarch.[44]

The history of the religious area on the south slope of Mount Parnassus replicates the pattern of cultural revisionism that took place in the eighth century B.C.: the site of Apollo's great temple a short distance to the west of the Castalian Spring contained no important sanctuary before the century of Homer.[45] The chief religious site in the late Bronze–early Iron Age was in fact down the slope to the east of the spring, in what is now the sanctuary and terrace of Athena Pronaia, where the Mycenaean tradition was renewed by the construction of temples in the seventh, fifth, and fourth centuries. Three columns of her fourth-century Tholos have been restored and stand as one of the attractions for the modern visitor, but Athena's demotion to an accessory remains in the name of this latter-day sanctuary "before the temple" of Apollo, Athena Pronaia.

Delos, the sacred island of Apollo in historical times, was first sacred to a Cycladic goddess; the temple of Apollo was erected on fresh ground, but the temple of his sister, Artemis, is on the site of an earlier Mycenaean shrine.

A similar displacement took place at Olympia, where "the entire country is full of temples of Artemis, Aphrodite, and the Nymphs" (Strab. 8.3.12) and the presence of a no longer active oracle of Zeus (Strab. 8.3.30) suggests a history like that at Delphi. In historical times Olympia was dedicated to Zeus, though his temple there was not completed until 457 B.C. The sanctuary of Artemis Kokkoka (*kokkos* = pomegranate seed, grain, or genitals) at Olympia (Paus. 5.15.7) and of Artemis Kordax (a cheerfully indecent country dance) nearby indicates something of the early religious character of the place.[46] What remains of the female tradition is a temple of Zeus' consort, Hera, begun in the late seventh century B.C.

The century of Homer is the best available date for the establishment of a clearly defined Hellenism that downgraded the powerful older goddesses and set aside oriental traditions such as a single goddess of love and war. But such Panhellenic modernism was counterbalanced by two powerful opposing tendencies. One was the tenacious conservatism of religion, particularly the local cults that exempted themselves from the leveling, modernizing forces of the larger centers such as Athens. These are the eccentric varieties attested by Pausanias, the Hellenistic scholiasts, Strabo, and others, collected at the end of the nineteenth century by Farnell. Even the big cities had their divergent religious traditions, such as the temple prostitutes at Corinth. The other opposing tendency was orientalism itself, which enjoyed a powerful revival (stimulated by renewed eastern contacts) about the

Figure 3.6. During Homer's time and the following century, a multiform type of goddess, one clad and the other nude, appears at Aegean and mainland sites, illustrating the tension between the eastern naked goddess and a less overtly sexual type. This ivory pair is from the temple of Artemis Orthia at Sparta. (The Metropolitan Museum of Art, Gift of Pierpont Morgan, 1917. All rights reserved, The Metropolitan Museum of Art)

time of Homer. This "orientalizing revolution"[47] was more than a change of fashion in the decorative arts; it affected Hesiodic mythology, Homeric story patterns, and writing itself by promulgating the Phoenician-Greek alphabet. The eighth century was self-conscious enough for the Greeks to give their sexual culture a more distinctive definition, but at the same time unselfconscious enough to be "much more malleable and open to foreign influence than it became in subsequent generations."[48]

While it is risky to appraise a change from what is unrecorded to what can be known from a small body of literary text, Homer and Hesiod are clear witnesses of change. Homer's appraisal of the heroic tradition is at the same time enthusiastic and critical. The same can be said of his erotic point of view. Aphrodite is driven in tears from the battlefield and her power is made problematic, with emphasis on her power to hurt. Her mortal offshoot, Helen, becomes in Homer a person whose moral nature rebels at her erotic gift. If our reading of Hesiod is correct, Pandora is metamorphosed from the all-giving to the taker-away of reason and felicity, the original troublemaker. A similar process metamorphoses Artemis the unruly nature goddess into an asexual goddess of purity suitable for the neurotic fixations of a Hippolytus, blinding or killing any man unfortunate enough to see her nude. These developments are patriarchal and restrictive, but they leave erotic culture less categorically excluded than do the Hebrew Scriptures. Helen is no whore of Babylon; her erotic charisma elevates her (and Menelaus) to immortality, scrutinized but left as intact as the heroic deeds done for her sake. Homer deals with an even hand, leaving his sexual figures a glamour that is beyond simple moralizing.

CHAPTER FOUR

Greek Patriarchy

THE SEVERE STYLE

Go therefore back in the house, and take up your own
work, the loom and the distaff, and see to it that your
handmaidens ply their work also; but the men must see
to discussion, all men, but I most of all. For mine is the
power in this household.

ODYSSEY 1.356–59, TR. LATTIMORE

When Telemachus begins his quest for father and identity at the
beginning of the *Odyssey*, he does so with this rebuke to his
mother, Penelope, who has asked Phemius to stop singing sad songs
about Troy. He repeats the words in book 21 almost verbatim, during
the contest with Odysseus' bow. He has, in the meantime, found his
father and established his adult male identity where first he could only
assert it. The speech is a tag from the *Iliad*, where Hector sends
Andromache away after a touching scene with Astyanax (6.490–493).
The words are especially striking because in none of their occurrences
do they rebuke a woman who has exceeded her proper authority. To
the contrary, Penelope and Andromache are models of the Greek
wifely ideal. In the form of the rebuke quoted here, Telemachus
substitutes "discussion," μῦθος, for "war," πόλεμος, in the *Iliad*; later,
in book 21, it is "the bow," τόξον. Commentators have understandably objected that elsewhere in Homer, especially in the *Odyssey*,
discussion is freely shared with the women.[1] The explanation, I believe,
is not psychological but cultural. In representing a past heroic age in
which grand ladies behaved grandly, Homer had to straddle the gap
between a bygone era and the modern values that give a point to his
story. Sparta and Scheria, where Helen and Arete are full participants
in the royal court, are slightly unreal, one because it is remote (Scheria,

"far away from men who eat bread"), the other (Sparta) because it is—in the *Odyssey*—a survival from the age of bronze. The *Odyssey* is about the age of iron: when Athena comes to rouse Telemachus in Ithaca, she does so in a male guise as Mentes, an iron trader. For all its instances of female power, the world of Odysseus is a man's world.

This is not to say that a world controlled by women lay anywhere in the background. No one has ever found a matriarchy in real life, though some have felt the need to invent one.[2] Men have arrogated the power to direct the organization of work, the assignment of rank, the allocation of food, the conduct of warfare, and other political arrangements in every culture. Whether the result of men's greater physical strength or of the extra burdens of childbirth and infant care to which the human female is subjected from menarche to menopause, the biological nature of our species predisposed archaic societies toward a certain sexual asymmetry; the decided tendency of culture, which in some other respects may try to counteract nature, has been to institutionalize the power of the male. Nevertheless, men have not always perceived the human cosmos as a man's world—social evidence to the contrary. The urge to create a higher role for the female is a persistent feature of human culture. Some cultures are matrilineal, as motherhood is more surely determinable than fatherhood; others are matrilocal, with women owning the home in which their husbands live. Most create privileged categories within which women are attributed special powers: every modern Greek male will insist that his wife rules supreme in the home, even if that is only half true. Women are put on pedestals, idealized, and symbolically venerated, sometimes in reverse proportion to their real status. The Neolithic culture of the Balkans venerated a symbolically female nature, as evidenced by the majority of their figurines. The civilizations of the Bronze Age in the Near East acknowledged patriarchal gods such as El, but their religion assigned power and autonomy to goddesses as well, and to their priestesses and female votaries.

Eighth-century Hellenism had little such veneration for the feminine. Its programmatic statements called for a realignment of old myths, as the last chapter argued. Although only fragments of the process survive in Homer and Hesiod, the evident general effect of this adjustment was to demote the great goddesses of the Mycenaean age known in mythology as Hera, Aphrodite, and Artemis to the status of troublemakers,³ or to assign them diminished ambits of power, and simultaneously to promote male deities representing subordination, rationality, and political order. The Apollonian emphasis of this shift had the overall effect of depressing the value of women and of powers traditionally associated with their gender. The formula of rebuke quoted at the beginning of this chapter is a pointed reminder of the lower Hellenic status of women. Necessarily, the greater distance this put between the sexes came at some cost to the bond between men and women.

As recorded in the previous chapter, the revival of a higher culture in eighth-century Greece included the transformation (in 776 B.C.) of a local ritual in the western Peloponnese to the Panhellenic Olympic Games and the adaptation of the Phoenician alphabet to Greek writing (no later than 750 B.C.). To these should be added a general flowering of religious sanctuaries and a dramatic increase in the number of votive offerings almost everywhere in the Greek world⁴ and the combination of short, heroic, oral lays into long, serious epics written in the old oral style. These developments coincided with revived trade with Phoenicia, intensified contact with easternized Greek communities on the coast of Anatolia, and a colonizing movement that extended the reach of the Greek world to the Danubian coast of the Black Sea, up and down the Adriatic, and into what would become known as Magna Graecia in southern Italy and Sicily. Greeks rivaled Phoenicians as shippers and traders. The most important transformation was economic, as commercial agriculture displaced subsistence farming: dry, rocky soil unsuited to grain production was planted with vines and olive trees, and surplus production was exchanged for imported cereal grains.⁵ The entrepreneurial class that made this transformation possible began to impinge on the old landed families. The mainland Greeks found themselves at the center of an increasingly cosmopolitan, Greek-speaking *oikoumenē* in which a peasant culture was no longer central to their life.

A significant paradox of this newly polis-centered culture of enterprise is the way it continued to focus on its rustic past and the culture of neediness. Instead of a modernist movement that declared the past irrelevant, traditionalist Greeks constructed parts of their mythology on a romanticized past not altogether unlike the Old West fabricated by Americans. Besides diminishing the Aegean and Near Eastern goddesses, mythmakers such as Homer and Hesiod used their archaic poetic dialect to reinforce an ethos of rugged, masculine poverty. The self-image so created continued to be popular well into the Classical age, and it was not altogether misleading. A culture of poverty existed in Archaic Greece no less than self-reliance in the Old West, but the idea of the thing became as important as its historical substance. Greek advertisement of their own poverty began as early as Homer, where it contrasted with the glamour of the Bronze Age. In the *Odyssey*, it lies behind the tireless concern of Odysseus and Telemachus to protect their property, whereas the heroes of the *Iliad* earned status by giving it away. Odysseus is acquisitive to the core, always looking for a gift when he is abroad; the first thing he does when he awakes after reaching Ithaca is look for the gifts he brought with him from Phaeacia. Telemachus, as we have seen, is reluctant to accept the costly gift of three horses offered by Spartan Menelaus because there is no place to run them properly on rocky Ithaca—an observation later repeated by Athena (4.606–607, 13.242). It is no whim that makes a beggar's rags the favorite disguise of Odysseus. Helen reports that he flogged himself and dressed as a beggar to sneak into Troy during the war (4.244–248). He repeats the act with several variations when he returns to Ithaca. His is no feeble poverty: Homer is at pains to emphasize the rocklike sturdiness with which he endures the suitors' physical abuse (17.235, 463–464); he himself cannot help showing off his muscle by beating the beggar Iros to a pulp. Nor is this sturdy poverty indolent: the disguised Odysseus brags to Eumaeus about his capacity for hard labor despite a youthful indisposition for work (14.222, 15.317–324). Odysseus' posture is typical of a Greek tendency to make the most of their simple past, as Texans love to brag about their ancient poverty while flaunting their new wealth. Beggar's rags set off a pose that was dear to Odysseus' countrymen for centuries afterward.

Hesiod is a significant figure in this cultural imagery. He draws a picture of a peasantry that could only have been peripheral to the civilization developing around him. His rhetorical posture in the *Works and Days* invites us to imagine a way of life in which personal relationships, pleasure, and an accommodation to nature are overshadowed by a single-minded attention to business:

> Let not a woman with buttocks attractively covered deceive you,
> charmingly pleading and coaxing while poking into your barn.
> He who trusts in women is putting his trust in deceivers.[6]

Sexual Culture in Ancient Greece

Hesiod advocates what Plato would have called a banausic, mechanical life in a mechanical if not totally predictable natural world. It is a joyless if practical way of life, unattractive but believable. He represents the leathery smallholder in a chronically poor society on the fringe of a commercial economy. His account of farming-cum-seafaring in the *Works and Days* tells of part-time seasonal trading by sea; his father, he says, had been a failed merchant seaman from Anatolia near Lesbos. Hesiod's is a classic hard luck story: the family farm near Mount Helicon in Boeotia is "nasty in winter, disagreeable in the summer, never good," its austere life forced on his family by hard times or more successful competition. Taken as a story, it bears comparison with the lying tales of Odysseus at Ithaca. The returning hero disguises himself as a feckless war veteran and drifter down on his luck, and he holds up his bad experience as a warning to the loutish suitors of Penelope:

> I myself once promised to be a man of prosperity,
> but, giving way to force and violence, did many reckless
> things, because I relied on my father and brothers. Therefore,
> let no man be altogether without the sense of righteousness . . .
> (18.138–141, tr. Lattimore)

In the *Works and Days*, Hesiod lectures his wastrel brother Perses with similar themes:

> Perses, hearken to Justice and don't honor Hybris.
> Hybris is a bad thing for the poor man, for not even the rich man
> easily bears it but staggers under its weight and
> meets with calamity. . . . Justice wins over Hybris,
> finally coming in victor. The fool by suffering learns this.
>
> . . . .
>
> Perses, you great fool, I shall advise you and try to improve you.
> One can get Failure for oneself in pressing abundance
> easily: smooth and exceedingly short is the road to her dwelling.
> But the immortal gods require us to sweat in order to reach Success.
> (213–218, 286–290, adapted from Frazer)

The beggar and Perses are parallel fictions, as are the real Odysseus and Hesiod. They are projected on rural communities—Ithaca and

Ascra—that scarcely typify the centers of enterprise such as Ionia, Athens, Aegina, and Corinth, where they became authoritative texts: country myths for city people.

This paradox is a familiar one to Americans raised on Norman Rockwell art, Old West movies, country music, and Bible belt religion. But rustic mythology does not necessarily dictate sexual repression. Theocritus' pastoral world is laced with sex, and American country music, bred in the poorest corners of rural Appalachia, could scarcely get by the first truck stop without a woeful song of sexual infidelity. The strict limits on eroticism in Hesiod's Ascra and Homer's Ithaca were less a matter of personal necessity than of cultural choice. The severe style that is identified with Athenian art of the early Classical period has its roots in a culture of restraint. The artistic movement can be linked with a style of poverty that was in its essence more a cultural artifact than an economic fact of the period to which it belonged.

It is in the spirit of this cultural style that Herodotus has the exiled Greek Demaratus tell Xerxes why his Persians cannot subdue the Greeks: "Poverty," he says, "has always been endemic to Greece, while valor [*aretē*] is an acquired virtue . . . by which she resists both poverty and slavery" (7.102). Homer contrasts Odyssean ruggedness with the genteel luxury of the Phaeacians, and Herodotus is suspicious of the luxurious Persians of Anatolia. These postures are fraught with contradictions. The Greeks from Hesiod in the seventh century to Thucydides in the fifth dreaded poverty and considered it a disgrace not to do everything possible to escape it: "As for poverty," says Thucydides' Pericles, "no one need be ashamed to admit it: the real shame is in not taking practical measures to escape from it" (2.40.1, tr. Warner). Private magnificence, argues Thucydides' Alcibiades, demonstrates public prosperity.[7] Their inability to resist the temptations of wealth and comfort rendered Spartan envoys notoriously corruptible. As for the Athenians, the importation of educated and talented hetaeras from Anatolia eroded the one-eyed masculinity of Athenian life. But in spite of their celebrated ruggedness, the Greeks suffered from an intolerance for wage labor that bound them to a slave economy; their famous rationality was beset by a scorn of useful knowledge that crippled their technology and by failures of observational method that curtailed their achievements in science, including their understanding of gynecology.[8] Anyone who looks at the Greeks for long will see that their behavior vacillates between a principled indifference to the senses and a passion for beauty and luxury. A similar dualism exists between extreme patriarchy and an affinity for the feminine.[9] The cult of poverty and Spartan austerity are one side of that dichotomy. Sparta took this side to such an extreme that a guest from Sybaris exclaimed after eating one of their communal meals, "Now I understand why the Spartans are not afraid to die!"[10] But it is significant that other Greeks, particularly in Athens, mythologized Sparta into a utopian state.

In Archaic literature after Homer and Hesiod up to the early fifth century, the masculine side of the dichotomy expressed itself in choral lyric celebrating athletic victories, the patriotic poetry of Aeschylean tragedy, and elegiac monodists such as Theognis, Solon, and Tyrtaeus. These set forth the energizing myths of an elitist, competitive, patriarchal community of warring city-states that prized their independence and throve on the challenges of combat-oriented athletic contests and organized violence. The other side of the dichotomy appears in the lyric poets of the Aeolic and Ionian Greek East. Although the religious artifacts of the mainland (especially near Sparta and Argos) maintained a feminine imagery in this period, mainland literature for the most part adopted a masculine bias with its attendant postures.[11] This tendency was less pronounced in Athens and Corinth, the former because of its close ties with the Ionian East, the latter because of its trade relations with Phoenicia, Egypt, and other eastern states.

In addition to its ascetic ethnic persona, one of the central features of Hellenism is a degree of individualism that would have been collectively disabling had it not been for the counter-institution of the polis. As the tragedy of Achilles shows in the *Iliad*, extreme individualism is the enemy of strong personal attachment, and it is not until Patroclus has fallen victim to Achilles' egomania that the hero of the *Iliad* realizes how he has cut himself off. It was not until Aeschylus portrayed Achilles and Patroclus as lovers in the lost *Myrmidons* that this conflict of self-love with love of another was put in erotic terms, but the collision of eros with strong personal identity took many literary shapes in the two centuries between Homer and Aeschylus. Once it goes beyond the purely physical, eroticism invades personal boundaries and compromises the self. As a Dionysiac state, an erotic condition is the enemy of the self-possession that stands at the center

Figure 4.1. Three views of bronze Egyptian statuette found at the temple of Hera at Samos, ca. 700–630 B.C. Especially in the islands, Crete, and the southern Peloponnese, nudes of the eastern type persist at temples of goddesses well into the historical period. (Copyright by DAI Athens, neg. nos. Samos 5281, 5282, 5283)

Figure 4.2. The nude goddess with her lions, from a bronze shield fitting found in a cult cave of Zeus (the Idaean Cave) on Crete, dated c. 700 B.C.—about the time of Homer's *Odyssey*. The style is oriental, evidence of the continued vitality of eastern religious traditions in the Greek world of historic times.

Figure 4.3. A geometric Mistress of the Animals, πότνια θηρῶν, clad in the mainland Greek fashion and relieved of her voluptuous curves. Boeotian amphora from the neighborhood of Thebes, the area and approximate date of Hesiod (ca. 680 B.C.). (National Archaeological Museum, Athens, no. 220)

Figure 4.4. The Love Goddess as the Girl Next Door. Plastic artists were working at the same time as Homer to Hellenize the Near Eastern goddesses. The sexual and maternal voluptuousness of the naked goddess had been reduced in this slim, chaste version of the Astartes from which this ivory figurine is derived, ca. 740–730 B.C. Though a generation earlier than fig. 4.2, this Athenian figurine shows a more advanced stage of Hellenization. From the Kerameikos Cemetery, Athens. (Copyright by DAI Athens, neg. no. NM 3282)

Figure 4.5. The soul of modesty, this orant or goddess from an unknown find-spot is styled in a manner typical of the latter half of the seventh century, 650–625 B.C. Alert and intense, she anticipates the erect grace of the late Archaic Athenian korai. (Photograph © Christian Larrieu at Musée du Louvre)

of Greek cultural ideology; it corrodes the shell of personal identity, the Apollonian ideal of self-knowledge, and the competitive ideal of *aretē*. Love is also in conflict with the Hesiodic work ethic, as poets and comedians noted.[12] Iconographically, Eros, the winged spirit of love pictured as Aphrodite's companion, is related in Greek art to Hypnos, the winged spirit of sleep, and Thanatos, the winged spirit of death.[13] Alexander the Great is said to have remarked that he felt his mortality most strongly when he slept and when he made love.[14] Where the Asiatics combined love and war in their great goddess, the Greeks constructed an iconography that brought love and death into conjunction. Eros is the death of the self.

The Archaic monodists found two strategies for confronting this problem. One was the dissenting attack of poets like Mimnermus of Colophon, who flourished about a century after Homer. His best-known poem uses Homeric language to defend a position equating eroticism with life and youth:

> But what is life, what pleasure without golden Aphrodite?
>   May I die, when I no longer care about that,
> the secret joy of love-making, gentle gifts, and bed,
>   which are flowers of youth to be seized
> by men and by women. When painful old age
>   arrives, which makes a man ugly and vile,
> always vile fears press in around his heart
>   and he gets no pleasure looking at the sunlight;
> boys hate him, women ignore him.
>   That's how awful god has made old age.

The initial δέ (but) of this elegy (fr. 1 West) implies a rhetorical context that Mimnermus specifies by borrowing Homeric language: a green old age of the sort predicted for Odysseus is all very well, but there is no substitute for erotic youth. Mimnermus' first elegy is not a languid Ionian "Ode to Youth" (what is life without love, tra la la) so much as a debating contention that sex is the fulfillment of life at its best rather than a distraction, as it was for Odysseus on his way home from Troy. Whatever its personal meaning, Mimnermus' poem is significant as part of a public dialogue about sex, life, and death. It is a statement of value as authentically Greek as the severer statements previously considered.[15]

Sappho, a lonely eminence of women's eroticism in Archaic poetry, has survived in such a fragmentary state that a reconstruction of her point of view must rely on a very small body of evidence. A prolific poet, her works were collected in antiquity into nine books, all but the last of which (wedding songs) were distinguished by meter rather than genre. She is regularly described as a monodist whose poems describe personal experience and are written for a small audience in which girls and young women (*paides* and *parthenoi*) figure prominently, and her lyrics are variously described as sympotic,[16] public,[17] or instructional.[18] Until twentieth-century readers learned to accept Sappho's homoerotic themes, it was explained that she was a schoolmistress presiding over a *thiasos*, or small group of girls or younger women. If we can detach this explanation from the image it once promoted of a nonsexual school-marm, it may not be entirely off the mark. Some of the most challenging and illuminating readings of Sappho are today coming from feminist critics who see in her language a distinctive idiom of desire: "Her model of homoerotic relations is bilateral and egalitarian, in contrast to the rigid patterns of pursuit and physical mastery inscribed into the role of the adult male *erastēs*, whatever the sex of his love object."[19]

If more of Sappho's work is ever recovered, it might be harder than ever to summarize her views precisely because she seems to be committed to the complexity of erotic experience. Part of her testimony is to the violence of sexual feeling, like a cold, sudden, violent fit, causing a strong mind to reel: "Eros shook my wits, like mountain wind falling on the oaks" (47 LP); "Once again Eros the weakener of limbs shakes me, the bittersweet, impossible beast" (130 LP). This is not a mild protest, or a celebration of love's joy. It is, in fact, close to what Christopher A. Faraone calls "erotic seizure," more curse than blessing.[20] Sappho's eroticism is an encounter with an altered state in which one may be caught in a dilemma between pleasure and a loss of control: "I do not know what I want: I am of two minds" (51 LP). She expresses the conflict in her culture between Apollonian self-possession and Dionysiac instinctualism. Love and death come together in her fragments: "I simply want to die . . . some longing to die possesses me, to see the shores of Acheron dewy with lotus" (94, 95 LP). This is not an Aeolic Keats, half in love with easeful death, or a melancholic, suicidal Werther—though later biographers had it that she jumped off a cliff in a frenzy of unrequited love.[21]

Her poems included marriage songs, moral advice, and at least one song about the death of Aphrodite's consort, Adonis,[22] an eastern theme with erotic elements. The impersonality that is typical of the epic, choral, and dramatic literature is not a part of the genre in which she writes, and the word that appears most frequently in positions of emphasis—the beginning or end of a line—is one form or another of ἐγώ, "I." The self-consciousness that goes with this idiom is ironic rather than romantic, self-mocking rather than self-dramatizing, confessional rather than priestly, even in her formal prayers of invocation to Aphrodite (1, 2 LP). Though the way she sees when she is in love is noteworthy,[23] her erotic sense is more than visual: "I fell in love with you Atthis, long ago . . . a small girl you seemed to me, and without grace" (49 LP); "a handsome man is only handsome to look at, but one who is also good will be handsome also" (50 LP). But it is also physical, both when she suffers sexual pain (as in the ode to Anaktoria, 31 LP) and when she enjoys sexual pleasure (as in the remembrance of things past, 94 LP). A highly developed eroticism exposes its possessor to pains of loss and unattainment, and the rumor took hold generations later that she was short and physically unattractive.[24] Like Mimnermus in the fragment quoted—in fact, like ancient Greeks in general—her eroticism is not gender-specific in its object: she does not need to make distinctions between a passionate feeling for one of her own sex and one of the opposite. Because Greek society was segregated by gender, she records strong emotional attachments to her usual associates, who were girls and women. The English terms "lesbian" or "homosexual" are misleading when applied to her world because the experience she records is not profoundly different from other kinds of female eroticism. The use of a female voice is, however, untypical; and though the special features of female erotic sensibility in her poems are particularly interesting, much of the erotic pathos she expresses was far from alien to Sappho's ancient male audience.

While the historical existence of Sappho requires no special proof, the survival of her memory, notwithstanding the manifest excellence of her poetry, calls for some explanation. Mere facts had little chance of surviving in Archaic memory unless they fit some recognizable category. Among the reasons why Sappho and her poetry survived is that they fit the belief that intense eroticism, particularly toward women, is a feminine category—not uniquely feminine, but specially so, as women were thought especially vulnerable to erotic seizure.[25] Eumaeus' nurse in the *Odyssey* had a sexual encounter "which beguiles the judgement of female women, even one who is a skilled worker" (15.421 f.) For the historical Greeks, the gender of Sappho is as fitting as that of Aphrodite, her declarations especially credible as those of a woman.

The eroticism of women has another spokesman in Alcman of Sparta, a contemporary of Mimnermus and the earliest choral writer to survive in enough quantity to provide some sense of his work. Alcman's poetic medium is the *partheneion*, or maiden song, that was popular among a number of male poets including Pindar, Simonides, and Bacchylides.[26] His singers are girls in a chorus performing in a competition honoring the local goddess Orthria (in the longest fragment), and part of their song is in praise of their own loveliest fellow singers. Fragment 3 expresses the beauty of one such girl in subjective and erotic language:

> . . . with desire that looses the limbs, and she darts a glance
> more melting than sleep or death. Nor is she sweet to no
> purpose. And Astymelousa does not answer me, but holds
> the garland as if she were some shining star flying through
> the heaven, or a golden branch, or soft down . . .

The fragment illuminates the proximity in Archaic rhetoric of praise to erotic statement. One function of Alcman's *partheneia* is to praise girls in a cultic dance in honor of a goddess. It is not personal monody, like much of Sappho's, but public rhetoric, and the chorus's erotic statement serves rather to praise the loveliness of a girl in their performance than to suggest a private feeling.[27] The eroticism is normative: to see Astymelousa is to fall in love with her, whether you are man, woman, or child. The emotion is erotic without being homoerotic, pedophiliac, or even sexual an any particular way. As sometimes in Pindar, erotic and encomiastic discourse are closely linked. Eros here informs and fulfills the expression of *aretē* in a girls' chorus in a way that is typical of Greek sexual culture. Thus erotic statement in Alcman leads in a direct line to Plato's equation in the *Symposium* of eros with philosophy.

While these lyric voices are significant for mainstream Greek culture, another persistent voice of these years conveys the sense that love is not the perfect fulfillment of human life, as it seemed with Mimnermus' description of youth's sexual prime, or with the dazzling girls of Alcman's Maiden Songs. Later Greek thinkers would articulate the Sapphic view that love is a *pathos*, something that comes over you.[28] Homer anticipated this when he represented the sexuality of Helen or Paris as something that comes from Aphrodite—like other mental states in Homer, whether a bad idea or a godlike virtue, love was god-given. In the lyric monody of later generations, individuals come forward to take credit for what they are and to protest against anything that interferes with that. Sappho belongs to this type, even though like Alcman she finds the links that join sex, love, and beauty. But because she is not the complete romantic, her relation with the eros that inspires her poetry is often painful. The Anactoria Ode resolves itself into a catalog of debilitating physical symptoms: "I see nothing with my eyes, my ears hum, sweat pours from me, a trembling seizes me all over, I am paler than grass, it seems to me that I am not far short of death." This "I've-got-it-bad-and-that-ain't-good" description of eros is bolstered by many Archaic poems and fragments. Prominent among the poets battered by love and war is Archilochus, who became well known in antiquity for his invective. Fragments of his epodes complain about love: "I am wretchedly involved in desire, riddled to the bones with awful pains sent by the gods."[29] The theme of love's violence became proverbial in Archaic poetry: "Once again Eros has hit me like a blacksmith with a big axe, and plunged me into a wintry torrent."[30] In keeping with this theme, Simonides made Eros the son of Ares and Aphrodite (70 Page), recalling the liaison Homer gives them in the *Odyssey* (8.266–366) and the Near Eastern link of the sex goddess with warfare. Aphrodite has her comic side; but eros, abstract or personified, is less often comic than sinister and violent. Romantic views of the Archaic Greek spirits of love contradict the testimonia.

Moreover, Hesiod's attention to the frailties of womankind bore its own sour fruit in Semonides of Amorgos' seventh-century B.C. invective against women, comparing various types to the sow, the vixen, the bitch (who won't stop yapping even when her husband knocks her teeth out with a rock), mud, the sea, a donkey, a weasel, the mare, a monkey, and finally (the only good kind) the industrious bee, who takes no pleasure in other women's conversations about sex. Scraps of Archilochus, Hipponax, and Anacreon hint that this kind of invective was as popular in Archaic Greece as it is today.[31] Although lyric should not be misread as social history, the thread of misogyny and sexual conflict is unmistakable. Homer is more balanced. The love-hate that Helen feels for Paris in *Iliad* 3 is unlike the loving scene in *Iliad* 6 between Hector and Andromache. The infidelity of Aphrodite with Ares in Demodocus' song in *Odyssey* 8 is a foil to Penelope's fidelity to Odysseus. The harmony of Odysseus and Penelope contrasts with the bickering between Zeus and Hera near the end of *Iliad* 1, where Zeus threatens his wife with violence. The sexual reunion at the end of the *Odyssey* contrasts with Hera's sexual manipulation of Zeus to distract his attention in *Iliad* 14. Conjugal warfare on Olympus is not a positive archetype of mortal sexual unions.

Yet most of the human bonds in Homer are not strongly sexual. The most erotic, that between Helen and Paris, is problematic, as we have seen. It is contrasted with many nonerotic bonds; Hector and Andromache are less erotically than conjugally bonded; Achilles' captive concubine, Briseis, is bound to him by the fortunes of war; she hopes to consummate this after the war as a regular marriage, with Patroclus' help. Achilles is attached to Briseis by his love of the glory she represents to him as the top prize of a raiding expedition. There is no ambivalence about any of these nonerotic bonds, each of which is fervently described by all of the participants themselves. They are all bonds of love, and there are many others in the *Iliad*. The most powerful of many ardent bonds in the *Iliad* comes as a surprise, because the relation between Achilles and his henchman, Patroclus, is taken for granted until it is shattered by the latter's death. Patroclus has all the compassion that his master lacks, and it is his death while defending the Achaeans in Achilles' place that ruptures the self-absorption of "the best of the Achaeans." Without Patroclus, Achilles has no wish to go on living, glory or no glory. The tragedy of the *Iliad* is that its hero cannot have the glory he craves without sacrificing the person dearest to him.

PINDAR'S EROTIC

Like Renaissance enthusiasts who sought to relive the romance of chivalry in jousting matches, the Greeks of the sixth century reconstructed Homeric glory in a less lethal form. The Olympic Games had for two centuries translated into athletic contests the heroic ethos pictured by Homer. Open only to boys and men of the ruling class with the leisure to train intensively in combat skills, they placed so much stress on the glory of winning and the disgrace of losing that cheating was a regular feature from an early date. In the sixth century, Panhellenic imitators sprang up at Delphi (starting in 586 B.C.), Isthmia (starting in 581 B.C.), and Nemea (Panhellenic from 573 B.C.). Pindar made himself the poet laureate of this neoheroic movement within a century of its proliferation, hiring out his extraordinary poetic voice to celebrate the victors and their families in epinician odes. He made it his business to show how their victories kept alive the grand tradition of *aretē* as the special province of a Junker-style elite. A poet of consummate skill and tact, Pindar wrote what his patrons wanted to hear with such rhetorical craft that his victory odes are valued among the best poetry written in Greek.

Pindar's rhetorical sparkle fades in translation, but his mastery of lyric places him in the top rank of Greek poets.[32] The victory odes are valuable testaments of a severely masculine life. Except for an ancestress who contributes to the founding of a noble family by being raped by Apollo (Cyrene in *Pyth.* 9), a princess who aids a hero (Medea in *Pyth.* 4), and similar supporting roles, women have little place in a Pindaric world resplendent with male nobility, single-mindedness, effort, personal youth and beauty, and (of course) success in exclusively masculine endeavors. Glamour is a male attribute; Pindar evokes an erotic, sensuous mystique both for the language of praise itself and for the athletes who earn praise by their victories.[33] But there is nothing either soft or feminine about this erotic mystique. As often in Greek literature, feminine eroticism is tinged in Pindar with a carnality that renders it prone to treachery. Like Eumaeus' Phoenician nurse in the *Odyssey* (15.417 ff.), Pindar's Clytemnestra is mentally tainted as a result of her illicit liaison (*Pyth.* 11.25). Coronis in *Pythian* 3 is a sexual overreacher. She makes love with Apollo and is thereby destined to bear the healer Asclepius, but before the happy event she accepts a mortal lover "in the waywardness of her wits," ἀμπλακίαισι φρενῶν. Female eroticism is a Pandora's jar, beyond a woman's power to control once broached. This dogma underlies the social control of women in Classical Greece. There was no appeal to a woman's own moral restraint in sex (as there was in Roman culture), as it was believed first that the ethical powers of a woman, being weaker than a man's, were inherently no match for her sexual urges, and second that those urges were stronger than a man's.[34]

Male eros may also be wrongheaded, as when in *Pythian* 2 the infamous Ixion is remembered as conceiving a desire for Hera and making "an attempt on the couch of Zeus" (as always in questions of rape, the crime is more against the male proprietor than against the female object). Whether male or female, eros, like our "lust," may be any strong desire and therefore dangerous. At its best, though, Pindar's eros blends sexual magnetism with the desire for success, as in the opening lines of his eighth Nemean ode in honor of a sprinter from Aegina named Deinias:

> Lady Youth, harbinger of Aphrodite's immortal liaisons,
> you who sit on the eyelids of girls and boys: one man you
> lift with the gentle hands of necessity, another you lift with
> other hands. It is something to admire when a person misses
> no opportunity and can win the object of his better desires
> [τῶν ἀρειόνων ἐρώτων].

The eros of Pindar's perfect young athletes is for victory; the lesser female breed lust after the victors themselves, as they can aspire to attain only the possessor of *aretē*, not the virtue itself. A victor's fame is the ultimate aphrodisiac: a sports celebrity after winning a race for boys, Hippocleias is "an object of care among young girls. For surely different desires provoke different minds" (*Pyth.* 10.59 f.). Telesicrates enjoys a similar adulation in *Pythian* 9: "the girls watched as you won the highest honors, and each prays silently that she will have a beloved husband like you, or a son."

Pindar's victors combine beauty and physical achievement in equal amounts, unlike Homer's Paris, who has looks but no courage (*Il.* 3.45) or Nireus of Syme, who is second only to Achilles in beauty but ineffective (ἀλαπαδνός, *Il.* 2.675). Beauty is as beauty does: the wrestler Epharmostos is "in the bloom of his youth and fair—and fairest in his deeds" (*Ol.* 9.94); Alcimedon, winner of boys' wrestling, is "fine to look at, and in action not refuting his looks" (*Ol.* 8.19); Aristocleides, winner of the tests of strength at Nemea, "is handsome, and does things worthy of his looks" (*Nem.* 3.19). Another winner of the *pankration* is Strepsiades of Thebes: "astonishing in strength, shapely to look at, and he bears an areté no worse than his build" (*Isthm.* 7.22). This muscular beauty, given special emphasis on Greek vases (see, e.g., fig. 5.5), is the kind that men also found arousing. The code for this in *Olympian* 10 is an allusion to Ganymede, the pretty young Trojan prince spirited off by Zeus to be his personal attendant on Olympus: "Archestratus' lovely son, fair in form and imbued with the youthfulness that once saved Ganymede from ruthless death with Aphrodite's aid," is a winner at boys' boxing. Like the young wrestler Alcimedon, his state of development is one that Greek men (and perhaps women as well, though their views on the matter are not recorded) particularly admired in a sexual way.

THE RULING CLASS CULT OF PEDERASTY

Because Greek culture was bisexual, there were no taboos restricting gender in sexual attraction. The ruling elite, which most rigidly segregated the sexes, consigned women to a lower caste and set themselves off from the general population by making a class cult of male love. Like ruling-class fashions everywhere, this became more generally emulated in Archaic Greek circles, and the cult hung on for centuries afterward. The general population was more than tolerant of homosexuality among women as well as men, making no invidious distinctions about the gender of sexual partners. For example, when Sappho writes in fragment 94 about past good times with a departing friend, there is no indication in line 23 about the gender of the person with whom that friend satisfied her desire; likewise, when Mimnermus (fr. 1, quoted above) writes about the humiliation of age, he pairs the disinterest of boys with that of women (line 9). Eroticism is regularly perceived as having both homosexual and heterosexual aspects, with prejudice toward neither.[35] At the same time, the love of boys by men took on the baggage of class bigotry some time in the sixth century B.C., so that by the time of Pindar in the first half of the fifth there was an erotic social code. The basic feature of the code was to make the love of boys an emblem of the ruling class and its ideals and to devalue the love of women.

Sexual Culture in Ancient Greece

Much of the language about sexual deportment that survives from the fifth century B.C. has to do with this class code and the ethics of the *kalokagathoi*, the wealthy and privileged "beautiful people" who maintained it. Part of the mythology of boy love was that it was inimical to tyranny because (like Freemasonry and Christianity) it took precedence over politics. It laid claim to a variety of what are loosely referred to as "spiritual values." The Pederastic Code distinguished the upper crust from the hoi polloi as decisively as the patriarchal myths embraced by Homer and Hesiod distinguished the Hellenes from the "barbarians" of the Near East. It was part of an ideology contemptuous of everything unmilitary on which the polis depended: labor, commerce, and other financially gainful employment. In its purest form, it affected a distrust of anything foreign, feminine, heterosexual, or common.[36] The Pederastic Code excluded women and regarded any attachment to them, any lack of enthusiasm for boys, as the symptom of a servile temperament. Like the rules of any gentlemen's club, the code was studiously artificial because its adherents felt themselves able to put themselves at a distance from the gross requirements of nature. The private gatherings of the *kalokagathoi* were symposia in the *andrōn*, or men's quarters, of the best and largest private homes. The literary voice of the symposium became the skolion and the epigram, while Pindar made the victory odes the public literary voice of the *kalokagathoi* in their public gatherings as sponsors of the Panhellenic games and the suppliers of their contestants. His victory odes, archaic throwbacks in the Classical fifth century, set out the ideology of his patrons in its most beautified form. Fragments of other poems show that his role as poet laureate of the first families extended into other types of poetry. He was always the poet of praise, but the ideological agenda is never far from the surface.

Fragment 123 is an encomium in which the ideology of the Pederastic Code is so densely interwoven that it is nearly impossible to translate clearly:

> It is proper to pluck the flowers of love in season, my soul,
> in the prime of life. But whoever darts a glance at the rays
> shining from the eyes of Theoxenus and does *not* swell with
> desire, such a man's heart is forged from steel or iron—a
> black heart in a cold fire—and he is unhonored by glancing

Aphrodite; he either drudges laboriously after material gain, or he has no more courage than a woman and is swept along every chilly path of servitude. But because of Aphrodite I melt like the wax of holy bees bitten by the sun's heat when I look at the young limbs and the youth of young boys.

Like other first-person statements in choral poetry, this is less auto-biographical than protreptic in intent, designed to instruct and per-suade. Like the chorus in a play, the speaker is an ideal spectator voicing the appropriate sentiment toward the person to be praised and admired. To fail to admire Theoxenus is to fall short of the Pederastic Code and the values it encapsulates: (1) it is permissible for a man of any age to fall in love with a boy; (2) to fail to do so in this instance is symptomatic of impotence and sexual retardation, and signals (3) that he belongs to that regrettable class of people who must work for a living, (4) that he is effeminate and a coward, and finally (5) that he is a drifter with the moral turpitude of a slave, more fit to be our slave than one of us. By contrast, "I," that is, every right-minded gentleman here present, am an enthusiastic pederast. Biographical critics who disregard the conventions of this poetry deduce from the Theoxenus encomium that Pindar was in love with Theoxenus. Nothing in frag-ment 123 excludes that possibility, but the content of the language is not autobiographical. Pederasty is a litmus of "true nobility," which is above all a social category. The meaning of the encomium is that young Theoxenus is one of us in the best sense of the word, that we should all admire him without reservation, and that anyone who fails to do so is a rank outsider.

It is instructive to compare the forceful conviction of the Theoxenus encomium with fragment 122, in honor of Xenophon of Corinth on the occasion of his dedication of fifty sacred prostitutes to the Corinthian temple of Aphrodite to mark his double victory at Olympia. This was a difficult commission to fulfill, because sacred prostitutes do not exactly fit the categories of the Pederastic Code. Though the evidence for it is disputed, sacred prostitution was itself probably a Near Eastern institution, established in Greece only at Corinth by virtue of its ancient trading connections with the East. It catered traditionally to outsiders, such as the merchant seamen who crowded the port of Corinth, and was associated with Aphrodite in her most universal and least discriminating aspect: Aphrodite *pandemos*, goddess of all the people. "Going to Corinth" was axiomatic for the enjoyment of sexual high times throughout antiquity.[37] The prostitutes of Corinth were one of the civic groups that publicly commemorated Aphrodite's aid in saving Corinth from Persian invasion in 480 B.C.[38] Now, in 464 B.C., Xenophon of Corinth is adding fifty to their number, probably fifty young slave women purchased in Asia Minor:

> Hostesses of many, girls attendant on persuasion in rich Corinth, who burn yellow tears of pale frankincense, often flying in your thoughts to heavenly Aphrodite, mother of the loves, to you, children, she has granted without reproach on lovely beds to pluck the fruit of tender youth. But with necessity, everything is fine. . . . [there is a break in the text]
>   Yet I wonder what the masters of the Isthmus will say to me for devising such a beginning of sweet song as a companion to public women. (Fr. 122)

The opening is graceful and ornate in the manner for which Pindar was famous. It concedes, with a touch of humor, that what the young women do is in this case "without reproach" and in any case done "with necessity" and therefore "fine," καλόν. But the subject does not fit the seamless masculinity of chivalric pederasty, and the poet acknowledges that his theme is a delicate matter—not because it is sexual, but because it is heterosexual, commercial, and (for him) un-Greek. They are, after all, "public women" who come into the genteel, closed world of the victor and his thank offering. Always in step with his patrons and his audience, Pindar admits the awkwardness of an offering more appropriate to the plebeian element of Corinth than to the genteel aristocrats who patronize the games.

The embarrassment Pindar expresses on behalf of his audience has nothing to do with a belief that prostitution was immoral. There is no evidence of such a belief until very late antiquity. It comes rather from a distinction he draws between the noble and the common worlds, which is comparable to the religious difference between sacred and profane, or the epic distinction between the ordinary and the epic world. As Homer never allows us to see his heroes eating anything but roasted meats, Pindar avoids subjects not germane to the strenuous nobility of upper-crust athletes.

WOMEN'S PLACE

The segregation of the sexes grew out of a related impulse. Though Homer represents an earlier society in which women had a larger public role to play than in his own time, women were expected to withdraw from "men's business." Women (Helen, Briseis) are objects of contention in the *Iliad* but are excluded from its deliberations. At the end of his scene with his wife and son in book 6 of the *Iliad*, Hector prays that Astyanax will grow up to be a great warrior and bring in bloody spoils to "delight the heart of his mother" (481), but when he sees Andromache weeping with fear for him he anticipates her objection with the lines paraphrased by Telemachus at the head of this chapter: "Go therefore back to our house, and take up your own work; . . . but the men must see to the fighting" (6.490–493). Aeschylus uses a similar formula in the *Seven Against Thebes* (467 B.C.),[39] and "the men must see to the fighting" is mockingly quoted by Aristophanes in *Lysistrata* 520 (411 B.C.) as the husband's typical response when Lysistrata objects to the incessant belligerence of Athens. In Homeric language the οἶκος "house," to which Telemachus dismisses his mother is the living quarters upstairs as distinct from the megaron, or great hall, below. A domestic room, a bedroom or storage chamber, is regularly a *thalamos*, usually under female control. Women control the keys: Penelope has the key to the *thalamos* where Odysseus' bow is stored, her housekeeper, Eurycleia, to the basement *thalamos*, another storeroom in the *Odyssey* 2.337 ff. The Homeric household is divided into spheres of influence, at least when the male proprietor is home, with the man in charge of the public hall, or megaron, where entertainment took place. When a man goes to bed he goes *up* to it not only in the sense that he "mounts" it like a chariot or a ship but also because he goes up into the domestic quarter.[40] When Homer tells about the killing of Agamemnon by Aegisthus the ambush takes place at a banquet in the megaron (ἐν μεγάροισιν, 4.537, cf. 11.410), that is, in the male part of the house.

When Aeschylus has Clytemnestra do the killing in the *Agamemnon*, it happens in the bath (1128–1129), and the stricken king cries out "I am struck a deadly blow *inside*."[41] Part of the drama in the scene where Agamemnon and Clytemnestra stand outside the palace entrance debating whether the conquering hero will walk over the purple tapestry she has laid out for him is that we see him losing control just at the point where he is entering his wife's domain. Sex in the Archaic and Classical world was spatially defined.

The separation of the home into male and female spheres persisted throughout antiquity wherever a house was large enough to admit such segregation. The *andrōn* became the men's banqueting hall and adjoining rooms, the *gynaikōn* the women's apartments. The precedent was Homeric, but the structuring of domestic as well as public life to preserve the separation of the sexes deeply marked the erotic part of Greek culture.[42] It did not prevent husbands from enjoying sexual relations with their wives when they chose to do so, but it permitted them to enjoy an entirely separate erotic life at home. Athenian law guaranteed a husband the right to keep a concubine at home, but it severely punished a wife's adultery. The sexual life of a man was as open as the man's part of the house, the woman's as closed as was her part of the house, farthest from the street in the "nook" (μυχός; see n. 41) of the house where things are kept safe.

The tendency to relegate male and female categories to opposite poles resulted less in an attraction of opposites than one of homogenes. Homer's Achilles is furious at the confiscation of his girl Briseis but inconsolable at the death of Patroclus, whom Aeschylus represented as his lover in his lost *Myrmidons*. War naturally breeds strong attachments between the men who share its risks together. It also breeds a mystique of elitism among those who share the greatest risk, and a tendency to value least those who are least exposed. The Greek cult of war as the natural state of men and cities[43] made the polarization of the genders even more pronounced[44] and led to the intensification of male bonding to a degree never anticipated by Homer, who has no male lovers. The preference for male companionship was rationalized according to the belief in female carnality, weak-spiritedness, and forgetfulness of absent men. Athena capitalizes on this when she wants Telemachus to hurry home from Sparta:

No property must go out of the house, unless you consent to it.
For you know what the mind is like in the breast of a woman. She
wants to build up the household of the man who marries her,
and of the former children, and of her beloved and wedded husband,
she has no remembrance, when he is dead, nor does she think of him.

(*Od.* 15.19–23, tr. Lattimore)

This is scarcely true of Penelope, who exemplifies the Greek truism
that there is nothing better than a good wife,[45] but it is enough to
bring Telemachus home in a hurry. Athena appeals to the assumption
that the female species is magnetically dependent on the male. Homer's
poetry tends to support this view. Achilles' Briseis is completely
attached to her captor. She can think of nothing better than to marry
him, and there is no hint from Homer that she harbors any resentment
that Achilles and his fellow raiders destroyed her home and her family
before reducing her to the status of booty.

Although the strong female characters in the *Odyssey* offset the
masculine *Iliad*, both poems play an important part in the construction of male and female as distinct identities. Intercourse between the
genders is less important than the understanding of what makes them
distinct. Hesiod goes so far as to call them a different species.[46] Archaic
poetry puts great emphasis on the social and ethical dimorphism of
the genders, with female nature dependent on the male; men depend
on each other, but the cardinal mandate is for a well-defended male
personal identity. As they continued to articulate a common sense of
life, Archaic poets recognized separate categories of place for men and
women that persisted for centuries afterward. Intimacy came to be
defined in terms that made relations between men more personally
and socially significant than those between the sexes. Women were
dismissed "up into the *oikos*."

CHAPTER FIVE

Education of the Senses from Solon to Pericles

We have hetairas for the sake of pleasure, concubines for
the day-to-day care of our body, and wives for the
begetting of legitimate children and the trustworthy care
of the home.

APOLLODORUS, *AGAINST NEAIRA*[1]

It is likely that Athens, which on all the evidence enjoyed the highest
general culture of mainland Greece, also had its highest sexual
culture. Not only were Athenian writers verbally articulate about sex,[2]
reflecting on eros in itself and as a metaphor for the other passions;
Athens also produced one of the richest schools of pictorial erotica in
the history of world art. Its medium was the red-figure vase, invented
in Athens by about 530 B.C.[3] Its most exuberant period lasted little
more than a generation, until about the second decade of the fifth
century, when the "severe style" of monumental, athletic idealism
supplanted it in the early Classical period. Athens exported this as it
did other cultural forms: Attic red-figure erotic art is as well known as
it is because a large quantity was exported to Italy, where it was preserved in Etruscan tombs. Greek sexual culture was also expressed in
its nude male kouroi and its gorgeously clad female korai, though the
erotic content of this public art was less overt and its production less
uniquely Athenian, being produced in many other parts of the Greek
world as well.

What does seem to have been particularly Athenian, especially on
the mainland, is a departure from the austerely masculine culture
implicit in Homer, Hesiod, and Pindar. While the ruling class maintained its solidarity with the Junker ideology glorified by Pindar, it did

not do so to the exclusion of an Athenian ethos described more than a century later by Thucydides in Pericles' funeral oration: "Our love of what is beautiful does not lead to extravagance; our love of things of the mind does not make us soft."[4] If Thebes and Sparta were like Prussia, Athens was more like Paris or Vienna.

The cultural leadership of Athens in the late Archaic period grew out of many causes, not least of them its close contact with Asia Minor. The Ionian dialect group to which the Athenians belonged encouraged their sense of kinship with Ionian Greeks in the Asiatic cities of Smyrna, Ephesus, Miletus, and Halicarnassus as well as with the islanders of Chios, Samos, and Naxos. Commercial relations were also close, with the result that the Athenians had immediate access to the luxuries for which the East had long been famous. The cosmopolitan affluence of Asia Minor produced more than refined sensuality among the Greeks who lived there. It had also made the Ionian coast an intellectual seedbed in which the beginnings of systematic, rational thought took root. Homer himself wrote of Asia Minor with the intimate knowledge of a native.[5] Historiography is also rooted in the Greek East: Herodotus of Halicarnassus, the southernmost capital of the Ionian mainland, based his historical methods on those of Ionian logographers such as Hecataeus of Miletus. The Ionian enlightenment, itself informed by contacts as far afield as Egypt and Babylonia, implanted habits of skepticism and debate that made all Ionians something more than passive consumers of ideas. The fourth-century achievements of Plato and Aristotle are unthinkable on ground unprepared by the Ionians Thales, Anaximander, and Anaximenes of Miletus, Xenophanes of Colophon, and Heraclitus of Ephesus.

Athens' open door to the East brought other benefits besides a taste for luxury and a love of ideas. The economic activity generated by a demand for imports changed the region from a freestanding agrarian community to a mixed economy of commerce, manufacture, and agricultural export, with the result that the power of the old landed families of Attica had to make room for commercial interests and the political power base widened as nowhere else in Greece. In Athens more than anywhere else, the demos, a new coalition of small landowners with commercial interests, won a secure place in the running of the polis. Athens' nearby Dorian rivals, Aegina, Megara,

Sexual Culture in Ancient Greece

and Corinth, did not respond in the same way to similar patterns of economic development and trade.

Urbanization was one result of this complex of developments. Not only did the native population grow independently of Attica's ability to feed itself; besides the natives, there was a large population of resident aliens, or metics, attracted to Athens by job opportunities in commerce, manufacturing, crafts, and shipping that proliferated around the port. Moreover, the political openness of Athens made it a place of refuge for discontents from parochial tyrannies and oligarchies elsewhere in the Greek world. These conditions not only resulted in simple population growth, but the growth of a self-selected population of in dividuals not satisfied with the life of peasants and underlings. What New York was to Europe in the nineteenth century A.D., Athens was to the Aegean in the sixth century B.C. By the beginning of the Peloponnesian War in 431 B.C., Athens was about three times larger than Corinth, her largest rival, and about five times the size of Thebes, Argos, and Corcyra.[6]

These changes did not take place overnight, and even if our data for the sixth century were not so sparse, it would be hard to judge exactly when the first urban civilization of Greece reached its takeoff point. One set of milestones is the series of constitutional reforms beginning with those of Solon in the first half of the sixth century B.C., when the aristocratic Eupatridai were forced to concede power to the farmers and tradesmen and wealth rather than birth or occupation became the criterion of eligibility for office. Other reforms, such as the adoption of a coinage and the assignment of a definite role to a citizen assembly, marked the needs of a developing economy from which more than a few were gaining strength. Plutarch represents Solon as solidly middle class, though the son of a ruined aristocrat, and although biographies of ancient figures should be considered more symbolic than factual, it is worth noting the type of statements made about him. Whether or not he was by birth or occupation a "demotic" of the middle class (*Sol.* 16), he is clearly billed as a merchant's man, who put through as much legislation favoring mercantile culture as possible, reducing the risk of indebtedness, promoting education in craft skills, and encouraging the naturalization of businessmen with families.

One interesting note in Plutarch is Solon's enjoyment of pleasure, which the biographer describes as a part of his mercantile culture:

> Solon's expensive and luxurious way of life, and his more vulgar than philosophic way of talking about pleasure in his poems, is thought to come from his mercantile life; having many great dangers, he demanded in return certain pleasures and amenities. (*Sol.* 3)

As it happens, nothing survives of Solon's poetry that is either vulgar or philosophic on the subject of sexual pleasure, but at least one account survives from antiquity that he admired the poetry of Sappho.[7] There is also a tradition that Solon purchased and set up "girlies" (*gynaia*) in houses "because of the culmination [*acmē*] of young men."[8] If it is correct to interpret this as a government provision rather than one of Solon's business enterprises, the implication is that Solon instituted prostitution as a measure for the common good.[9] While this may not conform to everyone's definition of the common good, it must be remembered that it was differently regarded in the ancient world, even as something better than a concession to inevitable vice. If prostitution became instituted as an officially sponsored enterprise during the time of Solon, it is a fair guess that Athens was by this time a center of population like Corinth and that public order (if nothing else) required such facilities for unattached males. It can also be seen that a public monopoly or investment in prostitution was a proven source of funds, as it had doubtless been for generations in the Near East. Was this a form of temple prostitution, like the establishment at Corinth referred to by Pindar a century later in 464 B.C.?[10] Something close to it, if Nicander of Colophon is referring to Athens when Athenaeus (13.569d) quotes him as saying that Solon built the first temple to Aphrodite Pandemos from the profits earned by the women in charge of the prostitutes' houses. The difference at Athens is that the temple appears to have followed rather than preceded the prostitutes and that the institution remained secular.

Whether or not he was a voluptuary or established prostitution on the Corinthian model, Solon promoted something other than the narrow Eupatrid formulas in adapting Athens to the realities of a city. With her strong eastern ties, Athens developed a distinct sexual culture.

Joined by a chain of Aegean islands to the Ionian coast of Asia Minor, she was buffered from the alien East by fellow Ionians who had lived next door to the Lydians and Carians for centuries, intermarried, and adopted their customs. Miletus, Ephesus, Priene, Colophon, Chios, and a dozen other Ionian coastal cities were founded by Greeks in the Ionian Migration at the end of the Mycenaean age. The islanders of the Cyclades between Athens and Asia Minor were Ionians from Athens, according to Herodotus (7.95.1). In this way, the Athenians enjoyed a unique bridge to the Near East.

The Lydian empire founded by Alyattes early in the sixth century enjoyed an economic growth in which the subject Ionian cities participated. The first electrum coinage was introduced at this time or slightly earlier, and Alyattes' son, Croesus, remains legendary for his wealth. That Alyattes' wealth attracted a professional class of prostitutes is indicated by Herodotus' account that his grave mound bore pillars recording the contribution made by each class to the monument. The prostitutes' share was the largest.[11] The Lydian empire fell to the Persian Cyrus soon after the middle of the sixth century. Writing some one hundred fifty years later, Xenophon idealized Cyrus and the disciplined sturdiness in which he was supposedly educated, contrasting it with the softness and luxury of the Medes.[12] In Xenophon and repeatedly at the hands of Greek writers early and late, easterners were tarred with the same brush of luxury (ἁβρότης, θρύψις, τρυφή) in dress, music, dance, cuisine, and sex. Luxury at its worst is a sexual offense, making a man effeminate (θῆλυς and related compounds— the same word means feminine, soft, gentle, weak). As a characteristic of Homer's Phaeaceans, luxury was un-Greek and self-explanatory: "always the feast is dear to us, and the lyre and dances and changes of clothes and our hot baths and beds."[13] Though Homer's fellow Ionians were not so averse to these tastes, mainlanders would draw their own conclusions. The damning link that the architects of "muscular Hellenism" forged between the feminine, eroticism, and decadent luxury continues to affect the way we think about these subjects.

It is impossible now to reconstruct the process by which the Athenians modulated the harshness of this ideology; zealots like Plato never relaxed their grip on it.[14] But in late Archaic Athens, an enriched way of life made inroads into the old ideal. An eastern style of refined luxury, *habrotēs*, confronted the arduous *aretē* of traditional Hellenism,

Education of the Senses from Solon to Pericles

with results that permanently changed Greek civilization. Shrapnel from that confrontation is preserved from the comedians by Athenaeus. A comedy presented in 434 B.C. by Callias called *The Cyclopes* (in which it may be supposed the Cyclopes are of the austere mainland type) makes fun of Ionia as "luxurious and fair-tabled," τρυφερὰ καὶ καλλιτράπεζος. Hermippus' *Soldiers* (ca. 422 B.C.) mocks the slack, unsoldierly look of troops from Abydus, a colony of Ionian Miletus; Aristophanes satirizes the Ionian passion for pretty boys in a fragment of his *Triple Phales*;[15] in *Ecclesiazusae* 883, an "Ionic ditty" is a dirty song, and in 918 f. a woman's desire to scratch herself "in the Ionian style," τὸν ἀπ' Ἰωνίας τρόπον, is to use a dildo.[16] An "Ionian speech" is slightly off-color, like a Milesian tale; an "Ionian poem" is licentious.[17] Polybius 32.11.10 uses the phrase "Ionian profligacy," Ἰακὴ ἀσωτία. The stereotype was indelible: the author of the Hippocratic *Airs, Waters, Places* joins in with the contention that the soft climate of Asia Minor is debilitating: "Courage, endurance, industry, and high spirit could not arise in such conditions, either among the natives or among [Greek] settlers, but pleasure must be supreme."[18] The common belief of the anti-Ionians, as Athenaeus goes on to illustrate, was that the soft self-indulgence of the Ionians led to their enslavement by tyranny; the same point of view cast Harmodius and Aristogeiton as tyrannicide lovers who freed Athens from the Pisistratids—a fable that both Herodotus and Thucydides refuse to accept.[19] In this way the cultural debate between the old *aretē* and the elegant new Ionian *habrotēs* took a sexual form, pitting the romanticized pederasty of the old mainland elite against the less narrow eroticism of the eastern Greeks. In this debate the comedians played both sides, and Herodotus and Thucydides refused to make common cause with the party of Pindar and the oligarchic elite.

Though it appears that "Ionian" became synonymous with anything luxurious or sexually licentious regardless of origin, some evidence points to the role of cultured hetaeras from Ionia in expanding the horizons of wealthy Athenians beginning in the late Archaic period. The euphemism itself (hetaera = female companion) may have originated in a Syro-Phoenician usage in Cyprus or Ugarit and may have referred to a "companion" or protégée of Astarte. Some form of sacred prostitution, probably adapted from Syro-Phoenician cult, was practiced in Classical Corinth as well as in Western Locri, a Greek

Sexual Culture in Ancient Greece

colony in Italy.[20] A late Classical inscription in Phoenician at Kition, Cyprus, lists women understood to be sacred prostitutes among the temple personnel.[21] Strabo's account of temple prostitution in Pontic Comana compares it to Corinth: "The inhabitants live in luxury, . . . and there is a multitude of women who make gain from their persons, most of whom are dedicated to the goddess, for in a way their city is a lesser Corinth."[22] The women who came from the Ionian cities to Athens may have been hierodules, or have been trained by them; if so, any original distinction between sacral sexual service and commercial prostitution had probably become clouded, and their position in Athens was secular, though they were at one time affiliated with the temple of Aphrodite. Shrines of Aphrodite Hetaera at Athens and Ephesus are among the evidence linking Athenian sexual culture to Ionia.[23] Ephesus, Samos, and Miletus are likely Ionian centers of the hetaera industry; it may not be a coincidence that two of these were important cult centers—one of the many-breasted "Ephesian Artemis," the other of Hera—and the third, Miletus, had a temple described by Strabo (14.1.5) as the largest in the world, μέγιστον νεῶν τῶν πάντων. As cult prostitution was not uncommonly associated with religious centers in commercial cities of the Near East, hetaeras in these cities would be attracted from them to wealthy Greek mainland cities such as Athens and Corinth. Herodotus also mentions Naucratis, an Ionian trading center near the mouth of the Nile, as famous for its hetaeras; it was here that Sappho's brother, Charaxus, fell in love with Rhodopis and spent a large amount of money to buy her freedom, much to the distress and annoyance of his sister.[24] Herodotus gives details of this episode that provide an interesting view into the life of a hetaera. Rhodopis, he says, was of Thracian birth, and was brought to Egypt by a Samian trader named Xanthes. After her affair with Charaxus, she remained in Egypt as a free woman and amassed a great fortune, spending a tenth of it on a dedication in her name at Delphi. Herodotus dates her prime to the reign of Amasis, soon after 570 B.C.

The hetaera's work was a refined form of erotic entertainment like that of a Japanese geisha. The nature of her art is expressed in words written by E. M. Forster to describe Cleopatra's cultivation of Mark Antony: "Voluptuous but watchful, . . . she never bored him, and since grossness means monotony she sharpened his mind to those more delicate delights, where sense verges into spirit."[25] Hetaeras became known for their art of repartee, as is attested by numerous anecdotes in book 13 of Athenaeus' *Professors at Dinner*, which quotes the books Περὶ Ἑταιρῶν by Apollodorus and Gorgias and Machon's Χρεῖαι, "Maxims."[26] The hetaera Phryne is identified as the model for Apelles' *Aphrodite Rising from the Sea* and two statues of Praxiteles: his famous Cnidian Aphrodite and a portrait statue in gold set up at Delphi.[27] Hetaeras figure prominently in the love stories of New Comedy (about which more in a later chapter); they were the lovers of some famous men and mothers of others.[28] The Greek fascination with hetaeras lasted until well into the Christian era, appearing in extant titles such as Alciphron's *Letters of the Hetaeras* and Lucian's *Dialogues of the Hetaeras*. Athenaeus lists a total of six authors who had written books about hetaeras.[29]

As hetaeras belonged to the most well trained elite of their profession, it would be useful to know more than we do about how and where they acquired the skills by which they made their way in the world. It is easy enough to imagine how this might have worked for Rhodopis, purchased from a Thracian slave dealer by a Samian trader. Perhaps after a period of training at Samos,[30] he installed her at Naucratis, where, as we have seen, she caught the eye of a man (Sappho's brother, Charaxus) who bought her freedom. A likelier form of tutelage would be available to the daughter of a hetaera, who would be trained by her mother and thereafter support her in her old age. Others were obtained by purchase, either from slave traders or (as still today in the Far East) from impoverished parents unable to provide for a daughter. Some lines of Alexis' comedy *Fair Measure* preserved by Athenaeus tell how hetaeras who have become rich "take into their houses fresh hetaeras, who are making their first trial of the profession. They straightway remodel these girls, so that they retain neither their manners nor their looks as they were before."[31] Apollodorus' *Against Neaira* tells of a former slave, Nikarete, who purchased seven girls as small children and raised them to work as prostitutes, later selling them off as we may presume the Samian Xanthes sold Rhodopis to Charaxus. In the early stages of her career, a future hetaera might attend symposiums as a flute girl or dancer. Such entertainers could be auctioned off to be taken home for the night by the highest bidder.[32] This might begin before a girl's puberty: Apollodorus charges that Neaira began working as a prostitute before puberty. We are told that the famous hetaera

e 5.1. Hetaeras began their training young. In this tondo from an Attic red-figure cup, a
g girl named Kallisto, wearing the transparent silk gown of an adult hetaera, holds up her
and dances for a symposiast named Philipos, who sings and slaps his knee to keep time.
ase for the man's pipes, which he holds in his left hand, hangs on the wall behind him.
.notty stick leaning against the wall indicates that he is a guest at another's house. Brygos
er, ca. 480 B.C. (British Museum, no. E68)

Laïs, taken as a slave from Sicily to Corinth, was brought to a symposium by the painter Apelles while still a girl.[33]

The best early evidence of the Athenian demimonde is on Athenian
red-figure ware, where hetaeras are seen performing sexual acts and
otherwise catering to their employers' needs. While the medium is not
well suited to illustrating the more personal and cultural dimensions of
their role, it is clear that among the variety of positions for both vaginal
and anal sex, some of those represented were more personal than others.
Illustrations of face-to-face intercourse tend to suggest greater intimacy,

Education of the Senses from Solon to Pericles

Figure 5.2. Size is usually an indication of age in erotic vase painting. Here a young man prepares to kiss a very young hetaera who meets his gaze and reaches up to return his embrace. Attic red-figure cup by the Kiss Painter, late sixth century B.C. (Staatliche Museum, Berlin, no. 2269)

and in some paintings it appears to be the intention of the artist to show a degree of mutual appreciation as the sexual becomes erotic.

The usual erotic scene in sixth-century Attic vases is located in the *andrōn*, or men's section, of the private home, specifically the party room, the scene of symposia catered to by hired boys and women who served wine, sang, danced, played the flute, and were sexually available. Because boys of good family might also attend symposia, the rules of

Figure 5.3. Young men and hetaeras in a symposium scene. Between the couples, a case for an aulos hangs on the wall of the symposium room. Red-figure kalpis by the Dikaios Painter, late sixth century B.C. (Musées Royaux d'Art et d'Histoire, Brussels, no. R.351)

chivalric conduct that governed sexual relations between men and boys[34] are usually observed in sexual scenes with boys. Because the condition of being penetrated was regarded as a debasement intolerable for a free male, intercourse of men with boys is between the thighs (intercrural), whereas women have oral and anal as well as vaginal intercourse. In accordance with the understanding that these domestic revels are for the benefit of men, there are no scenes of sex between women. In short, both the early Attic black-figure vases and the later red-figure pottery (beginning ca. 530 B.C.) represent the sexual culture

Figure 5.4. In sharp contrast to the preceding scenes of erotic sentiment, this red-figure cup by the Pedeius Painter shows an orgy scene. The purely physical nature of this scene suggests the women involved are common *pornai*, who would be more available and at a lower price for such activities. Late sixth century B.C. (Photograph by Pedeius Pariter, Musée du Louvre)

of the Athenians as they saw themselves or were willing to be seen.[35] They represent nothing that we know was considered perverse or otherwise divergent from the usual behavior of well-to-do Athenians of the period. Though these vase paintings illustrate a much wider range of behavior than some would approve for their own sons and daughters, there is a disarming frankness about them, and (on balance) an interest in human value that makes them something more than indecent curiosities. What the Athenians exported on their pottery was a way of life that their privileged male citizens enjoyed and others admired. To own an Attic vase was to participate vicariously in the pleasures of the most fortunate citizens in the Greek-speaking world.

The *kōmos*, whether Dionysiac or domestic, represented sexuality as a pleasure enjoyed among friends, with the sexual pursuits, wild dancing, intoxication, animal energy, and physical extravagance that have made the classical orgy (usually in its better-draped Roman

Figure 5.5. Boy love was an important part of Greek sexual culture. This red-figure cup by the Brygos Painter, 500–475 B.C., shows the erotic ideal. A helmet hung on the wall behind the bearded lover (ἐραστής) shows he is of the warrior class. His chest and thigh are exaggerated to show his fitness; the boy, his beloved, or ἐρόμενος, is given the pectoral muscles of a man, showing that he has been properly trained in the wrestling school, where such liaisons were traditionally initiated. In his left hand, the boy holds a bag of "Kydonian apples," or quinces, symbolic of awakening sexual readiness. (See Bowra, 1961, 260 ff., Ar. *Clouds* 978, and Dover's note 1968, 216 ff.) (Ashmolean Museum, Oxford, no. 1967.305)

Figure 5.6a–b. Sex and eros. Greek vases, like Keats's Grecian urn, sometimes show opposite aspects of their subject on opposite sides. On one side of this Attic black-figure *pelike,* a satyr seizes a maenad. Satyrs were grossly phallic, goatish beings who could think of nothing but the satisfaction of their lust. Though they are represented masturbating and copulating with animals, they are never shown getting their way with a maenad. Cf. fig. *1.18.* The woman on the other side shares an embrace with her lover.

Figure 5.7. Flanked by sirens and standing on a lion, this nude goddess supporting a mirror is iconographically related to Phoenician Astarte, but she has the small breasts and narrow, boyish hips preferred by the Greeks. Found at Hermione in the Argolid, it dates to the later sixth century B.C. She resembles the ivory figurine in the previous chapter (fig. 4.4), which wears a similar headpiece (*polos*) and is dated a century earlier. Nude females appear only in private art before the fourth century. (Staatliche Antikensammlungen und Glyptothek, Munich, no. 3482)

Figure 5.8. "Kalos" vases were commissioned as love gifts from male lovers to a boy or man, even when decorated with a heterosexual scene. The masculine adjective *kalos*, "fair," appears beneath the couch. The lovers brace their feet on the edges of the tondo on this Attic red-figure cup found in Etruria. The woman wears a garter on her left leg, and earrings; her fancy coiffure is held in place by a tasseled ribbon. Ca. 470 B.C. (City Museum, Tarquinia, by permission of Etruria Meriodonale, Minister of Culture, Rome)

variety) the modern cartoonist's stock-in-trade. Along with these group pleasures, beginning in the late sixth century, sometimes on the opposite side of a jar or the inside of a cup, there begin to appear more personal encounters, both pederastic and heterosexual. Pride of place with such topics belongs to the idealized pairing of a man with a boy. Some vase paintings of this type show a restrained eroticism, such as that of the schoolboy facing his teacher in the cup by Douris at the Getty Museum (fig. 6.1). The love of male nudity as an emblem of the leisured class and the Hellenic love of the human body gives an erotic coloring even to these controlled encounters.

Sexual Culture in Ancient Greece

"I forget who our cult actually worships, but we have a hell of a good time."

Figure 5.9. "I forget who our cult actually worships, but we have a hell of a good time." (The Cartoon Bank, James Stevenson © 1987 from The New Yorker Collection. All rights reserved.)

More openly erotic are courtship paintings that show exchanged caresses, as in figure 5.5 above. These were so common that there were conventions for such pictures: the older man, the *erastēs*, approaches from the left, with one hand extended to caress the genitals of the younger *erōmenos*. In all such encounters there is an indication (greater size, a beard) that the man making the advance is the older of the two. The man may offer the younger a cock or a dead hare, the traditional love gifts. The boy is sometimes seen modestly restraining the man's

Figure 5.10. A *kōmos* on a black-figure amphora from the second quarter of the sixth century B.C. One of the figures, on the extreme left, resembles a satyr. Sexual themes are sometimes associated with Dionysus by the presence of grossly phallic satyrs, vines and grape clusters, and dancing. (Staatliche Antikesammlungen und Glyptothek, Munich, no. 1432)

Figure 5.11. Detail from obverse of the Attic amphora above (fig. 5.10); two revelers combine dancing and sex. Female figures are painted white, male red, perhaps under the influence of the Egyptian male = red, female = white convention. The face-to-face position is uncommon in heterosexual scenes this early. (Staatliche Antikensammlungen und Glyptothek, Munich, no. 1432)

Figure 5.12. Homoerotic group sex. In each of the three couples pictured here, there is an older *erastēs*, or lover, and a younger *erōmenos*, or beloved. The *erōmenos* on either side holds a cock given as a love gift by his *erastēs*. The lover in the center is entering between the thighs of his *erōmenos*; this intercrural union was the only approved form of sexual union with a boy of free birth. The odd man out in this happy scene has a potbelly. Attic black-figure amphora by the Painter of Berlin 1686, ca. 540 B.C. (British Museum, no. W 39)

too ardent address. In a fragmentary vase at Boston, there is a little dialogue written in: the man says "Allow me!" (*eason*); the boy, who according to the convention was not supposed to show desire, replies, "Won't you stop?" (*ou pausei?*). They are all acting out the chivalric code of boy love.

Not surprisingly, there are fewer restrictions on a man's actions with a woman. Purely mythological painting had already made it clear in scenes from the sack of Troy that the laws of Greek chivalry do not extend to women. The gesture of seizure, a hand grasping the victim's arm (Fig. 5.13a), may denote any form of sexual approach. Indeed, the same gesture may precede deadly violence and rape, as well as less threatening moves, including marriage. Another gesture of seizure is an armlock around the victim's waist, generally found in mythological scenes (figs. 5.14, 5.15) and in paintings representing the efforts of satyrs to take advantage of maenads (figs. 5.6, 1.18). There are also scenes of sadism toward prostitutes in scenes of group sex (fig. 5.16). In spite of all this, and the obviously male orientation of vase paintings centered on a male erotic sensibility, it is not a foregone conclusion that male heterosexuality was categorically abusive of women.

The earlier the date of an Attic vase painting, the more narrowly masculine its point of view, the more orgiastic its mood, and the less likely it is to represent feelings gentler than those of an average college fraternity party. As works of purely formal design, even the early black-figure vases represent a considerable achievement. But as documents of human life, in particular of sexual culture, they represent a still callow sensibility. Beginning in the last decades of the sixth century there appear indications of a heightened self-consciousness and an awareness that the good life requires more than the *euphrosynē* of masculine mirth and merriment. An education of sense and sensibility begins to appear in pictures of Athenians enjoying themselves and each other. Many of these changes became embedded in the conventions of vase painting, and because they are conventional we must be careful not to take them as statistically representative of actual sexual behavior but as generally indicative of how male Athenians liked to view themselves and to be seen by others.[36]

The first development is the increasing importance of women as sexual partners for male lovers. The old black-figure vases emphasized love scenes between males, but by the fourth quarter of the sixth

a

b

Figure 5.13a–b. Matrimonial gestures of seizure. In these representations of the *hieros gamos*, Zeus signals his spousal proprietorship of Hera. In Sparta and other Greek states the marriage ceremony included a mock abduction, of which the present custom of carrying a bride across the threshold of her husband's home is a distant survival. Fig. 5.13a is a metope from the temple at Selinus, Fig. 5.13b a Pompeian wall painting. (Farnell, *The Cults of the Greek States*, 1896, by permission of Oxford University Press)

Figure 5.14. Abducting the bride: the parents of Achilles. Homer has it that the gods themselves gave the sea nymph Thetis to Peleus; here he locks his arms around her waist and prepares to sweep her off her feet, while sea snakes and a lion come to her aid. Signed by Peithinos, with the inscription *Athenodotos kalos* (Athenodotos is beautiful), a type of love dedication found on many Attic cups and vases. On the outside of this red-figure cup the artist has painted scenes of pederastic courtship. Late sixth century B.C. (Staatliche Antikensammlungen und Glyptothek, Munich, no. 2279)

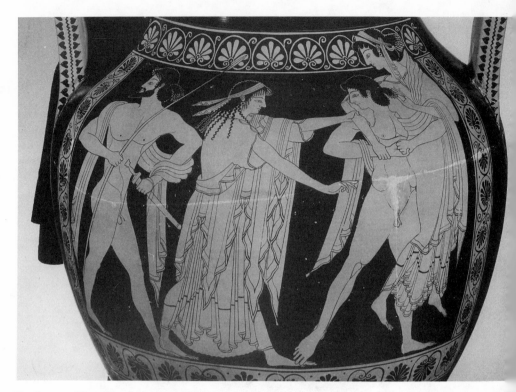

Figure 5.15. Theseus abducting Helen, who fondles his hair while Korone tries to rescue Dover (1978, 71) remarks on the similarity of hair, face, and thigh as illustrating the tende before the middle of the fifth century to make women look like men. Red-figure amphor Euthymides (late sixth century B.C.). (Staatliche Antikensammlungen und Glyptothek, Mun no. 2309)

century, heterosexual scenes came into their own. A second development was the practice of painting contrasting scenes on the same piece of pottery (e.g., figs. 5.6 a–b). While most of this may be simply a taste for juxtaposing lively with quiet scenes (as on Keats's imaginary Grecian urn), it is possible to see an ethical undertone that displays scenes of affection and mutual pleasure (fig. 5.3) instead of one-sided or merely physical encounters. Moreover, the inside/outside structural dichotomy noted in chapter 4 (p. 113) can be detected in cup painting where the tondo inside a cup represents a personal encounter (e.g., fig. 5.8) while the outside pictures the more social side of the symposium. Third, late Archaic ware develops a greater variety of sexual positions, including the less athletic face-to-face positions in which

Sexual Culture in Ancient Greece

Figure 5.16. Lords of discipline in the *andrōn*. The prostitute in the center is threatened with a stick, while on the right a man holds a lamp to burn another. On the wall behind them hangs a pleated dress of Amorgos silk, which was famous for seductive outfits. Cup by the Brygos Painter, first quarter of the fifth century B.C. (Soprintendenza Archeologica per la Toscana-Firenze, no. 3921)

personal intimacy was better able to enrich sexual encounters between men and women. Though human females are anatomically "designed for frontal copulation," most early vase paintings show lovemaking from behind.[37] Whether or not this reflects actual sexual practice, the convention of representing copulation in this reversed position suggests that the early artists and their clients consciously or otherwise devalued sexual intimacy between men and women, demoting it, in effect, to a casual party diversion stripped of emotional content.[38] The tension between the old, impersonal sexual style and the face-to-face positions that go with erotic intimacy suggests a cultural change in progress during the Archaic period. The tendency to represent lovers in pairs as opposed to groups is another sign of mature Archaic style that points to the growing interest in man as a sentient being.

Education of the Senses from Solon to Pericles

The cups and vases of the period from 530 to about 470 B.C. are the fullest record of erotic life in all Greek art; outside of Japan, there is little to rival it for sheer bulk or variety. The way of life that it represents continued throughout antiquity, but great changes in the way the Athenians perceived themselves and their art cut short the vase painting that brings it to life so vividly. The vase paintings, always a minor art because of their private ambit, ceased to represent the main current and mood of Athenian life, and the erotic themes all but completely drop out of sight within a decade of the last of the Persian Wars, the defeat of Mardonius at Plataea in 479 B.C. The gaiety of the Archaic yielded to the seriousness of the Severe Classical, and erotic art all but disappeared. We will have occasion later in this chapter to consider the long-term effects of the life that the elite men of Athens shared with the women imported for their pleasure, but first it is necessary to consider the events that precipitated Athens into the most turbulent and creative century of its history.

Under the dictatorship of Solon's younger kinsman, Pisistratus (d. 527 B.C.), and his sons, Athens confirmed its identity as a commercial power with interests beyond its own borders. The old aristocrats lost in public power what they may have gained in private pleasures, and the assets of the city continued to develop as public amenities: a large public water supply and fountain (the Enneakrounos), several religious monuments including the great temple of Olympian Zeus (so ambitious it was not completed until the second century A.D.), and the great city festivals of the Panathenaia and the City Dionysia, the latter of which became the famous drama festival. Pisistratus and his sons bought their power in part by making Athens a more public property than ever; the private good times of the old elite became less and less relevant to the public culture taking root. Pisistratus' younger son, Hipparchus, acted as his elder brother Hippias' patron of the arts, bringing in celebrated literary figures of the time such as the love poet Anacreon[39] and the choral poet Simonides and further promoting the development of Attic red-figure vase painting. Himself addicted to the life of pleasure that those paintings depicted, he was assassinated in 514 B.C. as a result of a sexual misadventure in which he fell victim to the lovers Harmodius and Aristogeiton, and within four years the last of the Pisistratids was expelled and Athens was once again a democracy.[40] The political reforms of Cleisthenes made it so in practical fact as well

Sexual Culture in Ancient Greece

as in name by establishing a representative government free of both tribal and regional factions. This new polity was soon to undergo the most demanding trial any Greek state had encountered, this time from without and against seemingly overwhelming odds.

In accounting for the victory of disunited and numerically inferior Greeks against the large and splendid forces of their adversary in the Persian Wars of 492–479 B.C., Herodotus invokes various metaphysical, political, and cultural explanations. Demaratus the Spartan, in a passage already quoted (chap. 4, p. 94) cites poverty, valor (*aretē*), wisdom, and respect for law as Greece's secret weapon (7.102). These remarks of a native informant are meant to explain the Greeks in general. In an earlier passage, Herodotus explains the powers of the Athenians in particular after the restructuring of their political system under Cleisthenes:

> So Athens had increased in greatness. It is not only in respect of one thing but of everything that equality and free speech are clearly a good; take the case of Athens, which under the rule of princes proved no better in war than any of her neighbors but, once rid of those princes, was far the first of all. What this makes clear is that when held in subjection they would not do their best, for they were working for a taskmaster, but, when freed, they sought to win, because each was trying to achieve for his very self.[41]

Athens went into the Persian wars as a freshly reconstituted state, its ordinary citizens energized by the belief that they were the direct beneficiaries of the new arrangement of power. The power of the great dynastic families was curbed; Athens belonged more than ever before to its ordinary citizens. An important new collective asset was discovered at about this time that confirmed this belief in a commonly held wealth. Like the North Sea oil that strengthened the British economy in the 1970s and the wells in the North Slope that made Alaska for a while the richest American state, the new silver found at Maronea about 483 B.C. in the old Laurion mining district of Attica suddenly made Athens (and hence all the Athenians) rich as a polity, whereas before she had been rich only as a collection of more or less successful families and individuals. Instead of distributing its profits among the citizens, Themistocles persuaded his fellow Athenians to invest the money in a navy of two hundred new triremes. Besides making Athens a major naval power in just two years, this navy made it possible, in fact made it necessary, that citizens without the wealth to buy weapons or armor or horses should take their place as oarsmen in the defense of their state. To a degree never before achieved, Athens became τὸ κοινόν, a respublica, or public thing, whose political and military base of power extended far down into the general population of citizens. War had long since stopped being the chivalric privilege it had been for Glaukos and Sarpedon in the *Iliad*. It was a universal enterprise and (as it was to prove) a pathway to citizenship, sometimes even for slaves.

The effect these developments had on the style of Athenian culture was considerable. Combined with the crisis of the Persian invasion, which tested Athenian democracy, it led to a more sober way of life and a heroic, idealizing idiom in art. The Athenians, though possessors of wealth and power as never before, faced dangers and challenges from their own demoted aristocrats within and from Persian "barbarians" without; either could be counted on to reinstate the old oligarchs as their client rulers. Hence the luxurious *euphrosynē* of the affluent aristocrats and their fancy hetaeras became anathema to the commoners. The red-figure vases that flaunted the life of *kōmos* and symposium went out of fashion, and a plain-living common man morality interposed itself as the approved style. This was not all political posturing: the Persian Wars are the point that marks the end of the Archaic age for all Greece. The unchallenged rule of oligarchs was on the wane. At its high water mark, the Persian invasion reached the Athenian Acropolis and put it to the torch in 480. But Xerxes was defeated in the same year at Salamis, and the remnants of his army were expelled the following year. The Acropolis was rebuilt on a larger scale, and in the leveling of its ground many symbols of the old life and its religion were buried (including the korai unearthed at the end of the nineteenth century). Though the "golden age" of Athens deserves its name, it was from a contemporary perspective a period of great difficulties. Herodotus writes that the three generations comprising the reigns of Darius (beginning 521 B.C.), his son Xerxes, and his grandson Artaxerxes (ending in 424 B.C.), "more ills befell Greece than in all twenty generations before Darius. Some of these came about through the Persians, and some by the acts of the chief peoples of Greece warring against one another."[42] Life for the Athenians became more deadly earnest than ever before, with predictable results for their erotic culture. But its development in the Archaic age had civilized all Greece in ways that brought further changes in the Classical period.

THE DOMESTICATION OF EROS

If the small evidence available from the later fifth century is of any use, the effect of the courtesan's art was not lost on the wives of the Athenian men who employed hetaeras in the *andrōn* for their pleasure. Wives were at a substantial disadvantage in claiming their share of life's pleasures, having had little education beyond the performance of weaving and household tasks, no knowledge of music or dance, and little exposure to the conversation of their educated spouses. Appearing seldom in public, they had little need for the ornaments regularly worn by hetaeras, saw little of the world, and, because women were thought incapable of sexual continence that was a type of *sōphrosynē*, they were strictly overseen during their childbearing years to prevent sexual contact with anyone other than their assigned spouses. Usually in their early teens when they were paired off by their father in an arranged marriage, they were placed in the role of household managers and breeders of legitimate children. Except for what we learn from male comedians (who had their own purposes as entertainers), we know very little about the sexual life of Greek women of the citizen class.

There is no evidence, though, that Greek wives rebelled openly at their low erotic status. If modern societies are any guide, women internalized the restriction placed on them and took it on themselves to see that their peers adhered to the law of continence. When, in Euripides' play of 428 B.C., Aphrodite infects Phaedra with an uncontrollable passion for her stepson, Hippolytus, Phaedra's chief preoccupation is the shame incurred by what she describes as a pollution or miasma.[43] The social contract exchanged a wife's sexual autonomy for social and economic security provided by her spouse. Women of the demimonde had no such security, but they enjoyed the freedom of the city and commanded the attention of men who had little power over them. Evidence of a later period suggests, in fact, that the less

Figure 5.17. Tall and svelte, the ideal hetaera was a Mediterranean exotic. In this scene, one anoints her partner with perfume as they prepare for their evening's work. Representation of the breasts is still naive. Painters of this period had not yet mastered the representation of breasts (cf. the center hetaera in fig. 5.18 and the one on the right in fig. 5.19 below). Their Amorgos silk chitons lie bundled on a stool. Attic red-figure cup by Apollodorus, ca. 500 B.C. (City Museum, Tarquinia, by permission of Etruria Meriodonale, Minister of Culture, Rome)

power men had over the most glamorous women, the more irresistibly they were attracted. Hence the cult of the hetaera, which grew steadily over time and created celebrities who were immortalized in art, anecdote, and history. Scraps of evidence support the view that respectable Athenian women learned to imitate the styles of their despised rivals.

That female entertainers removed genital and other body hair is shown by vase painting and literature. Part of the new dispensation proposed in the *Ecclesiazusae* (392 B.C.) is that slave prostitutes should not be allowed to remove their pubic hair to get an advantage over free women.[44] Aristophanes refers in the *Frogs* to dancing girls "in the

Figure 5.18. Any wife examining her husband's collection of erotic pottery might envy some part of the hetaera's life. Hetaeras had their own erotic fun at symposia. The inscription on this psykter signed by Euphronius (520–505 B.C.) reads *tin tande latasso, Leagre,* "This one's for you, Leagros!" indicating that the hetaera in the center is dedicating her throw of the *kottabos* to the famous beauty Leagros, a favorite of the Pioneer Group of painters to which Euphronius belonged. The woman in the center has removed some of her pubic hair. (The State Hermitage Museum, Leningrad, no. 644)

Figure 5.19. A vase painter's sex fantasy. In this picture, hetaeras are playing *kottabos*, w involved hitting a target with drops of wine cast from an emptied cup, usually for a sexual p The inscription *soi tendi Euthymidei kaloi* suggests that the winner of the throw would lik pleasure of taking care of the famous vase painter Euthymides (Boardman 1975, 30). The in this painting and in fig. 5.18 above has paid attention to the finely woven cushions which the couches of the *andrōn* are furnished. Red-figure water jar by Phintias (fl. 52 B.C.). (Staatliche Antikensammlungen und Glyptothek, Munich, no. 2421)

bloom of youth and recently plucked."[45] But by this time the practice may have spread. Wives disguising themselves as men in *Ecclesiazusae* 60–67 have let their armpit hair grow and discarded their razors "to get bushy all over and be no longer like a woman." Depilation is part of the seductive preparations designed to torment the husbands in *Lysistrata* 150 f.:

> we'll sit inside well-anointed, naked in our chitons from
> Amorgos, with our delta plucked . . .

Sexual Culture in Ancient Greece

Figure 5.20. A hetaera performs music in the nude for two delighted clients; the one on the right is dedicating a throw of the *kottabos* to her. A lyre, which women of her calling also learned to play, hangs on the wall of the *andrōn* behind her. This hetaera is larger-breasted than usual, and her pubic hair has been completely removed (cf. the woman in fig. 5.18 above). Aristophanes indicates in *Lysistrata* 151 (411 B.C.) that citizen wives plucked their pubic hair in the same manner. Cup by the Foundry Painter, a member of the Brygos Painter's Circle (first quarter of fifth century B.C.). (Fitzwilliam Museum, Cambridge, no. Lewis.103.18b)

The chitons from Amorgos were the diaphanous outfits (διαφανῆ χιτώνια, *Lys.* 48) in which red-figure vases of the previous century represented hetaeras entertaining men at parties (see figs. 5.1, 5.21).[46]

Makeup was another cosmetic attraction associated with the demimonde. A fragment of Alexis[47] gives a list of cosmetics applied to hetaeras' faces: black eyeliner made from soot, ἄσβολος; white lead, ψιμύθιον, used to set off eye shadow or to lighten a dark or suntanned complexion; rouge, interestingly called "boylove," παιδέρως, or ἄγχουσα, alkanet. The comedian Eubulus contrasts decent women with slatterns described in a fragment from the *Wreath-sellers*:

Figure 5.21. A full-service hetaera helps a symposiast who has had too much to drink. She wears a two-piece outfit of Amorgos silk. Red-figure cup by the Brygos Painter (fl. 490–470 B.C.). (Photograph by K. Oehrlein. Martin von Wagner Museum, Universität Wurzburg, no. L.479)

> "They are not, Zeus knows, plastered over with layers of white lead, and they have not, like you, their jowls smeared with mulberry-juice; if *you* go out on a summer's day, two rills of inky water flow from your eyes, and the sweat rolling from your cheeks upon your throat makes a vermillion furrow, while the hairs blown about on your faces look grey, they are so full of white lead.[48]

The objection to the use of such cosmetics by married women became a topos at least as early as Xenophon's *Oeconomicus*, where Ischomachus describes his misguided young wife's getup:

She had made up her face with a great deal of white powder [ψιμυθίῳ, lead carbonate] so that she might seem paler than she was, and with plenty of rouge so that she might seem to have a more rosy complexion than she truly had. And she wore platform shoes so that she might seem taller than she naturally was.[49]

The disapproval of the ancient (male) sources no doubt reflects their disapproval not so much of cosmetics but of their use by women whose appearance was expected to be sharply at variance with that of public women.

Xenophon, writing in the early fourth century about a wife's personal adornment, adds credibility to Aristophanes' jokes on the same subject not many years earlier. The talent of Athenian wives for erotic arrangements is a source of humor at several points in Aristophanes' *Lysistrata* (411 B.C.), such as their use of boudoir outfits in 44–48, and the unconsummated conjugal encounter of Myrrhine and Kinesias in 829–953. While the husband's requirements are simple enough (934, βινεῖν βούλομαι), his wife Myrrhine (whose name, also a common hetaera name, is cognate with the word for perfume) keeps postponing the desired moment to arrange some additional comfort—including, of course, perfume. By the last quarter of the fifth century, city women had adopted a sexual culture that men had originally designed for their own use. The comic protagonist of the *Clouds* (425 B.C.) is a rustic who married a sexually accomplished urbanite, "smelling of perfume, saffron dye, tongue-kisses, expense, gourmandise, Aphrodite Kolias, and the goddess Genetyllis" (51–52). The sexually demanding wife, an emergent cliché of the comic stage, is in Aristophanes an erotic sophisticate. Perilous as it is to draw social history out of comedy, the weight of evidence suggests that Athenian women did not remain sexual innocents as the culture of Athens developed around them.

PERICLES AND ASPASIA

Thucydides has Pericles end his famous Funeral Oration with advice to women: "the greatest glory of a woman is to be least talked about by men, whether they are praising you or criticizing you."[50] Though the meaning of these words may apply only to women in mourning for the dead, they invite a wider interpretation and were so understood in antiquity. It is ironic that such a dismissal should be attributed to Pericles, for his attachment to Aspasia, who was much talked about, is the most notable example of personal attachment in the fifth century—the more notable because of its defiance of convention. Plutarch records that Pericles amicably divorced his regular wife, a close relative, and agreed to her remarriage, thereafter living the rest of his life with Aspasia. Plutarch calls his attachment to her "rather of an erotic sort": μᾶλλον ἐρωτική τις ἡ τοῦ Περικλέους ἀγάπησις γενομένη πρὸς Ἀσπασίαν. As evidence of Pericles' extraordinary love (ἔστερξε διαφερόντως), Plutarch offers the report that he gave Aspasia a hug and a kiss each day on leaving for the Agora and on returning.[51] Trite as this may seem to anyone familiar with the modern rituals of married life, it was unusual enough to call for a mild disclaimer even from Plutarch (whose Antonine audience was more accustomed to the ideal of marital affection): ὥς φασι, "so they say."

Aspasia was a member of a prominent Milesian family related by marriage to the elder Alcibiades, according to a recent reconstruction of the family tree.[52] Born about 470 to the Milesian aristocrat Axiochus, she was the younger sister of the elder Alcibiades' second wife and came to Athens in his household at the end of his ostracism in 450. Though this is a reconstructed account, it is more credible than the tradition that she was a Carian prisoner of war[53] or a hetaera from Miletus.[54] Comic authors, exploiting the chronic unpopularity of Pericles, attacked him through Aspasia, calling her a "new Omphale," a Deianeira, a Hera, because of her supposed influence. Pericles had carried a law in 451/50 forbidding citizens to marry women of noncitizen birth and denying citizenship to children born of such unions. Besides stabilizing Athenian citizenship at a time of uncontrolled growth, this would prevent family alliances with rival city-states and resultant conflicts of interest. When, soon after passing this law, he divorced his wife and attached himself closely to the daughter of a prominent Milesian, his enemies were quick to accuse him of "tilting" Athenian policy, for example, in favoring Miletus over Samos in their dispute over control of Priene.[55] In a parody of Herodotus, Aristophanes accuses Pericles of passing the Megarian Decree of 432 to avenge Aspasia for the Megarian theft of two of her prostitutes (she was also accused of being madame to a string of brothels).[56]

A radically different view is put forward by Plato and Xenophon, who cast her not as a sexual opportunist, still less as an entrepreneur in the girlie trade, but as an intellectual and professor of rhetoric. An ancient commentator on Aristophanes' *Clouds* identifies her as a female sophist, σοφίστρια, to Pericles and his instructor in rhetorical doctrine. Another adds that she made Lysicles, the man she married after Pericles' death, an expert orator.[57] Plato's *Menexenus* represents Socrates reciting a funeral oration recited to him by Aspasia, composed extempore (we are told) with pieces added that were left over after she composed Pericles' funeral oration reported by Thucydides—an unkind joke at Pericles' expense. Xenophon cites her as an authority on practical aspects of relations between the sexes, on matchmaking in the *Memorabilia* (2.6.36), and on the partnership of husband and wife in household management in *Oeconomicus* 3.14.

It is difficult to separate a plausible account from such contradictory sources; ancient biography is a treacherous medium, especially when its object is a woman. The role given Aspasia by Plato in the *Menexenus* is part of the testimony that she was a member of the Socratic circle and is chiefly responsible for the tradition that she was an expert rhetorician.[58] This is not, however, such friendly testimony as may first appear, as Socrates' admiration in the *Menexenus* is ironic. Aspasia is guilty, if not of sexual pandering, then of rhetorical: "The speech is no doubt good of its kind, but its kind is not good: it is base rhetoric," flattering instead of enlightening.[59] Like the *Gorgias*, Plato's *Menexenus* is an attack on the meretricious tendencies of rhetoric, and it appropriately places at its focus a woman known as the companion of the greatest practical rhetorician of his century.

It is not difficult to understand why Aspasia attracted so much hostile witness. The Athenians liked their women invisible, domestic, and submissive, tolerating female assertiveness only in tragedy or the fantasy plots of Old Comedy. Aristotle described the relative freedom of Spartan women as "indiscipline."[60] The foreign Aspasia did not conform to local custom, and her irregular union with Pericles was a further affront to Athenian sensibilities, flouting as it did the spirit of Pericles' own law prohibiting foreign marriage. If she did own bordellos, as Aristophanes claimed, such ownership would have been another violation of convention for a woman of her position, though it is possible that Aspasia—like some modern feminists—may have seen prostitution as one means by which a woman could (like the former slave Rhodopis) gain freedom and independence. In Periclean Athens, it was perhaps the only means.

More suspicious to traditional Greek thinking was Aspasia's participation in intellectual life. It is a joke when Praxagora and her companions take over the Ecclesia in Aristophanes and put their political ideas into action. But there is a note of reality in an earlier play when Lysistrata says, "I am on the one hand a woman, but on the other I have a mind."[61] Sexual refinement was not the only development to which Athenian wives were becoming attuned. The theme of the "wise woman" appears twice in Plato, its other occurrence being in the *Symposium*, where the speech of Diotima of Mantinea, far from being ironic, is a brilliant philosophic summation. Ancient sources credit Aspasia with a kind of wisdom beyond the rhetorical skill attributed in the ironic *Menexenus*. Plutarch says she impressed Pericles "as an expert in politics," ὡς σοφήν τινα καὶ πολιτικήν, adding that Socrates' friends brought their wives (τὰς γυναῖκας) to hear her talk.[62] In Xenophon's *Memorabilia* 2.6.36, Socrates is made to quote Aspasia on matchmaking; he quotes her again on the economic partnership of husband and wife in *Oeconomicus* 3.15. Both are likely topics of conversation in Europe's first salon. As these works are roughly contemporaneous with Plato's middle dialogues, they may be independent, and they strengthen the possibility that Aspasia may have been an associate of Socrates. How well this sat with Socrates' male associates would be clearer if more scraps survived from works titled *Aspasia* by Antisthenes and Aeschinus. Plato, as we have seen, though too young to belong to Socrates' inner circle, was not enthusiastic.

As Greece's leading orator, Pericles found his perfect match in an articulate woman who defied convention, was a keen observer of politics, studied the rhetorical art in which he excelled, and encouraged the women who came with their husbands to hear her and to share her ideas. The match, while never popular, was prophetic for later generations. Xenophon was the first of many who would present marriage as a true partnership. If the ancient testimonia are to be trusted, Pericles' life with Aspasia was erotic in the highest sense, combining sexual attraction with mental affinity.

CHAPTER SIX

Idealizing Love

PLATO, SEX, AND PHILOSOPHY

Erotics is the only subject I understand.

οὐδέν φημι ἄλλο ἐπίστασθαι ἤ τὰ ἐρωτικά.

SOCRATES, IN PLATO, *SYMPOSIUM* 177D

While the cultivation of Athenian sensibilities was bringing a sense of the erotic closer to the mainstream, the pioneers of ethical philosophy in the Sophistic movement who made human *physis* their concern began to address sexual love as a moral question. "Erotics" (*ta erōtika*), an expression unattested before Plato, became an abstract noun and a major category of ethics in the first quarter of the fourth century.[1] This concern lasted into the Hellenistic era. In his account of Greek philosophers down to the time of Epicurus, Diogenes Laertius lists eighteen works on eros by philosophers such as Aristotle, Theophrastus, Diogenes of Sinope, Zeno, Chrysippus, Cleanthes, and Epicurus himself.[2] All of these have been lost; this chapter discusses what can be recovered of philosophies that put a positive value on sexual love.

Although the Classical period is sometimes perceived from the outside as an era of serene fixity, the period from the Persian War to the death of Alexander the Great in 323 B.C. is better understood as a time of ferment and sweeping change. Serene fixity was an ideal that artists and architects sought to achieve in spite of this ferment, and they sometimes did so with considerable success. In the early Classical period (490–450 B.C.), this effort is reflected in the concentration of the "severe" style of sculpture, in which close observation of human anatomy produced a canon of ideal bodily proportions. The epic and tragic spirit of the theater that developed around Aeschylus and

Sophocles reflects the period's monumental seriousness. The battles of Marathon, Thermopylae, and Salamis became in retrospect symbols of a heroic nobility that was uniquely Hellenic. Every effort was made to preserve that essence and to unify around it. The Olympic Games, founded as a Panhellenic institution during the eighth-century Greek renascence, took on renewed significance, as important now to the eastern Greeks as they had always been to the Greeks of Corcyra and Sicily. The Delphic oracle also, in spite of having compromised with the invading Persians, enjoyed something of a golden age in the half century after the war.[3] The Pythian Games, founded a century before, now reached the peak of their distinction; states and individuals vied with each other to erect statues not just at home but on the common ground of Delphi's Sacred Way and the sanctuary of Apollo to which it led. The fusion of regional cultures is evident in the combination of dialects in tragedy, where the iambic dialogue in Attic Greek alternates with choral lyrics in Doric. Panhellenism was not yet as explicitly formulated as it would later be in the speeches of Isocrates and the politics of Alexander, but the feelings that underlay the doctrine were present throughout the fifth century. Even while the city-states constantly maneuvered for advantage against each other, unity, synthesis, and order had a strong symbolic appeal to the generations after Marathon and Salamis and were cleverly manipulated by Athens.

Although it is never possible to reduce the impulses of an era to a single drive, the need for logical coherence and purposeful movement toward a goal is a common note in many of the notable achievements of the fifth century. It was also a legacy to the great philosophic movements of the fourth century. In politics, the polis had become a transcendent ideal capable of controlling the rampant individualism of the Greeks. In architecture, the trend is seen as the establishment of self-contained form expressed in the Doric order and the canon of rules applied by Ictinus to the design of the Parthenon. Its sculptural counterpart was rules of ideal proportion applied to human anatomy. In philosophy, it was the continued search for the underlying form of physical matter and the laws of its behavior. In the emergent field of ethics and human behavior, the attempt to distinguish knowledge from opinion and to define the good life as a goal expresses this same need for coherence. The last of these endeavors had an obvious bearing on the most mutable but least escapable of all human exigencies:

"erotics" became a field of ethics from the start. It remained one of the chief concerns of philosophy throughout the following century and into the Hellenistic period, in fact to the end of antiquity. Erotics had this recognition precisely because the sex drive seemed least in conformity with the need for order. Sex was a loose thread in the fabric of nature.

It is noteworthy, therefore, that this is the only area of knowledge in which Plato's Socrates, who made it his profession to disclaim all knowledge, claims expertise. This may be because there was a fixed set of traditions governing elective sexual behavior—behavior not locked in by marriage prescriptions—that Socrates could apply with little modification to the virtuous philosophic life. By following these traditional erotic rules, Socrates could describe a regimen for the pursuit of knowledge and the good life. Like all Socratic positions, this was fraught with irony, because the virtues of the philosopher were ascetic and called for the subordination of physical pleasure to rigorous and unceasing discipline. But the same irony was inherent in the pederastic tradition that Plato's Socrates invoked on behalf of philosophy.

Like other dialogues, Plato's *Symposium* reaches its goal after examining a variety of traditional views of its subject, which is the praise of eros. Rather than totally debunk these views, Plato allows us to see how they contribute to a correct understanding of philosophy as the highest form of erotic life. In so doing he demonstrates more about the virtues than the defects of the erotic tradition he scrutinizes. He demonstrates that, like other kinds of culture in the fifth century, sexual culture has a serious side. If nothing can be accepted as an end in itself but must be judged by its *telos*—by the good toward which it ultimately leads—then eros too must have its justification beyond mere *euphrosynē*. This undertaking is symptomatic of fifth-century high seriousness.

Conjugal eros was self-evidently justified because it led to the birth of children who would strengthen both family and state. In this formula, physical pleasure was a by-product essentially unrelated to the good that resulted. What required justification was erotically driven behavior that did not produce children. In this category fell all casual sex for pleasure alone. To call this "recreational" would be an anachronism, because re-creation of the person for further purposeful activity is the end that justifies the activity. The pleasures of literature and theater were traditionally justified because they held up images of heroic behavior that inspired emulation, thus improving society. But physical pleasure (*hēdonē*), including sexual pleasure, had no ulterior motive in traditional Greek thought: it was an end in itself. To understand the mind-set of the culture it is useful to compare it with that of England, America, or Western Europe in the late nineteenth and early twentieth century, when a rapidly expanding middle class and a growing industrial economy developed utilitarian standards of behavior. In that world, nothing that was not an "improving" activity in some moral or practical sense was altogether wholesome. This was the context in which the ideal of "recreation" was invented to justify the physical pleasure of sports. The battles of the British Empire were won on the playing fields of Eton, while in America the YMCA promoted sports as a sanitary antidote to the unhealthy new urban environments of the industrial East. In that culture, sex had its utility within marriage beyond the conception of children, but it was a private rather than a public good. Outside of marriage, it was unconscionable, and casual sex, euphemistically called "recreational," still carries pejorative connotations.

The fifth-century Greek counterparts of this busy bourgeoisie did not consider sex outside marriage unconscionable, and they were receptive to an ideology that would make it an "improving" activity. The low position to which the Greeks had relegated women made it difficult to imagine moral improvement proceeding from intimacy with this mentally inferior and carnally overloaded vessel. The contemporaries of Socrates were further hampered by the lack of erotic romanticism, the myth that enabled the European bourgeoisie to find in marriage the love that redeems us from our vices. While no man of the Victorian age ever fell so low that he could not be saved by the love of a good woman, men of the Periclean age had no such refuge. There was no pedestal for women in classical Greece. If sexual love had a transcendent moral function to perform, it must be between males. Here the advantage was with the Greek in contrast to the Victorian, because no structure of taboo had been erected that made invidious distinctions between heterosexual and homosexual feelings. On the contrary: the leisured elite of the previous century had erected a chivalric code that gave one form of homosexuality a privileged status.

As was seen in chapter 4, the most celebrated variety of homo-eroticism was a traditional social construct long before the Classical period began. It was something men of the better class did together apart from women of the better class. As often in sexual relationships, there was an understood distinction of roles; the older partner, the initiator and aggressor, the active "lover," or *erastēs*, dominated the younger, passive, modest *erōmenos*. The role of the *erastēs* was to comport himself with moderation and restraint, whereas the young *erōmenos* was to display no sexual desire of his own, reciprocating his lover's eros with simple goodwill, *philia*. If he accepted a lover's atten-tions he was perceived to "gratify" (*kharizesthai*) his suitor out of gratitude (*kharis*) rather than sexual desire, but the gratitude was less for love gifts (never for money) than for the elder man's time and attention. In return for being "gratified" through intercrural sex (as in fig. 5.12), the older man would introduce the younger boy to adult society and social skills; through this means the *erōmenos* would take his place in the male world of wellborn aristocrats, the "beautiful and good" *kalokagathoi*. For the adolescent boy, it was both an education in the customs of his class and a rite of passage to privileged society. In traditional archaic Greece, this was a closed society whose member-ship was as carefully guarded as admission to a London club in 1900.

In fifth-century Athens this social arrangement was more ambig-uous. Because the population of citizens possessing wealth and access to power was larger than ever before, the city was a much larger and hence less tightly knit polity, with the special character of a society whose old upper crust, though stripped of traditional privileges, was disliked and distrusted by the new middle class. Besides the old aristocrats, there were among the successful men in Athens many arrivistes who were scornful of the arrogant *kalokagathoi* but irresis-tibly attracted to their rituals.

Because political and sexual culture were linked, one possible response was to defend the chivalric ideology surrounding boy love and to emphasize its value to society. Another was to expose the insti-tution to ridicule. The choice probably had less to do with personal sexual preferences than with one's social role. Plato, belonging to a class that had the leisure to cultivate intellectual virtues, saw the educa-tional advantages of being undistracted by the day-to-day needs of ordinary life. Practical, "banausic" work was considered degrading in his intellectual circle. The unreflective esteem of ordinary people was a source of embarrassment, as it suggested one had played the toady to the mob. In Plato's exclusive circle, personal associations were purely elective, as there was supposedly no need to get ahead or earn money. His world was one in which like-minded men had little to do with outsiders, but their bonding to each other was strong. This tiny Brahmin elite maintained their solidarity from one generation to the next by literally courting the boys of their class when they came of age. Sexual and political seduction went hand in hand. The personalized, erotic method of winning hearts and minds was a strategy well suited to the training of a new type of intellectual elite. Plato's idealization of the love of males was not a mindless class reflex but an assimilation of an institution of his class to what he saw as its highest calling: the pursuit of wisdom via the one-on-one method of dialectic.

Aristophanes, about whom we know less personally, made fun of the same institution as a part of his role as a writer of popular theater. Whatever his personal tastes in sex, he was a competitor in the drama contests while still in his teens. This meant pleasing the crowd that Plato so distrusted, and though the politics of Aristophanes were in many ways conservative, he regularly made fun of anyone in power or with any claim to authority, whether political (the dead aristocrat Pericles as much as the living demagogue Cleon), literary (the old-fashioned Aeschylus as much as the newfangled Euripides), or intellectual (the old authoritarian pedagogues as much as the antitraditional Sophists). The technique of Old Comedy was in fact to spread its mockery as widely as possible, thereby to delight as many people as possible. Though these traditions called for a political style of comedy, Aristophanes tended to avoid the bitterest and most dangerous of Athens' political tensions, that between the oligarchic faction and the established regime of the demos.[*] This did not prevent him from making fun of chivalric pederasty as distinct from ordinary bisexuality. It is more than a coincidence that he does this in the same play that makes fun of the old and new styles of education.

The *Clouds* (423 B.C.) makes Socrates the representative of a movement caricatured as vaporous novelty, abstract intellectuality, religious subversion, and petty opportunism. The Socrates character is a trickster of the Groucho Marx type, who pays for his evil ways in the end by seeing his Idea Factory burned to the ground. In the

Sexual Culture in Ancient Greece

Figure 6.1. Paideia, in particular the education of boys, was a central concern of the elites who ruled the city-states of Greece. In this cup signed by Douris (ca. 480 B.C.), a bearded man wearing a chiton (through whose folds his genitals are clearly shown) faces a boy in his early adolescence, whose chiton is modestly covered by a himation. The boy's modesty is further shown by his lowered gaze, and he holds in his hand a tortoise-shell lyre, suggesting that he is receiving instruction in *mousikē*, the art, music, and literature in which every member of his class was educated. The restrained sexuality on both sides stresses the high ideals of this educational tradition. (Attic red-figure Cup Type B from the Collection of The J. Paul Getty Museum, Bareiss Collection, signed by Douris as painter, potted by Python, ca. 480 B.C., Terracotta, 11.9 cm. X 38.9 cm.)

debate scene his school of thought, represented by a punk philosopher named Worse Doctrine (Hēttōn Logos), gets the better of a traditionalist named Better Doctrine (Kreittōn Logos). Their debate focuses on the education of boys, with comic emphasis on sexual deportment. The defender of old-fashioned education stresses its encouragement of physical hardiness, obedience to tradition and authority, and physical modesty. His opponent advocates physical comfort, moral nihilism, and sexual indulgence: "Stick with me and indulge your nature!" (1077 f.). The debate is designed to make both sides ridiculous. Part of the Sophistic liberalism parodied by Worse Doctrine is the belief that the suppression of youthful sexual needs interferes with their acquisition of wisdom—or at least their success in politics.[5] A Hellenistic derivative of their view can be read in Micio's defense of permissive education in Terence's *Adelphoi*.[6] One of the emergent doctrines of the late fifth century was that a respect for nature (*physis*, as quoted above) should be allowed to guide our behavior. Denial of natural sexual needs, by this view, is likely to lead to poor moral choices and intemperate behavior. Better Doctrine's position, in turn, is a distortion of the traditional blend of physical with mental education and of the belief that moral virtue requires the self-discipline to ignore physical discomfort.[7] Aristophanes adds another note of mockery in making the spokesman of ancient virtue an ardent pederast, if not an outright sex maniac: his preoccupation with the graphic details of sexual decorum expose him as a dreamy old man given to peeking at boys.

> When they sat in the gymnasium boys had to keep their thighs forward, so as not to show anything that would torment men on the outside looking in. And when one stood up, he had to sweep the dust so as not to leave an imprint of his youthful parts for lovers to see. No boy would anoint himself with oil in those days below the navel, so the dewy fuzz blossomed on their genitals as on hanging fruit. (973–978)

Far from making fun of homosexuality, this is a hit at the preoccupation that Aristophanes' audience will identify with the old oligarchs. In the parabasis of the *Wasps* (422 B.C.) Aristophanes denies wasting his own time hanging around the wrestling grounds to gawk at the pretty boys but claims to have satirized men who did so and to have refused their offers of hush money (1025 ff.; cf. *Peace* 762). Socrates himself is accused of hanging around the same haunts, if only to steal cloaks (*Clouds* 179). Love dedications on Greek vases include the names of many prominent fifth-century Athenians, among them some members of Socrates' circle (Henderson [1975] 1991, 216). Because the traditional function of Old Comedy was to mock figures of authority, it singles out pederasty as a characteristic pleasure of the old oligarchic class and attacks it less as a perversion in itself than as a type of idle frivolity.

As a rule, the only sexual practice attacked as a demeaning perversity is passive anal sex by men, the "wide-asses" (*euryprōktoi*) who willingly submit to another man's assertiveness. In this society, any form of submissiveness was considered unworthy of a free man.[8] While all understood that a woman is naturally to be penetrated by a man, it was considered acceptable only for a slave or a male prostitute to submit in this way to another male. Part of the universal abuse dished out in the *Clouds* by Worse Doctrine is the claim that these pathics, εὐρύπρωκτοι, constitute a majority of legal advocates, poets, politicians, and theatergoers. Better Doctrine admits that he is right on that point, causing the audience to roar with delight and mock indignation.[9]

While at the beginning of the fourth century it was considered mildly scandalous for a man of position to keep a slave boy for sexual purposes (Lys. *Or.* III.3), a restrained erotic relationship between males of the same rank was an honored tradition. We have already seen the elevated language with which Pindar praised young Theoxenus in fragment 123 (chap. 4, pp. 109–110) and the innuendo with which he condemns those who do not participate in this socioerotic ritual. This is the tradition that Plato invokes in the *Symposium* when he has Phaedrus cite the story that Achilles and Patroclus were lovers.[10] A more significant fifth-century legend brought up in the same speech is the story of the tyrannicides Harmodius and Aristogeiton. The story that these lovers killed the tyrant Hipparchus to avenge an insult to Aristogeiton's *paidika* Harmodius was tirelessly repeated in *skolia* sung at symposia, and though it was debunked by both Herodotus (5.55–61) and Thucydides (6.53–59) on the grounds that their act was simply a personal vendetta that did more political harm than good, it was the standard myth in support of the proposition that the love of men for each other is a kind of erotic freemasonry that accompanies a love of freedom and the hatred of tyranny: good sex is good politics.

> Gratification of [pederastic] lovers in Ionia and other places ruled by barbarians is actually held to be shameful, along with philosophy and the love of exercise, due to their tyranny; for it is not, I think, to the advantage of rulers to have great thoughts engendered in those ruled, nor strong friendships and associations, that Eros above all others is especially wont to instill. Tyrants, in fact, have here learned this by actual deeds; for the Eros of Aristogeiton and the friendship of Harmodius, steadfastly abiding, overthrew their rule."

From our distance in time, the story has the look of a self-serving oligarchic fable in which "freedom" represents the ascendancy of the class that promoted this form of attachment. Because the Persians tended to favor oligarchic parties in Greek areas under their control and because the upper class was often suspected (with reason) of enlisting Persian aid against local democratic factions, any tale representing the most salient social ritual of the oligarchic class as hateful to the Persians was politically useful to its defenders. Far from collaborating with the enemy, wellborn men who formed erotic attachments with younger peers were haters of all tyranny—or so the myth ran.

In addition to such legends and pseudohistory, defenders of the pederastic tradition could appeal for precedent to the loves of the gods. The love of Apollo for Hyacinthus ends in the tragic death of the latter and his mourning by Apollo. The love of Zeus for Ganymede results in the boy's transference to Olympus, where he serves as cupbearer to the gods—fly now, pay later, as one recent wag put it. It is Zeus and Ganymede, therefore, who are usually cited as archetypes of human *erastēs* and *erōmenos* respectively. The pattern was apt: Zeus as the ultimate aristocrat, Ganymede as the handsome princeling, worthy by rank as well as by his good looks of being brought into the most exalted circles. In both stories, the youth is immortalized, one as a flower and hero of the eponymous Spartan festival of the Hyacinthia, the other as an Olympian who forever attends the feasts of the gods.

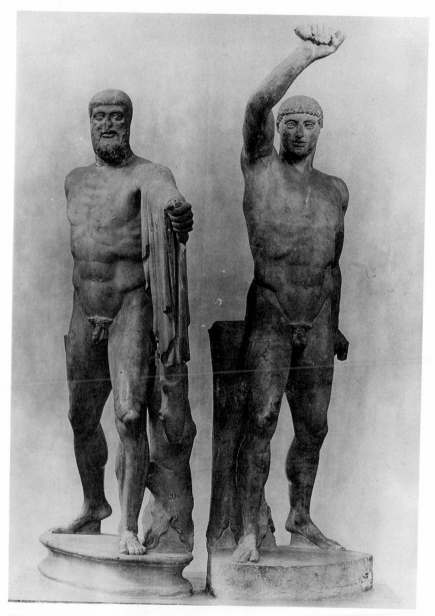

Figure 6.2. Harmodius and Aristogeiton, the lovers credited by tradition with having overthrown the Pisistratid tyranny in 514 B.C. This group, originally cast in bronze by Kritios and Nesiotes in 477/6 B.C., is considered the first great example of the severe style in early Classical sculpture. (Deutsches Archaologisches Institut, Rome, no. 58.1789)

Both of these legends are Dorian, one from Sparta and the other from Crete.[12] Though neither has an educational or initiatory component, the fourth-century B.C. geographer Strabo notes the following erotic rite of passage among the Cretans.

> They have a peculiar custom in regard to [pederastic] love affairs, for they win the objects of their love, not by persuasion, but by abduction; the lover tells the friends of the boy three or four days beforehand that he is going to make the abduction; but for the friends to conceal the boy, or not to let him go forth by the appointed road, is indeed a most disgraceful thing, a confession, as it were, that the boy is unworthy to obtain such a lover; and when they meet, if the abductor is the boy's equal or superior in rank or other respects, the friends pursue him and lay hold of him, though only in a very gentle way, thus satisfying the custom; and after that they cheerfully turn the boy over to him to lead away; if, however, the abductor is unworthy, they take the boy away from him. And the pursuit does not end until the boy is taken to the *andreion* [communal male mess hall] of his abductor. They regard as a worthy object of love, not the boy who is exceptionally handsome, but the boy who is exceptionally manly and decorous. After giving the boy presents, the abductor takes him away to any place in the country he wishes; and those who were present at the abduction follow after them, and after feasting and hunting with them for two months (for it is not permitted to detain the boy for a longer time), they return to the city. The boy is released after receiving as presents a military habit . . . and other things so numerous and costly that the friends, on account of the number of the expenses, make contributions thereto.[13]

This has the earmarks of a traditional wedding, and it is probably in fact a mock wedding with masculine trappings. For the Cretan boy, as for boys generally in Archaic societies, the passage into the adult world is not his wedding (as it is for a girl) but a species of "prewedding" in which the initiand's partner is a mature person of his own sex.[14] Such

Sexual Culture in Ancient Greece

Figure 6.3. Zeus carrying off Ganymede. Greek pederasty anchored its justification of boy love in this divine precedent. Found in shattered fragments at Olympia beginning in the nineteenth century, this terracotta group (ca. 470 B.C.) shows Ganymede holding Zeus' love gift, a rooster, in his left hand. (Olympia Museum, Athens)

Figure 6.4. The ideal type of the Archaic *erōmenos*, this Ganymede holds his love gift in one hand while he rolls his hoop—a child's toy—with the other. The circle emphasizes the boy's genitals and thighs, but as in all such erotic art the torso is well developed, bespeaking hard training in the wrestling school where boys were usually courted. Berlin painter, early fifth century B.C. (Musée du Louvre)

a ritual is possible in a society without taboos against homoeroticism. From this point of view, the abduction of Ganymede (lit. shining genitals) by Zeus matches the abduction of Persephone's daughter Korē (The Girl) by Hades. This is not the only Greek rite of passage in which the assimilation of a female role is required of the boy. Strabo's emphasis of the point that manly decorum is a more important qualification than good looks corresponds closely to the ideal requirements of a bride: her mastery of feminine virtues and demure comportment define her readiness for marriage.

The institution of pederasty as a Dorian custom adopted by Ionians and other upper-class Greeks is not to be confused with ordinary homosexuality, or with the ordinary pederasty of a bisexual culture (it has least to do with pedophilia, that is sexual attraction to children). As Greece developed from a congeries of tribes, villages, and warlords to an urban civilization, pederasty developed from a rite of passage to an educational institution that was at once ethical, strongly personal, and elitist. Its emphasis on physical virtues applicable to warfare gave it an ascetic cast, though it was driven by an erotic and therefore inherently sensuous energy.[15] Initiatory homosexuality of this general type has been studied elsewhere in the world (Australia, Siberia, South America, and Bantu Africa). Although it may involve only a small number of males in a society—as for example in the initiation of a shaman or members of a warrior elite—it is not a deviant practice relative to its own culture. It is, instead, the most intensive form of initiation a society that offers it can have.

This brings us back to Plato, who as a member of Athens' upper class knew Greek pederasty of a type that has loosely been termed "initiatory."[16] It is not by any means to be taken for granted that Plato had any personal taste for boys; in his latest writing he condemned all homosexuality: "the crime of male with male, or female with female, is an outrage on nature and a capital surrender to lust of pleasure" (*Laws* 1.636c). In two of his earlier dialogues, however, he makes "initiatory" pederasty the opening wedge of a metaphor by which to explain the nature and spirit of philosophic inquiry. The *Symposium*, written sometime after 385 B.C. but given a dramatic date of 416, consists of a series of panegyrics of love that take the reader through some traditional thinking about the blessings of eros, a characteristically fanciful myth put in the mouth of Aristophanes, and a climactic speech delivered by Socrates but attributed to an otherwise unknown and probably fictitious woman from Mantinea named Diotima.

In asking us to imagine Socrates' erotic instructor as a woman, Plato is probably not suggesting that his master had a mistress in love but rather acknowledging the intellectual parity of women and perhaps identifying with them a sex-linked discursive position available to men in the pursuit of philosophy.[17] He would also be reminding his audience of Aspasia, one of the eminent intellectuals of the period just before the dramatic date of the *Symposium*.[18] Whatever the implications, Diotima is Socrates' alter ego as surely as Socrates is Plato's. This may be reflected in the short shrift Diotima gives heterosexual love: "those who are physically procreative turn more to women and are erotic in that way . . . but there are those who are spiritually procreative and do their begetting in spirit rather than in body" (*Symp.* 208e–209a).[19] There is at any rate nothing personally erotic about Diotima, nor is she particularly interested in personal relationships except as a means to a transcendent *telos* that supersedes everything on earth. Her conception starts with a man's boy love and ends with disembodied, impersonal, otherworldly knowledge:

> When someone, ascending from things here through the right love of boys, begins to see *that*, the Beautiful, he would pretty well touch the end. For this is the right way to proceed in matters of love, or to be led by another—beginning from these beautiful things here, to ascend ever upward for the sake of *that*, the Beautiful, as though using the steps of a ladder, from one to two, and from two to all beautiful bodies, and from beautiful bodies to beautiful practices, and from practices to beautiful studies, and from studies one arrives in the end at *that* study that is none other than the study of *that*, the Beautiful itself, and one knows in the end, by itself, what it is to be beautiful.[20]

In this scenario, Plato has shifted the emphasis from the boy, who was traditionally the one who learned what his lover taught, to the man, who learns from the boy the rudimentary form of beauty. The boy receives no instruction, having served temporarily only as the paradigm of merely physical beauty for the aspiring philosopher. This is an inversion of traditional Greek pederasty, in which the lover provided his young companion with examples of masculine virtues. Moreover, Diotima, Socrates, and Plato overshoot the mark by going from sexual to erotic and then continuing on to philosophic, like students of literature so consumed by aesthetics and criticism that they no longer read literature.

Plato's theory of eros has less to do with eros than with philosophy. But as Foucault has argued, the austere regimen posed by "an erotics centered on an ascesis of the subject and a common access to truth" require "a symmetry and reciprocity in the love relationship" in which "the dissymmetries, the disparities, the resistances, and the evasions that organized the always difficult relations between the *erastēs* and the *erōmenos*—the active subject and the pursued object— in the practice of love no longer have any justification."[21] Plato always thought the work of philosophy to be adversarial, which explains his use of the dialogue form; but in his philosophy of eros the object of domination is the self and the objective pursued is a mutual goal rather than the gratification of a dominant partner.

Plato's Diotima illuminates the higher type of eros by imagining the love god not as an exquisite, winged boy-nymph with milky thighs but as the needy child of Poverty and Contrivance, a divine street urchin:

> He is rough and hard and homeless and unshod, ever lying on the ground without bedding, sleeping in doorsteps and beside roads under the open sky. Because he has his mother's [Poverty's] nature, he dwells ever with want. But on the other hand, by favor of his father [Contrivance], he ever plots for good and beautiful things, because he is courageous, eager, and intense, and clever hunter ever weaving some new device. . . . What is provided ever slips away so that Eros is never rich nor at a loss, and on the other hand he is between wisdom and ignorance.[22]

This characterization of a Faustian Eros, never satisfied with what he has but always in need of more, represents the Platonic philosopher who is never satisfied with the state of knowledge he has already attained; it symbolizes philosophy as a dynamic process of search rather than a static possession of knowledge. It is the greedy *pleonexia* (ambition) that Thucydides condemned in Athenian politics, raised to the level of a philosophic virtue. But the eros it adumbrates is not entirely satisfactory as a social or personal construct; it is rather too much like the perpetually erect satyrs in vase paintings or the dirty old men Aristophanes makes fun of who hang around wrestling schools trying to cop a peek at a pretty boy's downy genitals. We would call such an insatiable eroticism compulsive because it cannot find a satisfactory human object.

But this love of persons is not Plato's eros. In Plato it is a metaphor, like the eros Pericles wants his fellow Athenians to feel for their city.[23] The love of which Plato speaks is closer to Pindar's eros for *aretē* than to a lover's eros for a person. It is desire rather than love because its object is an ideal. The most literary of all Plato's dialogues has used sex to sell philosophy, catching our attention with a symposium (the traditional scene of sexual bouts) and a program of speechifying on Everybody's Favorite Subject. The erotic hook then catches the philosophic fish. The same rhetorical hook works again in the *Phaedrus*, a later dialogue of the period between 387 and 367 B.C., where Plato draws us in with the question of whether a boy should "gratify" a lover in the heat of passion or grant his favors rather to an older friend who is not in love. Socrates entertains Phaedrus by arguing both sides of the question with the skill of a trained Sophist, but he makes it clear that the passionate lover is preferable because he is possessed by *enthusiasmos*, a divine madness that he shares with prophets, healers, and poets. The love of Beauty that possesses the *erastēs* is the highest form of such "enthusiasm"; it distinguishes the philosopher from all other men, and association with it benefits the *erōmenos*. Once again love turns out to be philosophy: love of beauty and not of a person. The *erōmenos* is loved not for himself but for the "Beauty" of which he is the vessel. He is like the goose that lays the golden egg, prized for what he gives off. The human relation is incidental to the metaphysical symbiosis. Somewhere in Plato's symbolism is the friendly relation of teacher and pupil and the process of dialectic by which Plato represents his old teacher winnowing out error and refining philosophic truth. But authentic, sexual, chemical eros in the technical and literal sense of the word does not exist for Plato. It is only a metaphor for intellectual passion, with or without goodwill toward a partner in inquiry.[24]

Plato's discussions of eros in the *Symposium* and the *Phaedrus* are no more substantive than his discussion of poetry in the *Ion*. His real concern is with the ethical pursuit of beauty and truth, which is only symbolically related. But his rhetorical use of erotics is symptomatic of a widespread sympathetic interest in the subject at the end of the fifth century. The erotic themes of the dramatists are the subject of chapter 8. Here the point of interest is the perception that love's proper *telos* is good, that its violence can be controlled by wise management, and that it is part of nature (*physis*) in a cosmos that is beautiful and orderly.

Among the philosophers of Socrates' generation, the great debate about the claims of *nomos*, or man-made justice, versus those of *physis* was colored by a certain cynicism on the part of those who believed in *physis*. "It is a general and necessary law of nature to rule wherever one can," says an Athenian representative to the Melians just before his forces massacre all Melian men of military age and sell their women and children into slavery.[25] Altruistic champions of *physis* had against them its association with oligarchic radicals[26] and intellectuals who declared that war was the natural state of cities.[27] At the same time, there was a humanitarian appeal to natural law, as early as Antigone's appeal to the unwritten laws (*agrapta nomima*) of family duty in Sophocles' play (441 B.C.). Arguing for the forgiveness of involuntary error in the fourth century, Demosthenes says "nature herself has decreed it in the unwritten laws and in the hearts of men" (*De Cor.* 275), and in Plato's *Protagoras* the Sophist Hippias speaks to his friends as bound to him "by *physis*, not by *nomos*; for like is kin to like by *physis*, while *nomos*, the tyrant of mankind, does much unnatural violence" (337c–d). The conception of *physis* as having its own organic law became a tenet of Stoicism and is to this day regularly renewed in appeals to "natural law" as justifying this or that public policy.

One response to the belief of fourth-century teachers that virtue consisted in living according to nature was to demonstrate the simplicity of nature and its dictates. The virtuous life was the simple life, in which nature's requirements were taken care of in a quick and rudimentary way. Diogenes of Sinope (404–323 B.C.), the flamboyant philosopher who lived in a tub and went about with a candle in search of an honest man, demonstrated that sex is one of the most easily appeased demands of nature by masturbating in public and remarking to the gathered crowd, "Would that we could relieve hunger by rubbing the belly."[28] This utilitarian minimalism found its way into New Comedy of the antisentimental type. These lines of Philemon praise the women stationed in the houses attributed to Solon:

They stand there naked, so you won't be deceived: see it
all! Perhaps you're not quite up to form, a bit upset?
Nonsense! The door's open; just one obol, folks—jump
right in! No prudery, no twaddle, no sudden retreats. Just
quick service, any style you like, then you're out of there.
Tell her to go hang; she's nothing to you!²⁹

It became a commonplace of fourth-century philosophers to
debate whether the wise man falls in love, risking or avoiding pertur-
bation of spirit.³⁰ The number of treatises written on love in the late
Classical and Hellenistic periods suggests that the question was not
settled simply. Everybody was interested in pleasure, sex, and love,
including the philosophers. Aristippus of Cyrene, the first of Socrates'
pupils to charge fees, believed that the good life was one passed as
easily and pleasantly as possible; his school of Cyrenaic hedonism
glorified physical pleasure (*hēdonē*) according to the doctrine that
"only the feelings [*pathē*] are knowable with certainty." At the same
time, he advocated sex with emotional detachment. When twitted
about his liaisons with the famous hetaera Laïs, his reply was, "I possess
Laïs, she does not possess me."³¹ The Stoics countered hedonism with
the argument that pleasure was at best only a by-product of living in
accordance with nature, rather than the actual *telos*. As a rule, pleasure
is merely an irrational elation at getting what appears desirable; delight
is the soul's turning toward weakness, euphoria the dissolution of
virtue (Diog. Laert. 7.114). Eros is a craving that serious men do not
have (7.113). But Aristotle is said to have taught that the wise man will
fall in love.³² Epicurus advanced a brand of hedonism that declared the
greatest good to be the greatest pleasure, but he went on to prove that
the greatest pleasure was intellectual rather than emotional or physical,
requiring, therefore, that anything likely to produce emotional turmoil
be avoided and that merely physical pleasures be severely rationed so
as not to interfere with the higher pleasures. As a practical matter,
Epicureanism was as ascetic a regimen as Stoicism. Both aimed at an
emotionally cool self-possession and were therefore antierotic.

At the same time, the early Stoics preserved the ideals of disinterested pederasty that Plato and the oligarchic class had passed on
from earlier generations.³³ Zeno of Citium (335–263 B.C.), who founded
the Stoic school, wrote in his *Politeia* that Eros is a god who supplies

Sexual Culture in Ancient Greece

assistance toward the safety of the state[34] because he prepared the way for *philia*, harmony, and even freedom. This can be best understood as an extension of Pausanias' statement in the *Symposium* (182b–c; p. 00 above) citing the amorous friendship of Harmodius and Aristogeiton as proof that tyrants have reason to fear such attachments. Diogenes Laertius gives the Stoic definition of right eros as "an effort at friendliness motivated by the appearance of beauty; its goal is not intercourse, but friendship [*philia*]" (7.130). In his treatise *On Eros*, the Stoic chief Chrysippus (280-207 B.C.) defined this enlightened type of eros as having its goal in friendship.

It would be of the greatest interest to know which of the Hellenistic authors of treatises on Eros admitted the possibility that such "Platonic" love could exist between men and women, if it could coexist with sexually consummated love or with emotional attachment beyond the rational goodwill of *philia*. Antisthenes (ca. 445–ca. 360 B.C.), the Socratic who wrote one of the dialogues titled *Aspasia*, is said to have written a treatise titled *On the Begetting of Children, or On Marriage; A Discourse on Love.*[35] Aristotle includes erotic love as a form of *philia*.[36] His *Nicomachaean Ethics*, written sometime between 335 and his death in 322 B.C., contains the remarkable assertion, "*Philia* seems to come naturally to men and women, because man is by nature more a pairing animal than a political animal, inasmuch as the home is prior to and more necessary than the state, and the begetting of children more common to living beings" (1162a 16–19). A younger Socratic, Xenophon (ca. 428–354 B.C.), wrote in his *Oeconomicus*, a handbook on estate management, about the kindly relationship between a mature man and his young wife. Custom dictated marriage between men and women of disparate ages, requiring the husband to be as much teacher as spouse. Such statements broke important ground, as it had been the traditional view that eros was a *pathos*, an uncontrollable impulse that deprived its victims of their sense and belonged more in the category of curses than of blessings.[37] It will be shown in chapter 8 that the romantic plots of New Comedy took up the idea of benign heterosexual erotic bonding, but intellectuals in the fourth century were not necessarily of one mind about this aspect of human nature.

One focus for the more optimistic view of heterosexual eros was the mythological figure of Helen, revived as a faithful and loving wife to Menelaus in Euripides' *Helen* (412 B.C.). A self-obsessed and manipulative hedonist in the *Trojan Women* (415 B.C.), she is now a prototype of the heroine in romance, rescued from Paris by Hermes and protected by the Egyptian king Proteus, then menaced by the advances of Proteus' son, Theoclymenus. Meanwhile, her husband, Menelaus, himself lost for seven years following the Trojan War (fought over an empty image of Helen created by Hera), arrives shipwrecked and in rags. Following a tearful reunion, the married lovers plot an escape in which they trick the stupid barbarian Theoclymenus with the aid of his sister, Theonoë. Helen was the title character of several plays in the next few decades.[38] Gorgias of Leontini had previously defended Helen's conduct in his *Encomium of Helen*. A generation after Euripides' play (ca. 370 B.C.), Isocrates wrote his own *Encomium of Helen* in which he rapturously praises the beauty of Helen as "the most venerated, most precious, most divine of goods, . . . the most beautiful of the ways of living" (54.3–11),whose virtue is proven by its motivation of Greece's triumph over Asia.

But it was not the grand illusions of public life that were to hold the attention of the Greeks in the fourth century. By the time Alexander the Great was triumphing over Asia, private interests had replaced politics. The political themes of Old Comedy had yielded in Aristophanes' own lifetime to domestic themes, from which evolved the love plots of New Comedy. Philip of Macedon had reduced the city-states from sovereign poleis to municipalities, not entirely masters of their own destinies. Ethics had become the most important branch of philosophy, and the suitable conduct of personal life was the first task of the wise man. Privatism became an attractive refuge for the inhabitants of late Classical and Hellenistic Greece.

For the sexual historian, a coda to the old, exclusively masculine erotic culture can be found at the Battle of Chaironea in 338 B.C., Alexander's first battle (under his father's command) and the last stand of the Classical city-states against the expanding Macedonian kingdom of Philip. The youthful Alexander is said to have been the first commander to defeat the Sacred Band of Thebes, an elite battalion of three hundred male lovers formed earlier in the fourth-century by Gorgidas. The idea was that such a band would never retreat because no *erastēs* could tolerate having his *erōmenos* see him with a wound in his back; the masculine bond of *erōtikē philia* would make lovers so ashamed to play the coward before their beloved that together they would be undefeatable.[39] When Philip surveyed the field of Chaironea after the battle, he stopped where the three hundred were lying, and on being told that this was the Sacred Band, he wept and declared, "May they die an evil death who suspect these men did or suffered anything disgraceful!"[40] Although this is the kind of pretty tragedy that storytellers required, the bonding rituals of Archaic oligarchs and their boyfriends had receded into philosophic vapors having little to do with the realities of Hellenistic life. The citizen-soldier was a distant memory, and private life was everybody's business.

What remained from the ideals of pederastic ritual was the onetime oxymoron of erotic friendship. It was playwrights rather than philosophers who popularized *erōtikē philia* as a humanistic sexual value in which the bonding was not of warriors but of men and women.

CHAPTER SEVEN

Sexual Beauty

THE NUDE IN GREEK ART

A woman is the most beautiful thing there is.

γυνὴ γὰρ τῶν ὄντων ἐστὶ κάλλιστον.

AESCHINES, *DE FALSA LEGATIONE*

A central feature of Greek art, the nude suggests some central features of Greek civilization as well. It symbolizes a desire to contemplate the essentials of a subject, a tendency that we associate with the best Greek thinking. Expressive of a well-developed physical culture, the perfect nude argues a life lived in accordance with nature, which the Greeks believed contains principles of order, balance, and beauty that guide human ethics. It also marks the ready acceptance of sexual nature, with all its perils. Finally, the nude is the aesthetic form that best states a human scale of values. An icon of Classical humanism, the nude is unadorned human truth, stated in an idiom as concrete as the Greek language itself.

From an early date, nude and partially nude human figures became a kind of cultural marker that set the Greeks aside from other peoples of the ancient world. Only the nude female figurines of the Near East may be compared to what the Greeks developed, but it is precisely this nude—the female—that the Greeks for centuries rejected. Some archaic religious figurines of naked goddesses persisted, in testimony to the strongly conservative bent of Aegean religion; but it was the male nude that first caught the Greek imagination. It became an emblem of Hellenism during the Archaic period and was introduced in public athletics as well as art. Thucydides (1.6.5) says that the Spartans were the first to strip naked for their athletic exercises. Spartan girls wore scanty athletic clothing, but this proximity to female nudity was distasteful to the same Greeks who accepted full nudity in male athletes.[1] Ancient sources date the first athletic nudity from the fifteenth Olympiad, 720 B.C. Though both Thucydides and Plato, representing a date near 400 B.C., say athletes began regularly competing in the nude only a few years before their own time,[2] vase paintings show runners competing in the nude more than a century earlier. Various reasons have been proposed since antiquity for the institution of athletic nudity, such as ritual traditions and primitive hunting practice, but ancient testimony is unanimous that it was not an immemorial practice: it was correctly thought to have been instituted within historical memory.[3]

Having discovered an admiration for male nudity, Greek artists began to read it back into earlier history. This tendency is particularly evident in red-figure vases illustrating scenes from Homer, where heroes on both sides of the Trojan War are regularly represented as wearing nothing but footware and greaves below the waist. Such nakedness, which is (to say the least) foolhardy while less vulnerable parts of the body were protected by armor, is nowhere hinted in Homer, or illustrated in early art. As elsewhere in the ancient world, nakedness in the *Iliad* is a disgrace, for example, when Odysseus threatens to strip the loutish Thersites, "the ugliest man who came beneath Ilion," and send him "bare and howling back to the fast ships."[4] Odysseus' nakedness when he comes ashore in Scheria is symbolic only of his helplessness, and of the girls who encounter it, only Nausicaa has the presence of mind to remedy it with clothing from the royal laundry basket.

Male nudity became a convention in monumental art from about the middle of the seventh century when kouroi, large dedicatory statues of young, muscular, athletic male nudes, appeared throughout Greece. The male nude became what one recent art historian has called "the central genre of Greek sculpture, a prime index of value for Greek society, and a prime source of other satisfactions as well."[5] Ancient writers were well aware that this was a cultural feature. As Herodotus (1.10.3) remarks, "among the Lydians, as with nearly all other barbarians, even for a man to be seen naked brings the greatest disgrace." This non-Greek aversion to nudity is confirmed in general by Plato (*Rep.* 452c) and specifically by the archaeological record in the region of ancient Lydia.[6]

Figure 7.1. Greek artists of the late Archaic period projected male nudity back into Homeric themes. In this red-figure calyx crater by Euphronius (ca. 520–505 B.C.), Sleep and Death lift the nobly wounded Sarpedon's corpse from the battlefield while Hermes, who takes souls to the underworld, looks on. In Homer, it is Sarpedon who explains why heroes go to war (*Il.* 12, 310–328). Small genitals were an anatomical ideal, befitting the ascendancy of physical over sexual *aretē*. They were considered emblematic of good decorum (Ar. *Clouds* 1014). (The Metropolitan Museum of Art, Purchase, Bequest of Joseph H. Durkee, Gift of Darius Ogden Mills and Gift of C. Ruxton Love, by exchange, 1972 [1972.11.10])

Figure 7.2. Even when wearing armor, the Homeric warrior pictured by the Sosias Painter (ca. 510–500 B.C.) is nude below the waist. In this cup, a handsome young Achilles bandages the arm of his older companion, Patroclus. (Staatliche Museum, Berlin, no. F2278)

More than a form of art, male nudity became a form of costume displayed by a social elite, as Larissa Bonfante has shown.[7] Except in art, where as early as the time of Homer a decided emphasis on the male nude was established by convention, nakedness was normally tantamount to helplessness, representing deprivation of even the lowest denominator of culture. It was also a mortal state, immediately preceding death (e.g., Patroclus when stripped of Achilles' armor, *Il.* 16) or coming soon afterward (the fallen warrior stripped of his

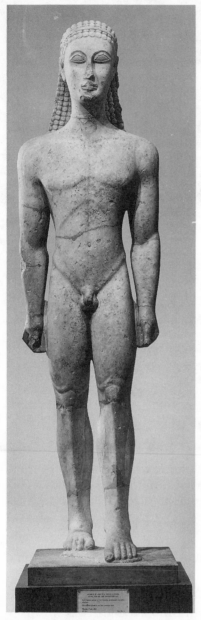

a   b

Figure 7.3a–b. Kouros from Attica, ca. 600–575 B.C. The advanced left foot is a convention probably of Egyptian origin. Early kouroi had more schematic anatomical features, such as the sharp ridge along the shin, V-shaped pelvic lines, oversize eyes, and an "Archaic smile." (The Metropolitan Museum of Art, Fletcher Fund, 1932 [32.11.1])

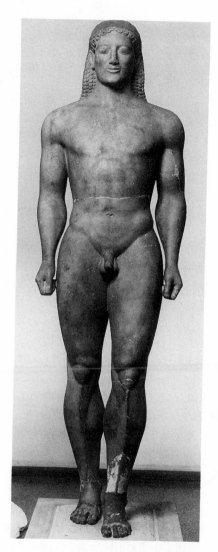

a

b

Figure 7.4a–b. Attic kouros from Anavysos, ca. 540–525 B.C. Anatomical observation contributed to the development of sculpture throughout the Archaic and Classical periods. The powerful musculature of the lower body is a common feature of the genre. (National Archaeological Museum, Athens, no. 3851)

armor). Priam imagines an old man fallen in battle as a wretched corpse whose genitals are mutilated by dogs.[8] The Greek word for genitals, *aidoia*, implies shame, *aidōs*. But, perhaps under the influence of pictorial conventions that displayed male nudes as early as the time

Sexual Beauty

of Homer, a curious inversion of social custom developed in the Archaic period when young aristocrats adopted nudity as a form of social display. Exercising regularly outdoors in the nude, they developed deep tans and conspicuous muscles. Well protected by their social rank, they were fearless of physical attack by an enemy; the safety from enemies thus implied was a proclamation of solidarity within the class to which these *kalokagathoi* and their admirers belonged. These were the "beautiful people" of their age, honored by the *kalos* dedications on red-figure ware described in chapter 5 (see figs. 5.8, 5.14). As for the traditional shame of nakedness, *honi soit qui mal y pense*. It has been argued that phallic display was a gesture of masculine ascendancy over women,[9] and it follows that where nudity is an exclusive privilege of males, women would indeed be subordinated. But such an argument, I believe, overlooks the meaning of the display. It is not directed against women, who were already thoroughly subordinated to men, but against outsiders, non-Greeks as well as any fellow citizens who were not privileged to exercise in the palaestra, develop well-balanced muscles, and keep their bodies clean and oiled.

It may also be noted that the penis itself is not an especially prominent part of the display in art that represents male nudity, though painters regularly positioned males to display rather than conceal the genitals (e.g., fig. 7.2). Except for special subjects such as Pan (fig. 1.17), satyrs (fig. 5.6 a–b), orgiasts (figs. 5.4, 5.10) and barbarians (fig. 7.5), the penis is small to the point of daintiness (figs. 6.1, 6.4, 7.5, 7.8). Infibulation, the practice of protecting the penis during exercise in the nude by tying the foreskin down over the glans with a leather string, may have had a cosmetic effect because it made the penis appear smaller (figs. 7.6, 7.7).[10] The penis is usually an aspect of male nudity rather than its focus. In contrast to traditional magical symbolism (such as the oversize erections of phallic Herms, figs. 1.16, 1.17), the human body itself is the image of power. The deemphasis of the phallus is consistent with the Greek subordination of eroticism to other virtues. The sturdy kouroi display *aretē* in their muscles, and the penis is not a muscle.

The male "cult of nakedness," as Oswyn Murray calls it,[11] is connected to the aristocratic custom of boy love and the cult of youth that developed in the Archaic period and remained an ideal through the Classical age. It is also part of the mystique of the athletic victor at the

Figure 7.5. In this painting of Heracles killing the attendants of King Busiris, the artist contrasts the bloated, circumcised penises of the barbarian stooges with the small, uncircumcised penis of the Greek hero. Pelike by the Pan Painter. (National Archaeological Museum, Athens, no. 9683)

Figure 7.6. Infibulation of the penis for protection during exercise was believed to ma[ke] it better-looking, though the retreating girl in this cup by the Penthesilea Painter [is] unimpressed. (Object in the collections of the American Philosophical Society. Phot[o]graph courtesy of the University of Pennsylvania Museum)

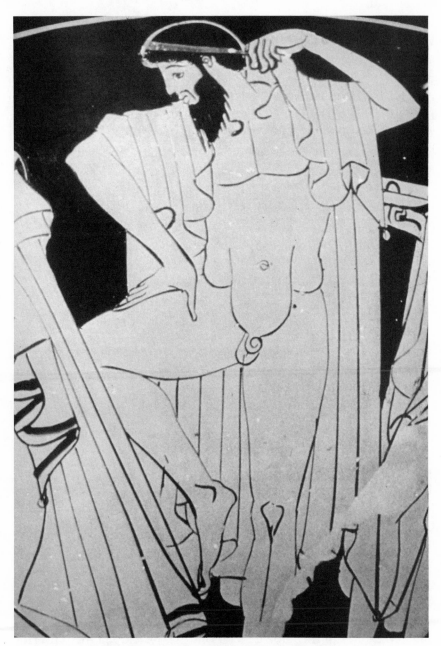

Figure 7.7. The reveler in this Attic red-figure cup by Douris (480–470 B.C.) wears a band on his head and a kunodesmē on his penis, giving it an ornamental curl. (Staatlich Museum, Berlin, no. 2289)

Panhellenic games celebrated by Pindar and Bacchylides. Life imitated art. Though pederasty as an oligarchic social ritual faded in the daylight of democratic Athens, its memory lived on in the fourth century and became a permanent fixture of Greek sexual culture where the erotic and the aesthetic seem to merge. At the beginning of the *Charmides*, Plato records a conversation in which Socrates sees the beautiful young Charmides entering a wrestling school and discusses the boy with his friends:

> Socrates: At the moment I saw him I confess that I was quite astonished at his beauty and stature. All the company seemed to be enamored of him. Amazement and confusion reigned when he entered, and a second troop of lovers followed behind him. That grown-up men like ourselves should have been affected in this way was not surprising, but I observed the boys and saw that all of them, down to the very smallest, turned and looked at him, as if he had been a statue.
>
> Chaerephon called me and said, "What do you think of the young man, Socrates? Has he not a beautiful face?"
>
> "Most beautiful," I said.
>
> "But you would think nothing of his face," he replied, "if you could see his naked form; he is absolutely perfect."[12]

Though the link between beauty and sexual enchantment is too subtle for positive analysis, some conclusions seem likely. Male-centered Greek canons of thought admitted male nudity as an ideal aesthetic form just as they admitted pederasty as an ideal erotic form. Plato is not the most reliable index of typical Greek thought, as he himself is quick to emphasize; but the linkage he makes in the *Charmides* between nudity, sexual magnetism, and statuary is far from idiosyncratic.

An admiration of the female body is also well attested among the oligarchic elites in the same generations that developed the powerful kouroi and other male nudes. We must assume that the Attic red-figure ware representing nude women who entertained men in symposia (see figs 5.1–5.4, 5.8) belonged to a secondary order of art. As the civilization of the polis subordinated the purely private to the public, activities enjoyed in the relative privacy of the symposium were

Figure 7.8. Divine nudity. This cast bronze Zeus or Poseidon, made at the height of the Classical "severe style," ca. 470 B.C., presents the nude as an expression of supreme power. Though larger than life, with arms elongated for effect, this statue shows a close observation of anatomy and a lithe muscularity that contrasts with the heavily schematic, static form of the Archaic kouros. Ca. 470–450 B.C. (National Archaeological Museum, Athens, no. 15161)

subordinated to public life and to the ideal forms exhibited in public. As chapter 5 showed, the symposium was a privileged arena where female nudity appeared side by side with male; but males displayed themselves also in more public places such as the palaestra and other outdoor exercise areas. While it has been argued that female nudity in the red-figure vases carries a different meaning (e.g., the helplessness

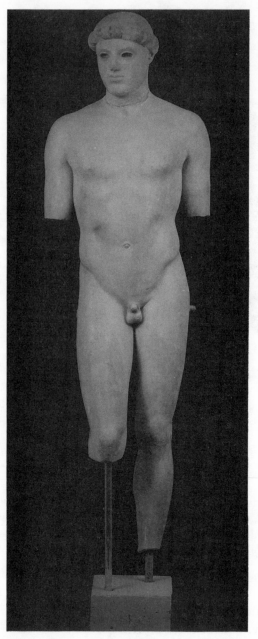

Figure 7.9. The "Kritios Boy," ca. 490–480 B.C., a late and crowning example of the kouros style, is less aggressively modeled than earlier kouroi and contrasts with the powerful god in the previous illustration. Sensuous in a wholly new way, his face shows an inward, contemplative character unimagined in the Archaic style. The position of the legs is reversed, with the weight on the left leg slightly tipping the pelvis and giving a slightly relaxed look to the figure as a whole. The curved line of the back contributes to an impression of articulated grace rather than monolithic strength. (Acropolis Museum, Athens, no. 698)

and humiliation of the hetaeras and other women present as hired entertainers), the type of *euphrosynē*, or good feeling, represented is not overtly sadistic or violent.[13] Male heterosexual pleasure took a visual form even among the aristocrats who made a cult of pederasty.

Even in public art, it is arguable that statues of women had a sexual content. In the later Archaic period the kore, a type of dedicatory statue representing robust, richly clad young women, emerged as a sister art to that of the male kouros. Inspired (like the kouros) by large statues that Greek travelers saw in Egypt after that country opened its doors to foreigners about 660 B.C., they were set up, apparently at private expense, in public places such as the Acropolis at Athens as dedications and memorials. Though at first not as popular a dedication as the kouros, the kore became a favorite at Athens under the Pisistratids in the last half of the sixth century B.C. Originally stiff and formulaic in execution, they gradually evolved toward more naturalistic forms but always maintained their forward-looking, columnar posture. The glory of the kouros is his splendidly powerful body, uncluttered by adornment and undiluted by concealment. The corresponding glory of the kore is the very adornment shunned by the kouros. Like male nudity, the kore's attire was in part a display of social position. Her rich Ionian layered costume, elaborate coiffure, and jewelry set off the radiant face of a cherished daughter in the prime of marriageable youth; little else of her person is frontally presented to the viewer. With this concealment, aesthetic dimorphism parallels sexual. Kouros contrasts with kore as the powerful, "masculine" simplicity of the Doric order contrasts with the elegant scrolls and complex fluting of the "feminine" Ionic.[14] The overt sexual features of the kore are muted, perhaps to compensate for the stronger sexuality attributed to women. As if the erotic power of the nude female were too much for public scrutiny, it is veiled and mediated with ornament. But taken as a whole, the kore is not altogether without its erotic character, difficult as that may be to gauge from our point of vantage. As it happens, Homer provides a context that suggests the erotic effect of these Ionic costumes. Although it precedes the korai by about two centuries, a scene in the *Iliad* suggests how his audience might picture a seductive female costume. When Hera wishes to seduce Zeus and induce a postcoital nap while their brother, Poseidon, aids the beleaguered Greeks, she outfits herself like a latter-day kore: she arranges her hair and puts on

> an ambrosial robe that Athene
> had made her carefully, smooth, and with many figures upon it,
> and pinned it across her breast with a golden brooch, and circled
> her waist about with a zone that floated a hundred tassles,
> and in the lobes of her carefully pierced ears she put rings
> with triple drops in mulberry clusters, radiant with beauty,
> and, lovely among goddesses, she veiled her head downward
> with a sweet fresh veil that glimmered pale like the sunlight.
>
> (14.178–185, tr. Lattimore)

Though as a rule he is not interested in clothing, Homer lingers on the details of this erotic "arming" scene: for his eighth-century audience, costume is evidently more captivating than seductive exposure. The "veil" in Lattimore's translation is in Greek a κρήδεμνον, an opaque kerchief or wimple that combines modesty with allure.[15] The dressing-up of female sexual allure contrasts significantly with the nudity of young male aristocrats. When not completely nude in the Near Eastern manner, sexual figures may show the opposite tendency. This is not a novelty, however. Elaborate coiffures (fig. 3.3) and complicated, flounced skirts beneath bare breasts (fig. 3.2) are early features of Aegean religious art. Moreover, complexity is a persistent feature of Aphrodite and her avatars: it is an aspect of her ambiguity that is linked to her ornamented appearance.[16]

Another aspect of the ambiguity or complexity of some korai is that when looked at from the left or behind, they are not as heavily draped as they appeared when seen head-on (figs. 7.12, 7.13 a–b). Their seminudity anticipates an increasing interest in the female nude during the latter half of the Classical period, when parts of a woman's body are revealed through the thin drapery that alternately conceals and reveals what is beneath. In a real sense, the history of the female nude in Greek sculpture begins with the kore.

Whatever the erotic content of the kore as originally conceived, she was much else besides, and cannot be fully appreciated unless seen in the round. Her columnar shape and its sometime use as a caryatid, or columnar support (named after priestesses of Artemis at Caryae), calls to mind a line in Homer's "Penelope leitmotif," repeated five times in the *Odyssey*: "she stood by the pillar that supported the roof with its joinery."[17] In her own way, the kore in her solidity is like the

Figure 7.10. Korai (like kouroi) were a Panhellenic genre of large statuary, placed as dedications at temples of Apollo or Artemis throughout Greece. The best examples were unearthed on the Acropolis where they were used as landfill after the Persian destruction of 480. Found in 1896 northwest of the Erechtheum, this kore wears a short Ionic himation over a belted chiton, hung in such a way as to reveal parts of the body beneath. She holds in her right hand an apple or pomegranate, an ancient sexual symbol. Traces of paint show the bright colors in which these statues were originally displayed. (Acropolis Museum, Athens, no. 680)

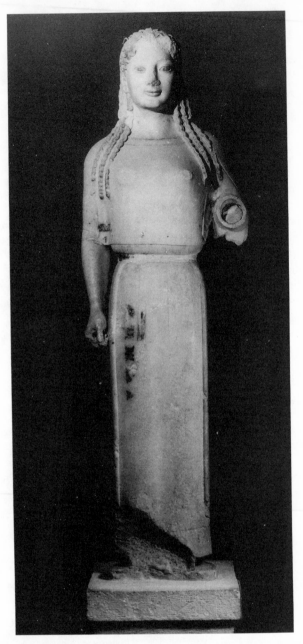

Figure 7.11. "The Peplos Korē," 540–530 B.C., is an early example of its kind. So called from the woolen peplos worn over her chiton, her strongly molded face contrasts with the columnar features of the rest: narrow hips and simple drapery that conceals the body beneath. (Acropolis Museum, Athens, no. 679)

Figure 7.12. The Antenor Korē seen from behind. According to a common convention, many korai held their chiton bunched in their left hand as if about to step forward. The result was an additional ornamental fall of drapery in front and the opportunity to combine drapery with underlying anatomy behind. Like the painted vase that expresses contrasting aspects of the same subject on opposite sides, the kore's body is concealed by its costume in front but revealed through the same clothing when seen from behind. The legs are, from a modern point of view, surprisingly heavy and powerful. (Acropolis Museum, Athens, no. 681)

Figure 7.13a–b. Side nudity. This Acropolis kore (no. 682), seen from the left, reveals a body that seemed fully draped when seen head-on. The arm, thighs, and buttocks are powerful and athletic, in contrast to the lighter physique of the hetaeras in the red-figure erotic vases. (a: Acropolis Museum, Athens, no. 682)

a

b

a

b

c

Figure 7.14a–c: This kore, dedicated by Euthydikos, represents the simpler style of the latest period of such sculptures, ca. 480 B.C. The diagonally draped garment over her peplos gives the appearance of a bared left breast. Side views reveal contrasting aspects, as in the preceding figure. (Acropolis Museum, Athens, nos. 686, 609)

kouros, expressing strength as well as beauty and prosperity; but being feminine, she is given an inward quality the male figures generally lack. It will be useful here to recall the structural associations of gender noted in Chapter 4 (n. 41), where inwardness or interiority is a feminine quality. In the kore, this is expressed less in the body surfaces than in the complicated raiment draped over them, establishing a play between the rippled layers of costume and the smooth body surfaces beneath (making the female body more "interior"), and in the radiance of the face that expresses interior virtues. The luminosity of the kouros is of light falling on the surfaces of his body, while the radiance of the kore seems to emit its own light from within. As with the kouros, mass and detail are concentrated on the upper part of the body, giving the resulting mass an upward energy. The virtuosity of the sculptor that was expended on the musculature of the kouros is invested in the complex folds of drapery on the kore. Artistry, like sexual identity, works along lines that contrast the sexes without valuing one above the other.

The Persian devastation of the Acropolis in 480 created a break with the past clean enough to make it the customary watershed between the Archaic and Classical periods. Though Pindar and even Plato open windows into the Archaic past, a spirit that is at the same time more democratic and more serious expresses itself in the early Classical "severe style." Red-figure ware illustrating sexual pleasures of the symposium all but disappear, but by the latter half of the century sculptural forms begin to appear in which the female form assumes a new importance.

We have seen in the Archaic kouroi (figs. 7.3a–b, 7.4a–b) and the early Classical Artemisium Zeus (fig. 7.8) how important the projection of power was in male statuary. The strong legs that show through the drapery of the Acropolis korai (figs. 7.12, 7.13b) reveal that muscle was not an exclusively male attribute. This has early antecedents: for example, the "mighty (lit. thick) hand" that Homer ascribes elsewhere to Odysseus is Penelope's in the *Odyssey* 21.6, as it was Athena's in the *Iliad* 21.403 and 424. In the *Odyssey* 18.195, Athena adds to Penelope's sex appeal by making her "taller and thicker," μακροτέρην καί πάσσονα, as she had done for Odysseus in 8.20 to impress the Phaeacians. The old Aegean iconography of the female breast (figs. 1.2, 1.9, 1.30, 1.31, 1.36, 3.1), which had not entirely died

Sexual Culture in Ancient Greece

out in the early Archaic period (fig. 4.5), is echoed in the sixth century with the exposure or semiexposure of a single breast, for example, in the Acropolis korai whose diagonally draped overgarments emphasize their left breast beneath their himation (figs. 7.10, 7.13a, 7.14a), in the running girl on the Vix crater (fig. 7.15), in the fragmentary torso of a Nike from Syracuse, and later in the Lapith woman defending herself from a Centaur in the west pediment of the temple of Zeus at Olympia (fig. 7.16). These powerful images, erotic or not, evince feminine strength in a most positive way that is antithetical to another convention in which the bared breast is a sign of pathos and helplessness intended to evoke pity (e.g., when Hecuba holds out a bared breast in supplication to Hector, *Il.* 22.80). As in the Archaic period nudity was converted from a shameful and helpless state to a display of masculine beauty and power, later generations saw the exposed breast transformed into an image of feminine capability, recalling perhaps the powers it symbolized in the earliest periods.

So little art of the Classical period has come down to the present time that sculptures such as the bronze nude males found near Riace in 1972, or the silkily gowned male "charioteer" found in Motya (w. Sicily) in 1979, fit inexactly into traditional conceptions of Classical style. While it can be said with confidence that the main current of early Classical taste was uncomfortable with completely nude female statuary and preferred male nudes that project power, these tendencies would eventually reverse themselves as the female nude gained wide acceptance and the male nude evolved a popular variant that emphasized grace over power. Moreover, symptoms of this great sea change can be detected at or even before the very dawn of the Classical period. The "Kritios Boy" (fig. 7.9) almost literally steps away from the kouros style that forms its immediate antecedent. His right foot advanced instead of its left, the pelvis slightly tipped and head turned, he ceases to emulate the foursquare frontality of the traditional kouros. While he is still powerfully built, the artist no longer concentrates on muscles and substitutes a sensual softness in the body surfaces. We have seen how the draped korai of about the same decades (before 480 B.C.) come out of their modest frontal concealment to display features that lend credence to the cult of Aphrodite *kallipygos*, "of the lovely buttocks."[18] By the beginning of the fifth century, antithetical formulas of sexual differences were beginning to show signs of weakness,

Figure 7.15. A female athlete in an early type of gym dress. One of three or four such figures attached to the lid of a bronze vase, ca. 520 B.C. Found in Prizren, Albania. The Spartan custom of dressing female athletes with little or no clothing offended the Athenians, who were always ready to believe the worst of their Peloponnesian antagonists. (The British Museum, no. 209027)

at least in sculpture. In the second half, a male nude evolved whose slender, supple lines contrasted dramatically with the hefty kouroi of the previous century. The female body, though still partially concealed by drapery, was well advanced in a direction first apparent in the late Archaic korai. Before the end of the Classical period it would create a new ideal form, whose consequences for art in the Western world are difficult to exaggerate.

From Olympia as far west as Sicily and the southern part of Italy known collectively as Magna Graecia, acceptance of female nudity in

Figure 7.16. Western Greek sculptors had an earlier latitude in representing the undraped female form. This Lapith woman on the west pediment of the temple of Zeus at Olympia (468–460 B.C.) is defending herself against a marauding Centaur. With noteworthy anatomical precision, the artist has represented the enlarged deltoid muscle in the woman's left shoulder and well-developed pectoral muscles beneath her small breasts. The powerful, athletic feminine physique is comparable to what is illustrated in figs. 7.13b and 7.22.

sculpture came earlier, perhaps because of traditions brought there in the course of colonization from centers such as Corinth, Halicarnassus, and Miletus, where eastern traditions were strong. The Ludovisi Triptych (470–450 B.C.), showing Aphrodite being helped from the sea by two nymphs, exploits the look of "wet drapery," *draperie mouillée*, to expose the goddess's torso completely; the scene of Aphrodite's birth is flanked by two sculptures representing contrasting sexual ideals: one represents a veiled bride, the other a nude flute girl playing her instruments. A wounded Niobid (fig. 7.19) from the same area a generation later (ca. 430 B.C.) is all but totally nude.

Although the sculptural art of the fifth-century Athenians avoided female nudity, it throve on the play of thin, supple drapery over the nude body, adding an element of sensuousness to the virtuosity with which the complex folds and curls of fabric had been executed in the Archaic kore. The technical vocabulary of Athenian sculptors was expanding, as presumably was the taste of their public constituents.

Figure 7.17. Aphrodite helped from the sea by two nymphs in the centerpiece of the Ludovisi Triptych (ca. 470–450 B.C.), a southern Italian marble relief probably carved by an Ionian sculptor at Locri near the toe of Italy. The wide spacing of the breasts gives them emphasis when seen from the front. (Editions Gallimard)

Besides the hard, tensed musculature of athletic males, sculptors were creating soft, relaxed bodies. The softer lines of the female body provided a natural subject with which to work in this style. The figures of Poseidon, Apollo, and Artemis on the east frieze of the Parthenon (447–432 B.C.) are early examples; the Nike figures on the temple of Athena Nike (411–407 B.C.) show the "wet" technique applied selectively to conceal and reveal the female form for a decent but sensuous effect. This was not purely an invention of virtuoso stonecutters. If Aristophanes' *Lysistrata* (48, 150) can be relied on, chitons of diaphanous silk from Amorgos (figs. 5.1, 5.16, 5.21) were actually worn by women of the citizen class.

The first fully nude large-scale public sculpture of a woman was Praxiteles' famous but now lost Aphrodite of Cnidos, perhaps the greatest of its kind in antiquity, created about 364 B.C. According to Pliny (36.20–21), the Athenian sculptor had made and put up for sale at the same price two Aphrodites, one nude and the other draped. The

Figure 7.18a–b. A veiled bride on one side of the Ludovisi Triptych represents sex-in-marriage; her nude counterpart on the opposite side is a flute girl, representing sex-as-entertainment. As represented in this triptych and throughout Greek myth, Aphrodite was from the beginning in important ways a woman's goddess. (Editions Gallimard)

Figure 7.19. Female nudity in the western Greek tradition (cf. figs. 7.16–7.19). A wounded daughter of Niobe from southern Italy, ca. 430 B.C. (Editions Gallimard)

Figure 7.20. Poseid Apollo, and Arte on the east frieze (6) of the Parthen Athens, ca. 447– B.C. While the dra on Apollo's arr heavy and rev nothing of the that supports it, temis' light garn calls attention to breasts beneath. (tions Gallimard)

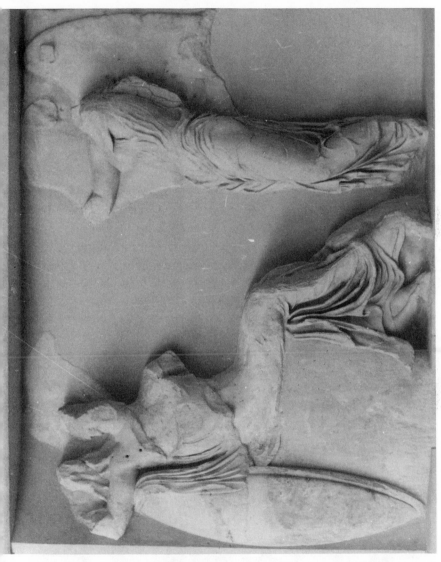

Figure 7.21. Dramatic, windswept drapery on a Nike at the Athenian temple of Athena Nike, 411–407 B.C. Comparison with the profile in fig. 7.13b, nearly a century earlier, shows the pedigree of this style, which is now even more complex and less rigidly erect. Virtuoso drapery work in stone as here and in fig. 7.26 was associated with the sculptor Callimachus (not to be confused with the Hellenistic poet of the same name). (Acropolis Museum, Athens, no. 989)

Figure 7.22. As in the preceding figure from the temple of Nike on the
Acropolis, where drapery was used to reveal the buttock and upper leg, here
attention is focused on the stomach and breast. This winged Victory from
the balustrade of the same temple is bending over to unlace her sandal so as
to make her offering with bare feet. (Acropolis Museum, Athens, no. 973)

islanders of Cos, who had the first choice, settled for the more conventional draped goddess. Their neighbors of Cnidus purchased the nude Aphrodite and placed her in an outdoor shrine where she could be viewed from all sides. Though several imitations of Cnidian Aphrodite survive from later centuries, many details of her appearance remain unknown and poorly understood today. The best-attested and most enigmatic of her features is the gesture of her right hand, which lightly shields her pubic area, both masking and calling attention to this part of her nudity. It is as mysterious as the Mona Lisa's smile. She soon became one of the great tourist attractions of the ancient world.[19]

The relaxed position in which she stands, with her hips on an inclined plane opposite to that of her shoulders, had been devised three quarters of a century earlier by Polyclitus for a male nude called the Spear-carrier, or Doryphoros. Polyclitus made this his "Canon" work, the basis of a textbook he wrote explaining the new relaxed style in which the lines were slanted and curving instead of vertical and horizontal, sinuous instead of columnar, graceful instead of powerful (Pliny 34.55–56). It is possible to date the change in taste to about the middle of the fifth century B.C., the end of the "severe" style, a century before Praxiteles' celebrated nude Aphrodite. One of the ramifications of the new, gracefully relaxed style is the change from a male to a female ideal of human beauty. From about this time, the male physique begins to imitate the female, reversing the earlier tendency to give female figures narrow hips and straight, boyish body lines. This was not a sudden revolution, but it set the course for the Greek art of the nude to the end of antiquity. It had corollaries as well in the general sensibilities of the Greeks regarding women.

While epochal changes in sensibility cannot be explained by appeal to a single cause, they can be understood in the context of related developments. During the fifth century, the tragedians wrote a number of plays in which a traditionally masculine conception of power is confronted by no less powerful feminine alternatives. Agamemnon's triumphal return from the Trojan War is cut short by his wife's vengeance (and that of the Furies) in the first play of Aeschylus' *Oresteia* (458 B.C.); Clytemnestra's role in the *Agamemnon* is the largest for any character in extant Greek tragedy; the trilogy pits female power against male in a way that can only be resolved in the end by a

Figure 7.23. The best-known Roman copy of Praxiteles' lost Aphrodite of Cnidos, the statue that launched the full female nude in Western art ca. 364 B.C. The goddess, perhaps surprised while bathing, is reaching for the garment that rests on the water jug to her left. (Alinari/Art Resource, New York)

Figure 7.24. The male nude feminized. Polyclitus' canon of antithetically balanced form, or contrapposto, is illustrated in Praxiteles' rendering of Apollo Sauroktonos or "lizard-slayer." The artist miniaturized Apollo's killing of the dragon at Delphi into a boy killing a lizard with the point of an arrow. The original of this bronze was created ca. 360–350 B.C. Beginning with the fourth century, Apollo and Dionysus are often represented as soft-bodied, almost effeminate young males. (Alinari/Art Resource, New York)

Figure 7.25. A bisexual culture found an erotic ideal in the Hellenistic hermaphrodite, which grew naturally out of the sexual ambiguity of figures such as the Sauroktonos (fig. 7.24). This is the "feminine" view of Hermaphrodite, as shown in most textbooks; s/he has male genitals. Ancient replica of an original dating in the first half of the second century B.C. (Alinari/Art Resource, New York)

goddess negotiating with female spirits of revenge, the Erinyes or Eumenides who give their name to the final play of the trilogy. Two plays of Sophocles produced not long after the *Oresteia* carry on the theme of female power. Male force is spent vainly in Sophocles' *Women of Trachis* (450s–440s B.C.), as Heracles' legendary sexual conquests turn back upon him to cause his death in agony:

> A woman, a female, in no way like a man,
> she alone without even a sword has brought me down.[20]

In the *Antigone*, a male regent, Creon, tries in vain to enforce his male authority over Oedipus' daughter, who insists on fulfilling her family obligation of burial for her brother, Polynices. He overreaches his power in condemning Antigone and is crushed by the suicides of his son and his own wife, Eurydice. Antigone's family love and duty, though fatal for her, win out against Creon's hate: "I was not born to join in hatred, but in love" (523).

With Euripides, the power of women (albeit for harm) assumes even greater importance, whether in conscious revenge for male sexual offenses (Medea, Phaedra) or in unconscious revenge for male hubris in power. In the *Bacchae* (ca. 406 B.C.), when Pentheus tries to suppress the cult of Dionysus by force, he is warned by Tiresias, "Do not boast that force is what has power for humankind."[21] In the end, he is torn to pieces by women under the spell of Dionysus, and his mother returns to Thebes bearing his head on her thyrsus.

The overruling of male power by women is a comic theme as well. The best known of Aristophanes' comedies in which women drive the plot is the *Lysistrata* (411 B.C.), in which the title character organizes a sex strike by wives to force the men of the warring Greek states to the bargaining table. Though Aristophanes has fun with the Greek belief that women are more sexually needy than men, somehow the men are brought to submission, and an actor costumed as a nude woman representing Reconciliation takes her place at Lysistrata's side "so that the men will have before their eyes an example of the pleasure they will have when they have ended the war."[22] In an earlier comedy of Aristophanes, the *Acharnians* (425), peace treaties were symbolized as jugs of wine; here we are given a nude.

Women seize power again in the *Congresswomen* of 392/1. No less a personage than Socrates had argued, it appears, that management of the public and private business was different only in degree and that in some, if not all, respects women were intellectually equal to men.[23] Such views were perhaps not uncommon in the late fifth century: Antisthenes (and later the Stoics) taught that men and women possess the same *aretē*, or that it is the same for both;[24] Pherecrates had written a comedy called *The Lady Ruler* (Tyrannis) when Aristophanes was still a boy that may have been the model for this play.[25] When Aristophanes' Praxagora tells her peers that women who are "stewards and treasurers" of their households (212) can govern the polis as well as the *oikos*, the women vote themselves a gynecocracy. That this was a good idea at least for the stage is testified by comedies titled *Gynecocracy* written by Amphis and Alexis within the century. Far from being despised and ignored, women were increasingly prominent in the Classical Athenian imagination.

During the years in which the female nude enters the idiom of public art, the power of women to excel in discourse becomes a noteworthy theme. We saw in chapter 5 that hetaeras attained a renown for their art of repartee. Reports that Pericles' companion (and later wife) Aspasia was an expert rhetorician (see p. 151) are persistent enough to deserve attention, if not to a biographical fact at least to the credibility of such a rumor about a prominent woman in the later decades of the fifth century. Aristophanes' Lysistrata presents her own intellectual credentials in a way calculated to win the belief of a male audience:

> I am a woman, but I have a mind
> and I'm not badly off for judgement of my own;
> to my father's and the old men's talk
> I've listened often, and my education is not bad.[26]

Similarly, Praxagora claims in the *Ecclesiazusae* (243–244) to have learned rhetorical skills while a refugee living on the Pnyx and listening to the orators. As if to illustrate the contention he would later make in the *Republic* that women have no less intelligence than men, Plato puts the climactic speech of the *Symposium* in the mouth of a female character, the fictitious Diotima of Mantineia.

Sexual Culture in Ancient Greece

The trend of Athenian history in the last third of the fifth century ran directly counter to the admonition that Thucydides puts in Pericles' funeral oration that women should shun attention. They became increasingly prominent in art and drama. Nor were they forgotten as a paradigm of nature. The old myths had kept alive the tradition of mother earth and father sky;[27] fifth-century rationalism had new myths of its own that contrasted a feminine *physis* with masculine *nomos*. These sexual linkages were not just a matter of noun gender: they were seen as extending to the natural affinities and social roles of men and women, justifying the traditional assignment of political roles to men and nutritional, procreative roles to women. But on a higher cosmic level, some of the pre-Socratics resurrected less parochial ancient memories of a goddess of life. Parmenides of Elea (fl. ca. 475 B.C.) had revived the idea of a female supreme being, "the goddess who steers all things" (fr. 12), who combined aspects of fire, Aphrodite, the goddess of Necessity, and Earth. Empedocles of Acragas (fl. ca. 450 B.C.) depicted a universe powered by two opposite feminine abstractions, love (*philotēs*) and strife (*eris*). The universe is alternately ruled by these powers; though strife is an important part of this cosmic dialectic, love is the harmonious, stable, and generative phase associated with good and desirable states.[28] The cosmogonic power that was a male Eros in Hesiod is in Empedocles a female *philotēs*. Not content with the abstraction, Empedocles often personifies the generative actions of nature as Cypris or Aphrodite. By the time of Euripides' *Hippolytus* (428 B.C.), the universality of Aphrodite's power over nature, stated by Phaedra's nurse, begins to sound like a commonplace:

> She wings her way through the air; she is in the sea,
> in its foaming billows; from her everything,
> that is, is born. For she engenders us
> and sows the seed of desire whereof we're born,
> all we her children, living on the earth.[29]

These maternal conceptions of the love goddess anticipate the *alma Venus* who was to preside over Lucretius' Epicurean cosmos just before the middle of the first century B.C.

A further projection of female power that receives special attention in the later fifth century and afterward is the goddess of Victory, Nike.

Figure 7.26. Slightly over life-size and designed to be seen from below at the high point of the site prepared for it at Samothrace, this winged Victory is the most memorable use of the female body as a symbol of transcendent power. The anatomical emphasis here is wholly on the midriff, centering on the navel. Rhodian, ca. 190 B.C. (Musée du Louvre, Giraudon/Art Resource, New York)

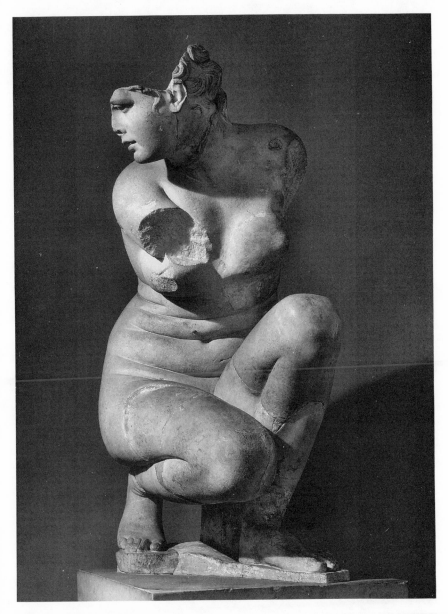

Figure 7.27. At the opposite pole from the large, heroic Victories, crouching nudes were slightly smaller than life-size. In a naturally modest position, this Aphrodite crouches while attendants pour bathwater over her. Doidalsas or Daedalsas of Bithynia is said to have done the original in Bronze in the third century B.C., and copies were made in quantity for private homes, courtyards, and fountains. This 250 B.C. Roman copy, from Hadrian's villa in Tivoli, is in the Museo Nazionale, Rome. (Editions Gallimard)

First mentioned in passing by Hesiod (*Th.* 384) as a minor attendant deity of Zeus, she was represented in the 430s B.C. by the great sculptor Pheidias as a miniature standing in the hand of a greater Olympian such as Zeus or Athena.[30] In about 420 B.C., the sculptor Paionios made a large Nike for Olympia who is virtually nude, partially clad in thin drapery that is blown back against her body. About the same time, Nike was given her own small temple on the Acropolis, which was finished before 408. Mentioned in Sophocles' *Philoctetes* (408 B.C.), and twice in Euripides' *Ion* (ca. 412 B.C.), she owes some of her prominence to Athens' military posture in the last third of the fifth century. But she is a decidedly feminine symbol, not an asexual armed goddess like Athena. No longer a Pheidian miniature, she appears in multiple full-size forms on the balustrade of her Acropolis temple, her nude form half-revealed beneath her drapery in the customary *draperie mouillée* style (fig. 7.22). In the Hellenistic period, Nike becomes a popular motif, usually winged and draped, like the famous Nike of Samothrace (ca. 200 B.C.) now in the Louvre (fig. 7.26).

The frequent emphasis in such figures on the abdomen may suggest maternal as well as sexual associations. Contrasting with the numerous crouching nudes that come to us from the Hellenistic and Roman periods, this triumphant type is one of an increasing range of styles for the increasingly popular female nude or seminude. The Nike is dramatic, energetic, and transcendent. Caught in an expansive moment of action—the Nike of Samothrace is about to alight on the prow of a ship—the later Classical and Hellenistic Nike figures come out of a world whose mental imagery had transferred its ideal conception of power from something masculine to something feminine. It is risky to project from this paradigmatic shift a radical change in social attitudes regarding gender. But it was a monumental development in the imaginative life of the West.

CHAPTER EIGHT

Erotic Friendship

ROMANTIC FICTIONS

The wise man does not fall in love.
FOURTH-CENTURY B.C. MAXIM

This is the very ecstasy of love,
Whose violent property fordoes itself
And leads the will to desperate undertakings
As oft as any passion under heaven
That does afflict our natures.
POLONIUS, IN *HAMLET*

Man is by nature more a pairing than a political being.
ARISTOTLE, *NICOMACHEAN ETHICS*

The female nude made her entry into Greek art in defiance of a strong and long-established distaste for female nudity; in a similar way, the entry of romantic love stories onto the Greek stage defied not only traditional canons but also the newer precepts of fourth-century philosophy. In the fifth century, Sophists had established three degrees of appetency, each more dangerous than its predecessor: *epithumia*, *eros*, and *mania*. The first of these ranges between inclination and yearning: *epithumia* includes sexual desire but in a more or less manageable strength. *Eros* is more urgent, denoting the same sexual passion it does today; in chapter 6 we noted a metaphorical use in Thucydides, where Pericles urged his fellow Athenians to have an eros for their city.¹ As we saw in Plato's *Symposium*, eros may be a metaphor of the philosopher's passion for beauty and truth. Mania is anything but philosophical, an uncontrollable craving that overrides the will. The pre-Socratic Prodicus explained, "*Epithumia* doubled is eros; eros doubled is mania."² It was axiomatic that a man or woman of good character stays aloof from all appetites, because they deprive us of self-control.

Because the individual was a cardinal focus of Greek thought, self-control was an important personal goal. For all its importance as a collective artifact, the democratic polis was most admired as a means by which individuals could achieve freedom, prosperity, and success.³ The priority of the individual is seen as early as the *Iliad*: nobody criticizes Achilles for subordinating the safety of the Achaeans to his personal vendetta against Agamemnon. The same attitude is illustrated generations later in Aristophanic comedy, when individual heroes like Dicaeopolis in the *Acharnians* find private solutions to political problems. Individualism was close to the core of most ethical philosophy in the fourth century B.C. and later, when the benefits of self-knowledge, self-sufficiency, and self-control were the subject of much written and spoken discourse. The achievement of these moral ends depended on a rigorous rationality that was capable of blocking mere emotions or appetites. By this means, the individual was thought to achieve true autonomy. The resulting freedom was the goal of every wise man, whether Cynic, Stoic, Skeptic, or Epicurean. No other culture that we know of in the ancient world was so fixated on personal freedom.

To remain free, the wise man avoids enslavement to wealth, power, fame, or physical pleasure. The only true pleasure is knowledge and the freedom from suffering that it makes possible. Stoic "apathy" is the freedom from every emotional *pathos* to which the flesh is heir, including the pathos of sexual love whose destructive power Euripides had so memorably dramatized. Epicurean *ataraxia* was a philosophic detachment that freed the wise from the confusion (*taraxis*) that clouded the minds of tyrants, the ambitious, the wealthy, gluttons, and lovers. To the Epicurean, love was "a tense straining for sexual satisfaction, coupled with frenzy and distress."⁴

Proud, autonomous, impregnable, the passionless sage of the later Classical and Hellenistic world possessed a cool impassivity that would not let him fall in love. When Aristippus said of his dazzling female companion "I possess Laïs, she does not possess me" (Ath. 544d), he was denying not physical but emotional intimacy: thus he maintained his claim to the good life as philosophy then defined it. A diffuse humanistic goodwill to men, *philanthropia*, tempered the chilly extremes of this outlook, as did the high value Stoics and Epicureans placed on *philia* between peers. To bridge the gap between the ideal of self-sufficiency and the fact of human interdependence, both Aristotle and the Stoic Zeno proposed that we consider a friend as "another self."[5] But the turbulence of eros, which Archaic monodists and Classical playwrights had depicted as a violent, diseased state, had no place in the philosopher's cool and rational life. Concerned as they were with sound mental hygiene, moralists for generations taught that eros was something to be got rid of. As early as Homer, heroes "put off their eros for food and drink" when they ate a meal.[6] Common sense dictated that erotic needs be taken care of before they could interfere with the business of living well. By the end of the fifth century, Euripidean plays carried warnings about eros that recommended quick accommodation before erotic disease, or *nosos*, becomes unmanageable. So Phaedra's nurse uses medical language to prescribe a homeopathic cure:

> Since you are sick, find a good way to subdue your sickness.
> There are such things as love-charms and beguiling spells;
> Some medicine for this disease will come to light.
>
> (*Hipp.* 477–449)

These charms and spells, like the magic Simaitha will try in Theocritus' second Idyll, will cure love's passion by helping to seduce the love object.

Sexual love was one of the central concerns of late Classical and Hellenistic ethics. As we have seen, the main tendency was disapproval of anything more than perfunctory carnal gratification. Diogenes of Sinope (ca. 400–ca. 325 B.C.), the flamboyant apostle of the Cynic sect, is said to have masturbated publicly in the Athenian Agora and remarked to bystanders how good it would be if it were possible to relieve hunger by rubbing the stomach.[7] The gesture was more original than the idea it dramatized: the standard opinion or platitude of philosophy in the fourth century was that the wise man does not fall in love. But the number of fourth-century and Hellenistic books titled *On Love* or something similar ascribed by Diogenes Laertius to various philosophers argues that the problem of love was not so easily dismissed. The disappearance of most philosophic writings from this time other than Plato and Aristotle prevents us from reconstructing the debate, but in the field of discourse shared by rhetoric and philosophy lay the contrarian proposition that the wise man *does* fall in love, or that eros is in one way or another socially or morally useful. Plato's *Symposium* was not alone in presenting this view. Zeno of Citium, the Hellenistic founder of the Stoic school, followed Plato in reviving the old oligarchic view that Eros is a god who provides friendship, concord, and even liberty; in his lost *Republic*, he added that Eros promotes the safety of the state (Ath. 561c). But what Zeno yields with one hand he takes away with the other: this same *Republic* also forbade marriage among the wise elite (παρὰ τοῖς σοφοῖς), substituting a community of wives to avoid the jealousies arising from adultery (Diog. Laert. 7.131). The sanitized Stoic definition of eros is "an effort toward friendliness due to visible beauty," and its goal of friendship takes precedence over sexual union.[8] Thus the Stoics kept eros in a diminished form that is scarcely distinguishable from *philia*, or friendship. A Hellenistic love epigram by Posidippus makes fun of the puritanical rigor of Zeno and his pupil Cleanthes: "Let Zeno, the learned swan, and Cleanthes' muse be silent, and let our care be for bittersweet love."[9]

Epicurean doctrine was equally grudging in the due it gave the devil love. Though Epicurus' book *On Love* is one of many Hellenistic treatises with this title that have been lost, he is quoted as saying in *On the Chief Good*, "I cannot conceive the good apart from the pleasures of taste, sex, sound, and form." But as we have seen, this theory of pleasure coexisted with a strong distaste for sexual tension, and in his *Letter to Menoeceus* he specifically excludes the sexual enjoyment of boys or women from what he calls pleasure, which is merely the absence of pain.[10] As if in reply to the Platonic and Stoic treatments of Eros as a god, Epicurus denied that eros was sent by the gods while affirming that the wise man does not fall in love, adding that sex never helped anyone and it was well if it did not actually do harm.[11]

Even the poets, following the antierotic rather than the romantic side of Euripides, exhibit a certain uneasiness about eros in the Hellenistic period. Apollonius of Rhodes plays the love interest to great effect in the *Argonautica*'s story of Jason and Medea, describing with great skill and psychological realism the stages by which a virginal Medea gives in to the effects of a *coup de foudre* administered by the bow of

Eros. The love god himself is on one level compounded of cute Hellenistic kitsch—he is shown beating the inexperienced Ganymede at knucklebones, a subject of popular art—but on another level we see a brat who habitually defies his mother and has to be bribed to commit a piece of mischief he enjoys for its own sake, the wounding of Medea. The poet allows us no pretty illusion about this nasty *putto*, apostrophizing him in words calculated to recall the anger of the Archaic monodists:

> Cruel Eros, great curse, great abomination to men, from you
> deadly quarrels and groans and wailings and numberless other
> pains in addition to these storm up. Arm yourself against the
> children of our enemies, demon, rising just as you did when you
> lay dreadful madness upon the wits of Medea.[12]

The madness, or *atē*, inflicted on Medea is represented in her dream (3.616–632), where she imagines herself rather than the golden fleece as the object of Jason's quest, and in the confused ramblings of her thoughts as she deliberates whether to kill herself (3.778–787). R. L. Hunter points out that the language describing Medea's mental and physical suffering "can almost all be paralleled from the fragments of Alcman, Ibycus, Anacreon, Archilochus, and Sappho, as well as from Alexandrian epigram."[13] From a viewpoint taken in the antierotic tradition of Greek poetry, Apollonius' treatment of the love story of Jason and Medea can be characterized as a *summa erotica*, reaffirming the sinister nature of love's affliction.

Though only metaphoric, Eros's wounding of Medea is more deadly than if it were literal, the victim herself becoming the killer: in the *Argonautica* itself, of her brother, Apsyrtus; and in the sequel earlier dramatized by Euripides, of her own children by Jason. Apollonius draws his readers in with a well-told love story without letting the reader or the characters themselves enjoy a moment's tenderness. The love of Jason and Medea is soured by its own guilty consummation. The story belongs to a now-common type of Western love story in which the first amorous excitement gives way to the tiresome routines of conjugal life. The *Argonautica*'s lovers share the dangers of an escapade that like an action romance in the movies leads to murder; but when at last they are united in marriage, there is only unhappiness.[14]

Though it is the most overtly ironic about the sexual passions, Apollonius' poem was not the first Hellenistic verse to pay equivocal tribute to the power of love. The literary culture of Alexandria that throve during the first half of the third century B.C. produced two new genres, pastoral and epigram, which seem to have made similar compromises between a reading public with an appetite for romance and an ethical distaste for erotic emotion. Apollonius knew what this public wanted, and was prepared to deliver the goods.

> She would have taken out her soul from her breast,
> and given it to him, so thrilled was she at his desiring her.
> Desire cast its sweet flame out from Jason's blond head;
> It captured her gleaming eyes. Her wits relaxed in its warmth,
> melting, fading, as the dew fades, warmed in dawn's early rays.[15]

Direct evidence about popular culture under the Ptolemies, who had made Alexandria the successor to Athens in the third century, is hard to find, but the mimes of Herondas and Theocritus—another new genre—offer glimpses into the life of a public who enjoyed erotic or romantic scenarios wherever they found them. In Theocritus' fifteenth *Idyll* two middle-class women, Gorgo and Praxinoa, go to see the annual rite of mourning for Aphrodite's consort, Adonis, and listen to a woman sing the dirge. This is performed under the patronage and in the palace of Queen Arsinoë, where a tapestry shows the dead Adonis: "how marvelous he is," exclaims Praxinoa, "lying in his silver chair with the first down spreading from the temples, thrice-loved Adonis, loved even in death!" A tableau is set out representing the goddess in bed with a still-blooming Adonis, who is described by the singer: "In Adonis' rosy arms the Cyprian lies, and he in hers. Of eighteen years or nineteen is the groom; the golden down is still upon his lip; his kisses are not rough. And now farewell to Cypris as she clasps her lover." This is a sexual show put on by women for women (though the poet who describes it is male). The erotic appeal of Adonis is his dewy youth: he is scarcely distinguishable from the downy softness of the young men pursued by oligarchic pederasts in an earlier age. He is further glamorized by a decorous and ornamental death that comes before maturity corrupts him ("his kisses are not rough"); he will return, newly gentle and innocent, the following year. Forever will she love, and he be young, an ideal sex fantasy for women married to men too old for them, with limited opportunities for firsthand sexual adventure.[16]

The ideal of mutual sexual desire in marriage enjoyed a special place in the politics of Alexandrian Egypt. When the Arsinoë who sponsored the Adonia described in Theocritus 15 married her younger brother, Ptolemy II Philadephus, sometime before 274 B.C., the ruling *theoi adelphoi* became living avatars of Isis and Osiris, Hera and Zeus. The match was far from a marriage in the familiar Greek style. Eight years older than her spouse, Arsinoë was as determined in this marriage as she had been in her first, to Alexander's companion, Lysamachus. She was the peer of her Alexandrian husband, if not the dominant partner, and like him took the title Philadelphus. Even before her death and official deification in 270 or 268, she was prayed to (like Isis) as a patron of sailors. This was one of her affinities with Aphrodite, whose cult had been promoted by her predecessor, Berenice I, wife of Ptolemy I Soter. In sponsoring the pageant of Aphrodite and Adonis, Arsinoë identified herself as a worthy successor, promoting the veneration of Aphrodite with a myth that represented the goddess as a sexually passionate partner. Aphrodite's dominance in the liaison with Adonis also gave color to the political role of Arsinoë as her spouse's active partner in politics as in love.

Kathryn Gutzwiller has shown that Arsinoë's successor, Berenice II, was no less deft in her manipulation of religious and erotic imagery. Like both her predecessors, she desired to be identified with Aphrodite.[17] The sexual passion she wished to be associated with her marriage to Ptolemy III not only helped to validate her partnership in rule, it linked her with the official cult of Aphrodite and the temple of Arsinoë Aphrodite at Zephyrium on the Canopic mouth of the Nile. Not least important for us, she enrolled the talents of the best available poet to celebrate and advertise her sexually charged marriage to the king.[18] Callimachus was probably in his sixties when he wrote *The Lock of Berenice* commemorating the votive lock of hair Berenice dedicated at the shrine of Aphrodite for the return of her husband from war and the lock's subsequent metamorphosis into a constellation. Though only pieces of the original survive, Catullus' Latin adaptation follows the Greek fragments closely enough to give us a clear impression of the original. In it, the lock speaks of its reluctance to be parted from its mistress and the intensity of Berenice's longing for her absent spouse. This is significantly not the official longing of a royal consort so much as the sexual *pothos* of a woman separated from her lover: "What god has changed your spirit so? [asks the Lock] Or is it that lovers do not wish to be long separated from the dear body of the other?"[19] The glamour of a royal romance was in this way enlisted to increase the popularity of Berenice among the literate Greeks of Alexandria. Gutzwiller argues that Berenice II followed the example of her predecessors by presenting her marriage in a way that had "a special appeal to feminine tastes" and that Callimachus planned *The Lock of Berenice* "to propagate a fantasy arising from female experience."[20] If so, she edified her female constituents is a way similar to that enjoyed by the women in Theocritus' *Idyll* 15, *Adoniazusae*.

Beginning in the late fifth century, Greek women had begun to play a significant role as consumers as well as objects of art: vases and ornamental mirrors for the boudoir, grave monuments commemorating their lives as wives and mothers, and jewelry. Their growing participation in cultural life may have included reading,[21] and probably the theater. Whether or not they can be thought of as influencing the market for literature, women certainly claimed an important share of what Hellenistic literature paid attention to. Much of this belongs to sexual culture, and the scenes put before Hellenistic readers often represented sex from a woman's point of view, or at least a view that was not exclusively masculine. Theocritus' *Sorceress*, his second Idyll, is written in the voice of a woman using a magic wheel, or *iunx*, to compel Delphis, a young man she met at a public festival, to resume a love affair in which he has lost interest. The poem is a confessional monologue, retelling the story of an independent woman's sexual adventure:

> I saw Delphis and Eudamippus walking together. More golden than helichryse were their beards, and their breasts brighter far than thou, O Moon, for they had lately left the manly labor of the wrestling-school. . . . I saw, and madness seized me, and my hapless heart was aflame. My looks faded away. No eyes had I thereafter for that show, nor know how I came home again, but some parching fever shook me, and ten days and ten nights I lay upon my bed. (77–86, tr. Gow)

After inviting Delphis to her house, she allows herself to be seduced:

> Ever too easily won, I took him by the hand and drew him
> down upon the soft couch. And quickly body warmed to
> body, and faces burned hotter than before, and sweetly we
> whispered. And to tell thee no long tale, dear Moon, all was
> accomplished, and we twain came to our desire. (138–143.
> tr. Gow)

Now Simaetha is unhappy, because Delphis has gone on to another liaison and she has nothing but her love charm to win him back.

Theocritus' contemporary Herondas also wrote sexual scenarios in which women are the central characters. Metriche, a housewife in "The Go-between," the first in a series of dramatic cameos or mimes, is approached by Gyllis, the title character, who comes to arrange an affair for her with an athlete who has taken a liking to her. Metriche's husband is absent on a trip to Egypt, but she declines the chance to have a fling. Bitinna, in the fifth mime, "The Jealous Woman," is about to flog and tattoo her slave-lover for carrying on with another woman but is persuaded to relent by her slave girl, Kydilla. The sixth mime is a conversation between housewives about an unusually good dildo that has been going the rounds. Metro wants to know who made it, as she wants to order one for herself. The eleventh, surviving in only three lines, is a conversation of συνεργαζόμεναι, "working girls" or prostitutes, and is probably comparable to Lucian's second-century A.D. *Dialogues of the Hetaeras.* This new subject matter is not exactly sentimental and was probably not written for women, but it opens a back door on a way of life in which women exercise considerably more personal autonomy than we imagine existed among the citizen class in Classical Athens. At the same time, it caters to an ancient Greek male stereotype of women whose lives are pervaded by thoughts about sex, and it constructs scenes around the stereotype. It is up to each reader to decide how believable such scenes are; their manner of presentation is realistic, and we view the scenes as if we were a fly on the wall. But as we are frequently reminded when characters in mime comment on works of art, it is the illusion of reality rather than reality itself that Hellenistic readers most admired. Literature of this period shows a curiosity about the lives of women that on the one hand

Erotic Friendship

borders on voyeuristic fantasy and on the other is more attentive to authentic female voices. A renewed interest in Sappho and the appearance of later female poets such as Anyte, Erinna, and Nossis in Hellenistic collections like Meleager's *Garland* attest to this concern.

The dramatic dialogues and monologues of Theocritus and Herodas were among the ways in which Hellenistic literature paid attention to private life and ordinary people. Like its philosophies, which counseled the development of enlightened privatism, Hellenistic taste concentrated on little things and personal rather than political events. By Classical standards, Hellenistic poetry had an escapist tendency, as is illustrated by the rustic vignettes Theocritus developed for urban readers. These pastoral idylls were not completely idyllic (Gk. *eidyllion* means simply "a little form"), but they conveyed a whiff of the life of herdsmen that was at the same time a little coarse and pleasantly simple, featuring inconsequential encounters between rustics with a taste for music and song. Here too sex plays an important part, providing ripples of interest in an otherwise placid and uneventful countryside that is isolated from the shocks of the outside world. Unlike the urban mimes that concentrated on the erotic lives of women, Theocritean pastoral encounters love through male characters, but it is still women who have the autonomy. Male lovers, like the Daphnis who dies of love in the first *Idyll*, are helpless (85 Daphnis is ἀμήχανος). The serenade to Amaryllis in *Idyll* 3 contrasts the singer's failure with the successes of male lovers in myth. Successful eros, like that of the unnamed old man in *Idyll* 4, is routine and mechanical, comparable to milling (58 μύλλει) and the rutting of the goats in *Idyll* 5.41 f. It is not, in fact, eros at all but a sexual act committed upon another, with a hint of debauchery and abuse (*Id.* 5.87 μολύνει, cf. 116 f.). When unsuccessful, it is the stuff of song, which is also its antidote: thus the song of Bucaeus in *Idyll* 10 and (more memorably) the lament of Polyphemus in *Idyll* 11, where the grotesque Cyclops "shepherds his love" for the sea nymph Galatea by singing it away. The futility of Polyphemus' unrequited love, the theme of two *Idylls* (6 and 11), is like that of Daphnis and the other lovers in pastoral. At its most successful, as in the flirtations of Comatas with Clearista and Lacon with Cratidas in *Idyll* 5 or Aratus with Philinus in *Idyll* 7, Theocritus' pastoral love has a preliminary, inchoate quality that is scarcely anything more than incidental ornament, not the main event."

Pastoral music in Theocritus is not the food of love, nor does song ever win the heart of someone loved. Pleasure is given and received by music, while love is a frightful evil (φοβερὸν κακόν, 8.57) that can be palliated or "shepherded" by music.

This conception of love has in common with the eros described by Diotima in Plato's *Symposium* that it does not possess the object of desire. In this "tense straining" defined by Epicurus, lovers are by definition sufferers because they do not have what they need to feel pleasure or be happy. It is a great paradox that the pastoral *locus amoenus* where pleasure is everywhere should also be the locus of love, the "frightful evil" about which Theocritus' rustics complain. But it was a paradox that Hellenistic readers found so pleasurable that poets invented an urban counterpart to pastoral escapism and placed the same erotic irritant there too. The urban world of love was the symposium illustrated in the red-figure ware discussed in chapter 5.

After the Macedonian conquest of Greece, Athens had lost its cultural hegemony, but as Hellenism spread over the formerly "barbarian" Near East, traditional Athenian institutions became the cynosure of civilized life. In much the same way as Chicago became the mythical gangster capital after the repeal of Prohibition had broken the gangsters' power, Athens supplied the cultural paradigms of Hellenism long after its political grip had been broken: every city that proposed to be taken seriously needed an Athenian-style *boulē* in which to conduct municipal business, a theater in which to replay Athenian drama, and a gymnasium in which to build and maintain the Attic shape. So powerful was the grip of Athens on the imagination of foreigners that they donated large public buildings such as the Stoa of Attalos (now rebuilt by another rich foreigner named Rockefeller) and the odeon of Herodes Atticus that the Athenians themselves could no longer afford. Law courts, civic councils, and theater festivals were useful institutions, but on another level they were also antiquarian rituals for the public display of liberal ideals. For private show, wealthy men of the *oikoumenē* built symposium rooms in which to entertain their friends in the traditional Greek manner. Around those symposium rooms and the sexual *euphrosynē* associated with them, poets built a world of love that belonged vicariously to anyone who could read the elegant elegiac couplets of the Hellenistic love epigram.

Figure 8.1. The rendering of the lovers' eyes, locked in a mutual gaze in this scene painted on a small red-figure jar by the Shuvalov Painter, illustrates the tendency to idealize sexual love beginning in the late fifth century B.C. (Staatliche Museum, Berlin, no. F2414)

The urban world of love was built in early-third-century Alexandria by Asclepiades of Samos, Callimachus of Cyrene, and a cohort of now unknown imitators anthologized for us by a latter-day master of this genre, the Syrian Meleager of Gadara, in his *Garland*. It is not so much an Alexandrian world as a region of the mind once vaguely identifiable with Athens. But unlike pastoral, which sometimes locates us in Sicily or Cos, and comedy, which typically names the scene of the action (often Athens), love epigram is placeless. Its little scenes place us only in a symposium room or in the street outside the house of the boy or woman sought by the lover. We may see the stars and the moon but never the city. The symposium room is a literary place, defined by already ancient drinking songs (*skolia*) and other lyrics of the Archaic period addressed to fellow revelers.[23] Its existence in the real world is confirmed by bits of comedy and mime,

Sexual Culture in Ancient Greece

Figure 8.2. Scene on a marriage bed from the Hellenistic period (ca. 130 B.C.). The emphasis on conjugal eros and the male lover's solicitude for his partner's feelings was a feature of New Comedy. (Musée du Louvre)

but the detachment of what happens in the world of love from the rest of life is almost complete. It is a sheltered world: the symposium room, like the grottoes and bowers featured in Hellenistic art and pottery, is a confined space, traditionally hung with ivy, vines, garlands, theatrical masks, and other paraphernalia of the arts. As such, it corresponds closely with the *locus amoenus* of pastoral, where an overhanging rock or tree, a grassy bank, and running water provide shelter from the noonday heat. The symposium, though, is a nocturnal world. The lover's world is also sheltered in epigram by the presence of friends. Instead of the persiflage of pastoral rustics, we get the encouragement of one lover to another to tell about the cause of one's distress:

Erotic Friendship

Drink, Asclepiades! Why these tears? What's the trouble? You're not the only one whom dreadful Cypris has plundered, nor has bitter Eros put on his bow and arrows for you alone.[24]

While the symposium is the characteristic locus of the love epigram, it is not the only one. Sometimes it is the bedroom, signaled by reference to a lamp; more often it is the *komos*, the outdoor revel and serenade where the emotional outbursts conventionally held in check at the symposium have freer rein. The lover departs the symposium and lurches through the streets to the house of his beloved, sometimes accompanied by friends and hired musicians from the symposium, sometimes alone. *Komos* epigrams often portray theatrical posturing:

I have drunk straight madness: quite drunk with words, I am armed with full frenzy for the road. I will go serenading; what do I care for thunder and lightning? If it strikes, I have love as an indestructible shield.[25]

Like the symposium, the *komos* was a real social institution of the demimonde, its objects the hetaeras and hired entertainers of the symposium. Its excesses, which included breaking down of doors, brawls, and other disorderly conduct, are chronicled in speeches written for the law courts and the plots of New Comedy,[26] but behavior in the love epigrams is never violent. As in pastoral, it is not the lover but the woman courted who is in control. It is easy to imagine that a hetaera who managed her career successfully would welcome frequent scenes outside her house as a form of unsolicited testimonial and would arrange real or imagined rivals to stimulate gift giving. But this aspect of the business is indicated only in comedy. Epigram concentrates on the woebegone lover, who is as helpless as Theocritus' Cyclops.

The *komos* of epigram concludes in lines spoken outside the woman's house door, the so-called *paraclausithyron* of the *exclusus amator*. The tone of this performance is wistful and maudlin, less noisy than the *komos*:

Sexual Culture in Ancient Greece

Night, I call you, no other, to witness how Nico's girl Pythias
outrages me, liar that she is. Summoned, not uninvited, I came.
May she some day stand at my door and complain to you that she
suffered the same.[27]

The convention was that the solitary lover would spend the night in
the beloved's doorway, hanging up his garlands and wetting the
threshold with his tears. How common these rituals were in the nightly
life of Hellenistic cities is anybody's guess, but they remained for
centuries a literary convention of erotic life outside epigram. When
Catullus' Attis mourns the loss of his past life as a much-courted beauty
of the Greek world, he remembers "my doorway was crowded, my
threshold warm, my house front wreathed with flowery garlands when
I left my room at sunrise" (C. 63.65–67).

The temptation to read social history out of these literary scenes
is held in check by the realization that love epigram represents an
urban world as artificial as the rustic world of pastoral. In some ways
it is an inverse image of reality as we would see it. Though early monodists such as Sappho and Ibycus are seconded by tragedians and
Hellenistic philosophers in describing eros as a violent disorder of the
mind, its fatality is mildly presented in epigram:

The cruel Philainion has wounded me, and if the wound is not
clear, still the pain reaches my extremities. I am gone, Loves,
destroyed; for in a reverie I stepped on a serpent. I know it, and I
have touched death.[28]

The world of love is crowded with metaphor. The pleasure seeker
becomes an innocent walker in a field, the woman on whom he is for
the moment fixated is a serpent, the pleasurable stimulation of love is
a painful death. The active *erastēs* becomes as passive as Apollonius'
Jason, while the passive *erōmenos* or *erōmene* is transformed into a kind
of predator, sometimes assuming the role of Eros himself:

Dorcion the lover of youths knows how like a tender boy to cast
the swift bolt of Cypris-of-the-marketplace as she flashes desire
from her eye—and hung over her shoulders with her sombrero,
her tunic revealed bare thigh.[29]

Dorcion, "little gazelle," knows what she likes and dresses up like a boy in a *chlamys* to get it. The boyish figure was a favorite; a piquant sexual ambiguity, punctuated by the sudden shift of tense in the final verb, emphasizes Dorcion's mastery. Reading between the lines, it is possible to read in Hellenistic love epigram a wish to find in the world of love a symbolic renunciation of the self-mastery men were taught to possess and a reversal of the sexual and class roles of the real world. The boys and women for whom the lovers pine are not social peers of the men who pine, nor do the loves blossom into relationships. The women and boys for whom we die in sport are only entertainers, and the conflicts most likely to provoke pain, rage, and jealousy are turned aside with a joke:

> White-cheeked Demo, someone has you next his skin. He's having fun, but my heart within me grieves. Yet if a Sabbath-keeper's love holds you, no great wonder. Even on frigid Sabbaths there is hot love![30]

The lover's world in Hellenistic epigram is not, then, so much different from Zeno's ideal republic, where wives are shared and no one is jealous for long. Critics who complain of the lack of *grande passion* in Hellenistic love epigram[31] are allowing their romantic assumptions about love poetry to interfere with their understanding of a preromantic genre. Grand passion was anathema to the Hellene of any period in the ancient world who hoped to stay in his right mind and keep his life under control. Hellenistic love epigram, like Hellenistic pastoral, is about pleasure. Part of that is literary and is provided by the craft and wit of the poetry; part is the refinement of sweetness from bittersweet love, which was achieved by confining its time, place, and object and by limiting the sexual involvements of lovers to this limited sphere, the world of love.

If it seems mean-spirited to wish that the effect of love on our spirit be not too strong, this wish came well recommended by authorities whom the Greeks of the third century trusted implicitly. *Aurea mediocritas* was especially desirable in the realm of love:

> Love must not touch the marrow of the soul.
> Our affections must be breakable chains that we
> can cast them off or tighten them.
> (Eur. *Hipp.* 253–257, tr. Grene)

Sexual Culture in Ancient Greece

Placed in the mouth of Phaedra's nurse, these words border on a platitude. They are, in fact, no more than the application to erotics of the
old Apollonian maxim "nothing in excess," which the nurse repeats a
few lines later in the same speech (265, μηδὲν ἄγαν).

Cynic poetry in the later third century put a coarse, wry spin on
this accepted wisdom. Cercidas, quoting or paraphrasing a passage
from Euripides similar to the one above (there must have been many),[32]
contrasts the harsh, ruinous Aphrodite with Aphrodite from the mar-
ketplace: "not a care in the world, whatever you want, whatever you
wish, no fear, no tumult. Lay her for an obol and think yourself the
son-in-law of Tyndarus [i.e., Helen's mate]."[33] Horace approved: "I
love the Venus that's accessible and easy to get" (Sat. 1.2.119, *para-
bilem amo Venerem facilemque*); he paraphrases a lost epigram of
Philodemus to the effect that such a "Venus" is better than a finicky
matron: "She's available for no great price and arrives promptly when
sent for. Straight and pleasant to look at, she is neat enough that she
wants to look no fairer or taller than nature made her. When she puts
her left side under my right, she's Ilia and Egeria," the erotic equiva-
lent of a first-class nymph. Moreover, he continues, there's no risk of
a nasty scene when the matron's husband shows up unexpectedly. The
theme goes back as far as Philemon, one of the most successful writers
of New Comedy, whom I quoted earlier as alleging that Solon provided Athens with public prostitutes. The fragment continues:

> They stand in nakedness, lest you be deceived; take a look at
> everything. Perhaps you are not feeling quite up to your form,
> something's bothering you. How could it? The door is open,
> price one obol. Jump right in! Not a bit of prudery, no nonsense,
> she doesn't snatch herself from under you. Go straight at it any
> way you like, any style you please. You go out: tell her to go
> hang, she's a stranger to you.[34]

In this way poetry and drama worked hand in hand with philosophy.
Sex had to be kept manageable, and the best sexual partner will be
someone you don't know. Philemon wrote in the same Cynic mode
as Philodemus and Cercidas.[35] But sometime in the fourth or third
century B.C., a different style of comedy grew up that, instead of
having its fun with gold-digging hetaeras and unscrupulous pleasure

seekers, indulged audiences with erotic plots involving young women of the citizen class.

The romantic brand of comedy is no less philosophic but plays to sentiments of *philanthropia*, a willingness to extend goodwill to the most unlikely human specimens and find redeeming features in the most unpromising encounters. It also juxtaposes contrasting models of behavior, often pairing rustic with urban households, authoritarian with liberal theories of discipline, submissive with entrepreneurial behavior by slaves. Though tolerant of human differences, romantic New Comedy constantly invites the audience to make ethical judgments, which it encourages with frequent moralizing. And like Cynic New Comedy, the romantic type is interested in human value and the bonds that connect people to each other. Moral dilemmas and surprises that upset our moral expectations are standard features of this genre.

A striking difference is the way romantic comedy treats sexual liaisons. Rather than devalue sexual bonds with women, treating them as casual at best, romantic comedy puts a premium on liaisons that lead to a permanent bond (marriage) between social peers. Moreover, it values love marriages over the arranged marriage that had been the historic norm in Greece between propertied families. Because the only approved form of sexual pleasure outside marriage was with women of lower rank—slaves and prostitutes—and because in Classical Athens the only legitimate marriage for a citizen was with another full citizen, plots needed to be contrived so that a young man's girlfriend turns out not to be a slave or "working girl" but the long-lost daughter of a citizen and thus a marriageable peer. By this means, the erotic bond is upgraded into a conjugal partnership. The slave who comes of citizen stock (or better) was a common feature of a society that had for centuries enslaved women and children taken in war. It was also a literary formula: Odysseus' most valued slaves in Ithaca, the swineherd Eumaeus and the old nurse Eurycleia, are from good families. We are given the names of Eurycleia's father and grandfather and are to presume that she was stolen by pirates as was Eumaeus' nursemaid, the daughter of a wealthy Sidonian. Eumaeus, the son of a king who is also able to name his father and grandfather, was also stolen. A common plot of New Comedy involves the discovery that the flute girl or the like with whom a young citizen has fallen in love is the victim of piracy or shipwreck, and what began as an irregular liaison can now be formalized as a marriage.

Sexual Culture in Ancient Greece

Sometimes the romantic young man defeats the system of loveless arranged marriages by rape. No plot is too bizarre for comedy, and rape was a common feature of a society that had small official regard for the autonomy of women. Nubile girls were closely guarded by parents who wished to marry them off advantageously, as virgins, to a man of good family. It was also assumed that as soon as a girl reached physical maturity she would not resist any sexual opportunity, and a man who takes furtive advantage of her condition is guilty of a form of theft, as he has deprived her father of a bargaining chip and left him with a liability. He has committed rape, even if the woman was a willing partner. Thus, Paris' "rape" of Helen was not the forcible abduction of an unwilling woman. Athenian law, in fact, treated seduction as a more serious offense than violent sexual assault.

Not only was traditional Greek society one that was able to live with rape, it had included rape in the symbolism of marriage. The *hieros gamos* of Zeus and Hera includes as a gesture of marriage Zeus' grasp of Hera's wrist in his right hand.[36] The Roman legend of the rape of the Sabines indicates that the association was known in Italy, and early Greek marriage rituals that enacted forcible abductions of the bride point to a tradition of some antiquity. The modern custom of carrying the bride across the threshold of her new home is a survival of marriage by abduction. In literature there are several variations of the theme. In virtually every case, the unwilling bride becomes the devoted marriage partner. Briseis in the *Iliad* hopes to become the wife of her captor, Achilles; Sophocles' Tecmessa, the captive bride of Ajax, is his devoted spouse in the *Ajax*; Deianira, who in her youth had (like Aeschylus' Danaids) "an agonizing fear of marriage" and prayed for death rather than marriage to her suitor, is in *The Women of Trachis* a similarly devoted spouse and uses what she believes is a love charm to keep the love of Heracles. Catullus' wedding hymns allude to the violent removal of a bride from her mother as if it were a part of the wedding ritual itself; but, he says, all will be well. One of the normative functions of myth was to show how unwilling brides become willing wives.

Hellenistic comedy offered an alternative myth that dispensed with the bride's unwillingness and made a simple plot device of her seizure. The hand of the girl next door is sometimes won in these plays as the result of rape at a nocturnal religious festival. This bizarre formula appears in some half dozen comic plots, and there are four other plays that are commonly interpreted as including incidents of rape. Rather than acts of violent hostility as we understand rape, these sexual assaults are lightly treated as misdemeanors committed under the influence of youth, darkness, wine, and even love. The perpetrators are not alienated felons but young men of good family whose clear intention, before or after the act, is as a rule to marry their victims.[37] The writers of New Comedy were not indifferent to the ethical questions raised by these assaults, but they were primarily interested in the romantic plots made possible by such episodes, and they tended to cloud the circumstances so as to diminish the sense of a terrible wrong committed. Though Menander's Greek, in the few cases where he chooses to be unambiguous, acknowledges the gravity of rape with words such as ὕβρις (outrage), βιασμός (force), and ἀδικεῖν (treat unjustly), we are often hard pressed for the kind of verbal evidence that would convince a jury that a crime had been committed. Only in the *Epitrepontes*, for example, do we hear anything of the victim's distress, and there is nowhere a word about other physical abuse of the victim. As a result, though we are ready to condemn the violence implied in rape, the playwrights often avoid clear indications that such violence has taken place. Intolerable as such waffling is to our sensibility, Hellenistic audiences were able to see acts of sexual force as the lesser of two evils when the greater evil was a seduction, which would have prejudiced audiences against the girl and spoiled the match.

These willful male offenses are useful plot devices because they produce a pregnant girl or a young mother who is innocent of wrongdoing, whose father is confronted with a fait accompli and must accept a marriage that he formerly opposed. Several of the sexual wrongdoings occur at nocturnal religious festivities. There are about six such incidents in plays that can be adequately documented, either plays by Menander or adaptations by Plautus. As with the other wrongful liaisons, the result is a baby, confusions of identity, recognitions (for example, by a ring snatched from the woman's attacker), and eventual marriage. There is no known precedent for such plot devices, though Euripides' *Ion* and *Auge* are sometimes cited as if they had set an example. To us, and perhaps to the audiences of New Comedy, there is something suggestively lurid about a nocturnal religious orgy with its provocative hints of unfettered sexual opportunities under cover of

Sexual Culture in Ancient Greece

darkness. But what would a nice girl be doing in a place like that? There is good evidence that nocturnal religious festivals did actually occur in Classical and Hellenistic Greece, though they were not necessarily orgies of promiscuous sex. They were celebrated chiefly by women, and the official absence of men, who had the most at stake in the supervision of women, meant that such occasions could be a rare (if chancy) sexual opportunity for an ardent youth. These "all-nighters" (παννυχίδες) honored any of several divinities: Dionysus, Demeter, Artemis, or Adonis. The Adonia, a favorite of hetaeras, was conducted on rooftops in the hottest nights of summer and was marked by a degree of sexual libertinism. Fragments from Alciphron and Diphilus suggest that women who were not hetaeras joined in Adonis parties— as Plangon does in Menander's *Samia*—and that they invited their lovers. Religious festivals were one occasion when the supervision of women was somewhat relaxed, and if an amorous encounter took place custom would assign the blame to the male perpetrator whether or not he had a willing partner. Like the sexual exploitation of a child under modern law, the offense was seen as statutory rape: the male was the offender, the female the victim without regard to the question of consent because she was not legally competent; technically, her character was left uncompromised. That—like the elopement of Helen with Paris—was "rape" in the ancient sense of the word (a trespass against the woman's *kyrios*, or proprietor), if not in ours. Like many unsanctioned erotic liaisons, ancient and modern, the offense was forgiven if the young man married the girl involved and the young man's passion that caused the trouble in the first place was requited by matrimony.[38]

If romantic comedy used bizarre plots to bring together lovers of equal social rank, it was in part because literature and social custom provided no mechanism for the voluntary selection of a spouse. All of the rituals of modern life that provide young people with the opportunity to choose a partner for an evening's entertainment or life partnership—cotillions, balls, proms, dating, casual social mixing, coeducation—were absent from ancient life because women were not allowed to participate in selection. Arranged marriages made little provision for the wishes of the bride, and if a process of enslavement and liberation or hanky-panky at a nocturnal festival provided even a slightly more elective alternative, audiences would see this as a happy ending.

The tumultuous and traumatic process through which the future bride must pass to win a loving husband was rough on her; but in comedy, all's well that ends well, and we may infer that audiences who had been subjected to old-fashioned arranged marriages appreciated the difference in the outcome. Though love marriages may in the end be no happier than arranged ones, they have always been the popular favorite.

Whatever its value as literature, New Comedy is a valuable index of shifting ethical and social values in the Hellenistic world. Slavery is another recurrent topic: Plautus' *Twin Menaechmi*, a Roman adaptation of an unknown Greek original, contrasts the willing slavery of Peniculus to pleasure (a common Cynic/Stoic theme) with the unwilling slavery of Messenio to Menaechmus of Syracuse. The unwilling but alert and enterprising Messenio is rewarded by manumission, part of the happy and morally edifying ending of the play. Terence's *Adelphoi*, an adaptation of Menander's second *Adelphoi*, sets the liberal authority of the urban elite against the authoritarian rule of the traditional rustic, generally to the disadvantage of the latter: the young brother Aeschines is more capable of benefiting others than his sibling, the helpless rube Ctesipho, who has learned only fear and obedience. These dramatizations of humane values are the means by which the new ideas of the philosophic schools were delivered to the general population. It is not far from the peripatetic flavor of Micio's lecture on enlightened moral upbringing to Cicero's Stoic declaration of the political power of *caritas*.

> MICIO [on Aeschinus, his adopted son]: He's my pride and joy—the only thing in life I really care about. And I do everything I can, too, to make him feel the same way about me. I give and forgive; I don't feel that I have to exert my full authority over him. . . . I've taught my son to tell me everything. . . . I think it's better to discipline children by developing their sense of decency and their gentlemanly instincts, than by making them fear authority. . . . The man whose devotion you've won by kindness acts out of conviction. He's anxious to give as much as he's received, and he's always the same, whether or not you're there. (Ter. *Ad.* 49–74, tr. Copley)

Sexual Culture in Ancient Greece

Of all the motives, none is better adapted to secure influence and hold it fast than love; nothing is more foreign to that end than fear. . . . Fear is but a poor safeguard of lasting power; while affection, on the other hand, may be trusted to keep it safe forever. Let us, then, embrace this policy, which appeals to every heart and is the strongest support not only of security but also of influence and power— namely, to banish fear and cleave to love. And thus we shall more easily secure success both in private and in public life. (Cic. *Off.* 2.23–24, tr. Miller)

These views on the power of *caritas* or *philia* may be contrasted with the views of fifth-century Athenian statesmen on the way to wield power:

Your empire is now like a tyranny. . . . All who have taken it upon themselves to rule over others have incurred hatred and unpopularity for a time; but if one has a great aim to pursue, this burden of envy must be accepted, and it is wise to accept it.(Pericles, Thuc. 2.63–64, tr. Warner)

When you give way to your own feelings of compassion you are being guilty of a kind of weakness which is dangerous to you and which will not make your allies love you any more. What you do not realize is that your empire is a tyranny exercised over subjects who do not like it and who are always plotting against you; you will not make them obey you by injuring your own interests in order to do them a favor; your leadership depends on superior strength and not on any goodwill of theirs. (Cleon, Thuc. 3.37, tr. Warner)

If we were on friendly terms with you, our subjects would regard that as a sign of weakness in us, whereas your hatred is evidence of our power. (Athenian delegates to the Melians, Thuc. 5.95, tr. Warner)

In what some Victorians condemned as a "loss of nerve," late Classical and Hellenistic thinkers substituted gentler virtues for the violent machismo of imperial Athens, using the pragmatic argument that goodwill is a more effective means of control than fear. Such is Micio's domestic argument in the *Adelphoi* and Cicero's political argument in *De Officiis*, but the appeal went beyond self-interest and became an end in itself as the glue that bonds people to one another. *Philanthropia* displaced jealous, competitive *aretē* and ambitious *philotimia* as the cardinal virtue, and personal relations were given a higher value. The sundering and restoration of personal bonds is a central feature in the plots of New Comedy. Another is personal interdependence. In Menander's *Dyskolos*, the misanthrope Cnemon's speech of recognition where he admits his *hamartia* (error), focuses on this.

> I think I've made just one mistake. That was
> to feel that I alone was self-sufficient and
> would need no one. Now that I see how death can be
> so swift and sudden, I know that I was wrong in this.
> A man needs someone standing by to help him out.
> I hadn't admitted that before, because I thought
> that every man around cared only for his own
> profit. By God, I thought there wasn't one of them
> who was concerned for other men. That was what blinded me.
>
> (713–722, tr. Moulton)

No man is an island. As we saw earlier in this chapter, the closely guarded boundaries of the self that Greek individualism required were relaxed in the declarations of Aristotle and Zeno that a friend is "another self." This realization worked its way into love epigram's language about the soul in love, where Asclepiades says that his soul is ebbing away: "That which is left of my soul, whatever it may be, Loves, that at least, by the gods, let me have in peace" (G-P 17 = 12.166); Callimachus took up the conceit with the playful declaration in G-P 4 = 12.73 that half his soul has gone off to be with some boy; Meleager goes farther in an appositive phrase to say that half his soul *is* his beloved Andragathus (G-P 81 = 12.52), using the Callimachean tag Ἡμισύ μευ ψυχῆς. This erotic conceit reverts to the language of friendship when Horace translates the Callimachean tag to describe his friend Virgil: *animae dimidium meae* (*Odes* 1.3.8). Like the earlier

Sexual Culture in Ancient Greece

writers of New Comedy, Horace blurred the distinction between erotic and companionate love.

In choosing to integrate eros with other forms of love such as *philia*, the comedians were no doubt influenced by the earlier form of erotic idealism that was thought to govern relations between a mature *erastēs* and a youthful *erōmenos* of the same sex. In archaic *Knabenliebe* such as that described in Plato's *Symposium*, the ideal love relation was not entirely symmetrical, but it joined persons of the same social class. It presumed a mutual wish to avoid disgrace in the other's eyes (*aidōs*, L. *pudor*) and evoked a solicitude for the honor and welfare of the less equal younger partner. Romantic love in New Comedy is built on a similar combination of eros and *philia*, which borders on an oxymoron because sexual passion was thought too irrational to allow room for disinterested considerations of goodwill. Among the Archaic warrior class, it was a quixotic virtue. Plutarch uses the phrase "erotic *philia*" for the bond that united the Sacred Band of Thebes,[39] but that was between men. Love in New Comedy differed from its antecedent in crossing the gender barrier and contemplating a lifelong bond with the expectation of a new family, made explicit more than once in Menander with the formula of betrothal "for the begetting of legitimate children."[40] A tattered scrap of papyrus found in Egypt preserves a dialogue from a comedy in which a young man tells a slave woman how he fell in love with his wife by a marriage arranged by his father—another bizarre comic plot, perhaps inspired by the account in Herodotus 1.8 of how Candaules fell in love with his own wife. The young man in this fragment is like Charisius in Menander's *Arbitrants*, who is in love with his wife of three months but is mad with grief when she has a baby that he thinks is another's (his error: it turns out he had raped her at a festival). The papyrus fragment, in which the young man tells how his heart was won by his wife's affectionate nature and good character, is unique in Greek literature in using *eros*, *philia*, and *agapē* at short intervals to describe the love between a man and a woman who are married to each other.[41] Romantic New Comedy, then, not only features the love-at-first-sight plots that culminate like the *Dyskolos* in a wedding but also presents lovers who are already married and then have a falling-out—always subject to the understanding that the hearts turn out to have been sundered by no greater evil than impulsive action, error, and misapprehension. Love is idealized in New Comedy not as

Erotic Friendship

a recreational activity but as a good to be sought for its own sake, most perfect when it combines the passion of sex with the union of true minds: a platitude to us but a fresh idea in the long history of Greek sexual culture.

It was not a complete novelty. As early as the *Odyssey*, we hear Odysseus conclude his first speech to Nausicaa,

> nothing is better than this, more steadfast
> than when two people, a man and his wife, keep a harmonious
> household; a thing that brings much distress to the people who hate them
> and pleasure to their well-wishers, and for them the best reputation.[42]

From one point of view, of course, the entire *Odyssey* is a conjugal romance. But it was not until the later fifth century that the matrimonial ideal began to have a popular appeal. So one would judge, at least, from fragments of lost plays by Euripides[43] as well as the *Helen* (412 B.C.), where the heroine proves not to have been unfaithful and is reunited with her spouse: the error anticipates New Comedy plots in which suspicions of infidelity turn out to be unfounded. Conjugal satisfaction was a subject for comedy as well as romance.

Aristophanes' *Lysistrata* (411 B.C.) is so full of sexual innuendo that readers may not at first realize that it is not the usual sexual license of Old Comedy. The humor in this play is all about conjugal sex. Both Euripides' *Helen* and Aristophanes' *Lysistrata* were sandwiched between the destruction of Athens' forces at Syracuse in 413 and the bloody oligarchic coup of 411. There can be little doubt that Aristophanes, at least, was playing to a disgust with military adventurism. Both plays hold up domestic happiness as the business to which people can best attend. Writing a generation later, Xenophon includes conjugal love among his types of eros: Niceratus, a guest at a Socratic symposium, is in love with his wife, and his love is reciprocated. In the *Hiero*, Xenophon argues against adultery on the grounds that it undermines the *philia* between married partners.[44] Ischomachus' young wife in the *Oeconomicus* is a better sexual partner than a slave woman would be whose services are compulsory: this is the work in which Xenophon described women as the peers of men in the capacity for memory, attentiveness, and self-control and in which marriage is described as a partnership in which one partner's deficiencies are made up by the

Sexual Culture in Ancient Greece

other's strengths.[45] Though a social and political conservative, Xenophon based his ideal of conjugal bonding on an opinion he ascribes to Socrates regarding the near-equality of the sexes. Aristotle too, though no upholder of sexual parity, said things about human nature that reflect the higher personal status of marriage in the fourth century. We have seen (chap. 7, n. 23) that he attributed to the females of every species a greater complexity and ability to intrigue; this may be a grudging tribute, but in the *Nicomachean Ethics* he talks about the *philia* between husband and wife in a way that not only recalls Xenophon's description of marriage but also adds to our appreciation of New Comedy as a dramatization of peripatetic ideas.

> The friendship between husband and wife appears to be a natural instinct; since man is by nature a pairing creature even more than he is a political creature, inasmuch as the family is an earlier and more fundamental institution than the state, and the procreation of offspring a more general characteristic of the animal creation. So whereas with the other animals the association of the sexes aims only at continuing the species, human beings cohabit not only for the sake of begetting children but also to provide the needs of life; for with human beings division of labor begins at the outset, and man and woman have different functions; thus they supply each other's wants, putting their special capacities into the common stock. Hence the friendship of man and wife seems to be one of utility and pleasure combined. But it may also be based on virtue, if the partners be of high moral character; for either sex has its special virtue, and this may be the ground of attraction.[46]

Aristotle's characterization of man as a pairing animal more than a political one is symptomatic of a refocusing of Greek values at the end of the Classical period, when the political life of independent city-states was checked by the power of larger kingdoms and personal life became the center of attention. The statement of Aristophanes in Plato's *Symposium* that "each of us is but the token of a human being, sliced like a flatfish, two from one, each ever seeking its matching half" (191d3–5), provided a poetic antecedent for Aristotle's pairing creature.

Erotic Friendship

As appraisals of human nature assigned higher value to marriage unions that combined eros and friendship, the two modes of attachment became less distinguishable from each other. In the *Nicomachean Ethics*, Aristotle says that love wishes to be the superlative degree of friendship;[47] it may be no coincidence that New Comedy plots exploit the theme of confusion between the two. In Menander's *Misoumenos*, the soldier Thrasonides sees his captive concubine, Krateia, embracing an older man whom he takes to be a lover. The supposed rival is in fact the woman's father, from whom she had been separated at the time of her captivity.[48] Glycera's sisterly embrace of Moschion in the *Perikeiromene* is mistaken by her lover, Polemon, as proof of her sexual infidelity. Such infidelity by a woman, in fact, almost never occurs in the plots of New Comedy, as sexual bonds are so implicated with personal loyalty as to preclude a woman's philandering. This idealization runs counter to another traditional belief, that women are morally and physically incapable of sexual continence.

It would be rash to conclude that either philosophy or popular comedy transformed the sexual culture of the Greek world, or even improved it. Plautus stated his own skepticism about the influence of moralizing comedies near the end of his *Rudens* when the fisherman Gripus says,

> Before now I've watched people in comedies mouthing wise
> sayings . . . and winning applause for preaching these upright
> morals to the audience; but when everyone scattered homewards,
> not a single one acted as the actors had urged.[49]

No one will doubt, however, that the combined testimony of philosophers and playwrights reflects a great transformation of cultural values relating to sexual bonding, marriage, and the role of women as peers to their spouses. New Comedy was the only Greek literary genre to turn against the philosophic disapproval of erotic entanglement while at the same time illustrating the humane ideals of erotic friendship. If the Cynic, Stoic, or Epicurean prude taught that the wise man does not fall in love, theater audiences voted for a folly that would outlast such philosophy.

It was comedy rather than philosophy that set the tone for Latin love lyric. From Catullus to Ovid, male lovers surrendered their autonomy willy-nilly to the women they loved. Even Horace, the most self-contained of the Latin lyricists, wrote of one Lyce "who stole me away from myself," *quae me surpuerat mihi* (*Odes* 4.13.20)—a statement not necessarily so autobiographical as symbolic of a way of loving that Catullus had made popular. Following the lead of Meleager, Latin poets subjectified love and did not attempt to represent themselves as lovers in control. They are not, for example, protected by wit or sympotic rules of engagement as they are in Hellenistic love epigram;[50] nor did they represent this loss of control as an altogether regrettable fall from grace. Catullus wants to marry his Lesbia, and he is devastated by her rejection of him. In Latin elegy, the lover abases himself to his *domina* in a way that Aristotle would have condemned as slavish and effeminate. Here we have the roots of medieval courtly love. Ovid's *Metamorphoses* includes a great variety of love stories: incestuous, adulterous, tragic, homoerotic. Among them he places mutually responsive passions that represent something like a conjugal ideal: Thisbe's devotion to Pyramus, the love of Cephalus for Procris, Alcyone's for Ceyx, even the pious domestic partnership of Baucis and Philemon. The latter are in strong contrast to pathological eros that isolates rather than joins. Ovid's idealized love stories represent what Brooks Otis has called "the ethical apex of Ovid's amatory scale," nowhere exactly anticipated in Classical, Hellenistic, or Roman literature.[51]

Between the first and the third century A.D., in a period of flamboyantly rhetorical writing called the Second Sophistic, five prose romances by Greek authors created a new kind of love story. In each of them, a young man and woman fall in love, are then separated by a series of misadventures, and are united in the end to live happily together forever after. David Konstan has recently shown that the protagonists in Greek love romance, invariably a young boy and a young girl of free status, are each equally enamored of the other and are not discriminated into an active and a passive partner in love.[52] Only rarely is the male lover allowed to play the rescuer or exercise a power that the other does not have. Erotic relationships in the Greek novel thus have a formal symmetry that is constitutive of the genre; that distinguishes it from both earlier and modern forms of love literature. Modern pulp romance, for example, is "conventionally based upon an unequal relationship, in which a male in a position of independence and authority attempts to subvert the virtue of a younger woman who has fallen under his sway" but is in the end converted to "a nobler love, with marriage as its aim."[53] In the Greek romance, a mutual infatuation ripens into the Hellenistic ideal of erotic *philia*. The parental opposition that was important in New Comedy is only vestigial; the lovers, though rooted in prominent families and famous cities, are free agents in a transnational *oikoumenē* ruled by a Roman Empire at the height of its power. Their independence of patriarchal and civic interests contributes to a focus in this literature on autonomous personal fidelity.

Much of this is peculiar to the age in which the writers of erotic romance lived. While the fantasies of Greek romance are no more representative of ordinary life under the Empire than contemporary Harlequin romances are of the way we live, they reflect real erotic ideals that began to appear in the late fifth century B.C. and matured in the Hellenistic world. Though Longus' *Daphnis and Chloe* owes something to Theocritean pastoral, the romances are chiefly indebted to New Comedy. And New Comedy, for all its reliance on peripatetic views of human nature, went beyond any philosopher we know about in drawing out its erotic ideal. The surviving plays of New Comedy and the five Greek romances are crafted more as popular entertainment than as high literature, but they are no less valuable for what they reveal. The erotic ideals they work with are, in their cultural milieu, as instinctual as the linguistic shifts that created Koine Greek. Developing more or less independently from any intellectual leadership we know of, romantic love actually defied the consensus of Stoic, Cynic, and Epicurean recommendations against erotic engagement. As if in response to a popular intuition, comedy valorized heterosexual love with an emphasis on marriage. Though it lacked the sexual symmetry perfected in the Greek romance, its lovers are, as a rule, members of the same class; its plots have an affinity for other types of symmetry, particularly when two ways of life are contrasted (e.g., liberal vs. authoritarian in the *Adelphoi*), or two forms of personal attachment (e.g., sexual vs. fraternal in the *Menaechmi*). One of the high points of Classical humanism seems thus to have been attained not by formal philosophy but by popular literature, in which the supreme sexual attainment is based on the parity of sexes and the equality of lovers.

Hand in hand with the pairing of equals in heterosexual love went the idealization of marriage that began in the age of Euripides and was further popularized in New Comedy.[54] Writing near the beginning of the second century A.D., Plutarch never tired of praising conjugal virtues. Three books of his, *Moralia, On the Virtues of Women, Dialogue on Love,* and *Marital Precepts,* promote the ideals that emerged during the Hellenistic age. His *Life of Pericles* portrays the love of Pericles and Aspasia, which he calls an "erotic affection," as illustrating the emancipated relation of equals.[55] Though his views may strike the reader today as little more than platitudes, Plutarch advocated a kind of symmetry in the erotic relation of men and women that is not often attained in any era. His doctrine of love was a combination of Hellenistic cultural syncretism in which nations merge their identities, and of Hellenistic science; in love, he said, individual identity is more liquid than solid:

> Just as with the mixing of two liquids, love seems at first to cause some effervescence and agitation, but as time goes on it settles down and is reduced and produces the best sort of stability. For this truly is what is called "integral amalgamation," that of a married couple who love each other; but the union of those who merely live together is like the contacts and interlacing of Epicurus' atoms, which collide and rebound, but never achieve the unity that Eros creates when he takes in hand a partnership in marriage.[56]

The metaphor, perhaps suggested to him by Antipater of Tarsus' treatise *On Marriage* (2d c. B.C.), recurs in *Marital Precepts* 34: "As the mixing of liquids, according to scientists, extends throughout their entire content, so also in the case of married people there ought to be a mutual amalgamation of their bodies, property, friends, and relations."[57]

That the ideals of Plutarch and the Greek romances were something more than literary postures is suggested by this inscription by one Praetextatus honoring his wife, Paulina, in the fourth century A.D.:

> To you I could entrust the fast-closed depths of my own mind . . .
> And so as friends we have been joined in trust,
> By long acquaintance, by shared initiations of the gods,
> All in one bond of faith, one single heart, united in one mind.[58]

CHAPTER NINE

Anerotic Religion

GREEK THEMES IN EARLY CHRISTIANITY[1]

> There are eunuchs who have been so from birth, and
> there are eunuchs who have been made eunuchs by men,
> and there are eunuchs who have made themselves
> eunuchs for the sake of the kingdom of heaven.
> CHRIST'S TEACHING, AS QUOTED IN MATTHEW 19:12

> Love of women is the root of all evils and the beginning
> of perdition; I tell you, it is the mania for sisters of the
> spirit, a root that sprouts perdition and blossoms with
> madness.
>
> BASIL OF CAESAREA, 4TH C. A.D.

My chronological survey of Greek sexual culture ends as it began, with a consideration of the sexual content of religion as an index of cultural values. As its title implies, this chapter concentrates on the intellectual currents that shaped early Christian doctrine, leaving aside whatever socioeconomic factors may have had a role. Largely because it has left a written record, late antiquity provides more on which to rest a case than prehistory does. This record declares a new religion's enmity to sex more passionately and insistently than any of the antierotic views noted in earlier Greek history. The fervor of early Christian pronouncements reflects a religion that had no tolerance for competing preoccupations of a sexual nature. Hence the title of this chapter. Though early Christianity was not monolithic, the marked tendency of its ideologues was to demand the total extirpation of eros from the life of the spirit.

This demand had something to do with the Hebraic traits noted in chapter 2 that Christian culture inherited, and it was influenced by a love of the absolute that is more Asian than Attic. But it was also the product of antierotic feelings in the Greek world that took hold during the Classical period.² Christianity put down its first strong roots in the Greek cities of Asia Minor and at its earliest stages was a sect appealing to Hellenized Jews. The language of its sacred testament was Greek. It was also to a great degree defined by its opposition to prevailing middle-class Greek mores, but it appealed to Greek ideas to overthrow them. The Greek asceticism with which Christians made common cause was deeply averse to a culture that was schooled in the love of beauty and that was increasingly eager, from the later fifth century onward, to enjoy private pleasures.

The last chapter showed how one thread of popular culture during these years grew into the romantic ideal of erotic friendship in New Comedy and finally into the symmetrical love affairs of Greek romance. This chapter takes note of another sexual thread: the various forms of erotica that appeared in the late fifth century and remained popular for centuries afterward. Some of this is obscure because it was later thought indecent; even some contemporary reaction was hostile. But these preoccupations, however inglorious, are essential to an understanding of the ancient world.

The growing importance of sexual culture in the fourth century went hand in hand with the privatization of Greek life, especially in Athens. Beginning with Socrates, ethics had become the most important branch of philosophy, and though Socrates died as a result of political entanglements on the part of his most notorious students, he himself counseled withdrawal from public life—as did his disciples and the philosophic sects they engendered. The last extant plays of Sophocles, the *Philoctetes* and *Oedipus at Colonus*, feature heroes who determinedly refuse to play a public role or accept public obligations. Aristophanes' comedies play off private interest against public discontent, becoming in the end more bourgeois than political. Even the art world responded to the decline of political culture, as patronage shifted in the fourth century from public and religious art to objects for private enjoyment. As a result, domestic and erotic subjects received an attention they had not had since the erotic art of the sixth-century red-figure vases. There were, for example, the erotic miniatures of Parrhasius in the late fifth century that were still famous in the age of Augustus.³ Testimony to the currency of such pictures ca. 428 B.C. is in Euripides, where Hippolytus says the only thing he knows about sex is what he has heard about or seen in pictures.[4] In the fourth century, we have word of erotic paintings by the Sicyonian painter Pausias and the sexually explicit illustrations, based perhaps on Pausias' originals, done on mirrors in Corinth. All but a few of the Corinthian bronzes are lost (see fig. 9.2). Like Japanese painters of the Edo period, some Greek painters seem to have shared the interest of writers in the "floating world," or demimonde: besides Parrhasius, Athenaeus mentions Pausias, Aristides of Thebes, and Nicophanes as "pornographers" or perhaps more accurately depicters of hetaeras and their world, as it would be rash to tar them as panderers with no more than etymological evidence.[5] One of their literary counterparts, named in the same passage, was Amasis of Elis. We learn elsewhere of a woman named Philaenis who wrote a treatise on sexual positions that circulated widely; this was translated into pictures on Pergamene vases, and centuries later it influenced Ovid's Latin Kamasutra, the *Art of Love*.[6] Philaenis' treatise is long lost; not so the love duet Aristophanes wrote for the young pair whose assignation is interrupted in the *Congresswomen*, which C. M. Bowra has argued is a parody of pop lyrics ca. 392 B.C.

> The one way to love
> lies this way, my love,
> so come this way to love,
> > my dear,
> With me, up above
> in bed, my love,
> you'll love away the night
> > right here.
> I throb with lust when I see the twist
> and the curl of your well-groomed hair.
> The oddest passion pervades my person;
> my maidenhood's abraded by its wear and tear—
> > So give way to love,
> > and don't wait to love,
> > relieve the weight of love
> > > up here.[7]

Sexual Culture in Ancient Greece

A less good-naturedly hostile witness is Thucydides, whose account of social change in Athens during the Peloponnesian War implicates the plague that devastated the city in 430 B.C. Besides the loss of life, says Thucydides, the plague brought with it a loss of moral fiber and a surrender to the pleasures of the moment.

> Athens owed to the plague the beginnings of an unprece-
> dented state of lawlessness [*anomia*]. . . . People now began
> openly to venture on acts of self-indulgence [*hēdonē*] which
> before then they used to keep dark. Thus they resolved to
> spend their money quickly and to spend it on pleasure [*to
> terpnon*], since money and life alike seemed equally ephem-
> eral. . . . It was generally agreed that what was both honor-
> able and valuable was the pleasure of the moment and every-
> thing that might conceivably contribute to that pleasure.[8]

Although it is plausible that a plague, like civil war or a tropical storm, might be accompanied by changes in social behavior, Thucydides generalizes the side effect of this episode into what he describes as a long-term social change. This is less plausible: passing crises have been known, for example, to trigger increased sexual activity, but they do not by themselves cause permanent changes in social mores.[9] By a poetic circularity of reasoning, the plague becomes in Thucydides a cogent metaphor of the anomie that he attributes to it. For the more prosaic historian, the plausible inference must be that the spirit of self-sacrifice and delayed gratification became less strong as the fifth century grew old and that all of this was accelerated by the stresses of plague and war.

One corollary of changing values in the late fifth century was a philosophic thesis advanced by Socrates' disciple Aristippus of Cyrene and his followers. The Cyrenaic school advocated freedom from the responsibilities of power and a life that is as easy and pleasant as possible. Cyrenaic hedonism differed from Epicureanism in holding that the supreme pleasures are physical rather than mental. But while popular culture had this philosophic support, much of the intellectual world was, as the previous chapter has showed, suspicious of things erotic and regarded most pleasure as problematic. The Cyrenaics were thus opposed by Antisthenes, Diogenes, and the Cynics, whose ragged cloak, staff, and beggar's pouch proclaimed their asceticism and cult of poverty. The philosophic controversy about pleasure was well known to Aristotle, who reports much difference of opinion about it.[10] Christian asceticism was to grow in large part out of this Greek opposition to *hēdonē*, set down more than four centuries before Christ and renewed by Neoplatonism. Plato, as we have seen, had sided with the ascetics; his way of doing so in the *Phaedo* ultimately had a deep effect on Christianity. He puts his words in the mouth of an otherworldly Socrates at the scene of his death.

> I have a firm hope that there is something in store for those who have died, and, as we have been told for many years, something much better for the good than for the wicked. . . . Ordinary people seem not to realize that those who really apply themselves in the right way to philosophy are directly and of their own accord preparing themselves for dying and death.[11]

This "training for death" is a kind of *askēsis*, or ascetic discipline. Plato then constructs a justification, probably influenced by Orphic doctrine, for separating the body from the soul, and for seeing them as each other's enemies.

> So it is clear first of all in the case of physical pleasures that the philosopher frees his soul from association with the body, so far as is possible. . . . In despising his body and avoiding it, and endeavoring to become independent, the philosopher's soul is ahead of all the rest. . . . The body fills us with loves and desires and fears and all sorts of fancies and a great deal of nonsense; . . . if we do not obtain any leisure from the body's claims and turn to some line of inquiry, the body intrudes once more into our investigations, interrupting, disturbing, distracting, and preventing us from getting a glimpse of the truth. . . . So long as we are alive, we shall continue closest to knowledge if we avoid as much as we can all contact and association with the body, except when they are absolutely necessary, and instead of

Sexual Culture in Ancient Greece

allowing ourselves to become infected with its nature, purify ourselves from it until God himself gives us deliverance. . . . Purification . . . consists in separating the soul as much as possible from the body.[12]

Plato's separation of the soul from the body, falling on ready ears, was a great philosophic watershed for European thought. The harmonious Classical partnership of mind and body gave way to their alienation from each other, a kind of warfare within each person in which the mortal body was constantly subverting the immortal soul. One of the most devastating consequences of this metaphysical construct was to be the destruction of physical and sexual culture, which was a key target of Christian zealotry. With them went the aesthetic values of the ancient world. The mutual hostility of man's spiritual and carnal nature is a persistent theme in the tirades of Saint Paul.

> I delight in the law of God in my inmost self; but I see in my members another law at war with the law of my mind and making me captive to the law of sin which dwells in my members. Wretch that I am! Who will deliver me from this body of death? . . . I of myself serve the law of God with my mind, but with my flesh I serve the law of sin. (Rom. 7:22–25)

> The desires of the flesh are against the Spirit, and the desires of the Spirit are against the flesh; for these are opposed to each other, to prevent you from doing what you would. (Gal. 5:17)

Plato is unlikely to have gotten this notion, which W. K. C. Guthrie ventures to call "essentially un-Socratic," from his teacher.[13] He himself refers to the esoteric doctrines of the Pythagoreans[14] near the beginning of the passage from the *Phaedo* quoted above; his contempt for life and the body is rooted in ideas that appeared sometime in the Archaic period. They are nowhere in Homer, who regarded the *psychē* as no more than a pathetic shadow that goes to Hades after the death of the body. The "self" (*autos*), as the *Iliad* has it, is the physical entity which is left behind, either to be honorably buried or for the dogs and birds to pick apart. But by the time of Pindar in the fifth century B.C., the soul has become an *aionos eidolon*, an image of life that is the only divine thing in us.[15]

Orphism, which began to spread sometime in the seventh and sixth centuries B.C. in Attica and southern Italy, derived human nature from our origins in the ashes of the Titans, who were incinerated after they devoured the divine child Dionysus. Our mixed nature is at one time divine and monstrously "Titanic." Plato, who was especially interested in this cult, attributes to the Orphics the jingle that man's *sōma*, his physical body, is his *sēma*, the tomb that buries his soul.[16] This antithetical notion of human nature—historically un-Greek though it is—had a powerful appeal in the later Greek world, even though many Greeks in antiquity despised the Orphics themselves as ridiculous ascetics and charlatans. Plato himself, for example, seems to have had little regard for the practicing Orphics of his own time.[17] The longing for purity that recurs in Orphic poetry is a striking feature of the writings of both Euripides and Plato. Euripides' Hippolytus is a strangely heroic fanatic in the play that bears his name (428 B.C.). His exclusive adherence to Artemis is presented as a neurotic monomania: "I worship Cypris from a long way off, because I am chaste [*hagnos*]. . . . God of nocturnal prowess is not my god!" With Hippolytus, the vain striving after purity takes an anerotic form that would seem no more than an idiosyncracy, did it not resemble Greek tendencies outside the world of the play. Hippolytus' father, Theseus, dimly recognizes this when he rejects his son's protestations of innocence.

> You are the veritable holy man!
> You walked with gods in chastity immaculate!
> I'll not believe your boasts of God's companionship:
> The gods are not so simple or so ignorant.
> Go, boast that you eat no meat, that you have Orpheus
> for your king. Read until you are demented
> your great thick books whose substance is as smoke.
>
> (947 ff., tr. Grene)

Hippolytus is not the Orphic groupie caricatured by Theseus, but the lines would have no meaning for theater audiences of 428 B.C. if such

Sexual Culture in Ancient Greece

persons were not as well known to most Athenians as they were half a century later to Plato.

Another sect active in the Greek world during this period promulgated similar religious doctrines. Pythagorean communes in Sicily and southern Italy shared the Orphic belief in the superiority of the soul to the body. An old Pythagorean maxim says that "pleasure is in all circumstances bad; for we came here to be punished, and we ought to be punished."[18] Pythagoras himself, who emigrated from Samos to Croton in southern Italy in 531 B.C., founded there a religious order whose regimen included purity, silence, self-examination, vegetarianism, and various other prohibitions, including sexual abstinence. Diogenes Laertius (8.9) quotes him as saying that sex is "always harmful and not conducive to health." Like Orphism, Pythagorean cult never became popular, but its beliefs were influential in Plato as well as in medical thought. The so-called Hippocratic oath, for example, is less Hippocratic than Pythagorean. Its prohibition of abortive pessaries, widely interpreted as a prohibition of abortion, runs counter to medical practice throughout antiquity,[19] as does its prohibition of assisted suicide, another common practice. The promise to abide by "purity and holiness" is cult language, never typical of the medical profession as a whole, which especially in the Hippocratic tradition avoided magico-religious tendencies.[20] In many respects, Orphic and Pythagorean beliefs ran against the grain of Classical Greek culture; but they anticipated beliefs that would redirect and profoundly alter the culture of ancient Greece.

The belief that sex contaminates a person, like the doctrine that the body is at war with the soul, requires a conception of nature that is diametrically opposed to the traditional assumptions of the Greeks from the earliest times. The changing culture of late antiquity thus called for a remodeled nature, and appeals to nature became an important part of the antierotic quest for purity. Euripides' Hippolytus seeks escape from the impurity of sex by living a hunter's life in the forest and dedicating himself to Artemis, the asexual goddess of the hunt. Plato based his late intolerance of homosexuality on the argument that it is unnatural: "when male unites with female for procreation the pleasure experienced is held to be due to nature [κατὰ φύσιν], but contrary to nature [παρὰ φύσιν] when male mates with male or female with female. . . . [T]hose first guilty of such enormities were impelled by their slavery to pleasure."[21] The Stoics disapproved of homosexual love for similar reasons: Cicero, an important popularizer of middle Stoicism, says at least that nature has allowed greater tolerance for the male love of women, and he quotes a verse of Ennius to the effect that the public display of male nudity in the Greek gymnasia was the beginning of infamy.[22] Musonius Rufus (1st c. A.D.) linked adultery with homosexuality as a violation of natural law: "Of all sexual relations, those involving adultery are most unlawful, and no more tolerable are those of men with men, because it is a monstrous thing and contrary to nature."[23] Living according to nature was a central goal of the fourth century and Hellenistic philosophers, and nature's only use for sex was procreation. Here too Plato seems to have anticipated the movement toward sexual fundamentalism modeled after a sentimentalized conception of nature.

> It is the law's simple duty to go straight on its way and tell our citizens that it is not for them to behave worse than birds and many other creatures that flock together in large bodies. Until the age for procreation these creatures live in continence and unspotted virginity; when they have reached that age, they pair together, the male with the female and the female with the male their preference dictates, and they live thereafter in piety and justice, steadfastly true to their contract of first love.

In an ideal state, says Plato's Athenian in the *Laws*, sexual indulgence should be checked by a sense of shame and by laws enforcing marital fidelity as well as forbidding men's "sterile and unnatural intercourse with males."[24]

The restriction of sex to procreative purposes prompted the Stoic view that intercourse during pregnancy—a practice in general approved by the Hippocratics—placed man lower than the animals.[25] An important corollary to this doctrine was the Stoic opposition to contraception and abortion, as it defeats the only legitimate pretext for sexual union. This opposition, absorbed into Christian doctrine, had lasting consequences, with a continued appeal to "nature." In the fourteenth episode of Joyce's *Ulysses*, Stephen Dedalus makes this argument against contraception: "What of those Godpossibled souls that we nightly impossibilize . . . ? We are means to those small creatures within us and nature has other ends than we."[26]

While reinventing "nature" to fit their beliefs, the moral revisionists of late antiquity had taken as their ultimate target the entire culture against which they fulminated, and they tended to assume a counter-cultural posture: the Cynics' rags proclaimed their rejection of material wealth and all related desires; their homelessness symbolized their rejection of civic loyalties; their public sexual displays advertised their rejection of everything erotic in favor of the simply carnal. Significantly, it was the radical, countercultural Cynic sect rather than the moderate, establishmentarian Stoics who experienced an influx of converts in the early years of the Christian era. Like the Hebrews, whose scripture repeatedly condemned the sexual abominations of the "cities of the plain," Cynics understood that eroticism is as much a cultural artifact as a natural instinct, and they fashioned a conception of anerotic nature along the lines indicated by the passage from Plato's *Laws* quoted above. In freeing themselves from a corrupted world, they placed special emphasis on sexual culture. But where the Cynics professed an indifference to eros, the Christians were obsessive in their denunciations. Some of this originated in Jewish tradition, where (as we saw in chapter 2) sexual metaphors and sexual taboos distinguished the tribes of Israel from the hated "Canaanites" around them. Like the authors of Deuteronomy and Leviticus, Christian preachers focused on sexual culture as the defining feature of the pagan world they despised. Saint Paul's letter to the Thessalonians thus equates holiness and purity with sexual deportment: "You know the rules we gave you in the name of the Lord Jesus. This is the will of God, that you should be holy: you must abstain from fornication [*porneia*]; each one of you must learn to gain mastery over his body, to hallow and honor it, not giving way to lust like the pagans who know nothing of God."[27] Although sexual vice is not the only sin, it is repeatedly targeted as the one most symbolic of the Greco-Roman culture the Christian must reject. It is given a special status, ironically as a sin against the body instead of the spirit: "Have nothing to do with fornication. Every other sin that one may commit is outside the body; but the fornicator sins against his own body."[28]

The dominant sexual culture against which the ascetics asserted themselves did not die out quickly. "Fornication," at least, seems to

Figure 9.1. While religious cultists fulminated against sex, its popularity spread in art, drama, and literature throughout the fourth century B.C. and for centuries later. The bronze mirror was a frequent medium of sexual art, as in this Aphrodite and Eros from the midcentury. The recurrence of erotic motifs in jewelry and boudoir furnishings suggests that women were important consumers of erotica. (Musée du Louvre)

have held its own against "purity" if one is to judge from the frequency of erotic representation between the third century B.C. and the third century A.D. The conventions of erotic art stressed heterosexual encounters in comfortable, secluded settings expressive of a growing,

Sexual Culture in Ancient Greece

Figure 9.2. Bronze mirrors were an important industry in fourth-century Corinth, which was something of a sex capital in the ancient world. Perhaps influenced by Parrhasius (ca. 460–380 B.C.) and the Sicyonian school of Pausias, these mirrors established a new iconography that distinguishes them from Archaic erotic art: (1) they are almost always heterosexual; (2) the couple are alone together in secluded quarters, not in a symposium room; (3) the appurtenances of physical comfort—bed, mattress, pillow—are prominently represented. These conventions, rarely violated, set the intimate, domesticated tone for the final stage of Greek erotic art. (Gift of E. P. Warren. Courtesy Museum of Fine Arts, Boston)

Figure 9.3. About the time of Euripides, Parrhasius painted the loves of mythical heroes and heroines; his work became the model for erotic art in later generations. The servitude of Heracles to the Lydian queen Omphale, who bought him chiefly for sex, was said to have included cross-dressing, in which he wore her dresses and she his lion pelt. Three cornelian intaglio gemstones survive from the later first century B.C. that illustrate their activities together. (Kunsthistorisches Museum, Vienna, no. III 19214.)

Figure 9.4. The Roman fondness for erotica is illustrated by molded terracotta bowls from Arrezzo made in the principate of Augustus by Marcus Perennius. Taking their subject from the bronze vases of the eastern Mediterranean, these bowls revive the calm simplicity of the Classical style. (Ashmolean Museum, Oxford, no. 1966.252)

prosperous urban bourgeoisie. Gentle and civilized rather than orgiastic, conscious of the proprieties of intimacy where both partners shared their pleasure, the sexual art of late antiquity is far from the group scenes, austere settings, and rough sex that had their place in Archaic vase painting. The emphasis on lovers as sentient beings, prominent in New Comedy and later in the prose romances, was implicit in art. But not all such love was idyllic. The potential for tragedy and unhappiness was eagerly taken up by the Romans at a formative time in their literary development. Parthenius of Nicaea, a Greek poet of some distinction during the first century B.C., became a leading guru for the *poetae novi* of Rome and wrote a collection of thirty-six prose love stories, *On Erotic Misfortunes*, as a sourcebook for Cornelius Gallus to use in epic or elegiac verse. Incest, adultery, and other forms of illicit love, nearly always heterosexual, are prominent in these tales, as are various kinds of betrayal. But a woman's devotion until death is a significant minor theme. Catullus' passion for Lesbia, recorded in lyric and elegiac verses just before the middle of the first century B.C., fit the Parthenian mold of erotic misfortune, with the special difference that the poems represent an unfolding personal calamity for the poet himself as he struggles with his infatuation for a married woman whose erotic agenda is more casual. The influence of Parthenius' unhappy stories can be felt in the *Aeneid*'s tragedy of Dido and many of the love stories in Ovid's *Metamorphoses*.

In a less tragic vein, the lurid, sensational tone of Parthenius had been anticipated in a collection of "Milesian Tales" written in the second century B.C. by Aristides of Miletus, popular enough to be translated into Latin by Cornelius Sisenna (d. 57 B.C.). "Their character was definite: they were erotic stories of a lascivious type. Their philosophy was that all men—and women—are sinners, and this belief was embodied in episodes from everyday life. Their amorality was such that the Parthian leader Surena was horrified when in the Parthian War of 53 B.C. a copy of the Milesian Tales was found in the pack of a Roman officer. Other short tales, for example those of Sybaris and of Ephesus, shared these characteristics of realism, irony, and disillusion."[29] The continuing popularity of Milesian tales among the Romans accounts for the inclusion of "The Widow of Ephesus" in Petronius' *Satyricon* (mid-1st c. A.D.) and Apuleius' description of his *Metamorphoses* (2d c. A.D.) as "a Milesian tale" or farrago of such tales. The amoral

Sexual Culture in Ancient Greece

insouciance with which these stories treat sexual peccadilloes gives color to the repulsion with which Christian purists regarded the pagan world.

Christians were not the only Romans who viewed sexual entertainment with distaste. Writing with the prudish emperor Augustus in mind, Ovid speaks disapprovingly of "adulteries of the stage," *scaenica adulteria*:

> foul-jesting mimes which always contain the sin of forbidden love, in which constantly a well-dressed adulterer appears and the artful wife fools her stupid husband. These are viewed by the marriageable maiden, the wife, the husband, and the child; even the senate in large part is present. Nor is it enough that the ear is outraged with impure words; the eyes grow accustomed to more shameful sights, and when the lover has deceived the husband by some novel trick, there is applause. . . . Because the stage is not moral, it is profitable to the poet.[30]

Propertius speaks with similar disapproval about erotic miniatures in the tradition of Parrhasius: "The hand that first painted lewd pictures [*obscaenas tabellas*], and set up objects foul to view in chaste homes, first corrupted the unsullied eyes of maids and refused to allow them to be ignorant of their own wantonness. . . . Not with such figures did men of old adorn their houses!"[31] Like the protestations of Ovid, this piffle was for the eyes of Augustus' morality police. As for the men of old, before Propertius and Ovid were born, Catullus—who had no need for profit or fear of censors—volunteered that he had written verses which "can stir up the itch for sex—not in boys, but for shaggy types who can't get their sluggish groins moving."[32] The Roman appetite for off-color wit is also well attested. Catullus was the first and greatest master of the versified sexual insult; Horace's earliest lyrics include two Epodes of similar character, 8 and 12, which were bowdlerized from school editions (and even the Loeb) for generations in the twentieth century. In the last decades of the first century A.D., Martial published some 1,561 epigrams, many of which employed sexual innuendo to make fun of individuals and types. From about the same time, a series of obscenely witty attacks called *Priapeia* have survived antiquity. The moralists had much to complain of in the less than two centuries of Rome's literary prime. But the use of sex for satirical purposes shows how ambivalent the Roman poets themselves were about the excesses of their age.

One does not need to look far to illustrate the early Christian repulsion. As can be seen in the epigraph at the beginning of this chapter, Christ himself is represented by the late-first-century Book of Matthew as countenancing self-mutilation in the name of holiness, and at least one church father, Origen, is said by Eusebius to have had himself castrated at the age of about twenty.[33] It became a common practice among young Christians seeking to silence the call of the flesh. Saint Paul's concessions to sexuality are at best grudging:

> It is well for a man not to touch a woman. But because of the temptation to immorality, each man should have his wife and each woman her husband. . . . I wish that all were [celibate], as I myself am. But each has his own special gift from God, one of one kind and one of another. To the unmarried and the widows I say that it is well for them to remain single as I do. But if they cannot exercise self-control, they should marry. For it is better to marry than to be aflame with passion.[34]

To the traditional Greek view that sexual desire, like other natural appetites, should be satisfied, Paul retorted, "The body is not made for immorality, but for the Lord, and the Lord for the body."[35] On the opposition of the spirit and the body, Paul took the traditional mystic's view:

> Now the works of the flesh are plain: immorality, impurity, licentiousness, idolatry, sorcery, enmity, strife, jealousy, anger, selfishness, dissension, party spirit, envy, drunkenness, carousing, and the like. . . . But the fruit of the Spirit is love, joy, peace, patience, kindness, goodness, faithfulness, gentleness, self-control; against such there is no law. And those who belong to Christ Jesus have crucified the flesh with its passions and desires.[36]

Sexual Culture in Ancient Greece

To set the mind on the flesh is death, but to set the mind on the Spirit is life and peace. For the mind that is set on the flesh is hostile to God; it does not submit to God's law, indeed it cannot; and those who are in the flesh cannot please God. . . . If you live according to the flesh you will die, but if by the spirit you put to death the deeds of the body, you will live.[37]

This line of thought bore fruit in subsequent centuries: Saint Jerome (347–419), whose works include a treatise (*Adversus Jovinianum*) in praise of virginity, believed girls should never take baths lest they see their own bodies naked (Epist. 107.11). The body's life was the soul's death, and salvation lay in mortifying it: "I am killing it because it is killing me," as a Desert Father put it, or, in the words of the Gospel of Thomas, "Woe to the flesh that hangs upon the soul! Woe to the soul that hangs upon the flesh!" (10). Often mortification of the flesh was aimed at expunging sexual desire. Hermits and monks starved themselves to deplete the physical reserves that maintained their libido. Dioscorus, abbot of monks in the desert around Egyptian Thebes, warned his charges not to fall into the slightest pollution of the flesh. A monk, he said, "must mortify the flesh and not allow an excess of seminal fluid to accumulate. We should therefore try to keep the fluid depleted by the prolongation of fasting. Otherwise, it arouses our sensual appetites."[38] Likewise, the isolation of monks in their cells and anchorites in the desert was an attempt to keep seekers of holiness away from sexual temptation. Sex thus became for many the synecdoche of choice for sin. This emphasis can be traced back to pre-Christian Hellenistic thought. As early as the third century B.C., the Septuagint had reordered the Ten Commandments to place adultery at the top of the list of sins against one's neighbor, before murder and theft.[39] For the most influential early Christians, sex became the world, the flesh, and the devil. All could be conquered, and holiness achieved, by the conquest of desire. In a religion that would be perverted and abused a thousand ways in the centuries to come, this was the first and most persistent degradation, if not the worst.

Christianity was not the first religion to accord special status to abstention from sex. As a *temporary* condition of ritual service, it was a common feature of Greco-Roman religion. Vestal virgins, for example, remained celibate for a finite period of service, after which they returned to normal life, which could include marriage.[40] They were chosen for a temporary role, not self-dedicated for life like Christian nuns. Likewise the children who participated in cult activities, such as the *puellae et pueri integri* who sing to Diana in Catullus 34 and the *virgines lectae puerique casti* in Horace's *Carmen Saeculare*. By the same token, adults might abstain from sex to meet a specific ritual requirement as they might abstain from certain food or drink, woolen clothes, or the pollution of death.[41] But such celibacy was ad hoc, a limited suspension of ordinary activity. Permanent celibacy was another matter. Besides being considered unhealthy, it would be an intolerable disruption of civic rights and duties, as unmarried persons would have no children to care for them in later life and provide the community with citizens and future parents. This was thought particularly true for males. Male asexuality did not exist in the Olympian pantheon, there being no male god corresponding to the asexual Hestia, Artemis, and Athena.

Given the importance of sexual activity to male identity in the classical world, voluntary religious castration of the type that became common in early Christianity was unthinkable. It entered from the eastern fringes of the Greek world, where its practice in the worship of Cybele, the Dea Syria, the Ephesian Hecate, the Syrian Aphrodite of Aphaca, and the Scythian mother goddess links it with the service of fertility goddesses.[42] The cult of Cybele was the first of this kind to reach Rome, where it became established ca. 204 B.C. Under the name of Magna Mater, her worship was tolerated under strict supervision: its priests were still orientals in the first century B.C., and citizens were not allowed to take part in its practice.[43] Like early Christianity, it was a religion of the lower classes, more or less ignored by the educated mainstream. Catullus may have seen some of its Asiatic rites during his tour of duty in Bithynia in 57–56 B.C. Whatever his firsthand experience, he put the collision of cultures into one of his most memorable longer poems, about a young Greek named Attis who sails to Asia Minor with a group of religious zealots who castrate themselves "with extreme hate of Venus," *Veneris nimio odio*, to serve Cybele. The next morning, he awakes to the chilling knowledge that he has cut away his culture as well as the sexual part of his body:

Sexual Culture in Ancient Greece

Shall I be absent from my country, possessions, friends, and parents?
—absent from the forum, palaestra, stadium, and gymnasia?[44]

The poem contrasts the warm complexity of Attis' past life with the bleak chilliness of his new home in the murky forests of Asia Minor. Now a feminized *ministra* of a barbaric goddess, Attis realizes too late the consequences of his religious zeal. Like the *Hippolytus*, this poem, written scarcely a century before the beginnings of Christianity, portrays the religious rejection of sexuality as irrational and violent. It is a kind of suicide that alienates man from his culture. Far from the temporary celibacy of Greco-Roman religion, the celibacy of eastern cult is permanent and deeply alien, a drastic rejection of everything considered rational and civilized.

Yet the very appearance of such stories acknowledges that a minority within the classical *oikoumenē* are embracing a type of religion that promotes the rejection of sexuality, and not long afterward such conversions were seen in a more sympathetic light. Apuleius' second-century A.D. story of Lucius' double metamorphosis, first into an ass and finally into a celibate priest of Isis, is calculated to appeal to readers who are sexually active but also yearn for religious meaning. Lucius' exchange of idle sexual adventures for a life of spiritual significance makes a powerful appeal to the imagination without categorically damning the pleasures of the body. While the most extreme expressions of this spirit are Christian and Gnostic, late antiquity witnessed a widespread revulsion against the body's "clay and gore" and preferred to see as "a filthy bag of excrement and urine" a human body that Marcus Aurelius' physician, Galen, viewed as the masterpiece of creation. With pagans such as Plotinus (205–270 A.D.) and Christians such as Paul, Jerome, and Origen declaring their contempt of the body, a religious consensus gave rise to a sexual revolution that set itself against the entire secular life of the Greco-Roman world.

Saint Augustine (354–430 A.D.) makes no secret of his anerotic spirituality in the story of his conversion, returning obsessively to the sexual appetites that he believed opposed his spiritual progress.

> Clouds arose from the slimy desires of the flesh and from
> youth's seething spring. . . . I was tossed about and spilt
> out in my fornications; I flowed out and boiled over in

them. . . . I, poor wretch, foamed over: I followed after the sweeping tide of passions and I departed from you. I broke all your laws, but I did not escape your scourges.[45]

While a student at Carthage, "a cauldron of shameful loves seethed and sounded about me on every side. . . . I defiled the very source of friendship by the filth of concupiscence, and its clear waters I defiled with the lust of hell." He describes himself in his thirtieth year as "caught fast in a disease of the flesh with its deadly sweetness, . . . a slave to lust."[46] Only after his epiphany on reading Paul's injunction to the Romans "Make not provision for the flesh in its concupiscences" does his mind become free from "scratching lust's itchy sore."[47]

Behind his weepy Asianic rhetoric, Augustine's readers have found vestiges of a classical education, such as the dialectic of opposite appetites within the soul that he shows impelling him in opposite directions. Although he outgrew his interest in a Manichaean contest between evil and good, he repeatedly shows his personal struggle for salvation as one between the sexual body and the divine soul in which one must win and the other lose. Some of the influence may be from Latin poetry. Kenneth Quinn speculates that Lucretius' stress of the sordid side of physical love in *De Rerum Natura* "played a part in shaping that obsessive horror [Augustine] came to feel for all the processes of sex and generation—*inter faeces et urinam nascimur*."[48] Another Roman influence was Virgil, who portrayed the calamitous results of a woman's *amor* in the tragedy of Dido and Aeneas and showed that a nobler destiny awaits the hero who steels his mind against its influence.[49] The structure of thought, however, is manifestly Greek. Although Augustine's absolutism in the description of his sexual appetites is unclassical, the belief that a physical pleasure has an opposing spiritual cost is a Greek way of structuring a problem that caught Augustine's imagination.

A significant corollary of the sexual dread that beset late antiquity was a persistent aversion to women. This prejudice lingered in spite of improvements in the social position of women and a growing ethical consensus regarding their equality with men. Most philosophers of the Hellenistic and Roman period held truly humane views about the moral and intellectual capacities of women. Musonius Rufus' Stoic teachings on this subject in the first century A.D. are unexceptionable by most modern standards. These views passed into Christian teaching, but ethical writers were quick to call attention to what they felt were female vices. Cicero, one of the first who popularized Stoicism in the Roman world, had equated moral weakness with "effeminacy" and good character with virile "maleness," *vir-tus*.[50] Clement of Alexandria (b. ca. 150 A.D.), a Greek convert to Christianity who was head of the Catechetical School at Alexandria, followed the teachings of Musonius regarding sexual equality. But he had special rules for female deportment, especially at parties: "A woman is quickly drawn into immorality even by only giving consent to pleasure. . . . Silence is the virtue of women." For Clement, faults are less forgivable in women than in men, because "for a woman knowledge of who she is, whoever she is, is in itself an embarrassment."[51] This distaste, perhaps augmented by traditional Hebrew attitudes, was shared by other early Christians; for some, being a woman disqualified one for salvation. In the Gospel of Thomas, when Simon Peter objects to the presence of a woman, "Let Mary leave us, for women are not worthy of [eternal] life," Christ answers that a woman who renounces her gender may be saved: "every woman who will make herself male will enter the kingdom of heaven."[52] That women did in fact attempt to renounce their gender in the name of holiness is attested by a decree of the Council of Gangra (340) forbidding the wearing of male attire by female ascetics. But the attitude lingered on; in his commentary on Paul's Epistle to the Ephesians, Jerome wrote that if a woman "wishes to serve Christ more than the world, she will cease to be a woman and will be called man." Ambrose and Augustine made similar statements.[53]

This misogyny is not entirely representative of early Christianity, which like the Hellenistic philosophical sects welcomed female members; women acted as patrons of local churches, heads of Christian families, and participants in Christian worship.[54] But the doctrine of the submission of women is a frequent note. The author of the Pastoral Epistle to Timothy writes, "Their role is to learn, listening quietly and with due submission. I do not permit women to teach or dictate to the men; they should keep quiet. . . . But salvation for the woman will be in the bearing of children, provided she continue in faith, love, and holiness, with modesty."[55] The Pauline Epistle to the Colossians is blunt: "Wives, be subject to your husbands; that is your Christian duty." Likewise to the Ephesians: "Wives, be subject to your husbands as though to the Lord; for the man is the head of the woman, just as Christ is the head of the church. . . . [J]ust as the church is subject to Christ, so must women be subject to their husbands in everything."[56] One of the Sentences of Sextus gives a Christian reason for opposing divorce: "A man who divorces his wife admits that he is not even able to govern a woman."

The ambivalence about women in late antiquity had an effect on sexual life even within marriage. For Saint Paul, it was a last resort to prevent a man from being consumed with passion, but until the second coming of Christ, "married men should be as if they had no wives."[57] The Encratites, so called because of their advocacy of *enkrateia*, continence, opposed intercourse even in marriage, and while like the pagan philosophers Christians tended to favor marriage itself, they most admired celibate marriage. The more sexually austere a marriage, the better its partners could attend to the spiritual demands of their religion. Paul suggests sexual abstinence during periods of devotion to prayer (1 Cor. 7:5). But married life, like the service of Mammon, is an attempt to serve two masters: "A married man is concerned with worldly affairs; his aim is to please his wife, and he is pulled in two directions. The unmarried woman or girl is concerned with the Lord's business; her aim is to be dedicated to him in body as in spirit. But the married woman is concerned with worldly affairs; her aim is to please her husband."[58]

Religious writers were not the only ones who believed that sexual activity depleted powers better put to other uses. Practiced to excess, it was even believed to make a man "womanish," an argument often used when the relative merits of boy love and heterosexual love were debated. Writing in the second century A.D., both Galen and Soranus held that men who abstain from sex will be better for it. Galen thought a method of castration that could somehow preserve vital heat would help Olympic athletes; Soranus stated that celibacy was equally healthy for men and women.

Virginity . . . is healthful, since it prevents the excretion of seed. Dumb animals also bear witness to what has been said; for of mares those not covered excel at running, and of sows those whose uteri have been cut out are bigger, better nourished, stronger, and firm like males. And this is evident in humans too; since men who remain chaste are stronger and bigger than the others and pass their lives in better health. . . . Permanent virginity is healthful, in males and females alike.[59]

Sexual austerity, approved by medical as well as spiritual authorities, became a dominant ethical theme in the early Christian centuries, even before Christianity percolated up into the ruling classes. Long present in Greek and Roman thought, it found expression in surprising quarters in the last century before Christ. When Catullus, adapting the words of Sappho, describes the effects of love on his person, he catches himself up in a final stanza and reproaches himself with *otium*, idleness. Eduard Fraenkel reminds us that three centuries earlier Theophrastus had defined love as "a pathology of leisure."[60] Cicero, writing about a decade after Catullus, is even harsher.

Just as those who are transported with delight at the enjoyment of sexual pleasures are degraded, so those who covet them with feverish soul are criminal. In fact the whole passion ordinarily termed *amor* . . . is of such exceeding triviality that I see nothing that I think comparable with it.[61]

The people of late antiquity lost more than carnal gratification when they rejected a sexual culture that had developed from earliest times and become increasingly humane in its final phases. Whatever damage was later inflicted by invaders or imported from alien cult, sexual renunciation—and the cultural renunciation that went with it—was a self-inflicted wound. Though celibacy may have won women a greater degree of autonomy in their childbearing years and helped to make those most subject to sexual exploitation more secure in their persons, it came in a countercultural package that uprooted the visual arts; the new ideology all but destroyed a literary tradition that even princes of the church admired, and outlawed international athletic contests along with the physical culture that such contests preserved. Though mortification of the flesh renewed the ancient virtues of self-control, it put human nature at war with itself and destroyed the equally ancient union of spirit and body that even theologians today count among the supreme conceptions of Greek thought.

Abbreviations

AJA   *American Journal of Archaeology*. Princeton: Archaeological Institute of America, 1897–.

ANET   James B. Pritchard, *Ancient Near Eastern Texts Relating to the Old Testament*. 2d ed. Princeton: Princeton University Press, 1954.

CAH   *The Cambridge Ancient History*. London: Cambridge University Press, 1970.

CISem   *Corpus Inscription Semiticarum*.

G-P   A. S. F. Gow and D. L. Page, *The Greek Anthology: Hellenistic Epigrams*. Cambridge: Cambridge University Press, 1965.

JIES   *Journal of Indo-European Studies*. Washington, D.C.: Institute for the Study of Man, 1973–.

K-A   R. Kassell and C. Austin, *Poetae Comic Graeci (PCG)*. Berlin: W. de Gruyter, 1983–.

PCG   *Poetae comici Graeci*. Ed. R. Kassell and C. Austin. Berlin: W. de Gruyter, 1983–.

RE   August Friedrich von Pauly, *Paulys Real-encyclopadie der classischen Altertumswissenschaft; neue Bearbeitung, unter Mitwirkung zahlreicher Fachgenossen hrsg. von G. Wissowa*. Stuttgart: J. B. Metzler, 1894–1980.

SVF   Hans Friedrich August von Arnim, *Stoicorum Veterum Fragmenta*. Collegit Ioannes ab Arnim. Stuttgart: B. G. Teubneri, 1968.

TAPA   *Transactions of the American Philological Association*. (Various places and publishers, most recently) Atlanta: Scholars Press, 1869/70–.

TGF²   August Nauck, *Tragicorum Graecorum Fragmenta*. Ed. secunda. Leipzig: Teubner, 1889.

Notes

CHAPTER 1. SEXUAL RELIGION:
THE ROOTS OF SEXUAL CULTURE

1. Nilsson 1950, 5, quoted with approval by Burkert, 1985, 15. But despite his emphasis on disparate elements in the archaeological record, Burkert concludes his brief discussion of Neolithic and Early Helladic religion with an affirmation of its later influence: "Although the many broken lines of tradition and the innumerable catastrophes of early times cannot be lightly overlooked, forces of continuity have always reasserted themselves, and probably nowhere as much as in the sphere of religion."

2. "Old Europe" is Marija Gimbutas's term for the pre-Indo-European cultural region covering central Italy to Sicily in the west and southeastern Europe from the Dnieper through the Balkans to Crete in the east. The key pictorial documentation for the Neolithic and early Bronze Age cultures discussed in this chapter are Gimbutas 1982; Ucko 1968; Demargne 1964; Marshack 1972; Mellaart 1975; Renfrew 1972; Trump 1980.

3. See Deubner 1932; Parke 1977; Simon 1983.

4. Fr. 44 Snell, from Ath. 13.600b. Cf. Hes. *Th.* 126 ff. For sexual ritual in a plowed field, see Hom. *Od.* 5.125–128; Frazer 1955, 2:97–119, "The Influence of the Sexes on Vegetation," places this in a larger cultural context.

5. For an illustrated catalog, see Ucko. Southeastern European, Balkan, and Aegean examples are illustrated in Gimbutas 1982. See also Patai 1967, 58.

6. See Hadzisteliou Price 1978. The epithet is applied to a number of goddesses not generally represented as maternal, including Hecate, Artemis, and Aphrodite.

7. Hor. *Odes* 3.13.4–8 (23 B.C.), for example, describes the promised sacrifice of a kid "whose forehead, swollen with first horns, foretells love and battles." This "offspring of the lustful herd," *lascivi suboles gregis*, like the libidinous goat (*libidinosus caper*) destined for sacrifice in *Epod.* 10.23, gains religious potency from its sexual condition.

8. On the sexual power of Hermes and herms, see Burkert 1979, 40.

9. See Borgeaud 1988, 74–87.

10. For a multicultural survey of hierogamy, see Frazer [1914] 1955, 2:chap. 12 (120–170). The tradition is better attested in the Near East (for which see Kramer 1969) than Greece (for which see Burkert 1985, 108 f.).

11. See Kramer 1969; Jacobsen 1970. In the Greek world, the ephemeral god was Adonis, whose annual Adonia was celebrated by women with lettuce and other green plants that grew and withered quickly. See Detienne 1977; Burkert 1985, 176–177. The eastern origin of Adonis is shown by its etymological link with Semitic *adoni*, "lord," of which the biblical variant is *adonai*.

12. The Virgin's youth was immediately noticed by critics, as it was understandably the usual practice to represent a more matronly type. In his later years, Michelangelo explained to his biographer Condivi that her youthful looks had been preserved by her "virginity and perpetual purity"— a conventional Neoplatonic view that Condivi took at face value. But recent scholars have reopened the question of the Virgin's youth, and the list of possible influences includes Greek models. Robert Coughlin (1966) notes that while the Virgin is much younger than her son, who is of normal proportions, she would be seven feet tall were she to stand. See Wind 1968, 185; Baldini et al., 1:92; Liebert 1983, 67–70.

13. "There is only one thing that feminist classicists are agreed upon: none of them, no matter how ideologically committed, believes in the historical existence of Amazons and matriarchies" (Skinner 1987, 23). But it remains a popular idea. Judith Ochshorn is one of many who have tried to lay the matriarchal myth to rest:

> The prominence of goddesses at any given time did not in itself signify the high status of women in the earthly societies of those same times. Sometimes the two seem to have gone together—as may have been the case in early Sumer with respect to upper-class women, or during some periods of Elamite and Egyptian history— but most often they probably did not. The worship of powerful goddesses during the Classical period of Athens seemed to bear little relation to the diminished status of upper-class Athenian women in real life, just as the later exaltation of the Virgin Mary by the early Church Fathers did not seem grounded in the actual status of most European women at that time, nor did the worship of Mary elevate that status. (1981, 107 f.)

14. 11.2, tr. Lindsay.

15. Its complexity, and its frequently sexual content, can best be appreciated by consulting Farnell 1896–1909.

16. See Aristophanes, *Acharnians* 237–279.

17. Schol. to Lucian 279, 24 (Rabe); Parke 1977, 98–99; Cook 1914–1940, 1:685; Deubner 1932, 65. For the making of phallic cakes at festivals in India, see R. C. Temple's foreword to Penzer 1923–1968, xxii.

18. Paus. 1.27.4; see Henderson 1987, 155. on *Lys.* 641; Parke 1977, 141 f.; Broneer, 1932, 31–55; Hampe and Simon 1981, 187 f.

19. For example, the site of the temple of Athena Alea at Tegea has yielded a number of naked female figurines "carrying water, controlling animals and with hands on breasts [which] suggest the fundamental qualities of a Fertility goddess and Mistress of Animals" (Voyatzis 1990, 269).

20. Farnell 1896–1909, 2:425. See also Lloyd-Jones 1983, 90: "In the earliest Greek religion, goddesses were little differentiated from one another: . . . the precise marking off of one deity from another in terms of attribute and function may not safely be attributed to the remote past." Cf. Voyatzis 1990, 269–270: "The location of the sanctuary [of Athena Alea] . . . seems to suggest that the cult was an ancient one which originally was not necessarily or specifically associated with a particular deity. Aspects of Artemis, Demeter, or Athena may have existed in some embryonic form from the beginning."

21. Farnell 1896–1909, 2:427–445; Burkert 1985, 149–152.

22. Lloyd-Jones 1983, 87 ff.

23. Farnell, 1896–1909, 2:444.

24. A view more popular among ancient commentators than modern philologists; see Fraenkel 1950, 490.

25. See Allen, Halliday, and Sikes 1936, 149–151; Apollod. 1.5.1; Farnell 1896–1909, 3:104; cultural parallels in Frazer [1914] 1955, 7:62, 116, and 8:17. On the sexual meaning of the pomegranate, see Allen, Halliday, and Sikes 1936, 168–170. An Orphic version of the story (fr. 215 Abel, 52 Kern) says that it was Queen Baubo of Eleusis who broke the ice by exposing herself to Demeter. Hesychius defines *Baubalion* as "a woman's vulva." For self-exposure as a gesture of abuse, see Hdt. 2:60 (in an Egyptian rite for "Artemis"); Theophr. *Char.* 11.2, Diod. 1.85.

26. The Sirens exemplify a pair that expands into a triad. Homer, our earliest source (*Od.* 12.39–54, 158–200), implies that they are a pair (12.52, the dual Σειρήνοιϊν); later sources make them a triad. See Zwicker in *RE* 2:3 (1927), 288–308; Gresseth 1970, 205 f.

27. The proximity of the Moirai to Aphrodite is suggested by the inscription seen by Pausanias (1.19.2) on the temple of Aphrodite in Athens: "Aphrodite Ouranios is the oldest of the Moirai." The antiquity of the

Athenian cult of Aphrodite is suggested by the aniconic form of her statue there, "like the figures of Hermes."

28. On Hesiod's Graces, see West 1966, 177, 406 ff;, 1978, 161 ff. For the allegorizing interpretation of the Graces, see Wind 1968, chap. 2; and on their role in Botticelli's *Primavera*, chap. 7. As we shall see in chap. 3, Hesiod has transformed Pandora "giver of all," a chthonic goddess of nature, into a troublemaker "gifted by all" the gods who made her. See West 1978, 164 ff.

29. *Quaestiones Conviviales* 744C3. See also H. Kees in *RE* 16 (1935), "Mousai," col. 687–688.

30. For the symbolism of clothing, see chap. 2 on the initiation of Enkidu.

31. On the goldenness of Aphrodite, see Friedrich 1978, 78, where it is related to her solar character; in this aspect she is like her eastern cognate Eos, the dawn goddess.

32. See Janko 1992 on *Il.* 14.214–217, and n. 24 in chap. 3 below. Even the Madonna in Michelangelo's *Pietà* wears one, embroidered with the artist's name (this is the only place the artist's name appears on any of his works).

CHAPTER 2. COMING-OF-AGE
IN THE ANCIENT NEAR EAST:
TWO SEXUAL MYTHS OF CULTURAL INITIATION

1. Gen. 2:18, RSV. For the sexual interpretation of the "fall" of man, see Hartman 1958; Bailey 1970.

2. The phrase "good and evil" is either a merism meaning "everything possible" or a formula meaning sexual knowledge (Gordis 1957, 130; cf. Bailey 1970, 144 ff., with bibliography). The phrase occurs in Gen. 2:17, 3:5, 3:22; Deut. 1:39; 2 Sam. 14:17, 19:35; 1 Kings 3:9; and Isa. 7:15 f. A Dead Sea Scrolls text stating the Rule of the Congregation (1 QSa [1.6–18]) states that a man may not have sex with a woman until "he is fully twenty years of age when he knows good and evil." Gordis 1957, 132, argues that "good and evil" refers to what was considered natural and unnatural sex. Many biblical interpreters (e.g., Midrash, Rashi, Milton, Pseudepigrapha) argue that Adam and Eve had sexual intercourse in Eden, but cognate myths in Greece would seem not to support such a view. The linkage of sexual experience with knowledge and wisdom but also divine wrath is made explicit in the Greek myth of Tiresias, who according to one myth (Hesiod fr. 275MW) is transformed for a time into a woman. He subsequently judges a dispute between Zeus and Hera

about sexual pleasure and is blinded by a wrathful Hera after declaring that women receive ten times more pleasure from sex than do men; another version (in Callimachus' *Bath of Pallas*) says that he was blinded after seeing Athena bathing in the nude (like Acteon, who was turned into a stag and killed by his own hunting dogs).

3. "For the Priestly writer [of Gen. 1:27] the idea that God might possess any form of sexuality, or any differentiation analogous to it, must be viewed, I believe, as an alien and repugnant notion" (Bird 1987, 35). Not all Israelites would have agreed: my colleague Benjamin Sommer points out to me that the Hebrew god YHWH is often called El in the Bible, and Ugaritic texts of the thirteenth century B.C. identify the Canaanite goddess Asherah as the consort of El. Even earlier Israelite inscriptions (8th c. B.C.) include a blessing dedicated to "YHWH and his asherah." Though the meaning of this is debated, the evidence does not support the priestly view of a monolithic, asexual Hebrew YHWH who was from the earliest times cleanly dissociated from a sexual Canaanite El. See Dever 1985; Miller et al. 1987, 138–139, 143–149. On the Canaanite mother goddess Asherah, see Olyan 1988; Ackerman 1992; Metzger and Coogan 1993, 62.

4. "Genesis 20:13 implies that Abraham's behavior was customary rather than exceptional. . . . Many nomadic peoples . . . use their women as a means of establishing relations with the sedentary population" (Pitt-Rivers 1977, 159).

5. Astour (1966) explains the Near Eastern religious context of the story in which Tamar poses as a sacred prostitute (Gen. 38) and suggests how that story may have been altered to fit the new morality of the later censors. The story "contains details that evoke associations with the legal and ritual prescriptions for temple harlots in Babylonia. . . .Sacred prostitution existed in Israel and Judah until the implementation of the religious reforms of the seventh and sixth centuries B.C." (p. 185). For an opposing view, see Frymer-Kensky 1992 and n. 9 below.

6. Jub. 33:20. The Book of Jubilees is a noncanonical book of the Hebrew Apocrypha, written in the second half of the second century B.C. Its obsession with fornication is a marked feature: see also 20:3–6, 25:7, 39:6, etc. For a comparison of ancient Hebrew law with Koranic law and modern customs in the Arabic world, see Patai 1967 passim.

7. For a discussion of attempts to date the Song of Solomon, see Pope 1977, 22–33. The editors of *The New Oxford Annotated Bible* (Oxford, 1977), 815, date its present written form to the third century B.C. but admit that "its material is much more ancient." Its attribution to Solomon is based on the tradition recorded in 1 Kings 4:32 that he "uttered three thousand proverbs; and his songs were a thousand and five."

8. For a history of the text and its analogues, see Tigay 1982.

9. She is identified in the texts by two words, *harimtu* and *shamhat*, both referring to women associated with Ishtar. Tigay (1982, 171) and Dalley (1989, 126 n. 14) take the latter to be her personal name, *Shamhat* being in particular "a type of cultic devotee of Ishtar in Uruk." Akkadian *šamhat* is cognate with "happy" in Semitic languages. It is sometimes inferred that she is a temple prostitute, a hierodule. Bailey (1970) cites the Babylonian proverb, "Do not marry a *harimtu*, whose husbands are innumerable." In Sandar's translation, she is "a wanton from the temple of love." Lerner (1986, 238–245) and Bird (1989, n. 2) dispute the connection between harlot and hierodule and the attempt to derive secular prostitution from sacred sexual service. See also Oden 1987, 131–153.

10. The suckling of milk and the refusal of beer are mentioned in the Old Babylonian Version (the Pennsylvania Tablet), quoted by Tigay 1982, 199. Quotations are from Dalley 1989.

11. The archetypes here are long-lasting. For the image of the woman as emblematic of civilization, see Zweig 1974, chap. 5. The other motif is forgetfulness. Odysseus' sexual involvement with Circe makes him forgetful of his home, and his men have to remind him (*Od.* 10.472–474). For a close reading of Shamhat's initiation of Enkidu and parallels in Genesis 2–3, see Bailey 1970.

12. Tigay 1982, 209, which cites in particular the Epic of Erra. See Dalley 1989, 305.

13. In Dalley's translation, the word translated "profound" is broken and hence bracketed; but the restoration is secured by a line five lines previous. See Gardner and Maier 1984, 80.

14. The metaphoric and symbolic structure of Enkidu's arrival is full of matrimonial suggestions: when he is first created he has long hair "like a woman's"; Gilgamesh's prophetic dreams suggest an attraction "like the love of a woman . . . you were drawn as though to a woman . . . you will love him as a woman." When Enkidu puts on man's clothing he appears "like a bridegroom," and his arrival in Uruk comes just as Gilgamesh is about to exercise his seigneurial *ius primae noctis* with a bride ritually designated for the occasion as a stand–in for Ishtar. His arrival puts an end to that unpopular custom: "I have come to change the old order" (Sandars 1972, 68). The biblical parallel to this matrimonial union of males is the companionship of David and Jonathan: "Your love to me was wonderful, passing the love of women" (2 Sam. 1:26). Cf. Homer's Achilles and Patroclus and Queequeg's "bridegroom clasp" of Ishmael at the beginning of Melville's *Moby-Dick*, chap. 4. This motif is further discussed in Halperin 1990, 75–87.

15. Besides pleasure, Siduri is recommending that Gilgamesh's fear of death can be answered only through procreation: the context of her advice is, "You will not find the eternal life you seek. When the gods created mankind they appointed death for mankind, kept eternal life in their own hands." Dalley compares Siduri's advice to that in Ecclesiastes 9:7–9: "Go, eat your bread with enjoyment, and drink your wine with a merry heart. . . . Let your garments always be white; do not let oil be lacking on your head. Enjoy life with the wife whom you love." For additional interpretations of this topos, see Abusch 1993.

16. It is interesting that Genesis assigns the woman's role in the Gilgamesh epic to a serpent, making Eve a deputy. Both are liminal figures, the serpent a pagan emblem of everlasting life or renewal that the Hebrew writers no doubt wished to demonize.

CHAPTER 3. HELENIZING GREECE: THE REVISION OF BRONZE AGE MYTHOLOGY

1. Nagy (1990) discusses the Hellenization of Indo-European poetics, myth and ritual, and social ideology. Important earlier works include Benveniste 1969, tr. Palmer (1973); Dumézil 1968, 1971, 1973.

2. Nagy 1990, 247; on p. 248, Nagy shows how Aphrodite, essentially an eastern (non-Indo-European) goddess, becomes a parallel of Eos in epic theme. Metrical and formulaic reasons thus contribute to the conflation of two more or less distinct traditions.

3. For a summary of the arguments for and against this reconstruction and further references, see Drews 1988.

4. Drews 1988, 152; Grottanelli 1986, 125; Ward 1968, 1970, 405–420.

5. The central action of the *Iliad*'s beginning is Achilles' abusive defiance of the supreme Greek warlord Agamemnon. When Athena prevents Achilles from murdering Agamemnon in the heat of their dispute, she does so by appeal rather than command. Her request, "Will you be persuaded?" αἴ κε πίθηαι, is mistranslated "Will you *obey* me?" by Lattimore. On Athene's tactful language, see Kirk 1985, 1:75, on *Il.* 1.207. Archaic Greek has an imperative but no word for "obedience."

6. Nilsson 1950.

7. "While the early assumption of a broad degree of religious uniformity within the Aegean no doubt once facilitated the identification of the main features of a 'Minoan-Mycenaean religion,' that term is now much too generalized, and no longer has any usefulness or validity for serious analysis" (Renfrew 1985, 394).

8. For a summary of the language problem, see Vermeule 1964, 60–64. The pre-Greek language is distinguished by distinctive possessive or locative suffixes in *-ssos* or *-nthos*, such as Parnassos, Hyakinthos, Corinthos, Hyancithos.

9. Vermeule 1964, 27, 44. For an example from Lerna itself of the type that seems to have died out, see fig. 1.16.

10. Vermeule 1964, 70, and chap. 2 and 3 passim, on which my own account of these problems is heavily dependent. See also Drews 1988 passim.

11. Gordon 1957a, 1957b, 1966, 37; Chadwick 1987, 44–61; Best and Woudhuizen 1988.

12. For the cult of Helen *dendritis* at Sparta, see Hooker 1980, 56–58. The attribution of divine power to Helen persisted in the story told by Plato that the Sicilian poet Stesichorus was struck blind for describing Helen's infidelity to Menelaus and regained his sight when he retracted his words in a palinode (*Phdr.* 243a). In the *Odyssey*, Menelaus tells of a prophecy by Proteus that he will live on forever in the Elysian field because he is Helen's spouse and thereby son–in–law to Zeus (4.561–570). We have it from no less an authority than Herodotus that Helen was still a goddess with a shrine at Sparta in the late sixth century B.C. (6.61); in 2.112 he identifies her with "foreign Aphrodite" (ξεινή Ἀφροδίτη), which if accurate would make her close to Astarte/Ishtar/Atargitis, the oriental nude goddess.

13. According to Paus. 3.26.1, Pasiphaë is a title of the moon; Ariadne is a Cretan moon goddess; the formation of her name suggests a Sumerian origin. Phaedra's name appears to be Greek, but it has a close Ugaritic cognate. See Astour 1967, 267 n. 2.

14. See Friedrich 1978, chap. 2.

15. Karageorghis 1982, 77–82.

16. Astour 1966, 186, cites *CISem* I, No. 86 = G. A. Cooke, *A Text-Book of North Semitic Inscriptions*, No. 20, B, line 10. The women are called *lmt*, "lasses, young women," the men *klbm* "dogs," so called not in contempt but because of their faithful service to the god. Cf. the prohibition in Deut. 23:18: "You shall not bring the hire of a harlot, or the wages of a dog, into the house of the Lord your God in payment for any vow," suggesting that prostitution may have been practiced in Syria–Palestine as a means of paying an ex–voto debt to the goddess for answering a prayer.

17. Gordon 1966, 19. The identification of *qdšm* with sacred prostitution in Phoenician religion is hypothetical and has been disputed. See Lerner 1986, 238; Drower *CAH* 2.2, 150; Bird 1989, n. 2: "there appears to be little or no evidence of confusion or interchange [of harlot and hierodule] in the primary ancient texts." Bird also objects to "the attempt to derive secular prostitution from sacred sexual service" in the ancient Near East, though the temple of

Aphrodite and commercial prostitution are closely linked in testimonia from the Classical world (Athens, Corinth).

18. Caquot 1965, 87; Gordon 1966, 95 f.

19. Text 76, Gordon 1966, 88–90.

20. Astour (1967, 128–138) derives Europa's name from a Semitic root that makes her a goddess of night who goes away into the sunset. He demonstrates her affinity with the love goddess Ishtar and with the evening star, which we call Venus, and emphasizes her identity with Pasiphaë. Ancient Near Eastern iconography at Ugarit suggests that the naked goddess on a bull's back is a prototype of the Greek Europa (Amiet 1980).

21. Whitman 1958, 38, n. 67. Martin Bernal has developed evidence along these lines to argue that Greek civilization was largely derived from what he calls an "Afroasiatic" or "Afrosemitic" cultural and linguistic complex that exerted its greatest influence between 2100 and 1100 B.C. This thesis, set forth in the two volumes of *Black Athena* (1987–1991), properly opposes the view that Greek civilization was a purely Indo-European development, but it greatly exaggerates the Egyptian and Near Eastern roles and wrongly implies that skin color was a significant element in the Egyptian cultures that contributed to Greece. See (among many in a similar vein) J. M. Weinstein's review in *AJA* 96 (1992): 381–383 and Lefkowitz 1996.

22. Trump (1980, 190) calls the Homeric Catalogue of Ships "a surprisingly good account of the political geography of the Aegean area in the 13th century B.C. and quite different from that of Homer's day in the ninth century." For an edition of this catalog with commentary, see Allen 1931; cf. Jachmann 1958; Page 1959, chap. 4; Simpson and Lazenby 1970.

23. On the early history of Helen, see Nilsson 1932, 73–76; Clader 1976 *passim*.

24. On the Near Eastern connections of these myths, see Astour 1967, 128–139 (Europa), 80–92 (Io), 137–138 (Pasiphaë), 267 n. 2 (Phaedra). For Ariadne, see Nilsson 1932, 172; 1950, 451 ff. Like characters being written out of soap operas, these Bronze Age figures are sometimes killed off: Homer has Artemis kill Ariadne because "Dionysos bore witness against her," perhaps because she was dedicated to Dionysus before her escapade with Theseus (*Od.* 11.321–325, one of only four mentions of Dionysus in Homer); Apollo kills the female serpent at Delphi, Narcissus dies by accident when his cult is replaced by that of Apollo (whom the myth represents as his grieving lover), and Euripides' Phaedra commits suicide when she fails to seduce Hippolytus.

25. Bonner 1949 shows the typology of this strap or saltire forming an x across her chest. Female idols so ornamented have been found in Mesopotamia, Syria, Iran, and India, dating from ca. 3000 B.C. to A.D. 250; the Sumerian love goddess Inanna is stripped of such a "breast decoration" when

she descends to the lower world (*ANET* 55). See also Brenk 1977; Faraone 1990; Janko 1992 on *Il.* 14.214–217.

26. Webster (1958, 86) describes this as originating in a Sumero-Accadian myth: Ocean and Tethys "are Apsu and Tiamat of the Akkadian story, and the Accadian (or rather Sumerian) pair quarreled because Apsu wanted to destroy all the younger gods, who made so much noise."

27. Farnell 1896–1909, 2:749. The Thessalian temple of "unholy" (*anosias*) or "murderous" (*androphonou*) Aphrodite (Ath. 13.589b; Plut. *Amat.* 768a), explained as stemming from the murder of the hetaera Laïs in her precinct by jealous women, is more likely to go back to an ancient armed Aphrodite.

28. Diomedes' taunt after he wounds her, εἶκε Διὸς θύγατερ, πολέμου καὶ δηιοτῆτος, resembles the warning of Apollo to Diomedes a few lines later, φράζεο, Τυδείδη, καὶ χάζεο (5.440), and Apollo's to Patroclus in book 16, χάζεο, διογενὲς Πατρόκλεες, etc. (707). Each time the warning phrase is followed by a patronymic (or similar phrase) and an explanation of why the person warned is out of his or her depth. Cf. Euphorbus' vain warning to Menelaus in 17.12–15, where the order of elements is altered.

29. The Ugaritic texts show some inclination to separate the dual aspects of the Astarte type: the bloodthirsty "Virgin Anath" of the Anath Text (Gordon 1966, 46–51) is distinguished from Lady Asherah of the Sea, Creatress of the Gods, the goddess who is usually associated with Canaanite erotic religion. (Anath is no virgin in the usual sense, however: she mates passionately with Baal and bears him offspring in Text 132 [Gordon 1966, 90 f. quoted above, p. ooo].)

30. The origins of Aphrodite are detailed in Friedrich 1978, chap. 2. For Aphrodite as dawn goddess, see also Boedeker 1974, 14 ff. It is possible that another dimension of Aphrodite's goldenness is fair hair. But Demeter is the only goddess so described (*Il.* 5.500), probably because of the ripe grain and straw with which she is associated, and of which her symbols are still made throughout Europe; Menelaus is routinely described as fair–haired—*xanthos* can mean yellow, tawny, or reddish brown—and Achilles and Odysseus are each twice described with the same word. This fair hair suggests a northern stock in historical Greece that had established itself in some places as a ruling elite. For pubic hair that is blond (*xanthos*) in an erotic context, see Archil. fr. S478 Page (P. Colon. 7511) 53.

31. On the etymology of *philomeidēs*, see West 1966, 88; Friedrich 1978, 202–204. On the sexual vulnerability of women, see *Od.* 15.421–422: "sex beguiles a woman's mind, even if she is a good worker." On the story attributed to Hesiod about Tiresias' finding that women get ten times more pleasure from sex than men (fr. 275 MW), see Lefkowitz 1986, 10. For a similar

myth in India, see O'Flaherty 1973, 113. American Indian beliefs about the lascivious and unstable character of women are summarized in Ellis and Abarbanel 1967, 1:92. Swahili women "are thought to be sexually enthusiastic and sexually irresponsible, given the opportunity" (Shepherd 1987, 243), a view close to that of many Greek men in antiquity.

32. Floral sexual vocabulary: *Hymn to Demeter* 6–14; Archilochus S478 Page (P. Colon. 7511) 27, 42 f.; Sappho LP95.11–12; LP 194; Tyrtaeus 10 West 28, Theognis 1276. Erotic dew in *dros-* compounds: Sappho LP 95.12, 71.8.

33. Homer also compares Nausicaa and Penelope to Artemis (*Od.* 6.102–109, 151; 17.37 = 19.54). The sexual power of Artemis is comparable to Aphrodite's in Homer's formula describing Penelope, "looking like Artemis or golden Aphrodite."

34. The Homeric *Hymn to Aphrodite* also reflects a view of the love goddess that is somewhat wary of her erotic potency. Focusing on Aphrodite's seduction of Trojan Anchises, it treats the episode as an embarrassment to her and a cause of dread to Anchises, whom she had tricked by saying she was the daughter of a well–known Trojan. See Lefkowitz 1986, 117 f.

35. Many Greek poets and philosophers followed his lead in this: Sappho (6th c. B.C., fr.198LP), Pherecydes (6th c. B.C., B3, A11), Empedocles (5th c. B.C., calling him *Philotēs*, B17.20 ff.), Parmenides (5th c. B.C., B13), and the Orphic tradition (fr. 28). Characters in Euripides (fr. 898, *Hyps.* fr. 57.23, p. 45 Bond), Aristophanes (*Birds* 700), and Plato (*Symp.* 195b–c) preserve the same tradition, which has a parallel in Phoenician cosmology attested in antiquity (West 1966, 195).

36. The derivation of Aphrodite's name from *aphros* is a folk etymology, but, in spite of a growing familiarity with ancient Near Eastern languages, nothing more scientific has been proposed. Most of the goddess's affinities are Near Eastern, one exception being the Indo–European dawn goddess Eos (Nagy 1990, 248; Friedrich 1978, 22, 28–49). The absence of Indo–European and Semitic cognates leaves open the possibility that Aphrodite is a local pre–Greek name originating in the southeastern European cultures of "Old Europe" (see Gimbutas 1982, 95, 149, on her affinity with water and birds; and Friedrich 1978, 9–12).

37. παρθενίους τ' ὀάρους μειδήματα τ' ἐξαπάτας τε
τέρψιν τε γλυκερὴν φιλότητα τε μειλιχίην τε.

Hesiod's lines bear comparison with the decorations on Aphrodite's sash in *Il.* 14.214 f.:

ἔνθ' ἔνι μὲν φιλότης, ἐν δ' ἵμερος, ἐν δ' ὀαριστὺς
πάρφασις, ἥ τ' ἔκλεψε νόον πύκα περ φρονεόντων.

38. In her chapter on misogyny, Lefkowitz (1986) gives a more nuanced view of attitudes in Greek authors from Hesiod to Aristotle than is provided by critics who dismiss them as misogynists: "Women are portrayed as being more readily susceptible to the effects of [sexual] passion (even) than men, and thus inevitably are considered to be potentially more dangerous" (p. 113). It is sex, not women, that is ultimately the source of trouble. For a discussion of the dangers associated with female nature, see Carson 1990.

39. Frs. 2, 4, 5; West 1978, 164–166. Hesiod's description of the male Eros at the beginning of his cosmogony, "surpassing every immortal in beauty,/ who, a loosener of limbs, brings all immortals and mortals/under his power and makes them unable to think as they should" (120–122, tr. Frazer), contrasts with his harsher picture of Pandora, the first woman, later in the *Theogony* (570 ff.). Instead of a figured sash, she is given a gold crown with monsters pictured on it.

40. See Loraux 1978 passim. Homer and Hesiod also call women a race, tribe, or class: φῦλον, *Il.* 9.130, 272 φῦλα γυναικῶν, Hes. *Th.* 1021 γυναικῶν φῦλον. In the absence of a word for gender, γένος continued to be used, e.g., Eur. *Hec.* 885, and the adjective θῆλυς. For a not-very-serious discussion of gender in language, see Ar. *Clouds* 658 ff.

41. Aesch. *Eum.* 2 ff., Paus. 10.5.5—though Lloyd-Jones tells me there are no physical remains to confirm this.

42. Fontenrose 1980, 13–216.

43. Parke and Wormell 1956, 1:7 f., 14 n. 12.

44. Latte (1940) shows, however, that there was no connection between Dionysus and the Pythia or her prophetic trances; the Pythia was probably, like Cassandra in the Trojan myth, taken to be Apollo's sexual partner whose intimacy with the god gave her the power to reveal the future. The Pythia's trance, whatever it was, is not demonstrably related to a goddess or to the kind of orgiastic mysticism associated with earlier cult. See also Parke and Wormell 1956, 1:15 n. 36.

45. Fontenrose 1980, 418.

46. Paus. 6.22.1. On the connection of Artemis with indecent dances in various parts of Greece, see Farnell 1896–1909, 2:569 n. 46; Nilsson 1961, 16, 38.

47. Burkert 1992 passim.

48. Burkert 1992, 8.

CHAPTER 4. GREEK PATRIARCHY: THE SEVERE STYLE

1. See Heubeck, West, and Hainsworth 1988, 120: "Certainly the favourable impression created by Telemachus' earlier observations is quite

destroyed by this adolescent rudeness, culminating in the outrageous claim that speech (μῦθος) is not women's business, quite contrary to Homeric custom as we see it in the courts of Menelaus and Alcinous, where Helen and Arete play a full part in the discussion after dinner."

2. Modern efforts date from Bachhofen's *Das Mutterrecht* (1861); popular books have projected matriarchal views into the Minoan and even the historical Athenian world. Matriarchy of a sort was imagined perhaps as early as Homer's Amazons, whom he calls ἀντιάνειραι (*Il.* 3.189, 6.186), "a match for men." Legend had it also that the Lemnian women killed their husbands and themselves ruled, but like the Amazons they lived in a single-sex society, which can be neither matriarchal nor patriarchal. See Ehrenberg 1989, 63–66; Cantarella 1987, 11–23; Dumézil 1924 passim; Frymer–Kensky 1992, vii.

3. Athena is a conspicuous exception to this rule. If she is "demoted" in any way, it is in the minimizing of whatever "feminine" features she may formerly have possessed. That she is virginal, a *parthenos*, does not necessarily by itself unsex her (as we have seen, the sexually charged Artemis is similarly unlinked to a consort), nor do her accoutrements of war (cf. the armed Aphrodites mentioned in the preceding chapter). But being born without a mother from the head of Zeus, her character is regularly patriarchal: "I favor the male in all things except in marriage," she says in Aeschylus' *Eumenides* (737).

4. Voyatzis 1990, 266; Østby et al. 1994, 141. The historical context of this development is given in Snodgrass 1980, 49–52.

5. Redfield 1978, 150.

6. *Op.* 373–375, tr. Frazer. Hesiod uses a coarser word than epic diction usually employs to describe this vamp: πυγοστόλος, "ass-rigged." See West 1978, 251.

7. Alcibiades argues in Thucydides that his displays of wealth at the Olympic Games and in Athens show off Athenian prosperity and increase its perceived strength (VI 16). Thucydides may in fact put these words in Alcibiades' mouth to suggest an arrogant abandonment of the old posture of poverty on the eve of the disastrous expedition against Sicily led by Alcibiades.

8. Little was known about ancient Greek gynecology a decade ago beyond Temkin's translation of Soranus' *Gynecology* (1956). See now Lloyd 1983; Hanson 1990a, 1990b, 1991, 1992. Not surprisingly, the shortcomings of Greek science are nowhere more baldly revealed than in their lack of knowledge about female sexual anatomy and physiology, not all of which is explained by their taboo against opening the body. For the lack of knowledge about the hymen in virgins, see Sissa 1990a, 1990b. Belief that the uterus may

wander about the body persisted until the second century A.D. and was revived in the Middle Ages. See Lefkowitz 1981, 12–25; Lloyd 1983, 58–111, 168–182. Articles by von Staden, Hanson, Dean–Jones, and Pinault in *Helios* 19 (1992) illuminate various aspects of ancient Greek gynecology.

9. These too are written into the personality of Homer's Odysseus, who has to be roused by his companions from the comforts of Circe's hospitality, *Od.* 10.472–474. For his love of hot baths, see 8.450–452. Odysseus' description of his tunic verifies his identity to Penelope: "it was like the dried-out skin of an onion, so sheer it was and soft. . . . Many of the women were looking at it in admiration" (19.232–235). W. B. Stanford notes in *The Ulysses Theme* (43 ff.) that Odysseus' closest personal relationships are with women. A close male companion is mentioned (Eurybates, *Od.* 19.244 ff.), but he plays only a bit part in Homer (*Il.* 2.183 f.). The Homeric scholiasts explained Ino's rescue of Odysseus by his love of women: Schol. *Od.* 5.333 ἦν φιλογύνης ὁ Ὀδυσσεύς; cf. Porph. *Quaest. Hom. ad Od.* 5.333.5; Eust. *Comm. ad Hom. Od.* 1.228.23, 234.12.

10. Ath. 138 f.

11. A significant exception is Alcman (late 7th c. B.C.), the Spartan poet whose choral songs for girls, *partheneia*, had an erotic tone that earned him the title "originator of love lyrics" (εὑρετής τῶν ἐρωτικῶν μελῶν) in the Suda. The austere style of life that the Spartans adopted to an extreme degree under the constitution ascribed to Lycurgus had not completely displaced Sparta's earlier traditions by the time of Alcman.

12. The most famous example is the girl's complaint in Sappho 102LP: "Sweet mother, I cannot do my weaving, overcome with longing for a boy because of slender Aphrodite." The motif recurs in Hor., *Odes* 3.12.4–5.

13. See, for example, Alcman 3, where erotic *pothos* is "more melting than sleep or death." The Sarpedon vase in the Metropolitan (fig. 7.1) shows a mortally wounded but otherwise perfect nude Sarpedon, every curling lock in place, being lifted by winged figures of Hypnos and Thanatos.

14. Plut. *Alex.* 22; *Mor.* 65F, 717F. With the moral disapproval of the ascetic, he said sleep and sex made him feel more sordid, ἀγεννέστερος, and more vulnerable, παθηκώτερος.

15. Compare, for example, Simonides fr. 79 Page (Ath. 512c–d): "What human life is desirable without pleasure, or what lordly power? Without it not even the life of the gods is enviable" (Loeb tr. Campbell). Born in 556 on the Ionian island of Ceos a few miles east of the tip of Attica, Simonides wrote extensively about the virtues of athletes and warriors, probably including the famous epigram to the Spartans who died at Thermopylae: "Stranger, report to the Lacedaemonians that we lie here in obedience to their orders."

16. Parker 1993.

17. "Sometimes the audience is clearly a public one including both men and women; . . . in other cases the outward form resembles what we know as public poetry. . . . Finally, in still other examples, she seems to depart altogether from the established mode of public discourse to a private, female-oriented world infused with the sights and smells of nature" (Snyder 1991, 17).

18. "The ultimate purpose of Sapphic song . . . was to encode strategies for perpetuating women's culture" (Skinner 1993, 135). Cf. Lardinois 1994, 80: "The model which can best be reconciled with the fragments, the historical period and the testimonia, is that of Sappho as an instructor of young women's choruses."

19. Skinner 1993, 133; citing Stehle 1990 and Foucault 1986, 38–93.

20. See Faraone 1993, 18.

21. Men. fr. 258 Koerte ap. Strab. 10.2.9 (Campbell 1982, 22).

22. Praxilla also wrote a poem to Adonis, who like Dionysus was a woman's god. See Atallah 1966; Detienne 1977.

23. Stehle 1990.

24. POxy. 1800 fr. 1: Campbell 1982, 2 f.

25. For another explanation of Sappho's appeal to the ancient male audience, see Skinner 1993, 136 f.

26. Skinner 1993, 133, citing Ps-Plut. De Mus. 17.1136 f.

27. Skinner (1993, 133) points out what may be more significant differences between Sappho and Alcman:

> The distinction . . . can be illustrated by juxtaposing Alcman's representations of girls in love with the desiring speakers portrayed in numerous Sapphic texts, most notably her fr. 31. The chorus's admiration of their leaders Hagesichora and Agido in Alcman fr. 1 is permeated with a spirit of eager rivalry, since they are competing with another chorus. Such agonistic tensions emulate the mindset of a male warrior society. Meanwhile, the yearning for Astymeloisa expressed in Alcman fr. 3 betrays an abject dependency quite foreign to Sappho herself.

28. The conception of love as a kind of mental illness made its way into the Renaissance via Stoicism:

> This is the very ecstasy of love,
> Whose violent property fordoes itself
> And leads the will to desperate undertakings
> As oft as any passions under heaven
> That does afflict our natures.
> (Polonius in *Hamlet* II.i.102 ff.)

The deprivation of selfhood was another indictment that stuck in ancient memory. Horace describes his former lover Cinara as one "who stole me from myself," *quae me surpuerat mihi* (*Odes* 4.13.20). One of the later philosophic arguments against falling in love was that it deprived the lover of self-mastery, Gk. ἐγκράτεια.

29. 193 West; cf. 191, 196. Archilochus' poetic statements were no less conditioned by the genre in which he wrote than those of other poets, whose personas were less autobiographical than representative of experience they wished to be seen as representative. The scarcity of Archaic poetry makes it difficult to reconstruct these genres, but it is clear that Iambic meters were associated with invective, while elegiac poems were less closely determined by their meter. The longest and newest fragment of Archilochus, preserved in a papyrus first published in 1974 (P. Colon. 7511), describes the narrator's meeting with a young girl, whom he persuades to have sex without penetration. The story is far from abusive and may belong to a genre that could be described as a type of erotic *pastourelle*. Although nothing else of this type has survived, it may have influenced the scene in *Odyssey* 6 where Odysseus encounters Nausicaa, and perhaps even Hera's seduction of Zeus in *Iliad* 14.292–351. Rather than emphasize love's violence, this tradition is gentle, courtly, and respectful of the woman's wishes. See Miralles and Pòrtulas 1983, chap. 5: "Archilochus and the young girl from Paros."

30. Anacreon fr. 68 Page, cf. 1 Page fr. 4, 51, 53; Simonides fr. 36 Page, Ibycus 5 and 6 Page.

31. Eust. *Comm. ad Hom. Il.* 4.835.15 (p. 1329.33) gives examples of such αἰσχρολογία: Archilochus 206 West; Hipponax 68, 135b, and 144 West; Anacreon 346 fr. 4, 396, 398 Page, Susarion ap. Stob. 4.22.68. For later examples of verbal abuse of the opposite sex, see Juvenal's Sixth Satire; Philip Wylie on "Mom" in *A Generation of Vipers* (1942); and the monologues of male and female standup comedians who specialize in this topic. The humor is perversely extreme, paranoid, and morally reckless but at the same time entertaining to people of both sexes.

32. The best translations are those of F. J. Nisetich (1980), R. Lattimore (1947, 1976), and C. M. Bowra (1969).

33. For the sensuous aspect of praise itself, see *Nem.* 7.32 *habron . . . logon*; *Ol.* 5.7 and *Isthm.* 1.50 apply the same adjective *habros*, "delicate, pretty," to *kudos*. Poetry is "soft," *malthakos*, in *Nem.* 9.4; in *Isthm.* 2.7–8, 31–32, songs are "soft-sounding," "lovely," and "sweet-sounding." Pindar describes his ode as "shedding delightful grace" at the end of *Isthm.* 4, but the pleasure of the victor in *Isthm.* 3.3 borders on the sexual: *eulogiais astōn memichthai*, "to hold intercourse with the praises of the townspeople." If sex was not a metaphor for poetry before, it became so with Pindar.

34. "Adultery, Women, and Social Control," chapter 6 of Cohen 1991, gives an excellent historical and regional overview of attitudes that influenced the treatment of women in Classical Athens, but he argues that the "oriental seclusion" in which Athenian women are alleged to have been kept is an unwarranted exaggeration: pp. 153–154.

35. For example, in the *Frogs* (405 B.C.), when Aristophanes has Dionysus confess a craving (*pothos*), Heracles asks him if it is for a woman or a boy (53 ff.). Aristophanes' mock accusations of his audience as sodomites and similar raillery may be interpreted as for the benefit of common people in the audience who were scornful of the erotic affectations of the upper class.

36. That this was affected is seen in the next chapter, which shows how many of these sometimes-scorned aspects of Greek life were cultivated by these same *kalokagathoi*. When the elite joined in revelry of the *kōmos*, they took on some of the eastern, effeminite ways that they professed to despise. Such, at any rate, is the meaning of the "Anacreontic" vases dating from 510 to 450 B.C. discussed in Frontisi-Ducroux and Lissarrague 1990, 229: "What the men of Athens as they are represented on their drinking vessels, seem to be searching for in the practice of communal wine–drinking, and in forms of music, song, and dance quite distinct from the forms of music, poetry, and dance that made up the education by which they had become citizens, is the chance to become other, to become—just a little bit—woman, Eastern, or barbarian. To have a party—the verb is *kōmazein*, 'to do the *kōmos*'—seems, if we can trust the images, to have meant to play at becoming other."

37. The Greek saying was οὐ παντὸς ἀνδρὸς ἐς Κόρινθον ἔσθ' ὁ πλοῦς, according to Aristophanes fr. 928 K-A, Aulus Gellius I 8.4, Strab. 8.6.20, and the scholiast to Horace *Epistles* I 17.36, who translates it *non cuivis homini contingit adire Corinthum*, "it does not fall to every man to visit Corinth." On the cult of Aphrodite and the sex industry at Corinth, see Salmon 1984, 398–400; Williams 1986. Corinth was to the Greeks and Romans what Paris was to Americans in the 1920s: a place to get pleasures not available at home. Strab. 8.6.20 (end of 1st c. B.C.) says there were more than a thousand of them, and he attributes the city's crowding and wealth to them: καὶ διὰ ταύτας οὖν πολυωχλεῖτο ἡ πόλις καὶ ἐπλουτίζετο. In the late sixth century and on into the Classical fifth, it was a likely conduit for prostitutes from Anatolia and points east.

38. Ath. 13.573d–e; scol. Pind. *Ol.* 13.23, calling them the "wives" (γυναῖκας) of the Corinthians; Campbell 1991, 3:530. The tradition is also significant because it implies an Aphrodite who can repel an armed force, like the warrior-sex goddess Ishtar/Inanna. For the cult of armed Aphrodite in Corinth, see Paus. 2.5.1; Strab. 8.6.20; Williams 1986. Figurines of Aphrodite

in Corinth resembling the Near Eastern Astarte have been found from as late as the second half of the fifth century B.C.

39. In the *Seven Against Thebes*, 230–232, it is religious consultation that is the special privilege of men: "This is the task of men, the sacrifice and consultation with the gods while making trial of the enemy. Yours [the women of Thebes] is to be silent and remain inside the house."

40. The regular Homeric verb for getting into bed is ἐπιβαίνω, used also of going up into the land from the sea and mounting a ship, horse, chariot, city wall, or pyre. In the domestic sphere, upwardness and inwardness (as in the following note) are more than physically directional; they imply movement into a female area. In New Comedy, Philemon uses εἰσπηδάω "leap in" of sexual entry (K-A fr. 3.13). The directionality of going to bed persists in our own language. We lie **down**, but we **climb** (or jump, or hop) into bed, particularly when the purpose is sexual.

41. The "inside" (ἔσω) of line 1343 is therefore ambiguous in a way that has bothered the commentators because it strains the normal usages of Greek. Agamemnon's deadly blow is deep inside his body, but as Weil remarked, the bald placement of the adverb at the end of the line would properly mean "inside the house." But the double sense was perhaps intended by the author. See Fraenkel 1950, 3:633.

The master bedroom of the Homeric house is regularly called the "nook," or μυχός (*Il.* 17.36, 22.240; *Od.* 4.304–305, 7.346; *H. Dem.* 143), and by extension it is any part of an enclosure where sleeping and lovemaking take place: the corner of the cavern where Odysseus and Calypso sleep (*Od.* 5.226), the corner of the tent where Achilles sleeps with (or without) Briseis (*Il.* 9.659, 24.675), the grotto where the Nymphs make love (*H. Aph.* 263). Praxagora refers to women's genitals in Ar. *Eccl.* 13 as "the secret nooks of our thighs," anticipating American slang in which sexual access to a woman is "nooky." The μυχός is also a place of safety or refuge (*Il.* 21.23; *Od.* 13.363, 23.41, 24.6). Inwardness is therefore also a female area, as when the author of the speech *Against Neaira* says "we have wives for the trustworthy guardianship of **things inside**" (τῶν ἔνδον, Ps-Dem. 59.122, cf. Aesch. *Sept.* 230–232). For inwardness and outward ness as female and male modes reflecting anatomical differences, see Keuls 1985, 97.

42. Slater (1968) argues that the sharp segregation of the genders and the low status of women in the fifth and fourth centuries B.C. led to extremes of a woman's dominance in the home and the focusing of that dominance on male children: "The house being divided into men's and women's quarters, her control over her own domain, which included the children, most of the slaves, and the economic heart of the household, was largely unchallenged, and made the male vulnerable indeed" (p. 9). The result, according

to Slater, was a kind of cryptomatriarchy that is reflected in Greek myth and tragedy and a pervasive male narcissism demanding high achievement.

43. See chap. 6, n. 24.

44. Redfield (1978) shows how this worked in Spartan society, where women fiercely enforced the warrior code ("Come back with your shield or on it") "but seem[ed] to be subject to no code themselves" (p. 149). The cult of permanent war led in Sparta to an especially sharp polarization of polis (a male sphere in which conformity was the rule) and *oikos* (a female sphere in which individual behavior was perceived elsewhere to border on license: Arist. *Pol.* 1269b12–70a15).

45. Hes. *WD* 702–703, Semonides fr. 6, Theog. 1225–1226. Such affirmations are not always balanced as they are in the Hesiodic example and in Simon. 7 by a reminder that there is also nothing worse than a bad woman. The tradition was renewed in Euripides fr. 164, 819.

46. *Th.* 590, γένος . . . γυναικῶν θηλυτεράων. Hesiod uses the same term for the "race" of the gods and the giants.

CHAPTER 5. EDUCATION OF THE SENSES FROM SOLON TO PERICLES

1. This widely quoted definition, from a law court oration delivered about 350 B.C., is the best short description of the conventional roles of women in the sexual culture of Classical Greece. But it is less precise than it appears, as the social and legal status of a concubine, or *pallakē*, is difficult to determine precisely. See Sealey 1984; Mossé 1991; Patterson 1991.

2. See, for example, Henderson 1991 on obscene language in Attic comedy and Dover [1978] 1989 on homosexuality.

3. Boardman 1975, 7. The interest in sexual subjects did not arise ex nihilo, however: "The art of the eighth and seventh centuries had been indifferent to sex, the early sixth displayed its urgency, and the middle added to its tenderness" (Cook 1972, 75). Brendel 1970 provides the best basic introduction to Greco-Roman erotic art.

4. 2.40, tr. Warner. The Ionian luxury of Athens became proverbial. Bacchylides' Dithyramb to Theseus addresses him as "lord of the luxuriously living Ionians," τῶν ἀβροβίων ἄναξ Ἰώνων (18.2 Snell); Heraclides Ponticus connects a luxurious life with Athens' finest years: Καὶ ἡ Ἀθηναίων πόλις, ἕως ἐτρύφα, μεγίστη τε ἦν καὶ μεγαλοψυχοτάτους ἔτρεφεν ἄνδρας (Ath. 512b).

5. Huxley 1966, 40.

6. The estimate is in Finley 1981; Bury and Meiggs (1978, 237, n. 29) quote Gomme's earlier estimate of 315,000 for all of Attica, "perhaps more

than twice as large" as Corinth. These basic estimates are still generally accepted.

7. Stobaeus' *Flor.* 3.29.58 quotes Aelian as follows: "Solon of Athens, son of Execestides, when his nephew sang a song of Sappho's over the wine, liked the song and told the boy to teach it to him; and when someone asked why he was so eager about it, he said, 'So that I may learn it and die.'" Loeb tr. D. A. Campbell 1982, 13.

8. Ath. 13.569d–e. The comedian Philemon is quoted (fr. 3 K-A) as saying in his *Brothers* that πρῶτος Σόλων διὰ τὴν τῶν νέων ἀκμὴν ἔστησεν ἐπὶ οἰκημάτων γύναια πριάμενος. The evidence would be weak coming from a comedian, but Nicander of Colophon is quoted as saying in his *History of Colophon* (F 9 Jac.) that Solon πανδήμου Ἀφροδίτης ἱερὸν πρῶτον ἱδρύσασθαι ἀφ' ὧν ἠργυρίσαντο αἱ προστᾶσαι τῶν οἰκημάτων. Cf. Eust. *Comm. ad Hom. Il.* 4.331.12 and Harp. *Lexicon* 233–234: Νίκανδρος ἐν Κολοφωνιακῶν Σόλωνά φησι σώματα ἀγοράσαντα εὐπρεπῆ ἐπὶ στέγης στῆναι διὰ τοὺς νέους, καὶ ἐκ τῶν περιγενομένων χρημάτων ἱδρύσασθαι Ἀφροδίτης πανδήμου ἱερόν. It would be interesting to know what this had to do with Colophon: were the prostitutes imported from this coastal city of Asia Minor?

9. Henry (1985) and others are skeptical of this story, but see Halperin (1989, 98–104), who argues that the provision of subsidized sex was a form of sexual empowerment with democratic overtones. What interests Halperin is less the literal truth of the story than the alleged "relation between prostitution and democracy." See also Humphreys 1993, xxxix n. 73.

10. See Chap. 4, p. 111.

11. Hdt. 1.93.3; Strab. 13.4.7. Cf. the Corinthian prostitutes' commemorative inscription honoring Aphrodite's defense of Corinth in 480 B.C., Ath. 13.573d–e; see chap. 4 above, p. 111 and n. 38. Herodotus adds that it is the custom among the *demos* of Lydia for young women to earn their dowries by prostitution and to choose their own husbands. Something like the same practice has recently been noted in modern Istanbul. Calling it "the Natasha syndrome," an April 17, 1993, *New York Times* article reported that thousands of Russian and Romanian women in Istanbul earn money by prostitution to start a business back home, with their fiancés' approval.

12. *Cyropaedeia* 8.15.

13. Lattimore's translation of *Od.* 8.248 f.:

αἰεὶ δ' ἡμῖν δαίς τε φίλη κίθαρίς τε χοροί τε
εἵματά τ' ἐξημοιβὰ λοετρά τε θερμὰ καὶ εὐναί.

The sexual meaning of εὐνή is prominent in Homer, e.g., in variants of the formula φιλότης καὶ εὐνή. In its erotic sense, εὐνή occurs nine times in the scene where Hera seduces Zeus, *Il.* 14.158 ff., though there is no actual bed. Heubeck, West, and Hainsworth (1988, 361) compare the structure of the *Odyssey* passage to lines in the *Iliad* describing the violence of Achilles and Ares, 1.177 = 5.891: αἰεὶ γάρ τοι ἔρις τε φίλη πόλεμοί τε μάχαι τε.

14. See, e.g., Plato's description in *Phdr.* 239c–d of the boy whose lover is motivated by pleasure: "a weakling rather than a sturdy boy, one who has a cozy, sheltered upbringing instead of being exposed to the open air, who has given himself up to a soft unmanly life instead of the toil and sweat of manly exercise," etc. (tr. Hackforth). Aristophanes makes fun of the old zealotry through a character named "Just Doctrine" in the *Clouds*, 889–1113. Contrast the more balanced view of Aristotle in *Eth. Nic.* 1147b27, where sex is good or bad according to the categories of profligacy (ἀκολασία) and temperance (σωφροσύνη).

15. Callias fr. 8 K-A, Hermippus fr. 57 K-A, Aristophanes fr. 556 K-A. See Ath. 524f–525c. The passage continues with quotations from the orator Antiphon, and others as early as Callinus and Archilochus. See also 517a (Men. *Trophonius,* fr. 397 Körte-Thierfelder): "The millionaire Ionian, living on Lydian pilaf, superscrew dishes," and Ar. *Thesm.* 163, Cratinus fr. 460 K-A.

16. Emlyn-Jones 1980, 170; Ussher 1973, 203. Miletus was famous for its dildoes, as we learn from Ar. *Lys.* 108 and fr. 62.1–31 Austin (fr. 592 K-A). Cf. the Ionian dildo maker "from Chios or Erythrae" in Herod. 6.58.

17. Ἰωνικὴ ῥῆσις, Ath. 573b; Ἰωνισὰ καλούμενα ποιήματα, Ath. 620e. On the Milesian tale, see Haight 1943, 5: "Their character was definite: they were erotic stories of a lascivious type. Their philosophy of life was that all men—and women—are sinners, and this belief was embodied in episodes from everyday life. Their amorality was such that the Parthian Surena was horrified when during the Parthian War of 53 B.C. a copy of the Milesian Tales was found in the pack of a Roman officer. Other short local tales, for example those of Sybaris and of Ephesus, shared these characteristics of realism, irony, and disillusion." The best-known Milesian tale is probably "The Widow of Ephesus" in Petronius' *Satyricon* 111–113; Apuleius calls his Metamorphoses (or The Golden Ass) a Milesian Tale: *ego tibi sermone isto Milesio varias fabulas conseram.* The genre began with the *Milesiaka* of Aristides of Miletus, ca. 100 B.C.

18. Chap. 12, adapted from the Loeb translation of W. H. S. Jones; cf. Ath. 625b, where the hard, spirited character of earlier Ionians is contrasted with their more voluptuous latter-day ways, ἤθη τρυφερώτερα, blamed in 624d on their barbarian rulers.

19. Hdt. 5.55, 6.123; Thuc. 6.54–59; commentary in Dover 1965, 57–68. Ath. 602a–e quotes the Peripatetic writer Hieronymus' examples of pederastic affairs that resulted in the downfall of tyrants.

20. On the ritual prostitution at Locri, see Just. 21.3, Prückner 1968; Ridgway and Scott 1972; Sourvinou–Inwood 1974. Strab. 6.2.6 also mentions a temple of Aphrodite at Eryx in Sicily which "in early times was full of female temple–slaves, who had been dedicated in fulfillment of vows not only by the people of Sicily but also by many people from abroad." (Loeb tr. Jones) But even in a temple of Aphrodite, a woman who is a hierodule is not necessarily a prostitute, sacred or otherwise.

21. Peckham 1968, 323; Karageorghis 1976, 107; 1982, 126. The word interpreted "sacred prostitutes," '*lmt*, may also be interpreted "maidens"— though this may be a euphemism. On the problematic link between sacred and secular prostitution in the ancient Near East, see chap. 3 above, n. 17. On prostitution in Corinth, see Salmon 1984, 398–400.

22. 12.3.36, Loeb tr. Jones. The hierodules belong to the temple of Ma, a goddess compared by Strab. 12.2.3 to the Greek Enyo, a war goddess linked in Homer with Athena (*Il.* 5.333) and Ares (*Il.* 5.592). In the eastern tradition, such a goddess would also be strongly sexual, like Astarte.

23. Ath. 559a, 573a. Eubulus fr. 2.178 Kock (Ath. 572a) compares the ugly eating habits of women with the dainty style of a "Milesian girl," παρθένος Μιλησία, possibly referring to a hetaera. Cf. the ambiguous Phoenician term in n. 17.

24. Hdt. 2.134 f.; Sappho frs. 5, 15(b); Page 1955, 45–51. Strab. 17.808 gives the hetaera's name as both Doricha (as in Sappho) and Rhodopis, the latter being probably her professional nickname.

25. Forster 1961, 28.

26. Ath. 577d (Machon, Gow fr. XII), 596f (Gorgias), 591c (Apollo-dorus). Strab. 8.6.20 includes such a piece of repartee in his account of Corinth.

27. Ath. 590f–591b. Pliny 35.86 f. reports the view that Apelles' model for the *Anadyomene* was Alexander the Great's mistress Pancaspe, with whom the artist fell in love and who was thereupon presented to Apelles as a gift. The romantic pairing of Praxiteles and Phryne is discussed in Havelock 1995, 42–49.

28. Ath. 591 f. names the orator Demades and the philosopher Bion of Borysthenes as sons of hetaeras; the list of famous men and the famous hetaeras who consorted with them occupies a large portion of Ath. bk. 13, which is devoted to hetaera lore.

29. Ath. 567a; the title Περι τῶν Ἀθήνησι Ἑταιρίδων is evidently a paraphrase of various titles attributed there to Aristophanes of Byzantium, Apollodorus, Ammonius, Antiphates, and Gorgias; at 591d he cites in addition Callistratus' Περὶ Ἑταιρῶν. See n. 20.

30. It appears from Menander's *Samia* that this had been a typical place of origin of women of pleasure. For the known facts about the woman who caught the attention of Sappho's brother, see n. 24 above.

31. Fr. 103 K-A = Ath. 13.568a, adapted from the Loeb translation of C. B. Gulick.

32. Ath. 607d–e.

33. *Against Neaira* 22, ἐργαζομένη μὲν ἤδη τῷ σώματι νεωτέρα δὲ οὖσα διὰ τὸ μήπω τὴν ἡλικίαν αὐτῇ παρεῖναι. On Laïs: Ath. 588c–d.

34. Dover [1978] 1989, 103.

35. No attempt is made here to appraise the popularity of Greek erotic vase paintings as reflected in the frequency with which they appear, as their survival is necessarily the result of accident. Sutton (1992, 7–8) notes that only about 150 of 30,000 to 40,000 vases represent actual acts of copulation (an additional 2,000+ have "a strong sexual element") and that more were found in Etruscan tombs than in Greek sites, showing that they were probably made for export to clients who were not Greek as well as for local consumption. Likewise, the iconography of such art cannot be known in detail, though it is hard not to see that they represent a mostly male point of view and that on the whole they take a positive view of sexual pleasure. It is not even clear that the nude women in these sexual scenes were hetaeras rather than women of the citizen class, or to what extent the erotic vases represent actual Greek life (Havelock 1995, 31–32 and n. 28). Kilmer (1993) describes the Attic red-figure erotic vase paintings of the period between 520 and 460 B.C., noting, among other things, that no more than 18 percent of the total show homosexual scenes of copulation. This compares with 14 percent found by Kämpf-Dimitriadou (1979) on vases portraying mythological love scenes.

36. On the social interpretation of Greek erotic vase paintings, see Sutton 1992, 32–34 passim.

37. See Fisher 1982, 95, on frontal copulation; Boardman 1971, 136, on sex from behind.

38. This needs to be qualified by the observation that some of the back-to-front copulation is anal, possibly at the insistence of hetaeras who needed to avoid pregnancy, like their temple counterparts in the ancient Near East who were forbidden by religious law to have children (Astour 1966, 191 and n. 40).

39. Anacreon deserves special mention as the poet laureate of the Archaic symposium and its life as pictured on the Attic red-figure vases. His lifetime begins about the time vase painting was becoming an Athenian craft industry (ca. 572 B.C.) and ends soon after the Battle of Marathon (490 B.C.), when Athenian culture turned away from the era of privilege, parties, and

pleasure. He grew up in Teos on the Asiatic mainland. Summoned from exile in Thracian Abdera to teach poetry and music to the son of Polycrates of Samos, he remained the tyrant's court poet until the Persian takeover (ca. 522), whereupon Hipparchus summoned him to Athens. Though his time in Athens could not have lasted longer than twelve years, his fame as the poet of wine, women, and song was so well established that he is depicted on three surviving red-figure vases (Beazley 1942, 31 no. 2, 40 no. 69, 123 no. 29), and his statue, standing next to that of Pericles' father Xanthippus, stood on the Acropolis for centuries (Paus. 1.25.1). A more graceful than profound poet, his wistful lines to a "boy with the look of a girl" (fr. 15 Page) speak of an eroticism in which the genders blended. See Bowra 1961, 268–307.

40. On the debacle that led to the end of the Pisistratid dynasty, see n. 17 above. According to Thucydides' account, Hipparchus, a younger brother of the Athenian tyrant Hippias, tried to seduce Harmodius, "a most beautiful young man in the flower of his youth, [who] was loved and possessed by Aristogeiton, a citizen who belonged to the middle class."(6.54.2, tr. Warner). When the rejected Hipparchus publicly insulted Harmodius' sister, the lovers plotted to overthrow the tyranny but succeeded only in assassinating Hipparchus. Both lovers were killed as a result, and the tyranny of Hippias, formerly an easy one, became harsher. It was not until the Spartans and the exiled Alcmaeonids intervened three years later that the Pisistratid regime fell, but popular memory attributed the overthrow to the lovers.

41. 5.78, tr. Grene.

42. Hdt. 6.98.2, tr. Grene.

43. Eur. *Hipp.* 244: αἰδούμεθα; 246: ἐπ' αἰσχύνην ὄμμα τέτραπται; 317: φρὴν δ' ἔχει μίασμά τι.

44. See Ussher 1973, 177, and Kilmer 1982, 106, on *Eccl.* 720 ff.

45. *Frogs* 516, ἠβυλλιῶσαι κἄρτι παρατετιλμέναι. See Kilmer 1982, 104 ff. Genital depilation was done by singeing (*Lys.* 823 ff., *Eccl.* 13 f.) and plucking (*Lys.* 87–89, 151).

46. See Richter 1929, 33 ff., and Henderson 1987, 85, on these expensive outfits. It is Richter's suggestion that Amorgos was the island through which silk was imported from the East; in the Roman period Cos had supplanted Amorgos in the sexy negligée business. See Butler and Barber 1933, 156, on Propertius 1.2.2, *Coa veste.*

47. Fr. 103 K-A = Ath. 13.568a; see n. 29 above.

48. Fr. 97 K-A = Ath. 557 f., Loeb tr. Gulick. This satirical topos, perhaps originating in Ar. *Eccl.* 878, where a superannuated woman shows up plastered with white lead, καταπεπλασμένη ψιμυθίῳ, is picked up by Hor. *Epod.* 12.9–11, perhaps Ovid's fragmentary *De medicamine faciei,* Juv. 6.461 ff., and much later Gregory of Nazianzus' pamphlet "Against Women Who Use Cosmetics."

49. *Oec.* 10.2, tr. Pomeroy (1994). Round tablets of lead carbonate have been found in women's tombs in Attica and Corinth dating from the third century B.C.: Pomeroy (1994, 305) notes that Greek art as early as the Bronze Age shows that cosmetics were used liberally by women of the highest rank: "Cosmetic containers found among women's grave goods reveal that cosmetics were considered essential for respectable women." Elevator shoes built up with cork are one of the enhancements employed by hetaeras in Alexis fr. 103 K-A = Ath. 13.568a (see n. 29 above). Pomeroy speculates that "Xenophon's censorious attitude was perhaps shaped by his experience in Sparta or by the Spartan ideal, according to which cosmetics, perfumes, and other bodily adornments were banished and beauty was the natural result of good health and hard work." See Xen. *Sp. Const.* 5.8; Plut. *Lyc.* 1.4.4; Ath. 686–687.

50. Thuc. 2.45.2, tr. Warner. See Hornblower 1991, 314, on interpretations of meaning.

51. Plut., *Per.* 24.6: καὶ γὰρ ἐξιών, ὥς φασι, καὶ εἰσιὼν ἀπ' ἀγορᾶς ἠσπάζετο καθ' ἡμέραν αὐτὴν μετὰ τοῦ καταφιλεῖν. The source of this report, according to Ath. 13.589e, is Antisthenes, whose testimony in the lost *Aspasia* was apparently favorable (Lucian *Imag.* 17 implies the dialogue was complimentary). Aeschines' *Aspasia* categorically dismissed all Ionian women as adulterers and fortune hunters, μοιχάδας καὶ κερδαλέας (Ath. 5.220b) but says that she made Lysicles, an otherwise undistinguished man, the first man in Athens (Plut. *Per.* 24.4). Plutarch is ambiguous about her reputation, except to say that it was formidable: τῶν τε πολιτικῶν τοὺς πρωτεύοντας ἐχειρώσατο καὶ τοῖς φιλοσόφοις οὐ φαῦλον οὐδ' ὀλίγον ὑπὲρ αὐτῆς παρέσχε λόγον: "she conquered the leading politicians and provided philosophers occasion to discuss her in no brief or paltry way" (*Per.* 24.1).

52. Bicknell 1982. For a comprehensive review of Aspasia and her biographical tradition, see Henry 1995.

53. Schol. Aristid. *Tett.* 127.16, 3.468 Dindorf; Bicknell 1982, 245. Had she been a slave, it is unlikely her son by Pericles would have been voted citizenship in 430/29 B.C., or that she could legally have married Lysicles after Pericles' death. It is also unlikely that the ancient sources would know and record her father's name.

54. So, e.g., Heraclides Ponticus fr. 51 Wehrli = Ath. 12.533c–d. The formula of the story in Athenaeus is a familiar one: a certain personage (here Pericles), preferring a life of pleasure, dismissed his regular wife and lived with a low woman (here the courtesan from Miletus), squandering the greater part of his property on her. The very triteness of the story, part of the tract *On Pleasure* (περὶ Ἡδονῆς), renders it suspect; virtually the identical account is attributed to Clearchus' *Love Stories* (Ἐρωτικῶν, Ath. 13.589d). Athenaeus is

full of tittle-tattle about the luxurious foibles (τρυφή, χλιδή) of the rich and famous, most of it uncritically quoted. But the tradition that she was a hetaera persisted in antiquity and is still widely accepted, e.g., Allen 1991, 19; Halperin 1990, 122; Humphries 1993, 56.

55. Plut. *Per.* 24.1.

56. *Ach.* 523 ff.; Dover 1972, 86 f.

57. Schol. Pl. *Menex.* 235e1: τὸν Λυσικλέα ῥήτορα δεινότατον κατεσκευάσατο, καθάπερ καὶ Περικλέα δημογορεῖν παρεσκεύασεν. The source is evidently Aeschinus of Sphettus as reported in Plut. *Per.* 24.4. See n. 51 above.

58. Ath. 13.569 f.; Schol. Ar. *Ach.* 526; Plut. *Per.* 24.3. Two members of Socrates' circle, Antisthenes and Aeschines of Sphettus, wrote works entitled *Aspasia*, one of them a Socratic dialogue. See Ehlers 1966.

59. Allen 1984, 321. Though some in antiquity took Aspasia's speech seriously as a model of serious patriotic oratory, Plutarch recognized that it was written in a playful spirit, μετὰ παιδιᾶς . . . γέγραπται.

60. Arist. *Pol.* 1269b12–70a15; Redfield 1978, 149.

61. *Lys.* 1124 f.: ἐγὼ γυνὴ μέν εἰμι, νοῦς δ' ἔνεστί μοι, /αὐτὴ δ' ἐμαυτῆς οὐ κακῶς γνώμης ἔχω.

62. Plut. *Per.* 24.3: τὰς γυναῖκας ἀκροασομένας οἱ συνήθεις ἦγον ὡς αὐτήν.

CHAPTER 6. IDEALIZING LOVE:
PLATO, SEX, AND PHILOSOPHY

1. Following the accepted chronology of Plato's works, the expression occurs first in the *Charmides* (155d5) and once in the *Lysis* (206a1). Repeated several times in the *Symposium*, it appears once thereafter, *Rep.* 403c6.

2. This includes only works clearly labeled Περὶ ἔρωτος, Ἐρωτικός, Ἐρωτικαὶ διατριβαί, and the like. Other works, such as Plato's *Symposium* and Diogenes' *Republic*, contained major statements about the uses of eros.

3. Parke and Wormell 1956, 180.

4. The notable exception is in the *Thesmophoriazusae*, produced in 411 B.C. just weeks before an oligarchic coup, where the Chorus curses people who attempt to substitute the established law and decrees with their own (361–362) and invokes Athena "who hates tyrants, as is proper" (1143–1144). See Dover 1972, 170 f.

5. We can see this doctrine reflected in the fragment of Philemon's *Brothers* cited in chap. 5, n. 6. Athenaeus quotes lines of the play that say that Solon's establishment of public prostitution was "a law for all mankind,"

which he goes on to call "a demotic thing to do, by Zeus, and good for public safety," δημοτικόν, ὦ Ζεῦ, πρᾶγμα καὶ σωτήριον (13.569e), using political buzzwords of the opposing political factions that make the line say, in effect, that Solon's measure was "a Democratic thing to do, and Republican as well." Good sex is good politics.

6. Micio's soliloquy in *Ad.* 49 ff. has more to do with paternal control through love than with the teaching of *sophrosyne*: "I think it's better to hold children with respect and generosity than with fear" (*pudore et liberalitate liberos retinere satius est credo quam metu*). But the boys-will-be-boys liberalism of New Comedy grows directly out of late fifth-century doctrines that virtue cannot exist except in conformity with nature, *physis*.

7. One historical irony of the "old-fashioned" position of Better Logic is that its emphasis on the virtues of physical hardiness anticipated the virtues Plato ascribed to Socrates in the *Symposium* (216d ff.) as well as the Cynic-Stoic belief in the virtue of ignoring pain.

8. In this connection it is informative to read the *Oxford Latin Dictionary's* definitions of *humilitas*, which was not yet a Christian virtue: 1: Lowness of stature, shortness, lack of height. 2: Lowness of position. 3: Lowness of rank or status, humbleness, humble condition, insignificance, unimportance. 4: Degradation, debasement, humiliation. 5: Unambitiousness, commonplaceness. 6: Submissiveness, subservience, humility.

9. *Clouds* 1085–1104, cf. *Ach.* 716, 843; *Wasps* 1070; *Thesm.* 200. See Dover [1978] 1989, 140; Henderson 1991, 77, 210, 213 f.

10. Sergent (1986, 250 f.) notes that the absence of this element in Homer could be a purely literary convention: "epic poetry, following the moral dictates of its tradition, eschews all mention of homosexuality." Since the relationship is not pederastic, it "cannot also be sexual." The erotic theme is first attested in the fifth century in Aeschylus' *Achilleïs* trilogy (*Myrmidons, Nereids,* and *Phrygians*). Achilles addresses the dead Patroclus as a respected sexual partner: "had you, ungrateful for my many kisses, no respect for [my] pure reverence of your thighs . . . ?" (fr. 228); in fr. 229 Achilles remembers "the reverent converse with your thighs." The mention in both fragments of Patroclus' thighs emphasizes the anatomical correctness of their sexual relationship. The multiple use of words for reverence, purity, and respect serves to make the love bond unmistakably proper and in some uniquely Archaic sense "Platonic." The lines were often quoted in antiquity as expressing the ideal of intense emotional and physical homoerotic love within strict physical limits. (Achilles and Patroclus are not yet lovers in fig. 7.2, which shows Patroclus as the elder, in the Homeric tradition.)

11. *Symp.* 182b–c, adapted from the translation of Allen 1991, 122. Eros, besides the abstract noun for sexual feeling, is the god of male love where

Aphrodite presides over the love of women. Only the older Aristogeiton feels eros; it is reciprocated by the younger Harmodius' *philia*.

12. Though Homer makes him a Trojan, Plato claims a Cretan origin for the myth (*Laws* 1.636c–d); Athen. 13.601 f. cites a Cretan historian Echemenes as authority that it was Minos rather than Zeus who abducted Ganymede. The legend of Zeus' birthplace on Crete is further circumstantial evidence. See Sergent 1986, chap. 22.

13. 10.4.21 (C 483–84), tr. H. L. Jones.

14. Christianity eventually created a symmetrical initiatory ritual for girls. The First Communion is a mock wedding in which the young initiate becomes a "bride of Christ."

15. Marrou 1956, 26–35.

16. Dover (1988) disputes the position developed by Bethe (1907), Bremmer (1980), Patzer (1982), Sergent (1986), and others that Greek homosexuality with boys derives from prehistoric Indo-European rituals of initiation. As insufficient evidence exists today to prove or disprove the initiatory thesis, it can be demonstrated only that "about 600 B.C. Greek poets, artists, and people in general brought homosexuality, both male and female, 'out of the closet'; not long after, females were put back into the closet, while males stayed out" (Dover 1988, 131).

17. Halperin (1990, 257–308) asks, "Why is Diotima a woman?" He argues that she is a construct designed by Plato "to represent the institutional and psychological conditions for the proper practice of (male) philosophy." Like Aspasia in her role as teacher or the Muses as the source of poetic inspiration, Diotima is a kind of liminal figure assisting her male hearers to achieve a higher level of understanding. Skinner (1993) asks the same question about Sappho's gender and comes to a similar conclusion about the character of her female discourse.

18. The similarities of Aspasia and Diotima were recognized in late antiquity, and modern writers have suggested that Diotima is a stand-in for Aspasia: Ehlers 1966, 131–136; Halperin 1990, 124. There are several reasons why Plato might have wanted to employ a different personality, as the biographical tradition suggests an Aspasia who was interested in sexual love for its own sake, whereas Diotima believes in it only as a metaphor and a means to a wholly different end.

19. Socrates belittles heterosexual love again in *Phaedrus* 250e, but the context makes it clear that what he condemns there as tantamount to bestiality is a surrender to pleasure, *hēdonē*, rather than association with women. In the same breath he condemns "unnatural" pleasure, by which he presumably means any form of anal sex. As a rule, Plato means homoeroticism

when he speaks favorably about eros, and he distinguishes his highly sublimated eros from mere pleasure.

20. *Symp.* 211b–c, tr. Allen.

21. Foucault 1985, 242–245.

22. 203c–e, tr. Allen 1991, 147.

23. Thuc. 2.43.1: "You should fix your eyes every day on the greatness of Athens as she really is, and should fall in love with her," ἐραστὰς γιγνομένους αὐτῆς. The metaphor may be drawn from Aeschylus' *Eum.* 852, γῆς τῆσδ' ἐρασθήσεσθε. The implications of this metaphor for the relation between citizen and city are developed in Monoson 1994. Rusten 1989, 169, compares Hdt. 3.53.4 τυραννὶς χρῆμα σφαλερόν· πολλοὶ δὲ αὐτῆς ἐρασταί εἰσι . . . : "power is a tricky thing: many have fallen in love with it." For other metaphoric extensions of eros and its cognates, see Dover [1978] 1989, 156.

24. Plato's doctrine on this point is not abundantly clear. His commitment to the spoken word over the written is rooted in the belief that the quest for truth is the cooperative effort of teacher and disciple united by a common love of truth, beauty, and goodness, which is *philosophia*. Socrates illustrates "boy love with philosophy" (*paiderastein meta philosophias, Phdr.* 249a) in a rhapsodic passage (250e–252c) describing the ecstasy of the philosopher's soul when it sees fresh beauty and is rewinged for spiritual flight by the resulting flood of passion. But here the transaction is between the soul of the philosopher and the beauty of the boy rather than between two persons. Plato's tendency is to avoid direct analysis of what we would call personal relationships.

25 Thuc. 5.105, tr. Warner.

26. Dodds 1959, 13 n.3: "*Nomos* was the watchword of good democrats like Protagoras and the Anonymous Iamblichi, while praise of *physis* is usually associated with an aristocratic bias, from Pindar onwards." But the notion that *arete* was inherited and could not be taught was becoming more tenuous with time; see Guthrie 1969, 251. On *nomos* versus *physis*, see Heinimann 1972.

27. Pl. *Laws* 626a: "by nature there is always a state of undeclared war between every state and every other," πάσαις πρὸς πάσας τὰς πόλεις ἀεὶ πόλεμον ἀκήρυκτον κατὰ φύσιν εἶναι. Cf. *Protagoras* 322b; Connor 1988 shows that warfare was neither constant nor unopposed.

28. Diog. Laert. 6.46: ἐπ' ἀγορᾶς ποτε χειρουργῶν "εἴθε," ἔφη, "καὶ τὴν κοιλίαν ἦν παρατρίψαντα μὴ πεινῆν." The story is repeated in 6.69.

29. Fr. 3 K-A. These sentiments are repeated with variations by other comedians quoted in Ath. 13.568d–569d. Cf. Hor. *Sat.* 1.2.101 ff.

30. Diogenes Laertius counts Aristippus and Epicurus among the anti-erotics (2.91.8, 10.118.9), Aristotle, Antisthenes, Zeno, Chrysippus, and

Apollodorus in favor—but the last three of these only if the beloved appears to be a boy of good character (7.129).

31. Frs. 57a–g, Guthrie 1969, 495; Ath. 12.544d, ἔχω καὶ οὐκ ἔχομαι. Other witticisms on his cohabitation with Laïs are recorded in 588e–f.

32. Diog. Laert. 5.31, ἐρασθήσεσθαι δὲ τὸν σοφὸν καὶ πολιτεύσεσθαι; cf. n. 27 above. The linkage of sex and politics is again noteworthy; what they both have in common is risk of disaster and confusion.

33. See n. 30 above: Zeno, Chrysippus, and Apollodorus advocated falling in love only if the beloved appears to be a boy of good character (Diog. Laert. 7.129, cf. Chrysippus *Frag. Mor.* 2.650.3, <ἐρωτικὸν εἶναι τὸν σοφὸν> καὶ ἐρασθήσεσθαι τῶν ἀξιεράστων, εὐγενῶν ὄντων καὶ εὐφυῶν).

34. *Stoicorum Veterorum Fragmenta* i.61, Diog. Laert. 13.561c.

35. Περὶ παιδοποιίας ἢ περὶ γάμου ἐρωτικός, Diog. Laer. 6.16.

36. Diog. Laert. 5.31, Arist. *Divisiones* 3 col. 1.13–16, 2 col. 2.11–14; although *Rhetoric* 1381b28 does not include eros among the forms of friendship, the four εἴδη (φυσικόν, ξενικόν, ἑταιρικόν, and ἐρωτικόν) were widely recognized: Chrysippus *Frag. Mor.* 112.13, Plut. *Amat.* 758C11–D4. Diogenes Laertius says in his life of Plato (3.81) that some philosophers admit the category of ἐρωτικὴ φιλία not recognized by Plato himself.

37. On erotic curses as well as erotic magic generally, see Faraone 1990, 1992, 1993.

38. Kassel and Austin (1983–, 8:378) name the tragedians Euripides, Theodectes, and Diogenes of Sinope and comedians Anaxandrides (fr. 12 K-A), Alexis (fr. 70 K-A), and Alexander (fr. 2 K-A) as authors of plays named *Helen*. Sophocles had written three plays about her: *The Demand for Helen, The Theft of Helen,* and *The Marriage of Helen*. A comic version of *The Demand for Helen* was written by Timesitheus, *The Theft of Helen* by Alexis (frs. 71–72 K-A); fragments also survive of Alexis' *The Suitors of Helen* (frs. 73–75 K-A).

39. Plato has Phaedrus state the theory fully in the *Symposium,* 178d–179a:

> I say then that a man in love, if discovered doing something shameful, or suffering it from another and failing through cowardice to defend himself, would not be so pained at being seen by his father or friends or anyone else as by his beloved. We see this same thing too in the beloved, that it is especially before his lovers that he feels shame when seen in something shameful. If then there were some device so that a city or an army might be made up of lovers and their beloveds, it is not possible that they could govern their own affairs better than by abstaining from all things

shameful and vying for honor among themselves; fighting side by
side, men of this sort would be victorious even if they were but
few against nearly all mankind. For a man in love would surely not
let himself be seen by his beloved, beyond all others, deserting his
post or throwing down his arms; he would choose to die many
times before that. (Tr. Allen)

The phrase *erōtikē philia* is used to describe the Sacred Band of Thebes in
Plut. *Pel.* 18.2.

40. Plut. *Pel.* 18, *Alex.* 9; Ath. 13.561 f., 602a. A statement of such a sort
is of course difficult to imagine unless the speaker felt that many would
consider such homosexual bonding disgraceful—as for example Plato states
in *Laws* 1.636c. The number three hundred was no doubt meant to recall the
band of three hundred Spartan hoplites who died holding the pass at
Thermopylae against the Persians in 490 B.C., Hdt. 7.224.

CHAPTER 7. SEXUAL BEAUTY:
THE NUDE IN GREEK ART

1. Euripides puts this bit of anti–Spartan propaganda into the
Andromache (ca. 425 B.C.):

No Spartan girl
Could ever live clean even if she wanted.
They're always out on the street in scanty outfits,
Making a great display of naked limbs.
In those they race and wrestle with the boys too—
Abominable's the word. It's little wonder
Sparta is hardly famous for chaste women.
(595–601, tr. Nims)

2. See Hornblower 1991, 27 f. on the passage in Thuc. 1.6.5, where
further discussions of athletic nudity are cited. Pl. *Rep.* 452c: "It is not long
since the Greeks thought it disgraceful and ridiculous, as most of the barbarians do now, for men to be seen naked."

3. For a discussion of the evidence from antiquity and theories ancient
and modern explaining Greek athletic nudity, see Sansone 1988, 107–112.5.

4. *Il.* 2.216, 263, tr. Lattimore. Harris (1972, 20) cites Xen. *Ages.* 1.28,
where the Spartan king displays naked Persian prisoners so his troops can see
their untanned, flabby bodies and lose their fear of the enemy.

5. Stewart 1990, 106.

6. Hanfmann 1983, 86: "It is noteworthy that we seem to have found no archaic Lydian representations of either naked men or naked women, and apparently no nude athletes."

7. Bonfante 1989. My own remarks, suggested in part by Bonfante's study of art and literature, have more to do with the social use of male nudity in Classical Athens. To what extent this occurred elsewhere in Greece remains unclear.

8. *Il.* 22.75 f.; cf. Tyrtaeus fr. 7.

9. Keuls 1993, 2: "The concept [of phallocracy] denotes a successful claim by a male elite to general power, buttressed by a display of the phallus less as an organ of union or of mutual pleasure than as a kind of weapon: a spear or war club, and a scepter of sovereignty."

10. Keuls 1993, 68: this was called a *kyōn*, "dog," or *kynodesmē*, "dog bundle" (κύων, LSJ VII, κύνοδέσμη, Photius apud Stephanus). One of many words in comedy for the penis was "dog," κύων (Pl. *Com.* fr. 188. 16 K-A, Hsch., AP 5.105.4 [Marc. Arg.], AP 12.225.2 [Strato]; see K-A on Aristophanes fr. 135, Henderson 1987 on Ar. *Lys.* 158, and Henderson 1991, 127).

11. Murray 1993, 215.

12. *Charmides* 154c–d, adapted from the Jowett translation.

13. For an exception, see fig. 5.16.

14. The differences have both regional and cultural aspects. The kore type, "heavily indebted to Oriental prototypes" (Ridgway and Scott 1977, 114), is Ionian by association (notwithstanding the Dorian *peplos* she sometimes wore), where the simple nudity of the kouros (though, as Stewart 1986, 66, notes, the type is curiously rare at Dorian sites) is rooted in Doric, Peloponnesian, and Cretan traditions. The ramifications lead anyone who is so inclined to see a division of Hellenism into masculine Doric and feminine Ionian tendencies. I am not aware that this analysis occurred to the Greeks themselves, but the Romans of the first century B.C. were fond of juxtaposing masculine Romans with feminine easterners: Septimius and Acme in Catullus 45, Caesar and Cleopatra in Hor. *Odes* 1.37, Aeneas and Dido in the *Aeneid*.

15. It is the same piece of headgear in which Homer poses Penelope when she appears before her suitors in *Od.* 1.334, 16.416, 18.210, and 21.65. For its symbolic combination of chastity and allure, see Nagler 1974, 44–63.

16. Sappho fr. 1 LP prays to an Aphrodite who is an elaborately throned weaver of wiles, ποικιλόθρον' . . . δολόπλοκε; Euripides uses similar language to express her duality in fr. 26 Nauck, calling her a goddess of many complexities:

τῇ δ' Ἀφροδίτῃ πόλλ' ἔνεστι ποικίλα·
τέρπει τε γὰρ μάλιστα καὶ λυπεῖ βροτούς.

17. *Od.* 1.353, 8.458, 16.415, 18.209, 21.64. Penelope fulfills her role as the prop and support of the household.

18. This tendency is best illustrated in Acropolis Korai nos. 598, 615, 670, 672, 674, 675, 678, 681, 682. The evidence for such a cult of Aphrodite is late: Ath. 554c–e. There is no additional ancient evidence for an actual cult, but see Säflund 1963 for the type of Aphrodite ἀνασυρομένη and the gesture of self-exposure ἀνάσυρμα, which may have ritual connotations. All of this is of course unrelated to the korai.

19. For more about of this statue and its influence, see Havelock 1995.

20. *Trach.* 1062–1063, tr. Jameson. On the contemporaneous dating of *Antigone* and *Trachiniae*, see Lloyd-Jones 1994, 8.

21. 310: μὴ τὸ κράτος αὔχει δύναμιν ἀνθρώποις ἔχειν.

22. Henderson 1987, 196. Greek Old Comedy had from the beginning dressed its male characters in a costume that included exaggerated phalluses on male characters: a "dangling thong of leather, red and thick at the tip" (*Clouds* 538 f., tr. Arrowsmith: see note ad loc. by Dover 1968). This is not unparalleled in ritual performances elsewhere in the world. On the nude female characters in Aristophanes plays, see Zweig 1992.

23. A rather conservative Socrates, as remembered by the conservative Xenophon, says in *Mem.* 3.4.12 (without mentioning women) that management of private business differs only in scale from that of public, τῶν ἰδίων ἐπιμέλεια πλήθει μόνον διαφέρει τῆς τῶν κοινῶν. In *Oec.* 7.26 his friend Ischomachus states that women have the same capacity for memory and attention (or management skill, μνήμη and ἐπιμέλεια) as men; Socrates says elsewhere that women are equal to men except in judgment (γνώμη) and physical strength, *Symp.* 2.9, but Plato's Socrates avers that except for physical weakness women are men's equals and equally suited to govern, *Rep.* 455d6–456a11. Aristotle generalized that male animals are in general "simpler and less cunning" (ἁπλούστερα καί ἧττον ἐπίβουλα) than females, and that these qualities extend to humans (*Hist. An.* 608b4).

24. Diog. Laert. 6.12: ἀνδρὸς καὶ γυναικὸς ἡ αὐτὴ ἀρετή. Cf. the Stoic view, *SVF* 3.59: οὐκ ἄλλην τοίνιν πρὸς τὴν ἀνθρωπότητα φύσιν ἔχειν ἡ γυνή, ἄλλην δὲ ὁ ἀνὴρ φαίνεται, ἀλλὰ τὴν αὐτήν· ὥστε καὶ τὴν ἀρετήν. . . . φιλοσοφητέον οὖν καὶ ταῖς γυναιξίν, ἐμφερῶς τοῖς ἀνδράσιν, κτλ. Cf. Lactant. *Div. Inst.* 3.25: Stoici . . . et servis et mulieribus philosophandum esse dixerunt, Epicurus quoque qui rudes omnium literarum ad philosophiam invitat.

25. Frs. 150–154 K-A; see *PCG* VII, p. 175, on the topic of the play.

26. *Lys.* 1124–1127. Cf. the women in the chorus of Euripides' *Medea* 1085 ff.

27. See, e.g., the fragment from Aeschylus' *Danaids* fr. 44 Radt and Euripides *TGF*² 648.

28. See Guthrie 1969, 2:175–176.

29. *Hipp.* 447–450, tr. Grene; cf. 1268–1281. These lines significantly expand the claims traditionally made for Aphrodite, for example, in the Homeric *Hymn to Aphrodite* (V), 1–6, where it is stated only that all creatures *have an interest in* (μέμηλεν) the works of Aphrodite.

30. Phidias' colossal statue of Athena for the Parthenon (438 B.C.) held a small Nike in her hand; a similar Zeus at Olympia, finished ca. 430 B.C., also held a Nike (Paus. 5.11.1).

CHAPTER 8. EROTIC FRIENDSHIP: ROMANTIC FICTIONS

1. P. 170 and n. 23.

2. Fr. B7 D-K; cf. Socrates in Xen. *Mem.* 3.9.7: "Just as they call a strong *epithumia* eros, so they name a great delusion mania."

3. This is the point of Herodotus' analysis of Athenian power under democratic rule:

> Thus Athens went from strength to strength, and proved, if proof were needed, how noble a thing freedom is, not in one respect only, but in all; for while they were oppressed under a despotic government, they had no better success in war than any of their neighbors, yet, once the yoke was flung off, they proved the finest fighters in the world. This clearly shows that, so long as they were held down by authority, they deliberately shirked their duty in the field, as slaves shirk working for their masters; but when freedom was won, then every man amongst them was interested in his own cause. (5.78, tr. de Sélincourt).

Cf. the Hippocratic *Airs, Waters, Places* 23 (probably contemporary with Herodotus): "Independent people, taking risks on their own behalf and not on behalf of others, are willing and eager to go into danger, for they themselves enjoy the prize of victory."(Loeb tr. W. H. S. Jones).

4. Hermias in Pl. *Phdr.*, 76 (fr. 483 Usener): σύντονον ὄρεξιν ἀφροδισίων μετὰ οἴστρου καὶ ἀδημονίας.

5. *Eth. Nic.* 1166a31: ἔστι γὰρ ὁ φίλος ἄλλος αὐτός. Cf. Zeno of Citium in Diog. Laert. 7.23, Cic. *Amic.* 80: *est enim [amicus] is qui est tamquam alter idem.* Aristotle also says that one's children are another self: *Eth. Nic.* 1161b28.

6. The formula αὐτὰρ ἐπεὶ πόσιος καὶ ἐδητύος ἐξ ἔρον ἔντο occurs seven times in the *Iliad* and fourteen in the *Odyssey*.

7. Diog. Laert. 6.46, 69. The Cynics did not discourage sex, teaching only that it must be consensual and that women have the same rights as men. Antisthenes advocated mutuality to the extent that he said men should have sex with women who will be grateful for it: χρὴ τοιαύταις πλησιάζειν γυναιξὶν αἳ χάριν εἴσονται, Diog. Laert. 6.3. See Rist 1969, 56 f., 59–62. When Diogenes' student Crates married Hipparchia, they conducted their sexual relations in public: ἐν τῷ φανερῷ συνεγίνετο, Diog. Laert. 6.97; Rist 1969, 61 n. 7.

8. Diog. Laert. 7.130: ἐπιβολὴν φιλοποιίας διὰ κάλλος ἐμφαινόμενον; cf. Cic. *Tusc.* 4.34.72: Stoici vero et sapientem amaturum esse dicunt et amorem ipsum conatum amicitiae faciendae ex pulcritudinis specie definiunt. Cleanthes' student Chrysippus taught that erotic love depends on friendship: εἶναι οὖν τὸν ἔρωτα φιλίας, Diog. Laert. 7.130, as illustrated for the Stoics by Menander's *Misoumenos* where Thrasonides does not force himself on his captive mistress because she dislikes him.

9. Posidippus G-P 1 = A.P. 5.134.

10. Ὅταν οὖν λέγωμεν ἡδονὴν τέλος ὑπάρχειν, οὐ τὰς τῶν ἀσώτων ἡδονὰς καὶ τὰς ἐν ἀπολαύσει κειμένας λέγομεν, . . . οὐδ' ἀπολαύσεις παίδων καὶ γυναικῶν. . . . Diog. Laert. 10.131–132.

11. On the good and sexual pleasure, fr. 67 Usener, cf. Ath. 12.546e, 7.280a, 278f; Diog. Laert. 10.6; Cic. *Tusc.* 3.41. On the wise man and heaven-sent love, Diog. Laert. 10.118.

12. *Argon.* 4.445–449. The opening words Σχέτλι' Ἔρως . . . ἐκ σέθεν κτλ. recall Theognis 1231–1232 Σχέτλι' Ἔρως . . . ἐκ σέθεν κτλ.; and Simonides fr. 54: Σχέτλιε παῖ δολομήδεος Ἀφροδίτας. . . .

13. Hunter 1985, 27.

14. Beye 1993, 206.

15. *Argon.* 3.1015–1021, tr. Beye 1993, 187.

16. On this scenario, in which the boring and unpleasant restraints of a married woman's life are vicariously exchanged for a sexual fantasy of undemanding love and delight, see Griffiths 1981. On the appeal of the Adonis cult to women, see Kraemer 1992, 30–35. The symbolism of the Adonia is discussed in Detienne 1977 and Winkler 1990, 188–209.

17. Gutzwiller 1992, 363–366.

18. See Theoc. *Id.* 17 and Asclepiades or Posidippus A.P. 12.77 = 39 G-P on the resemblance of Berenice I to Aphrodite; Callimachus 5 Pf. = 14 G-P and Posidippus 12–13 G–P on the shrine of Arsinoë Aphrodite at Zephyrium.

19. Quis te mutavit tantus deus? An quod amantes
    non longe a caro corpore abesse volunt?
    (Catullus 31–32)

20. Gutzwiller 1992, 361.

21. There is little on which to base a reliable statistical appraisal of female literacy in any period of Greek history, though it was certainly lower than that of males. Ischomachus' wife is able to read and write household inventories in Xenophon's *Oeconomicus* (9.10), but she belongs to the most privileged class. Like all other evidence from antiquity, this is purely anecdotal, and the evidence that women read literary texts is especially scant. See Harris 1989, 106–108; Cole 1981.

22. See Rosenmeyer 1969, 78 f.: "Matched against the goal of *otium*, love, in spite of the appeal of its genuineness and spontaneity, must always have an air of the preliminary or fairly ludicrous about it. Hence the mocking quality of love in Theocritus." The only exception to the rule of failure or inconclusiveness in Theocritean pastoral love is Daphnis' marriage to the nymph Nais at the end of *Idyll* 8.

23. For the pervasive influence of Archaic lyric on the Hellenistic epigram, see Giangrande 1968, 93–174.

24. Asclepiades G-P 16 = A.P. 12.50 (Gow and Page 1965 is the best edition and commentary); see also W. R. Paton's Loeb edition of *The Greek Anthology*, vols. 1 and 4.

25. Anon. G-P 6 = A.P. 12.115.

26. For the large range of ancient testimony on the *kōmos*, see Headlam 1922, 82 f.

27. Asclepiades G-P 13 = A.P. 5.164.

28. Asclepiades G-P 8 = A.P. 5.162.

29. Asclepiades G-P 20 = A.P. 12.161.

30. Meleager G-P 26 = A.P. 5.160.

31. For example, Ouvré 1894, 97, on Meleager, whose problem, thinks Ouvré, is that he is not a European: Et pourtant sachons gré à Méléagre d'aspirer à la grande passion. Il n'y peut atteindre, et se content de chimères. Bien des hommes en sont là, surtout chez les peuples de l'Orient et du Midi. Tandis que la poésie plane dans l'idéal, les moeurs restent brutales et vulgaires." See also Luck 1967, 405, where the oxymoron *sanfte Raserei*, "mild frenzy," is coined to describe the mixture of passion and control that is characteristic of this genre. Garrison 1977 deals in detail with the strictures that critics have put on Hellenistic love epigram in modern times and appraises the individual character of its three greatest masters, Asclepiades (who appears to have invented the genre), Callimachus, and Meleager.

32. See, e.g., *IA* 543–557.

33. Cercidas Meliamb 3.27–33 (Powell 1925, 207, fr. 2 Lomiento); Loeb ed. Rusten et al. 1993, 420 f.

34. Fr. 3 K-A, Ath. 13.569e–f, adapted from Gulick's Loeb translation.

35. The Cynic style in comedy is reflected in Roman adaptations such as Plautus' *Twin Menaechmi*, in which bonds based on marriage and sex (Menaechmus of Epidamnus, his wife, and the *meretrix* Erotium) are fraught with lies, suspicion, and opportunism while the kinship that bonds the twin Menaechmi survives years of separation and is completely disinterested.

36. See, e.g., the metope on the temple at Selinus, Sicily, illustrated in fig. 5.14a.

37. Terence's *Eunuchus* is a notable exception. Smith 1994 points out that none of the usual mitigations, such as drunkenness before the fact or remorse afterward, are present. The goal of harmony toward which a comedy regularly moves is compromised by the rash selfishness of the rapist Chaerea at the expense of Thais: the traits of Chaerea and his brother, Phaedria, "overwhelm and nullify the careful rationality of Thais and confirm the negative impression that Chaerea's actions, despite the youthful charm of his energy and impetuousness, have already made upon the audience" (p. 30).

38. Detienne 1977 is an exhaustive review of the Adonis rituals and their symbolism, much of which was sexual. Packman 1993 objects to the reluctance of handbooks and translations to use the word "rape"; but much of what happens in New Comedy falls into a gray area that the English word "rape" distorts. Most rapists, for example, are not eager to marry their victims. On rape in ancient law and theater, see Cole 1984; Harris 1990; Smith 1994.

39. *Pel.* 18.2: "A band that is held together by the friendship between lovers [ἐρωτικὴ φιλία] is indissoluble and not to be broken, since the lovers [οἱ ἀγαπῶντες] are ashamed to play the coward before their beloved, and the beloved before their lovers, and both stand firm in danger to protect each other."

40. See Gomme and Sandbach 1973 on *Dyskolos* 842 ἐγγυῶ παίδων ἐπ' ἀρότῳ γνησίων and *Perikeiromene* 1013.

41. See P. Antinoopolis 15 (Austin 240; Sandbach [1972] 1990, 327) and Lloyd-Jones 1964 (repr. in 1991, 94–114). Another verb of affection that takes on a romantic sexual tone beginning in the fourth century is στέργειν: see Page 1962 fr. 34.15 (Sandbach [1972] 1990, 328); Xen. *Symp.* 8.14.21, *Com. Adesp.* 284 Kock, Meleager GP 80 = 12.164 of Alexis and Cleobulus.

42. 6.182–185, tr. Lattimore. The topic became conventionalized; cf. Semonides 7 West 75f., Hor. *Odes* 1.13.17–20:

> Felices ter et amplius
> quos irrupta tenet copula nec malis
> divulsus querimoniis
> suprema citius solvet amor die.

The ideal of eternal fidelity was particularly attractive to the Romans, as was the combination of love and friendship. Catullus, echoing the theme of erotic *philia* in New Comedy, spoke of his love for Lesbia as an *aeternum sanctae foedus amicitiae*, C. 109.6. Cf. Prop. 2.6.42: *semper amica mihi, semper et uxor eris*. See Williams 1958, 25; Lilja 1965, 172 ff.

43. See Nauck TGF^2 (1889), frs. 164, 822, 823, 909. The marriage of Electra and Pylades at the end of the *Electra* is Electra's consolation and an end to her troubles: τοῖσδε μελήσει γάμος (1342).

44. Niceratus: *Symp.* 8.3 ὁ Νικήρατος . . . ἐρῶν τῆς γυναικὸς ἀντερᾶται. See *Hiero* 3.4 on the attachment of man and wife.

45. On the erotic superiority of a wife, *Oec.* 10.12, which opposes the Cynic formula that a slave woman is the best sexual partner; on conjugal partnership, *Oec.* 7.26–28, cf. Xenophon's *Symp.* 2.9 (where Socrates declares that except for *gnomē* and physical strength, woman's nature is not inferior to a man's) and Ar. *Eth. Nic.* 1162a16–29, quoted below.

46. *Eth. Nic.* 1162a16–29, Loeb tr. H. Rackham. This passage contrasts with Aristotle's claim in *Politics* 1253a19 that "the polis is prior in nature to the household [*oikia*] and to each of us individually. For the whole must necessarily be prior to the part." Later he says, "as between the sexes, the male is by nature superior and the female inferior, the male ruler and the female subject" (1254b13–15). Both of these views argue that book 1 of the *Politics* is an earlier work than the *Nicomachean Ethics*, or represents a historically earlier point of view.

47. 1171a12; this is close to the Stoic view reported by Diog. Laert. 7.130 that eros is a subset of *philia*; see n. 7 above.

48. See Arnott 1970. Significantly, this is the same play that the Stoics used to illustrate that eros grows out of philia: Thrasonides does not take advantage of his captive mistress because she does not like him.

49. *Rudens* 1249–1253, tr. Hunter 1985, 140.

50. These protective barriers are described in Garrison 1978, 33–47.

51. Otis 1970, 266.

52. Konstan 1994, 7.

53. Konstan 1994, 11.

54. See, e.g., the "for richer or poorer" speech of a young wife responding to her father's suggestion that she leave her husband because he has fallen on hard times: Papyrus Didot 1 (Greek in Sandbach [1972] 1990, translation in Miller et al. 1987).

55. *Per.* 24.5, where the key phrase is ἐρωτικὴ ἀγάπησις.

56. *Dialogue on Love* 769E–770A, where "integral amalgamation" is ἡ δι' ὅλων κρᾶσις. The translation is the Loeb version of W. C. Helmbold.

57. *Mor.* 142F–143A, adapted from the Loeb translation of Frank Cole Babbitt. See Antipater of Tarsus, *SVF* 3.63.15 ff. (p. 255), from his treatise *On Marriage*.

58. From H. Dessau, *Inscriptiones Latinae Selectae* 1259.4–5 and 10–11, 1:278, quoted in Brown 1988, 15. Further documentation of the affective bonds between spouses in Roman society is found in Saller and Shaw 1984, 134–135, and Veyne 1978, 33–63. Benecke [1896] 1970, 17, remarks that a woman, "regarded *merely* as a source of pleasure or convenience, can no more be an object of love than a bottle of brandy or a railway train."

CHAPTER 9. ANEROTIC RELIGION: GREEK THEMES IN EARLY CHRISTIANITY

1. Part of this chapter was first presented at a meeting of the Society for Ancient Greek Philosophy on October 26, 1987.

2. "Beginning in the later books of the Hebrew Bible and continuing through the New Testament, there is a general decline in the value of sexuality and a tendency toward exaggerating its sinfulness. This shift in attitude resulted less from the influence of apocalyptic religious thought than from the Greco–Roman cultural hegemony of the third century B.C.E. to the second century C.E." (McAffee 1993, 691). Foucault 1978, 1985, and 1986 detail Greco-Roman intellectual developments that emphasized the disadvantages of sexual activity.

3. Pinxit et minoribus tabellis libidines, eo genere petulantis ioci se reficiens (Pliny *HN* 35.72); Propertius believed it made his reputation: Parrhasius parva vindicat arte locum (3.9.12).

4. 1004 f., οὐκ οἶδα πρᾶξιν τήνδε πλὴν λόγωι κλύων / γραφῆι τε λεύσσων. We are apt to assume with Barrett that he saw Archaic vase paintings because these have survived. For Euripides' contemporaries, later paintings of the type we know were contemporary are more likely.

5. Ath. 13.567b. Whether "pornographers" means portrayers of famous courtesans (so *LSJ*) or creators of erotica (or both) has been disputed, but the latter is more likely. See chap. 5, p. 122, and n. 29 on the interest in hetaeras in later antiquity.

6. A.P. 7.345 and 450; Ath. 7.335c–e, 10.457e; P. Maas in *RE*, vol. 19.2, col. 2122, Gow and Page 1965, 2:4; Boardman and LaRocca 1978, 154. An Egyptian hetaera named Elephantis also wrote a book illustrated with twelve different sexual positions. See Weitzmann 1970, 67 f. The Suda reports that a serving woman of Helen and Menelaus named Astyanassa wrote the first

book on sexual positions, which were later imitated by Philaenis and Elephantis or Elephantina.

7. *Eccl.* 952–959, tr. Parker; see Bowra 1958.

8. *The Peloponnesian War* 2.53, tr. Warner. Hornblower (1991, 326) notes that the first verb in the Greek original, ἦρξε, is ambiguous: "The disorders about to be listed *began* with the plague in the chronological sense; but did the plague directly cause them all?" The ambiguity thus suggests by innuendo the interpretation in Warner's translation that the plague caused a cultural change, without actually stating as much.

9. On sexual license as a conventionalized response to danger in Archaic societies, see Durkheim [1915] 1976, 405; Briffault 1927, 3:201 f.; Thomas 1937, 264. Closer to home, news accounts noted an outbreak of sexual activity—and consequent pregnancies—along with the arson and looting that accompanied the New York City blackout of July 13, 1977.

10. *Eth. Nic.* 10.1.2; Aristotle devoted the last part of bk. 7 and most of bk. 10 to this problem. See Gosling and Taylor 1982 for a review of the controversy. Even Antisthenes, the founder of the Cynic sect, had contradictory views about pleasure that are difficult to reconstruct.

11. 63c5–64a6, tr. Tredennick.

12. 64e7–67c7, tr. Tredennick.

13. Guthrie 1971, 164.

14. ὁ ἐν ἀπορρήτοις λεγόμενος, that humans are posted, as it were, in a guard post, 62b3.

15. Fr. 131b: "Each man's body follows the call of overmastering death; yet still there is left alive *an image of life,* for this alone is from the gods. It sleeps while the limbs are active; but while the man sleeps it often shows in dreams a decision of joy or adversity to come" (tr. Dodds 1959, 135). Cf. Xen. *Cyr.* 8.7.21, which describes the same prophetic function, and Hippoc. *De diaeta* 4.86, where the soul is the sleeping body's housekeeper.

16. *Cra.* 400b9–c1 ff.; in *Grg.* 493a2 he attributes it to "one of our wise men."

17. *Rep.* 364e3 ff.

18. D-K 58 C4. Even the Pythagorean abstention from beans may have had a sexual pretext. Aristotle is quoted in Diog. Laert. 8.34 that Pythagoras warned against them "because they are like genitals, or the gates of hell." Porph. *Plot.* 44 and Lydus, *Mens.* 4.42 explained that a bean that has been bitten and exposed to the sun's heat for a while gives off the smell of human semen. On Pythagorean suspicion of women because they are synonymous with *tryphē* and prejudicial to *ponos,* see Detienne 1977, 123.

19. On the interpretation of the Hippocratic oath against abortive pessaries and the common practice of abortion, see Riddle 1992, 7–10.

20. See Edelstein 1967, 3–63, which concludes that "the Hippocratic oath is a Pythagorean manifesto and not the expression of an absolute standard of medical conduct." For the avoidance of magicoreligious medicine, see pp. 205–246, "Greek Medicine in Its Relation to Religion and Magic." On abortion in the ancient world, see Riddle 1992.

21. *Laws* 636b, Loeb tr. R. G. Bury. In 836b–e Plato returns to this topic, noting that the life of animals proves homosexuality to be unnatural, that it does not promote virtue, and should therefore not be countenanced by the laws.

22. *Tusc.* 4.70–71; Ennius fr. 341: Flagiti principium est nudare inter civis corpora.

23. Fr. 12, tr. Malherbe 1986.

24. *Laws* 840d, 841a–d, tr. A. E. Taylor.

25. For the Hippocratic approval of sex during pregnancy, see Rousselle 1988, 42, and *Oribasius Libri Incerti* 14. Sources for the Stoic view in Fox 1987, 738 n. 16.

26. *Ulysses* p. 319, 11.225–228 (1984 Bodley Head ed.). Dedalus's reference to the "small creatures within us" extends the doctrine of Tertullian that sperm is a child as soon as it is ejaculated (Veyne 1987, 12).

27. 1 Thess. 4:2–5, Revised English Bible.

28. 1 Cor. 6:18, Revised English Bible.

29. Haight 1943, xx.

30. *Tristia* 498 ff., Loeb tr. A. L. Wheeler.

31. 2.6.27 ff., Loeb tr. H. E. Butler.

32. *C.* 16.9–11.

33. Euse., *Hist. Eccl.* 6.8.2–3; Brown 1988, 168 and n. 44.

34. 1 Cor. 7.

35. 1 Cor. 6:13.

36. Gal. 5:19–22, RSV.

37. Rom. 8:6–8, 13, RSV.

38. *Historia Monachorum in Aegypto* 20, tr. Norman Russell; quoted in Rousselle 1988, 171; Rousselle's tenth chapter, pp. 160–178, illustrates the use of starvation to quell sexual appetites.

39. McAffee 1993, 691.

40. Beard 1980; Drijvers 1987; Brown 1988, 8 f. and n. 14.

41. Nock 1972, 11.

42. Nock 1972, 7.

43. Dion. Hal. 2.19.4–5; James 1959, 161 ff.

44. *C.* 63.59 f.

45. *Confessions* 2.1.2–4, tr. Ryan.

46. 3.1.1; 6.12.21 and 15.25, tr. Ryan.

47. *Confessions* 8.12.29 (Rom. 13:14), 9.1.1, tr. Ryan.

48. Quinn 1963, 144–147.

49. See O'Meara 1969, 53.

50. On moral equality, see chap. 7, n. 24; and von Arnim, *SVF* III 58 f., §5. On "effeminate" for weak or degraded, Cic. *Tusc.* 1.95.6 *nunc quidem cogitationibus mollissimis effeminamur*; 2.15.10: *enervatam muliebremque sententiam*; *Off.* 1.14.10: "Nature and Reason are careful to do nothing in an improper or effeminate fashion," *ne quid indecore effeminateve faciat*. Notwithstanding Cicero's prejudices, the Roman Stoa, particularly Seneca and Musonius Rufus, developed the strongest case for sexual equality. But philosophic and pseudophilosophic rant against the vices of women was evidently a commonplace in the first century A.D., e.g., Juv. *Sat.* 6 and Eumolpus in Petronius' *Satyricon* 110. Both emphasize sexual incontinence.

51. *Paedagogus* 2.2.33, tr. S. P. Wood; 2.7.58; 2.2.33: γυναικί, ἧ καὶ τὸ συνειδέναι αὐτὴν ἑαυτῇ, ἥτις εἴη, μόνον αἰσχύνην φέρει.

52. Saying 114, trans. T. O. Lamden, cited in Meeks 1993, 145. The quotations of Thomas are wrongly called a "Gospel," as they do not purport to narrate the life of Christ. But the title has become customary.

53. In *Patrologia Latina* 26.533; cf. Ambrose, ibid. 15.844: "She who does not believe is a woman and should be designated by the name of her bodily sex, whereas she who believes progresses to complete manhood, to the measure of the adulthood of Christ. She then does without worldly name, gender of body, youthful seductiveness, and garrulousness of old age." Cf. St. Augustine *De Trinitate* 12.7 in *Patrologia Latina* 42.1003–1005: "Only man is the image and glory of God. Since the believing woman cannot lay aside her sex, she is restored to God only when there is no sex, in the spirit."

54. Evidence of women's leadership and offices in Christian communities is given in Kraemer 1992, 174–190.

55. 1 Tim. 11–12, 15; Revised English Bible.

56. Col. 3:18; Eph. 5:22, Revised English Bible. Cf. 1 Pet. 3:1: "You women must submit to your husbands, so that if there are any of them who disbelieve the gospel they may be won over without a word being said, by observing your chaste and respectful behavior." All of these are conventional sentiments overlaid with a Christian rationale; in preaching the submission of women, Christian ideologues were simply endorsing conventional patriarchal morality. These New Testament "household codes," it has been argued, were written by followers of Paul, not Paul himself. See Abrahamsen 1993, 816. De Ste. Croix (1981, 103–111) cites and quotes many Judeo–Christian texts justifying the subjection of women.

57. 1 Cor. 7:9, 29.

58. 1 Cor. 7:33–34.

59. Galen, *De Semine* 1.8, p. 571 Kühn; Soranus, *Gynaecia* 1.7.30–32, tr. Temkin 1956, 27–30.

60. Catullus 51.13–16. Fraenkel 1957, 212. Theophrastus in Stob. *Flor.* 64.66: Θεόφραστος ὁ φιλόσοφος ἐρωτηθεὶς ὑπό τινος τί ἐστιν ἔρως, 'πάθος' ἔφη 'ψυχῆς σχολαζούσης.' Cf. Ter. *Haut.* 109: *nulla adeo ex re istuc fit nisi ex nimio otio.*

61. *Tusc.* 4.68, Loeb tr. King.

Selected Bibliography

Abrahamsen, Valerie. 1993. "Women: Early Christianity." In *The Oxford Companion to the Bible*, 814–818. New York: Oxford University Press.

Abusch, Tzvi. 1993. "Mourning the Death of a Friend: Some Assyriological Notes." In *The Frank Talmage Memorial Volume*, ed. Barry Walfish, 53–62. Haifa: Haifa University Press.

Ackerman, Susan. 1992. *Under Every Green Tree: Popular Religion in Sixth-Century Judah*. Atlanta: Scholars Press.

Allen, Reginald E. 1984. *The Dialogues of Plato*. Vol. 1: *Euthyphro, Apology, Crito, Meno, Gorgias, Menexenus*. New Haven: Yale University Press.

———. 1991. *The Dialogues of Plato*. Vol. 2, *The Symposium*. New Haven: Yale University Press.

Allen, Thomas W. 1931. *The Homeric Catalogue of Ships*. Oxford: Oxford University Press.

Allen, T. W., W. R. Halliday, and E. E. Sikes, eds. 1936. *The Homeric Hymns*. 2d ed. Oxford: Oxford University Press.

Amiet, Pierre. 1980. *Art of the Ancient Near East*. New York: Abrams.

Apollodorus. 1967. *The Library*. Loeb. Tr. J. G. Frazer. Cambridge, Mass.: Harvard University Press.

Arnott, Geoffrey. 1970. "Menander: Discoveries Since the Dyskolos." *Arethusa* 3:49–70.

Astour, Michael C. 1966. "Tamar the Hierodule." *Journal of Biblical Literature* 85:185–196.

———. 1967. *Hellenosemitica*. Leiden: Brill.

Atallah, W. 1966. *Adonis dans la littérature et l'art grecs*. Paris: Klincksiek.

Austin, Colin. 1973. *Comicorum Graecorum Fragmenta*. Berlin: de Gruyter.

Bailey, John A. 1970. "Initiation and the Primal Woman in Gilgamesh and Genesis 2–3." *Journal of Biblical Literature* 89:137–150.

Baldini, Umberto, et al. 1966. *The Complete Works of Michelangelo*. London: Macdonald.

Barrett, W. S. 1964. *Euripides Hippolytos*. Oxford: Clarendon.

Beard, Mary. 1980. "The Sexual Status of Vestal Virgins." *Journal of Roman Studies* 70:12–27.

Beazley, J. D. 1942. *Attic Red-Figure Vase Painters.* Oxford: Clarendon.

Benecke, E. F. M. 1896. *Antimachus of Colophon and the Position of Women in Greek Poetry.* London: S. Sonnenschein.

Benveniste, Emile E. 1969. *Le vocabulaire des institutions indo-européennes.* Paris: Éditions de Minuit. Tr. E. Palmer. Coral Gables, Fla: University of Miami Press, 1973.

Bernal, Martin. 1987–1991. *Black Athena: The Afroasiatic Roots of Classical Civilization.* New Brunswick, N.J.: Rutgers University Press.

Best, Jan, and Fred Woudhuizen, eds. 1988. *Ancient Scripts from Crete and Cyprus.* Leiden: E. J. Brill.

Bethe, E. 1907. "Die dorische Knabenliebe: Ihre Ethik und ihre Idee." *Rheinisches Museum für Philologie* 62:438–475.

Beye, Charles Rowan. 1993. *Ancient Epic Poetry.* Ithaca: Cornell University Press.

Bicknell, Peter J. 1982. "Axiochos Alkibiadou, Aspasia, and Aspasios." *L'Antiquité Classique* 51:240–250.

Bird, Phyllis A. 1981. " 'Male and Female Created He Them': Gen. 1:27b in the Context of the Priestly Account of Creation." *Harvard Theological Review* 74(2):129–159.

———. 1987a. "The Place of Women in the Israelite Cultus." *Ancient Israelite Religion: Essays in Honor of Frank M. Cross*, ed. Paul D. Hanson, Patrick D. Miller, and S. Dean McBride, 397–419. Philadelphia: Fortress Press.

———. 1987b. "Genesis I–III as a Source for a Contemporary Theology of Sexuality." *Ex Auditu* (Annual, Princeton Theological Seminary) 3:31–44.

———. 1989. "The Harlot as Heroine: Narrative Art and Social Presupposition in Three Old Testament Texts." *Semeia* 46:119–139.

Boardman, John. 1971. "A Southern View of Situla Art." In *The European Community in Later Prehistory*, ed. John Boardman et al., 121–140. London: Routledge & Kegan Paul.

———. 1975. *Athenian Red Figure Vases: The Archaic Period.* London: Thames & Hudson.

Boardman, John, and Eugenio La Rocca. 1978. *Eros in Greece.* New York: Erotic Art Book Society.

Boedeker, Deborah. 1974. *Aphrodite's Entry into Greek Epic.* Leiden: E. J. Brill.

———. 1983. "Hecate: A Transfunctional Goddess?" *TAPA* 113:79–93.

Bonfante, Larissa. 1989. "Nudity as a Costume in Classical Art." *AJA* 93:543–570.

Bonner, Campbell. 1949. "ΚΕΣΤΟΣ ΙΜΑΣ and the Saltire of Aphrodite." *American Journal of Philology* 70:1–6.

Borgeaud, Philippe. 1988. *The Cult of Pan in Ancient Greece*. Chicago: University of Chicago Press.

Bowra, Cecil Maurice. 1958. "A Love-Duet." *American Journal of Philology* 79:376–391.

———. 1961. *Greek Lyric Poetry*. Oxford: Clarendon Press.

Bremmer, Jan. 1980. "An Enigmatic Indo-European Rite: Paederasty." *Arethusa* 13:279–298.

Brendel, Otto J. 1970. "The Scope and Temperament of Erotic Art in the Greco-Roman World." In *Studies in Erotic Art*, ed. Theodore Bowie and Cornelia V. Christianson, 3–69. New York: Basic Books.

Brenk, F. E. 1977. "Aphrodite's Girdle." *Classical Bulletin* 54:17–20.

Briffault, Robert. 1927. *The Mothers*. 3 vols. New York: Macmillan.

Broneer, Oscar. 1932. "Eros and Aphrodite in the North Slope of the Acropolis in Athens," *Hesperia* 1:31–55.

Brown, Peter. 1978. *The Making of Late Antiquity*. Cambridge, Mass.: Harvard University Press.

———. 1988. *The Body and Society: Men, Women, and Sexual Renunciation in Early Christianity*. New York: Columbia University Press.

Burkert, Walter. 1979. *Structure and History in Greek Mythology and Ritual*. Berkeley: University of California Press.

———. 1985. *Greek Religion*. Cambridge, Mass.: Harvard University Press.

———. 1992. *The Orientalizing Revolution: Near Eastern Influence on Greek Culture in the Early Archaic Age*. Tr. M. E. Pinder and W. Burkert. Cambridge, Mass.: Harvard University Press.

Bury, J. B., and Russell Meiggs. 1978. *A History of Greece*. 4th ed. rev. New York: St. Martin's Press.

Butler, H. E., and E. A. Barber. [1933] 1964. *The Elegies of Propertius*. Hildesheim: Georg Olms.

Campbell, David A. 1982, 1988, 1991. 3 vols. *Greek Lyric*. Cambridge, Mass.: Harvard University Press.

Cantarella, Eva. 1986. "Dangling Virgins: Myth, Ritual, and the Place of Women in Ancient Greece." In *The Female Body in Western Culture*, ed. Susan Rubin Suleiman, 57–67, Cambridge, Mass.: Harvard University Press.

———. 1987. *Pandora's Daughters: The Role and Status of Women in Greek and Roman Antiquity*. Baltimore: Johns Hopkins University Press.

Caquot, A. 1965. "Western Semitic Lands: The Idea of the Supreme God." In Pierre Grimal, *Larousse World Mythology*, 85–95. New York: Paul Hamlyn.

Carson, Anne. 1990. "Putting Her in Her Place: Woman, Dirt, and Desire." In *Before Sexuality: The Construction of Erotic Experience in the Ancient Greek World*, ed. David Halperin, John J. Winkler, and From I. Zeitlin, 135–169. Princeton: Princeton University Press.

Chadwick, John. 1987. *Linear B and Related Scripts*. Berkeley: University of California Press.

Clader, Linda. 1976. *Helen: The Evolution from Divine to Heroic in Greek Epic Tradition*. Mnemosyne Suppl. 42. Leiden: E. J. Brill.

Cohen, David. 1991. *Law, Sexuality, and Society: The Enforcement of Morals in Classical Athens*. Cambridge: Cambridge University Press.

Cole, Susan Guettel. 1981. "Could Greek Women Read and Write?" In *Reflections on Women in Antiquity*, ed. Helene B. Foley, 219–245. New York: Gordon and Breach.

———. 1984. "Greek Sanctions against Sexual Assault." *Classical Philology* 79:97–113.

Connor, W. R. 1988. "Early Greek Land Warfare as Symbolic Expression." *Past and Present* 119:3–29.

Cook, Arthur Bernard. 1914–1940. *Zeus: A Study in Ancient Religion*. 3 vols in 5. Cambridge: Cambridge University Press.

Cook, Robert Manuel. [1972] 1977. *Greek Painted Pottery*. 2d ed.London: Methuen.

Coughlan, Robert. 1966. *The World of Michelangelo*. New York: Time.

de Ste. Croix, G. E. M. 1981. *The Class Struggle in the Ancient Greek World*. Ithaca: Cornell University Press.

Dalley, Stephanie. 1989. *Myths from Mesopotamia: Creation, the Flood, Gilgamesh and Others*. Oxford: Oxford University Press.

Demargne, Pierre. 1964. *The Birth of Greek Art*. New York: Golden Press.

Dessau, Hermann. 1954–1955. *Inscriptiones latinae selectae*. Editio secvnda lvcis ope expressa. Berlin: Weidmann.

Detienne, Marcel. 1977. *The Gardens of Adonis*. Hassocks: Harvester.

Deubner, Ludwig August. 1932. *Attische Feste*. Berlin: Keller.

Dever, W. 1985. "Asherah, Consort of YHWH?" *Bulletin of the American Societies of Oriental Research* 255:21–37.

Dodds, E. R. 1959. *Plato Gorgias*. Oxford: Clarendon Press.

———. 1965. *Pagan and Christian in an Age of Anxiety*. Cambridge: Cambridge University Press.

Dover, Kenneth James. 1965. *Thucydides Book VI*. Oxford: Oxford University Press.

———. 1968. *Aristophanes Clouds*. Oxford: Clarendon Press.

———. 1972. *Aristophanic Comedy*. Berkeley: University of California Press.

———. [1978] 1989. *Greek Homosexuality*. Cambridge, Mass.: Harvard University Press.

———. 1988. "Greek Homosexuality and Initiation." In *The Greeks and Their Legacy*, ed. K. J. Dover, 115–134. Oxford: Blackwell.

Drews, Robert. 1988. *The Coming of the Greeks: Indo-European Conquests in the Aegean and the Near East.* Princeton: Princeton University Press.

Drijvers, Hans J. W. 1987. "Virginity." In *The Encyclopedia of Religion,* ed. Mircea Eliade, 15:279–281. New York: Macmillan.

Dumézil, Georges. 1924. *Le crime des Lemniennes.* Paris: P. Geuthner.

———. 1968, 1971, 1973. *Mythe et épopée.* 3 vols. Paris: Gallimard.

Durkheim, Emile. [1915] 1976. *The Elementary Forms of the Religious Life.* London: Allen & Unwin.

Edelstein, Ludwig. 1967. *Ancient Medicine.* Baltimore: Johns Hopkins University Press.

Ehlers, Barbara. 1966. *Eine vorplatonische Deutung des socratischen Eros. Der Dialog Aspasia des sokratikers Aischines.* Zetemata 41. Munich: Beck.

Ehrenberg, Margaret. 1989. *Women in Prehistory.* Norman: University of Oklahoma Press.

Ellis, Albert, and Albert Abarbanel. 1967. *Encyclopedia of Sexual Behavior.* 2d ed. 2 vols. New York: Hawthorne.

Emlyn-Jones, C. J. 1980. *The Ionians and Hellenism.* Boston: Routledge.

Faraone, Christopher A. 1990. "Aphrodite's Κεστός and Apples for Atalanta: Aphrodisiacs in Early Greek Myth and Ritual." *Phoenix* 44:219–243.

———. 1992. "Sex and Power: Male-Targeting Aphrodisiacs in the Greek Magical Tradition." *Helios* 19:92–103.

———. 1993. "The Wheel, the Whip and Other Implements of Torture: Erotic Magic in Pindar Pythian 4.213–219." *Classical Journal* 89, no. 1 (Oct.-Nov.): 1–19.

Farnell, Lewis Richard. 1896–1909. *The Cults of the Greek States.* Oxford: Clarendon Press.

Finley, Moses I. 1981. *Economy and Society in Ancient Greece.* London: Chatto and Windus.

Fisher, Helen. 1982. *The Sex Contract: The Evolution of Human Behavior.* New York: Morrow.

Fontenrose, Joseph. 1980. *Python: A Study of Delphic Myth and Its Origins.* Berkeley: Univeristy of California Press.

Forster, Edward Morgan. 1961. *Alexandria: A History and a Guide.* Garden City, N.Y.: Doubleday.

Foucault, Michel. 1978. *The History of Sexuality.* Vol. 1, *An Introduction.* New York: Pantheon.

———. 1985. The Use of Pleasure. Vol. 2 of *The History of Sexuality.* New York: Pantheon.

———. 1986. *The Care of the Self.* Vol. 3 of *The History of Sexuality.* New York: Pantheon.

Fox, Robin Lane. 1987. *Pagans and Christians*. New York: Knopf.

Fraenkel, Eduard. 1950. *Aeschylus Agamemnon*. Oxford: Clarendon Press.

―――. 1957. *Horace*. Oxford: Clarendon Press.

Frazer, James G. [1914] 1955. *The Golden Bough*. 3d ed. London: Macmillan.

―――. 1918–1935. *Pausanias Description of Greece*. 5 vols. New York: Putnam.

Friedrich, Paul. 1978. *The Meaning of Aphrodite*. Chicago: University of Chicago Press.

Frontisi-Ducroux, Françoise, and François Lissarrague. 1990. "From Ambiguity to Ambivalence: A Dionysiac Excursion through the 'Anacreontic' Vases." In *Before Sexuality: The Construction of Erotic Experience in the Ancient Greek World*, ed. David Halperin, John J. Winkler, and From I. Zeitlin, 211–256. Princeton: Princeton University Press.

Frymer-Kensky, Tikva S. 1992. *In the Wake of the Goddesses: Women, Culture, and the Biblical Transformation of Pagan Myth*. New York: Free Press.

Gardner, John, and John Maier. 1984. *Gilgamesh*. New York: Knopf.

Garland, Robert. 1990. *The Greek Way of Life: From Conception to Old Age*. Ithaca: Cornell University Press.

Garrison, Daniel H. 1978. *Mild Frenzy: A Reading of the Hellenistic Love Epigram*. Wiesbaden: Franz Steiner.

Giangrande, Giuseppe. 1968. "Sympotic Literature and Epigram." In *L'Épigramme grecque*, 93–174. Genève: Fondation Hardt.

Gimbutas, Marija. 1982. *The Goddesses and Gods of Old Europe*. Berkeley: University of California Press.

Gomme, A. W., and F. H. Sandbach. 1973. *Menander: A Commentary*. Oxford: Oxford University Press.

Gordis, R. 1957. "The Knowledge of Good and Evil in the Old Testament and the Qumrun Scrolls." *Journal of Biblical Literature* 76:123–138.

Gordon, Cyrus H. 1957a. "Akkadian Tablets in Minoan Dress." *Antiquity* 31:237–240.

―――. 1957b. "Notes on Minoan Linear A." *Antiquity* 31:124–130.

―――. 1966. *Ugarit and Minoan Crete*. New York: Norton.

Gosling, J. C. B., and C. C. W. Taylor. 1982. *The Greeks on Pleasure*. New York: Oxford University Press.

Gow, A. S. F. 1952. *Theocritus*. Cambridge: Cambridge University Press.

Gow, A. S. F. and D.L. Page. 1965. *The Greek Anthology: Hellenistic Epigrams*. Cambridge: Cambridge University Press.

Gresseth, Gerald H. 1970. "The Homeric Sirens." *TAPA* 101:203–218.

Griffiths, Frederick. 1981. "Home before Lunch: The Emancipated Woman in Theocritus." In *Reflections on Women in Antiquity*, ed. Helene P. Foley, 247–273. New York: Gordon and Breach.

Grottanelli, C. 1986. "Yoked Horses, Twins, and the Powerful Lady: India, Greece, Ireland, and Elsewhere." *JIES* 14:125.

Guthrie, William Keith Chambers. 1969. *A History of Greek Philosophy*. 3 vols. Cambridge: Cambridge University Press.

———. 1971. *Socrates*. Cambridge: Cambridge University Press.

Gutzwiller, Kathryn. 1992. "Callimachus' Lock of Berenice: Fantasy, Romance, and Propaganda." *American Journal of Philology* 113:359–385.

Hadzisteliou Price, T. 1978. *KOUROTROPHOS: Cults and Representations of the Greek Nursing Deities*. Leiden: E. J. Brill.

Haight, Elizabeth Hazelton. 1943. *Essays on the Greek Romances*. London: Longmans Green.

Halperin, David M. 1990. *One Hundred Years of Homosexuality and Other Essays on Greek Love*. New York: Routledge.

Halperin, David M., John J. Winkler, and Froma I. Zeitlin. 1990. *Before Sexuality: The Construction of Erotic Experience in the Ancient Greek World*. Princeton: Princeton University Press.

Hampe, Roland, and Erica Simon. 1981. *The Birth of Greek Art*. New York: Oxford University Press.

Hanfmann, George M. A. 1983. *Sardis from Prehistoric to Roman Times*. Cambridge, Mass.: Harvard University Press.

Hanson, Ann Ellis. 1990a. "The Logic of the Gynecological Prescriptions." *Actas del VIIe Colloque International Hippocratique*. Universidad Nacional de Educación a Distancia, 1990.

———. 1990b. "The Medical Writers' Woman." In *Before Sexuality: The Construction of Erotic Experience in the Ancient Greek World*, ed. David M. Halperin, John J. Winkler, and From I. Zeitlin, 309–338. Princeton: Princeton University Press.

———. 1991. "Continuity and Change: Three Case Studies in Hippocratic Gynecological Therapy and Theory. In *Women's History and Ancient History*, ed. Sarah B. Pomeroy, 73–110. Chapel Hill: University of North Carolina Press.

———. 1992. "Conception, Gestation, and the Origin of Female Nature in the Corpus Hippocraticum." *Helios* 19:31–71.

Harris, Edward M. 1990. "Did the Athenians Regard Seduction as a Worse Crime than Rape?" *Classical Quarterly* 40:370–377.

Harris, Harold Arthur. 1972. *Sport in Greece and Rome*. London: Thames & Hudson.

Harris, William V. 1989. *Ancient Literacy*. Cambridge, Mass.: Harvard University Press.

Hartman, Louis F. 1958. "Sin in Paradise." *Catholic Biblical Quarterly* 20: 26–40.

Havelock, Christine M. 1995. *The Aphrodite of Knidos and Her Successors*. Ann Arbor: University of Michigan Press.

Headlam, Walter. [1922] 1966. *Herodas: The Mimes and Fragments*. Ed. A. D. Knox. Cambridge:Cambridge University Press.

Heinimann, Felix. [1945] 1972. *Nomos und Physis*. Darmstadt: Wissenschaftliche Buchgesellschaft.

Henderson, Jeffrey. 1987. *Aristophanes' Lysistrata*. Oxford: Clarendon Press.

———. 1991. *The Maculate Muse: Obscene Language in Attic Comedy*. 2d ed. New York: Oxford University Press.

Henry, Madeline Mary. 1985. *Menander's Courtesans and the Greek Comic Tradition*. Studien zur klassischen Philologie 20. Frankfurt: Peter Lang.

———. 1995. *Prisoner of History: Aspasia of Miletus and Her Biographical Tradition*. New York: Oxford University Press.

Heubeck, Alfred, and Arie Hoekstra. 1989. *A Commentary on Homer's Odyssey*. Vol. 2. Oxford: Clarendon Press.

Heubeck, Alfred, Stephanie West, and J. B. Hainsworth. 1988. *A Commentary on Homer's Odyssey*. Vol. 1. Oxford: Clarendon Press.

Hooker, J. T. 1976. *Mycenaean Greece*. London: Routledge & Kegan Paul.

———. 1980. *The Ancient Spartans*. London: Dent.

Hornblower, Simon. 1991. *A Commentary on Thucydides*. Vol 1. Oxford: Clarendon Press.

Humphries, Sarah C. 1993. *The Family, Women, and Death*. 2d ed. Ann Arbor: University of Michigan Press.

Hunter, R. L. 1985. *The New Comedy of Greece and Rome*. Cambridge: Cambridge University Press.

Huxley, G. L. 1966. *The Early Ionians*. London: Faber & Faber.

Jachmann, Günther. 1958. *Der homerische Schiffskatalog und die Ilias*. Köln: Sestdeutscher Verlag.

Jacobsen, Thorkild. 1970. *Toward the Image of Tammuz and Other Essays*. Cambridge, Mass: Harvard University Press.

James, Edwin Oliver. 1959. *The Cult of the Mother Goddess*. New York: Praeger.

Janko, Richard. 1992. *The Iliad: A Commentary*. Vol. 4, Books 13–16. Cambridge: Cambridge University Press.

Kämpf-Dimitriadou, Sophia. 1979. *Die Liebe der Götter in der attischen Kunst des 5. Jahrhunderts v. Chr.* Bern: Francke.

Karageorghis, Vassos. 1976. *View from the Bronze Age: Mycenaean and Phoenician Discoveries at Kition*. New York: Dutton.

———. 1982. *Cyprus, from the Stone Age to the Romans*. London: Thames & Hudson.

Kassel, R., and C. Austin. 1983–. *Poetae Comici Graeci (PCG)*. Berlin: W. de Gruyter.

Keuls, Eva C. [1985] 1993. *The Reign of the Phallus: Sexual Politics in Ancient Athens.* 2d ed. Berkeley: University of California Press.

Kilmer, Martin F. 1982. "Genital Phobia and Depilation" *Journal of Hellenic Studies* 102:104–112.

———. 1993. *Greek Erotica.* London: Duckworth.

Kirk, G. S., ed. 1985–1993. *The Iliad: A Commentary.* 6 vols. Cambridge: Cambridge University Press.

Konstan, David. 1994. *Sexual Symmetry: Love in the Ancient Novel and Related Genres.* Princeton: Princeton University Press.

Kraemer, Ross S. 1992. *Her Share of the Blessings: Women's Religions among Pagans, Jews, and Christians in the Greco-Roman World.* New York: Oxford University Press.

Kramer, Samuel Noah. 1969. *The Sacred Marriage Rite.* Bloomington: Indiana University Press.

Lardinois, André. 1994. "Subject and Circumstance in Sappho's Poetry." *TAPA* 124:57–84.

Latte, Kurt. 1940. "The Coming of the Pythia." *Harvard Theological Review* 33:9–18.

Lefkowitz, Mary R. 1981. *Heroines and Hysterics.* New York: St. Martin's Press.

———. 1986. *Women in Greek Myth.* Baltimore: Johns Hopkins University Press.

———. 1996. *Not Out of Africa: How Afrocentrism Became an Excuse to Teach Myth as History.* New York: Basic Books.

Lerner, Gerda. 1986. "The Origin of Prostitution in Ancient Mesopotamia." *Signs: Journal of Women in Culture and Society* 11:236–254.

Lilja, Saara. [1965] 1978. *The Roman Elegists' Attitude to Women.* Helsinki: Suomalainen Tiedeakatemia. Repr. New York: Garland.

Liebert, Robert S. 1983. *Michelangelo.* New Haven: Yale University Press.

Lloyd, G. E. R. 1983. *Science, Folklore and Ideology.* Cambridge: Cambridge University Press.

Lloyd-Jones, Hugh. 1964. "A Fragment of New Comedy: P. Antinoop. 15." *Journal of Hellenic Studies* 84:21–34. Repr. in Lloyd-Jones 1991, 94–114.

———. 1983. "Artemis and Iphigeneia." *Journal of Hellenic Studies* 103: 87–102. Repr. in Lloyd-Jones 1991, 306–330.

———. 1991. *Greek Comedy, Hellenistic Literature, Greek Religion, and Miscellanea: The Academic Papers of Sir Hugh Lloyd-Jones.* New York, Oxford University Press.

———. 1994. *Sophocles.* Loeb Classical Library. Cambridge, Mass.: Harvard University Press.

Loraux, Nicole. 1978. "Sur la race des femmes." *Arethusa* 11:43–87.

Luck, Georg. 1967. "Witz und Sentiment im griechischen Epigramm." In *L'Épigramme grecque*, 389–408. Genève: Fondation Hardt.

Malherbe, Abraham J. 1986. *Moral Exhortation: A Greco-Roman Sourcebook.* Philadelphia: Westminster Press.

Marrou, H.-I. 1956. *History of Education in Antiquity.* Tr. from the French 3d ed. New York: Sheed & Ward.

Marshack, Alexander. 1972. *The Roots of Civilization.* New York: McGraw-Hill.

May, Herbert G., and Bruce M. Metzger, eds. 1977. *The New Oxford Annotated Bible with the Apocrypha.* New York: Oxford University Press.

McAffee, Gene. 1993. "Sex." In *The Oxford Companion to the Bible,* 690–692. New York: Oxford University Press.

Meeks, Wayne. 1993. *The Origins of Christian Morality.* New Haven: Yale University Press.

Mellaart, James. 1967. *Çatal Hüyük: A Neolithic Town in Anatolia.* New York: McGraw-Hill.

———. 1975. *The Neolithic of the Near East.* New York: Scribner's.

———. 1978. *The Archaeology of Ancient Turkey.* London: Bodley Head.

Metzger, Bruce M., and Michael D. Coogan. 1993. *The Oxford Companion to the Bible.* New York: Oxford University Press.

Miller, Patrick, et al., eds. 1987. *Ancient Israelite Religion: Essays in Honor of Frank Moore Cross.* Philadelphia: Fortress.

Miralles, Charles, and Jaume Pòrtulas. 1983. *Archilochus and the Iambic Poetry.* Rome: Edizioni dell'Ateneo.

Monoson, S. Sara. 1994. "Citizen as Erastes. Erotic Imagery and the Idea of Reciprocity in the Periclean Funeral Oration." *Political Theory* 22, no. 2 (May): 1991. 253–276.

Mossé, Clause. 1991. "La Place de la pallaké dans la famille athénienne." In *Symposium 1990,* 273–279. Cologne: Böhlau.

Murray, Oswyn. 1993. *Early Greece.* 2d ed. Cambridge, Mass.: Harvard University Press.

Nagler, Michael N. 1974. *Spontaneity and Tradition: A Study in the Oral Art of Homer.* Berkeley: University of California Press.

Nagy, Gregory. 1990. *Greek Mythology and Poetics.* Ithaca: Cornell University Press.

Nauck, August. 1889. *Tragicorum Graecorum Fragmenta (TGF).* 2d ed. Leipzig: Teubner.

Nilsson, Martin P. 1932. *The Mycenaean Origin of Greek Mythology.* Berkeley: University of California Press.

———. 1950. *The Minoan-Mycenaean Religion and Its Survival in Greek Religion.* Lund: C. W. K. Gleerup.

————. 1961. *Greek Folk Religion*. New York: Harper.

Nock, Arthur Darby. 1972. *Essays on Religion in the Ancient World*. Ed. Zeph Stewart. Cambridge, Mass.: Harvard University Press.

Ochshorn, Judith. 1981. *The Female Experience and the Nature of the Divine*. Bloomington: Indiana University Press.

Oden, Robert A., Jr. 1987. "Religious Identity and the Sacred Prostitution Accusation." In *The Bible without Theology*, 131–153. San Francisco: Harper.

O'Flaherty, Wendy Doniger. 1973. *Asceticism and Eroticism in the Mythology of Siva*. New York: Oxford University Press.

Olyan, Saul M. 1988. *Asherah and the Cult of Yahweh in Israel*. Monograph series (Society of Biblical Literature) no. 32. Atlanta: Scholars Press.

O'Meara, John J. 1969. "St. Augustine's Attitude to Love." *Arethusa* 2: 46–60.

Østby E., et al. 1994. "The Sanctuary of Athena Alea at Tegea: First Preliminary Report (1990–1992)." *Opuscula Atheniensia* 20(8):89–141.

Otis, Brooks. 1970. *Ovid as an Epic Poet*. 2d ed. Cambridge: Cambridge University Press.

Ouvré, Henri. 1894. *Méléagre de Gadara*. Paris.

Packman, Zola Marie. 1993. "Call It Rape: A Motif in Roman Comedy and Its Suppression in English-speaking Publications." *Helios* 20(1):42–55.

Page, Denys L. 1955. *Sappho and Alcaeus*. Oxford: Clarendon Press.

————. 1959. *History and the Homeric Iliad*. Berkeley: University of California Press.

————. 1962. *Select Papyri III: Literary Papyri. Poetry*. Cambridge, Mass.: Harvard University Press.

Parke, Herbert William. 1977. *Festivals of the Athenians*. Ithaca: Cornell University Press.

Parke, Herbert William, and D. E. W. Wormell. 1956. *The Delphic Oracle*. 2 vols. Oxford: Blackwell.

Parker, Holt N. 1992. "Love's Body Anatomized: The Ancient Erotic Handbooks and the Rhetoric of Sexuality." In *Pornography and Representation in Greece and Rome*, ed. Amy Richlin, 90–111. New York: Oxford University Press.

————. 1993. "Sappho Schoolmistress." *TAPA* 123:309–351.

Patai, Raphael. 1967. *The Hebrew Goddess*. New York: Ktav.

Patterson, Cynthia. 1986. "Hai Attikai: The Other Athenians." *Helios* 13: 49–67.

————. 1991. "Response to Claude Mossé." In *Symposion 1990*, 281–287. Cologne: Böhlau.

Patzer, Harald. 1982. *Die griechische Knabenliebe*. Wiesbaden: Steiner.

Pausanias. 1971. *Guide to Greece*. 2 vols. Tr. Peter Levi, S.J. Middlesex: Penguin Books.

Peckham, Brian. 1968. "Notes on a Fifth-Century Phoenician Inscription from Kition, Cyprus (CIS 86)." *Orientalia* 37:304–324.

Penzer, Norman Mosley. 1923–1968. "Sacred Prostitution." Appendix 4 of Somadeva's *The Ocean of Story*, tr. Charles Henry Tawney. Vol. 1. 2d ed. Delhi: Motilal Banarsidass.

Pitt-Rivers, Julian. 1977. *The Fate of Shechem or The Politics of Sex.* Cambridge: Cambridge University Press.

Pomeroy, Sarah B. 1975. *Goddesses, Whores, Wives, and Slaves: Women in Classical Antiquity.* New York: Schocken.

———. 1994. *Xenophon Oeconomicus: A Social and Historical Commentary.* Oxford: Clarendon Press.

Pope, Marvin H. 1977. *Song of Songs.* The Anchor Bible. Garden City, N.Y.: Doubleday.

Powell, John U. 1925. *Collectanea alexandrina.* Oxford: Clarendon Press.

Prückner, Helmut. 1968. *Die Lokrischen Tonreliefs: Beitrag zur Kultgeschichte von Lokroi Epizephyrioi.* Mainz: P. von Zabern.

Quinn, Kenneth. 1963. *Latin Explorations.* London: Routledge.

Radt, Stefan, ed. 1977. *Tragicorum Graecorum Fragmenta (TrGF).* Vol 4, *Sophocles.* Göttingen: Vandenhoeck & Ruprecht.

———. ed. 1985. *Tragicorum Graecorum Fragmenta (TrGF).* Vol 3, *Aeschylus.* Göttingen: Vandenhoeck & Ruprecht.

Redfield, James. 1978. "The Women of Sparta." *Classical Journal* 73:146–161.

Renfrew, Colin. 1972. *The Emergence of Civilisation: The Cyclades and the Aegean in the Third Millennium B.C.* London: Methuen.

———. 1985. *The Archaeology of Cult: The Sanctuary of Phylakopi.* British School of Archaeology at Athens, Suppl. No. 18. London: Thames & Hudson.

Richter, G. M. A. 1929. "Silk in Greece." *AJA* 33:27–33.

———. 1960. *Kouroi.* Garden City, N.Y.: Phaidon.

———. 1970. *Korai: Archaic Greek Maidens.* London: Phaidon.

Riddle, John. 1992. *Contraception and Abortion from the Ancient World to the Renaissance.* Cambridge, Mass.: Harvard University Press.

Ridgway, Brunilde S., and R. T. Scott. 1972. Review of Prückner 1968 in *Archaeology* 26:43–47.

———. 1977. *The Archaic Style in Greek Sculpture.* Princeton: Princeton University Press.

Rist, J. M. 1964. *Eros and Psyche: Studies in Plato, Plotinus, and Origen.* Toronto: University of Toronto Press.

———. 1969. *Stoic Philosophy.* London: Cambridge University Press.

Rosenmeyer, Thomas G. 1969. *The Green Cabinet: Theocritus and the European Pastoral Lyric.* Berkeley: University of California Press.

Rousselle, Aline. 1988. *Porneia: On Desire and the Body in Antiquity.* Tr. Felicia Pheasant. London: Basil Blackwell.

Rusten, Jeffrey S. 1989. *Thucydides: The Peloponnesian War, Book II.* Cambridge: Cambridge University Press.

————, et al. 1993. *Theophrastus Characters, Herodas Mimes, Cercidas and the Choliambic Poets.* Cambridge, Mass.: Harvard University Press.

Säflund, Gösta. 1963. *Aphrodite Kallipygos.* Tr. P. M. Fraser. Stockholm: Almquist & Wiksell.

Saller, Richard P., and Brent D. Shaw. 1984. "Tombstones and Roman Family Relations in the Principate." *Journal of Roman Studies* 74: 124–156.

Salmon, J. B. 1984. *Wealthy Corinth.* Oxford: Oxford University Press.

Sandars, N. K. 1972. *The Epic of Gilgamesh: An English Version with an Introduction.* Rev. ed. Harmondsworth: Penguin.

Sandbach, F. H. 1990. *Menandri Reliquiae Selectae* (OCT). 2d ed. Oxford: Clarendon Press.

Sansone, David. 1988. *Greek Athletics and the Genesis of Sport.* Berkeley: University of California Press.

Sealey, Raphael. 1984. "On Lawful Concubinage in Athens." *Classical Antiquity* 3:111–133.

Sergent, Bernard. 1986. *Homosexuality in Greek Myth.* Tr. A. Goldhammer. Originally published in 1984 as *L'Homosexualité dans la mythologie grecque.* Boston: Beacon Press.

Shepherd, Gill. 1987. "Rank, Gender, and Homosexuality: Mombasa as a Key to Understanding Sexual Options." In *The Cultural Construction of Sexuality,* ed. Pat Caplan, 240–270. London: Tavistock.

Simon, Erika. 1983. *Festivals of Attica: An Archaeological Commentary.* Madison: University of Wisconsin Press.

Simpson, R. Hope, and J. F. Lazenby. 1970. *The Catalogue of Ships in Homer's Iliad.* Oxford: Oxford University Press.

Sissa, Giulia. 1990a. *Greek Virginity.* Tr. Arthur Goldhammer. Cambridge, Mass.: Harvard University Press.

————. 1990b. "Maidenhood without Maidenhead: The Female Body in Ancient Greece." In *Before Sexuality: The Construction of Erotic Experience in the Ancient Greek World,* ed. David M. Halperin, John J. Winkler, and Froma I. Zeitlin, 339–364. Princeton: Princeton University Press.

Skinner, Marilyn B. 1987. "Des bonnes dames et méchantes." *Classical Journal* 83:69–74.

————. 1993. "Woman and Language in Archaic Greece, or Why Is Sappho a Woman?" In *Feminist Theory and the Classics,* ed. Nancy S. Rabinowitz and Amy Richlin, 125–144. New York: Routledge.

Slater, Philip E. 1968. *The Glory of Hera: Greek Mythology and the Greek Family.* Boston: Beacon Press.

Smith, Louise Pearson. 1994. "Audience Response to Rape: Chaerea in Terence's *Eunuchus.*" *Helios* 21, no. 2 (Spring):21–38.

Snodgrass, Anthony M. 1980. *Archaic Greece: The Age of Experiment.* London: J. M. Dent.

Snyder, Jane McIntosh. 1991. "Public Occasion and Private Passion in the Lyrics of Sappho of Lesbos." In *Women's History and Ancient History,* ed. Sarah B. Pomeroy, 1–19. Chapel Hill: University of North Carolina Press.

Sourvinou-Inwood, Christiane. 1974. "The Votum of 477/6 B.C. and the Foundation Legend of Locri Epizephyrii." *Classical Quarterly* 24:186–198.

Stanford, W. B. 1963. *The Ulysses Theme.* 2d ed. Oxford: Basil Blackwell.

Stehle, Eva. 1990. "Sappho's Gaze: Fantasies of a Goddess and Young Man." *Differences* 2(1):88–125.

Stewart, Andrew F. 1986. "When Is a Kouros Not an Apollo? The Tenea 'Apollo' Revisited." In *Corinthiaca,* ed. Mario A. Del Chiaro, 54–70. Columbia: University of Missouri Press.

———. 1990. *Greek Sculpture.* New Haven: Yale University Press.

Suleiman, Susan Rubin, ed. 1986. *The Female Body in Western Culture.* Cambridge, Mass.: Harvard University Press.

Sutton, Robert F., Jr. 1972. "Pornography and Persuasion on Attic Pottery." In *Pornography and Representation in Greece and Rome,* ed. Amy Richlin, 3–35. New York: Oxford University Press.

Temkin, Owsei. 1956. *Soranus' Gynecology.* Baltimore: Johns Hopkins University Press.

Thomas, William I. 1937. *Primitive Behavior.* New York: McGraw–Hill.

Tigay, Jeffrey H. 1982. *The Evolution of the Gilgamesh Epic.* Philadelphia: University of Pennsylvania Press.

Trump, David H. 1980. *The Prehistory of the Mediterranean.* New Haven: Yale University Press.

Ucko, Peter J. 1968. *Anthropomorphic Figurines of Predynastic Egypt and Neolithic Crete with Comparative Material from the Prehistoric Near East and Mainland Greece.* London: A. Szmidla.

Ussher, R. G. 1973. *Aristophanes Ecclesiazusae.* Oxford: Clarendon Press.

Vermeule, Emily. 1964. *Greece in the Bronze Age.* Chicago: University of Chicago Press.

Veyne, Paul. 1978. "La famille et l'amour sous le Haut-empire romain." *Annales É.S.C.* 33:35–63.

———, ed. 1987. *A History of Private Life.* Vol. 1, *From Pagan Rome to Byzantium.* Cambridge, Mass.: Harvard University Press.

Voyatzis, Mary E. 1990. *The Early Sanctuary of Athena Alea at Tegea and Other Archaic Sanctuaries in Arcadia*. Göteborg: P. Åströms.

Ward, D. J. 1968. *The Divine Twins: An Indo-European Myth in Germanic Tradition*. Berkeley: University of California Press.

———. 1970. "An Indo-European Mythological Theme in Germanic Tradition." In George Cardona et al., *Indo-European and Indo-Europeans*, 405–420. Philadelphia: University of Pensylvania Press.

Webster, Thomas Bertram Lonsdale. 1958. *From Mycenae to Homer*. London: Methuen.

Weitzmann, Kurt. 1970. *Illustrations in Roll and Codex*. 2d ed. Princeton: Princeton University Press.

West, M. L. 1966. *Hesiod Theogony*. Oxford: Clarendon Press.

———. 1978. *Hesiod Works and Days*. Oxford: Clarendon Press.

Whitman, Cedric Hubbell. 1958. *Homer and the Heroic Tradition*. Cambridge, Mass.: Harvard University Press.

Williams, Charles K. 1986. "Corinth and the Cult of Aphrodite." In *Corinthiaca*, ed. Mario A. Del Chiaro, 12–24. Columbia: University of Missouri Press.

Williams, Gordon. 1958. "Some Aspects of Roman Marriage Ceremonies and Ideals." *Journal of Roman Studies* 48:16–32.

Wind, Edgar. 1968. *Pagan Mysteries in the Renaissance*. London: Faber and Faber.

Winkler, John J. 1990. *The Constraints of Desire: The Anthropology of Sex and Gender in Ancient Greece*. New York: Routledge.

Wylie, Philip. 1942. *Generation of Vipers*. New York: Farrar & Rinehart.

Zweig, Bella. 1992. "The Mute Nude Female Characters in Aristophanes' Plays." In *Pornography and Represnetation in Greece and Rome*, ed. Amy Richlin, 73–89. New York: Oxford University Press.

Zweig, Paul. 1974. *The Adventurer*. New York: Basic Books.

Index

Amorgos: silk clothing from, *139, 144,*
146, *148*, 200, 296n.46
Amos, 51
Amphion, 31
Amphis: *Gynecocracy,* 210
Anacreon, 104–105, 140, 289n.36,
295–296n.39
Anat, 19, 69
Anaxandrides: *Helen,* 302n.38
Anaximander, 116
Anaximenes of Miletus, 116
Anchises, 21, 283n.34
Andragathus, 238
Andromache, 89, 105, 112
Animals: associated with goddesses, *8,*
12, 28, 29, *97*; human nature and,
305n.23, 313n.21; as love gifts, 131, *134*;
neutering of, 268; religious sacrifice
and, 29, 273n.7; sex with, 52; women
likened to, 104
Antenor Korē, *193*
Antigone, 171, 209
Antipater of Tarsus: *On Marriage,* 245
Antiphates, 294n.29
Antisthenes: asceticism of, 250; *Aspasia,*
152, 173, 297n.51, 298n.58; *On the*
Begetting of Children . . . , 173; sex
and, 301–302n.30, 307n.7, 312n.10;
women and, 210, 297n.51
Anyte, 224
Apelles, 123; *Anadyomene,* 294n.27;
Aphrodite Rising from the Sea, 122
Aphrodite: Adonis and, 102, 220, 221;
Anchises and, 21, 83n.34; Ares and,
79, 80, 83, 104, 105; Astarte and, 68,
289–290n.38; bird imagery and, *33*;
birth of, 68, 84, 199, *200*; chest band
emblem and, *75, 76*; complexity of,
40, 62, 80, 88, 104, 190, 231, 304n.16;
Corinth and, 110–111; costuming of,
39–40; cult of, 27, *41, 42,* 68, 84, 197,
221, 275–276n.27, 305n.18; Cyprus
and, 68, 84; Cythera and, 68, 84;
demotion of, 90–91; duality of, *41,*

79; Eos and, 279n.2; Eros and, 100,
256; Ganymede and, 108; Graces and,
32; Helen and, 39, 73, 280n.12;
Hephaistos and, 79; Hera and, 39, 75,
78; as life-giving goddess, 10–11, 211;
name of, 283n.36; as nature goddess,
306n.29; nonmaternal nature of,
273n.6; origins of, 38, 46, 67;
Pandora and, 39; Phaedra and, 143;
prostitution and, 111, 281n.17; as
Queen of Conjugal Peace, 75;
Sapphic poetry and, 102; sea imagery
and, *14,* 69, 211, 221; as sex goddess,
72, 104, 221; statues of, 200, 205, *213*;
swan imagery and, *12*; temple of, 86,
121, 294n.20; war and, 88, 285n.3; as
war goddess, 282n.27, 289n.38; as
woman's goddess, *201*; women's love
and, 300n.11
Aphrodite, golden: fair hair and,
282n.30; Homeric usage of epithet,
29, 74, 80–81, 283n.33; iconography
of, 38–39; as poetic metaphor, 100;
solar character and, 276n.31; statue at
Hasanoglan, *77*
Aphrodite of Aphaca, 264
Aphrodite of Cnidos, 200, 205, *206*
Aphrodite Hetaera, 121
Aphrodite Kolias, 149
Aphrodite Ouranios, 275n.27
Aphrodite Pandemos, 111, 118
Aphrodite Paphia, 68
"Aphrodite's Girdle," 75
Apollo: artistic depiction of, 200, *202,*
207; cult of, 85–86; duality of, 28;
Hyacinthus and, 162; Narcissus
and, 281n.24; Patroclus and,
282n.28; Pytho and, 284n.44; rape
of Cyrene by, 106; rationality and,
91, 100, 101; as representative of
new gods, 4; sanctuary of, 154;
temple of, 86, *191*
Apollo Sauroktonos, *207–208*
Apollodorus (vase painter), *144*

Attica, 291n.6
Attis, 19, 229, 264–265
Augustine, Saint, 265–266, 267

Baal, 19, 69–70, 282n.29
Babylonia, 52, 116
Bacchylides, 103, 186, 291n.4
Barbarism: civilization vs., *19*, 225;
    depiction of genitalia and, 182, *183*;
    nudity and, 177, 303n.2; patriarchal
    myth and, 109; sexuality and, 162
Bathsheba, *51*, 53
Baubo of Eleusis, 275n.25
Baucis, 243
Beauty: aspects of, 107–108; Eros and,
    169; ethical pursuit of, 170; of human
    form, 186, *188*, 189–190, *193–194*,
    196–200, 205; linked with sex and
    love, 103, 104, 186, 218, 229; love of,
    95, 116, 170, 247, 301n.24; as philo-
    sophical construct, 168, 215; youth
    and, 106
Beer, 54, 55
Berenice I, 221
Berenice II, 221–222
Bion of Borysthenes, 294n.28
Bird imagery, *12, 33*
Birth of the Gracious Gods, 69
Bisexuality, 158, 167, *208*
Bitinna, 223
Black-figure ware, 125–126, *128, 132–134*,
    135. *See also* Vase paintings
Body, human: beauty of, 130, 186,
    205; death and, 251, 312n.15;
    female, *144, 147*; function of, 13;
    gender differences, 90; ideal
    proportions of, 153, 154; male, *127*,
    166, *178*; mortification of the flesh
    and, 269; sexual appetites of, 255,
    265–266; vs. soul, 250–252,
    262–263, 269
Book of Jubilees, 277n.6
Book of Matthew, 262
Botticelli: *Primavera*, 34, *36*

Boy love: beauty and, 301n.24; chivalric
    ideology of, 109, 157; effeminacy and,
    268; love gifts and, *130*; male cult of
    nakedness and, 182, 186; social class
    and, 108–109, 110, 111–112; spirituality
    and, 168. *See also* Pederasty
Boys: education of, 150, *159*, 167, 168,
    236; female roles of, 166; as objects of
    love, 164, 168, 170, 230, 293n.14; rites
    of passage of, 157, 166
Breast, female: Cycladic representation
    of, *16*; depiction of, *144*, 190, 197;
    goddess iconography and, *4, 7, 37*,
    196–197, 275n.19; maternal function
    and, 13; on Minoan figurine, 38; in
    Mycenaean art, *67*; on statuary, *195*,
    199, 200, 202, 204
Briseis, 105, 112, 113, 114, 233, 290n.41
Bronze Age: cultural developments of,
    3, 49, 50, 62–64, 70, 71; death in,
    281n.24; Eastern influences on, 5;
    goddess tradition of, *8, 12*, 38, 54,
    79–81, 85, 90; literature of, 49, 57;
    mythologizing of, 72, 73, 92;
    women's sexuality and, 58
Brygos Painter, *123, 127, 139, 148*
Brygos Painter's Circle, *147*
Bucaeus, 224
Bull: cult of, 68, 72; horns of, 17, 65;
    male virility and, *7*, 17, 69, 70; in
    mythology, 67, 69, 70, 281n.20
Busiris, *183*

Cadmus, 70
Caesar, 304n.14
Callias: *The Cyclopes*, 120
Callimachus (sculptor), *203*
Callimachus of Cyrene, 226, 238,
    308n.31; *Bath of Pallas*, 277n.2; *The
    Lock of Berenice*, 221–222
Calypso, 58, 83, 290n.41
Canaanites: religion of, 53, 69, 277n.3,
    282n.29; sexual culture of, 52, 59, 69,
    255; urban civilization of, 49, 50

Classical period: antieroticism of, 172, 217, 247; change during, 153–154, 174, 237–238; philosophy of, 216, 217, 241, 251; religion of, 235, 274n.13; "severe style" of art of, 94, 115, 140, *187*, 196, 197, *259*; women in, 38, 190, 232, 288n.34

Cleanthes, 153, 218, 307n.8

Clearista, 224

Cleisthenes, 140–141

Clement of Alexandria, 267

Cleon, 158

Cleopatra, 121, 304n.14

Clothing: Amorgos silk, *139*, *144*, 146, *148*, 200, 296n.46; civilization and, 55; for hetaeras, *123*, *144*; identity and, 286n.9; prostitution and, *139*; semi-nudity and, *159*; sensuality and, 54, 146–147, 190, 199, 279n.15; social class and, 179, 200; on statuary, *9*, *15*, *34*, 38, *67*, 189, *191*, *193*, 197; wealth and, 38, 119

Clytemnestra, 106, 113, 205

Cnidus: Aphrodite statue of, 122, 205

Cock: as love gift, 131, *134*, *165*, *166*

Colophon, 119, 292n.8

Comana, Pontic, 121

Comatas, 224

Comedy: Cynic style of, 309n.35; male bias of, 143; moralizing influence of, 242; phallic costume in, 17; politics in, 150, 158; satyr figure in, *22*; sexual culture and, 149, 226, 231–232, 242, 244, 288n.31; themes of, 120, 233–234, 309n.37; women's power in, 209–210

Coming of age, 48, 50

Contraception, 254–255, 295n.38

Corcyra, 117

Corinth: as commercial center, 94, 116–117; erotic bronzes of, 248; female nude and, 199; feminine imagery of, 95; hetaeras in, 121; population of, 117, 292n.6;

prostitution and, 110–111, 118, *257*, 281n.17, 289n.37, 292n.11; sacred prostitution in, 86, 120–121; trade with Near East, 110–111

Cornelius Gallus, 260

Cornelius Sisenna, 260

Coronis, 106

Cos, 205, 296n.46

Cosmetics, 147–149, 296n.48, 297n.49

Council of Gangra, 267

Courtship paintings, *127*, 131, *134*, 135

Crates, 307n.7

Cratidas, 224

Creon, 209

Crete, 65, 70, *97*, 164, 304n.14; goddess tradition of, 31–32, *35*, 67

Croesus, 119

Cross-dressing, 52, *258*

Croton, 253

Ctesipho, 236

Cults: change and, 68, 86; children in, 264; feminine themes of, 22; Homeric rationalization of, 72; local, 26–27; male, 182; orgiastic and, *131*, 284n.44; Pythagorean, 253; sexual, 58, 59, 67–68, 103, 120–121; sexuality and, *21*, *256*

Cybele, 19, 264

Cyclades, 62, 86, 119; figurines of, 13, *14*, *15*, 40, *44*, 63

Cyclops, 224, 228

Cynics, Cynicism: asceticism of, 250; comedic style of, 309n.35; individual freedom and, 216; love and, 242, 244; natural law and, 217; pain and, 299n.7; pleasure and, 236, 312n.10; sex and, 231, 255, 307n.7, 310n.45

"Cyprian, The," epithet for Aphrodite, 68

Cypris, 211

Cyprus: Aphrodite and, 67, 68, 84; development of, 71; goddess tradition in, *37*, *41*, *42*; hetaeras and, 120; sacred prostitution in, 121

Euthymides, *138, 146*
Eve, 47, 48, 49, 56, 279n.16

Fates, 31–34, *37*
Fertility: goddesses and, 51, 72; sex vs., 13; symbols of, *6, 7,* 38
Festivals, 27–28, 234–235. *See also specific festivals*
Figurines: Aphrodite, 289–290n.38; as cultural marker, 26, 176; Cycladic, *15, 16,* 38, 40, *44,* 63; female, 13, 275n.19; male, *19;* "Venus," *5, 7;* goddess, *4, 8–12, 17, 37,* 63, 68, *96,* 176; goddess of love, *98*
First Communion, 300n.14
Food, 54, 55, 119, 217, 279n.15
Fornication, 52, 255, 265, 277n.6
Foundry Painter, *147*
Friendship: eros and, 173, 302n.36; erotic love dependent on, 307n.8; language of, 238–239; love and, 310n.42; male bonds and, 56, 57–58, 164, 309n.39; philosophy and, 217, 218; politics and, 162
"Frying pan" artifact, 13, *14, 15,* 38, 63
Furies, 205

Galatea, 224
Galen, 265, 268
Ganymede, 108, 162, *165,* 166, 219, 300n.12
Garden of Eden, 47
Genesis, 48–51, 55, 58
Genitalia: artistic emphasis of, 13, 63, *159, 166, 178;* depilation of, 146, *147,* 296n.45; female, 144, *145,* 146, 205, 285–286n.8, 290n.41; literary reference to, 69, 160, 312n.18; male, 81, 84, 182, *208,* 304n.10; religious propriety and, 28; terms for, 181. *See also* Penis; Phallus; Vulva
Gilgamesh, 21, 54, 56, 57, 278n.14, 279n.15
Gilgamesh Epic, 47, 54, 56, 57, 58

Girls, 103, 167, 263; initiatory rituals of, 300n.14; love and, 287n.27; marriage and, 164, 233; sexual desire of, 286n.12; Spartan, 176, 303n.1
Glaukos, 142
Glycera, 242
Gnostics, 265
God (Hebrew/Christian), 50, 51, 52, 277n.3
Goddesses: cruciform representation of, *42, 43;* cultic dance honoring, 103; cultural power and, 72, 86, 88, 90–91; dawn, 21, 60, 81, 276n.31, 283n.36; differentiation of, 275n.20; earth, 63, 85; evening, 73, 281n.20; fertility/life-giving, 5, 26–29, 62, 64, 211, 264, 282n.29; Great, *7–8, 17;* as heroines, 65, 67; iconography of, *4, 9–10, 12, 14, 96–98, 99, 129,* 275n.19, 281n.20; love, *76–78,* 86, *98,* 211, 281n.20, 283n.34; love and war, 62, 79, 86, 100, 104, 294n.22; moon, 280n.13; nature, 19, 21, *24,* 28, 29, 30–40, *42, 43,* 72, 88, 211; Near Eastern, 23, 26–27, *37,* 62, 86, 100, 104; paired, *87;* prostitution and, 121, 280n.16; snake, 65; status of women and, 274n.13; tree, 72; triple, 31–36, 38; war, 282n.27, 285n.3, 289n.38, 294n.22. *See also specific goddesses;* Figurines; Religion, early
Gods, 72, *187;* demoted to heroes, 73; nature, 19, 21, 274n.11; pederasty and, 162, *165;* sexuality and, 218, 252, 264; sky, 60, 62–63, 211. *See also specific gods*
Gorgias, 151
Gorgias of Leontini, 122, 294n.29; *Encomium of Helen,* 174
Gorgidas, 174
Gorgo, 220
Graces (Charites), 31–34, *36*
Greek language, 60, 64, 70–72, 75, 88, 91, 247, 279n.5, 280 n.8
Gripus, 242

Gumelniţa lovers, *24*
Gyllis, 223
Gynecology, 94, 285n.8

Hades, 29, 166
Halicarnassus, 116, 199
Haloa festival, *6*, 27, 29–30
Harmodius, 120, 140, 161, 162, *163*, 173, 296n.40, 300n.11
Hasanoglan: "golden Aphrodite" statue from, *77*
Hasselmann Painter, *6*
Headpiece iconography, *8*, *9*, *17*, *31*, *35*, 38, *129*, 304n.15
Heavenly Twins, 61
Hebrews: culture of, 49–53; ethnic law code of, 62; Holiness Code of, 52, 53, 73; morality of women and, 267; religion of, 53, 68–69, 70; sexual culture of, 51–53, 59, 65, 81, 255, 276n.2, 280n.16, 311n.2. *See also* Judaism
Hecataeus of Miletus, 116
Hecate, 264, 273n.6
Hector, 74, 89, 105, 112, 197
Hecuba, 197
Hedonism, 172
Helen, 92, 112; Agamemnon and, 73–74; Aphrodite and, 39, 80; Artemis and, 82; beauty of, 174; divinity of, 280n.12; eroticism of, 72, 73, 88; Menelaus and, 48, 105, 173–174, 240; Paris and, 73–74, 82, 104, 105, 233, 235; plays about, 302n.38; Priam and, 73, 74–75; royal court and, 89, 285n.2; sexual power of, 29, 73–75, 79, 88; Spartan cult of, *67*, 72; Theseus and, *138*; as tree goddess, 65, 72; Zeus and, 74
Helladic periods, 63, 65, 71, 95
Hellenistic period: eros and, 173, 217, 218–219; love and, 172, *227*; nocturnal religious festivals of, 235; pastoral escapism and, 225; philosophy of,

216, 217; poetry of, 224; privatism of, 174; virtues of, 237–238; women and, 38, 223–224, 266
Hephaistos, 79
Hera: Aphrodite and, 79; Argive, 26; Aspasia likened to, 150; Athena and, 30; bronze statuette of, *96*; cattle and, 29; cult of, 27, 29, *45*, 86, 121; as goddess of marriage, 28, 75; Hellenic demotion of, 90–91; Ixion's desire for, 107; as nature goddess, 29; seduction of Zeus by, 29, 39, 75, *78*, 79, 81–82, 189–190, 288n.29; Trojan War and, 174; Zeus and, 29, *45*, 105, *136*, 233, 276–277n.2
Heracles, 61, *183*, 209, 233, *258*, 289n.35
Heraclitus of Ephesus, 116
Hermaphrodite, *208*
Hermaphrodite figurine, 13, *15*, *16*
Hermes, 17, 174, *178*
Hermione, *129*
Hermippus: *Soldiers*, 120
Herms, *20*, 21, 182
Herodas, 220, 223, 224
Herodes Atticus, 225
Herodotus of Halicarnassus: Aristophanes' parody of, 150; conjugal love and, 239; culture of poverty and, 94; hetaera's life and, 121; as historian, 68, 116, 119, 120, 141, 142–143, 161–162, 306n.3; nudity and, 177
Heroes: athletic contests and, 106; culture of poverty and, 92–93; ideals of, *57*, 61, 62, 174–175, 217; love and, *258*; in Minoan-Mycenaean cult, 65; private life of, 247; semidivine nature of, 54; tragedy of, 105; on vase paintings, 177, *178*
Hesiod: Aphrodite portrayed by, 68, 69, 81, 84; culture of poverty and, 92–93, 94; Eros portrayed by, 211, 284n.39; goddesses portrayed by, 90–91; masculine culture of, 80,

91–93, 109, 115, 284n.38; Nike and,
214; Pandora portrayed by, 39, 84–85,
88, 276n.28, 284n.39; portrayal of
women by, 83–85, 104, 114; *Theogony*,
32–33, 34, 38, 83–85; triple goddesses
portrayed by, 32–33, 34, 38; *Works
and Days*, 34, 84–85, 92–93

Hestia, 264

Hetaeras: Adonia festival and, 235;
Aspasia as, 298n.54; as consorts of
famous men, 294n.28; cult of, 144;
decline of, 142; depicted in art,
311n.5; as erotic entertainers, 121–122,
189, 228; ideals of, *144*, *147*, *194*,
294n.23, 297n.49; Ionian origins of,
120–124; life of, *145*; masculine cult of
poverty and, 94; Miletus and, 150;
nature of, 231–232; pornography and,
248; pregnancy and, 295n.38;
professional nicknames of, 294n.24;
sexual knowledge and, 311n.6; skills
of, 122, *123*, 143, 210

Heterosexuality: abuse of women and,
135; acceptance of, 156, 268; in erotic
art, 256, *257*, 260; idealization of,
226–228; mythological models for,
173–174; pairing of equals in, 173, 241,
244; philosophy and, 168; social class
and, 108, 111–112; Socrates and,
300n.19; visual depiction of, *130*, 189.
See also Love; Sex; Sexuality

Hierodules, 55, 58, 121, 278n.9, 280n.17,
294nn.20, 22

Hieronymus, 293n.19

Hierogamy (*hieros gamos*): male
dominance in, 18; as Near Eastern
tradition, 274n.10; as paradigm for
marriage, 18, *23*, *24*; Zeus and Hera
as model for, 28, 29, *45*, 82, 105, *136*,
233

Hipparchia, 307n.7

Hipparchus, 140, 161, 296nn.39, 40

Hippias, 140, 296n.40

Hippocleias, 107

Hippocrates: *Airs, Waters, Places*, 120,
306n.3

Hippocratic oath, 253, 313n.20

Hippocratics, 254

Hippolytus, 28, 67, 88, 143, 248, 252,
253, 281n.24

Hipponax, 104–105

Hittite language, 64

Holiness Code, 52, 53, 73

Homer: Achilles portrayed by, 73, 105;
Aphrodite portrayed by, 28, 29, 62,
73, 74–75, 88, 104, 105; Artemis
alluded to by, 29; Catalogue of
Ships, 71, 281n.22; cultural insights
of, 48, 61–62, *66*, 70, 81–83, 116, 119,
216, 299n.10; goddesses portrayed
by, 79–80, 90–91; Helen portrayed
by, 29, 38, 39, 65, 73–75, 79, 80, 88;
heroes portrayed by, 61, 62, 71–72,
82, 281n.24; heroic ethos of, 94,
106, 177, *178*, *179*, 217; *Hymn to
Aphrodite*, 306n.29, 382n.34; Hymn
to Apollo, 85; *Iliad*, 61, 62, 216;
lovers portrayed by, 81–82, 104, 105,
299n.10; masculine ethos of, 80,
91–93, 109, 115; mythmaking of, 72;
Nausicaa portrayed by, 283n.33;
Odysseus portrayed by, 286n.9;
Odyssey, 48, 82–83; Penelope portrayed by, 190, 196, 283n.33,
304n.15; Sirens portrayed by,
275n.26; Thetis and Peleis portrayed
by, *137*; women described by, 105,
112–114, 189–190, 196, 285n.2. *See
also Iliad; Odyssey*

Homoeroticism: good character and,
302nn.30,32; group sex and, *134*;
Plato and, 300–301n.19; politics and,
162, 296n.40; Sapphic, 101; social
class and, 161–162; as social construct,
157; taboos against, 166; warrior
bond and, 61, 95, 105, 239, 299n.10.
See also Boy love; Homosexuality;
Pederasty

Korone, *138*

kottabos, 146, 147

Kouros, kouroi, 177; anatomical conventions of, *180, 181,* 182; nudity of, 304n.14; as public art, 115; stylistic conventions of, *187, 188,* 189, 196

Kourotrophos (divine mother with child), *11,* 13, 18, *23, 26*

Krateia, 242

Kritios, *163*

"Kritios Boy," *188,* 197

Kydilla, 223

Lacon, 224

Laïs, 123, 172, 216, 282n.27

Lapith woman, 197, *199*

Leagros, *145*

Lemnian women, 285n.2

Lerna, *40*

Lesbia, 243, 260; 310n.42

Leviticus, 51, 52, 53, 255

Linear A script, 65

Linear B script, 65, 70–72

Lion as emblem, *8, 97, 129, 137*

Literature: critical studies and, 168; cultural insights in, 5, 61, 62, 102, 109, *159,* 220–224, 244, *256,* 269; justification of, 155–156. *See also* Drama; Poetry

Locri, Western, 120–121

Longus: *Daphnis and Chloe,* 244

Lot, 50–51

Love, 33, 75, 82, 171, 172; bonds of, 105; of city, 170, 215; courtly tradition of, 243, 288n.29; death and, 100, 101, 104; effects of, 102, 104, 230, 308n.22; emotional elements of, 102; as a feminine abstraction, 211; forms of, 152, 173, 239, 301n.23; friendship and, 238–239, 310n.42; ideals of, 239; marriage and, 156, 219; metaphor and, 229; nature of, 245; paternal control and, 299n.6; as a pathology, 170, 219, 228, 230, 269, 287n.28;

philosophy and, 170, 172, 216, 217, 218; pleasure and, 225; power of, 211, 237; romantic, 219, 222, *226,* 233–234, 239–246, 247; of self vs. other, 95, 100; sexual, 84, 143–149, 150, 153, 156, 216, 217; tragic, 260; unrequited, 224, 229; violence of, 103–104, 287n.28; war and, 100, 104; wisdom and, 217, 242

Love dedications, *137,* 161

Love gifts, *130, 131, 134,* 157, *165, 166,* 228

Love lyric, 242–243

Lucian, 27, 265; *Dialogues of the Hetaeras,* 122, 223

Lucius, 27, 265

Lucretius: *alma Venus* of, 211; *De Rerum Natura,* 266

Ludovisi Triptych, 199, *200, 201*

Lugalbanda, 21

Lyce, 243

Lycurgus, 286n.11

Lydia, Lydian empire, 119, 177, 292n.11, 304n.6

Lyric, 95, 106

Lysamachus, 221

Lysicles, 151, 297nn.51,53

Lysistrata, 112, 152, 210

Ma, 294n.22

Macedonia, 225

Machon *Maxims,* 122

Madonna, 13, 19, *25*

Maenads, *22, 128,* 135

Magic, sexual, 51

Magna Mater, 264

Maiden Song (*partheneion*), 103, 104

Manichaenism, 266

Marathon, Battle of, 154, 295n.39

Marcus Aurelius, 265

Marcus Perennius, *259*

Mardonius, 140

Marriage: abduction and, 233; adultery and, 223, 261; Aphrodite and, 75; Athenian laws on, 150, 151; bonds of,

309n.35; celibacy in, 268; conjugal love and, 156, 173, 221, *227*, 232, 235, 239, 242, 244; customs regulating, 173; divorce and, 268; eroticism and, 75, 84; feminine ideals and, 89, 167; friendship in, 241–242; Hera and, 29, 75; idealization of, 105, 244–245; inheritance and, 84; male bonds and, 278n.14; nocturnal religous festivities and, 234; as a partnership, 151, 152, 240–241, 244, 245, 310n.45; poverty and, 310n.54; rape and, 233–234, 309n.38; as rite of passage for girls, 164; Sappho's songs of, 102; selection of a spouse, 235–236; sex and, 50, 113, 135, 143–149, 150, 155, 156, *201*, 209, 262, 307n.16; tediousness of, 219; vestal virgins and, 264; views of, 218; violence and, *136*; women and, 22–23, 29, 314n.56. *See also* Hierogamy

Martial, 261

Mask, 17, 18

Masturbation, *128*

Mater Dolorosa, 19, *25*

Matriarchy, 22–23, 63, 90, 274n.13, 285n.2

Medea, 106, 209, 218–219

Megara, 116–117

Megarian Decree, 150

Meleager of Gadara, 238, 308n.31; *Garland*, 224, 226

Men: autonomy of, 242–243; bonding of, 61, 158; domestic segregation of, 102, 108, 109, 112–114, 124, 290nn.40,42; Egyptian association with red, *133*; eroticism and, 106, 107–108, 135, 186, 295n.35; homo-eroticism and, 157, 161, 278n.14; ideals of, 119, *127*, 166, 168, 176–177, 205, 240, 267, 293n.14; longevity of, 21; love and, 109–112, 217–218, 222–223, 230, 239–240; marriage and, 84, 173, 221, 241, 268; mythology of heroic age and, 91–93; nocturnal religious

festivals and, 235; phallic display by, 290n.41, 304n.9; power of, 90, 205, 209–210; religious consultation by, 290n.39; as sacred prostitutes, 68, 69; sex and, 101, 125–126, 135, 138–139, 157, 161, 264, 277n.2; sexual desire of, 13, 17, 81, 107, 172, 209, 216, 262, 284n.38; social roles of, 211; stereotyping of women by, 223; subordination of women to, 18, 143–144, 182, 268, 310n.46; symposia and, 124–125; violence and, 234; warrior bonds of, 174–175

Menaechmus, 236

Menander: *Adelphoi*, 236; *Arbitrants*, 239; *Dyskolos*, 238, 239; *Epitrepontes*, 234; *Misoumenos*, 242, 307n.8; *Samia*, 235, 295n.30

Menelaus: court of, 48, 92; Euphorbus and, 282n.28; fair hair color, 282n.30; Helen and, 67, 73, 74, 82–83, 105, 174, 280n.12; immortalized by Homer, 88

Menstruation, 52

Meriones, 61

Messenio, 236

Metriche, 223

Michelangelo, 274n.12; *Pietà*, 19, *25*, 276n.32

Micio, 160; *Adelphoi*, 236, 238, 244

Milesian girl, 294n.23

Milesian tales, 120, 260–261, 293n.17

Miletus, 116, 119, 121, 150–151, 199, 297n.54

Mime genre, 220, 223, 224, 226

Mimnermus of Colophon, 100, 104, 108

Minoan culture, 38, 65

Minoan-Mycenaean culture, 62, 65, 67–71, 85, 279n.7

Minos, 67, 70, 300n.12

Minotaur, 67, 69

"Minyans," 63–64

Mirrors, bronze, *256*, *257*

Mistress of Animals, *8*, 28, *97*, 275n.19

Moabites, 52

Moirai (Fates), 31–34, 275n.27

Monody, 95

Monotheism, 23, 26–27

Moschion, 242

Moses, 52

Muses, 31–34, 300n.17

Music: as a cultural expression, 289n.36; hetaeras and, 122; love and, 224, 225; as a luxury item, 119; sex and, 143, *147*, *201*; social class and, *159*; symposia and, 124

Musonius Rufus, 254, 266–267, 314n.50

Mycenae, 63, 72, 82, 86

Mycenaean culture, 61, 62, *66*, 68, 69, 71–72. *See also* Minoan-Mycenaean culture

Myrrhine, 149

Mythology, 17, 47, 49, 59, 61, 64, 72–73, 85, 91–94

Nais, 308n.22

Narcissus, 281n.24

Natural law (*physis*): as anerotic, 255; feminine power and, 211; homosexuality and, 253–254, 313n.21; human behavior and, 299n.6, 314n.50; philosophy and, 153, 174; procreation and, 173; sexual love and, 153, 217; social class and, 301n.26; warfare and, 301n.27

Nature: asexuality in, 253; goddess as representation of, 13; human life and, 38, 171, 211; regenerative cycle in, 19, 82, 220; sexual forces of, 47

Naucratis, 121, 122

Nausicaa, 29, 58, 83, 177, 240, 283n.33, 288n.29

Naxos, 116

Near East: Athenian influence on, 225; erotic power of women in, 58; goddess religions of, *12*, 18–19, 39, 67, 72, 79, 90, 104, 176, 281n.20, 283n.36;

hierogamy in, 274n.10; influence of, 5, 60, 71, 84, *96*, *97*, *98*, 109, 116, 281n.21; prostitution in, 110–111, 118; religious cults of, 63, 65, 68–69, 277n.5; serpent iconography of, 85; sexual culture of, 51, 53, 54, 73; trade with, 62; urban cultures of, 65

Nemea, 106

Neolithic: art of, 40, *44*; early Greek culture and, 50, 64; figurines of, *8*, *9*, *12*, 13, 17; Genesis and, 49; goddess traditions of, 5, 90; religious traditions of, 3, 5, *19*, 62, 64; revolution, 10; sexual imagery of, 13, 15–23

Neoplatonism, 250, 274n.12

Nereid, *14*

Nesiotes, *163*

New Comedy: abduction/rape in, 233–234; cultural values in, 216, 236, 238, 244, 299n.6; erotic friendship in, 242, 247, 310n.42; hetaeras in, 122; influence of, 244; *komos* and, 228; love in, 173, *227*, 232, 239–240, 242, 260; plot of, 174, 232; as popular entertainment, 244; prostitution in, 231; rape in, 309n.38; utilitarian minimalism of, 171–172

New Testament, 311n.2, 314n.56

Nicander of Colophon, 118

Nicophanes, 248

Nike, 211, *212*, 214, 306n.30; Nike statuary, 197, 200, *203–204*

Ninsun, 21

Niobe, 200, *202*

Nireus of Syme, 107

Nossis, 224

Nude, female: clothing as drapery on, 199–200, *202–204*, *212*, 214; erotic power of, 189; goddess religion and, 38, 64, *87*; iconography of, 23, 275n.19; in Neolithic, *8*; as object of veneration, 38; physical ideals of, *199*, 200, *212–213*, 214; as private art form,

219; mythmaking and, 91; non-Greek and, 5; Orphic, 252; *partheneion* as, 103; patriotic, 95; personal experience in, 101–102, 222; Pisistratids and, 140; Plato's *Ion* and, 170; public rhetoric in, 103; Roman, 260, 261–262, 266; sex as metaphor for, 288n.33; sexuality and, 231, 261; symposium and, 109; victory odes, 106–110. *See also specific genres*

Polemon, 242

Polis, 22, 95, 100, 109, 116–117, 141–142, 154, 216

Politics: Athenian, 140–142; cultural change and, 116–117; Eros and, 172–173; household vs., 310n.46; ideals of, 153, 154; individualism and, 241; love and, 237, 244; self-interest and, 169, 174, 306n.3; sex and, 51–52, 160, 161–162, 221–222, 292n.9, 299n.5, 302n.32; sexual culture and, *20*, 157–158; social class and, 140–142, 171; spiritual values and, 109; theater and, 158; triple goddesses and, 32–33; urban culture and, 225; women in, 210

Pollux, 31, 61

Polybius, 120

Polyclitus, 205, *207*

Polycrates of Samos, 296n.39

Polygamy, 52

Polynices, 209

Polyphemus, 224

Pomegranate as sexual symbol, 29, 86, 191

Pornography, 248, 311n.5. *See also* Art, erotic

Poseidon, 67, 69, 70, 75, 82, *187*, 189, 200, *202*

Posidippus, 218

Poverty: cult of, 94–95, 100, 141, 250, 255, 285n.7; eros and, 169; marriage and, 310n.54; mythology of heroic age and, 91–93

Praetextatus, 245

Praxagora, 152, 210, 290n.41; *Ecclesiazusae*, 144, 146

Praxilla, 287n.22

Praxinoa, 220

Praxiteles, 122, 200, 205, *206–207*

Priam, 74–75, 181

Priapeia, 261

Priene, 119

Primavera (Botticelli), 34, *36*

Procreation: betrothal and, 239; Demeter and, 29; divine prototypes of, *23*; eternal life and, 279n.15, 306n.5; heterosexual eroticism and, 168; natural law and, 173, 254; sex and, 155, 156; sperm and, 313n.26; symbolism of, 13; women and, 211. *See also* Children; Reproduction

Procris, 243

Prodicus, 215–216

Prometheus, 84, 85

Propertius, 261

Proserpine, 27

Prostitutes, prostitution: civilization and, 54–56, 58; Colophon and, 292n.8; commercial, 119, 121, *126*, 278n.9, 280–281n.17; Corinth and, 86, 110–111, 289n.37, 292n.11; democracy and, 292n.9; Hebrew, 51, 277n.5; hierodules and, 294nn.20,21; in Istanbul, 292n.11; liminality of, 58; Lydia and, 119, 292n.11; men as, 68, 69, 161; in Near East, 121, 280–281n.17; prayer and, 280n.16; public monopoly of, 118, 298–299n.5; sacred, 51, 68, 86, 110–111, 120, 121, 277n.5, 278n.9, 280–281n.17; sadism and, 135, *139*; sexual pleasure and, 232; slaves and, 144; social class and, 111–112; Solon and, 171–172; in Uruk, 55; Venus and, 231; women's independence and, 152, 223

Protagoras, 301n.26

Proteus, 174

Serpent iconography, 48, 50, 63, 65, 85, 279n.16, 281n.24

Sesklo, *19*

Sex: anal, 123, 161, 300n.19; art and, *133, 134, 257,* 291n.3; balanced view of, 293n.14; beauty and, 186; bonds of, 309n.35; carnal nature of, *128,* 224, 255, 269; degrees of passion in, 215–216; effects of, 102, 218, 253, 261, 268, 284n.38; as entertainment, *201,* 261; forms of, 288n.29; irrationality of, 239; justification for, 155; knowledge and, 276n.2; law of nature and, 171; life's pleasures and, 100; likened to sleep, 286nn.13–14; as luxury item, 119; male identity and, 264; moral function of, 156; philosophy and, 170, 172; poetic metaphor and, 10, 288n.33; politics and, 160, 161–162, 292n.9, 299n.5, 302n.32; procreation and, 155, 156, 254; public conduct of, 307n.7; as response to danger, 312n.9; as sin, 255, 263, 311n.2; slavery and, 310n.45; violence and, 234; war and, 104, 209; women's rights with, 307n.7; youth and, 104, 107, 160, 220, 224, 229, 234. *See also* Heterosexuality; Homosexuality; Intercourse, sexual

Sexual dimorphism, 197–198

Sexuality, 72, *127*; human vs. divine, 50, 58; male, 13, 17; regulation of, 51, 160

Shamhat, 54, 55, 58, 278n.9

Shuvalov Painter, *226*

Sicily, 285n.7

Siduri, 57, 279n.15

Simaetha, Simaitha, 217, 222–223

Simonides, 103, 140, 286n.15

Simon Peter, 267

Sins: Christian, 51, 255, 263

Sirens, 31, 275n.26

Skepticism, 216

Slaves, slavery, 94, 110, 171, 236, 297n.53; hetaeras and, 122, 123; prostitution and, 144; self-interest and, 306n.3;

sex and, 161, 223, 232, 240, 242, 310n.45; temple service and, 294n.20; warfare and, 142; women and, 290n.42

Sleep (personification of), *178. See also* Hypnos

Sleep, 100, 286nn.13,14, 312n.15

Smyrna, 116

Snake cult, 63, 65, 85, 72

Socrates: Aspasia and, 151, 152, 298n.58; beauty and, 301n.24; Diotima and, 167, 168; heterosexual love and, 300n.19; management of private business, 305n.23; *Phaedrus*, 300n.19; portrayed by Aristophanes, 158, 160, 161; portrayed by Plato, 167–168, 170, 186, 250; students of, 172, 249; virtuous philosophic life and, 155; women's intellect and, 210, 241, 310n.45

Sodomy, 51

Solomon, 51–52, 53, 277n.7

Solon: character of, 117–118; elegiac monody of, 95; Pisistratids and, 140; prostitution and, 118, 171–172, 231, 298–299n.5; Sappho and, 292n.7

Song, 33, 226, 286n.11, 289n.36

Song of Solomon, 53, 277n.7

Sophists, 153, 158, 160, 170, 215

Sophocles: *Ajax*, 233; *Antigone*, 171, 209; Classical theater and, 153–154; *The Demand for Helen*, 302n.38; family duty and, 171; female power and, 209; heroes and, 247; male power and, 209; marriage and, 233; *The Marriage of Helen*, 302n.38; Nike and, 214; *Oedipus at Colonus*, 247; *Philoctetes*, 214, 247; *The Theft of Helen*, 302n.38; *The Women of Trachis*, 209, 233

Soranus, 268

Sosias Painter, *179*

Soul vs. body, 250–252, 262–263, 266, 269

Oeconomicus, 148–149, 151, 152, 173, 240, 308n.21; Socrates and, 305n.23; women and, 297n.49, 308n.21

Xenophon of Corinth, 110–111

Xerxes, 94, 142

Youth: beauty and, 106; love and, 243; sex and, 19, 56, 104, 107, 160, 182, 220, 229, 234, 314n.53

Zeno of Citium: on eros, 153; friendship and, 217, 218, 238; homoeroticism and, 301–302nn.30,33; ideal republic of, 230; *Politeia*, 172–173

Zethos, 31

Zeus: Artemis and, 28; Athena born from head of, 285n.3; court of, 48; cult cave of, *97*; depicted in statuary, *187*, 196, 214; Europa and, 70; Ganymede and, 108, 162, *165*, 166, 300n.12; Helen and, 81–82, 280n.12; Hera and, 29, *45*, 105, *136*, 233, 276–277n.2; Indo-European origins of, 60; Nike and, 214, 306n.30; punishment of Apollo by, 85; seduced by Hera, 29, 39, 75, *78*, 79, 189–190, 288n.29; sexual conquests of, 29; temple of, 86, 140, 197; triple goddesses and, 32